Decision-Making and Judgment in Child Welfare and Protection

Decision-Making and Judgment in Child Welfare and Protection

and Protection

Theory, Research, and Practice

EDITED BY JOHN D. FLUKE,

MÓNICA LÓPEZ LÓPEZ,

RAMI BENBENISHTY, ERIK J. KNORTH,

AND DONALD J. BAUMANN

Oxford University Press is a department of the University of Oxford. It furthers
the University's objective of excellence in research, scholarship, and education
by publishing worldwide. Oxford is a registered trade mark of Oxford University
Press in the UK and certain other countries.

Published in the United States of America by Oxford University Press
198 Madison Avenue, New York, NY 10016, United States of America.

Library of Congress Cataloging-in-Publication Data
Names: Fluke, John, D., author. | López, Mónica López, author. |
Benbenishty, Rami, author. | Knorth, E. J. (Erik J.), author. |
Baumann, Donald J., author.
Title: Decision-making and judgment in child welfare and protection :
theory, research, and practice / John D. Fluke, Mónica López López,
Rami Benbenishty, Erik J. Knorth, Donald J. Baumann.
Description: New York, NY : Oxford University Press, [2021] |
Includes bibliographical references and index.
Identifiers: LCCN 2020005795 (print) | LCCN 2020005796 (ebook) |
ISBN 9780190059538 (hardcover) | ISBN 9780190059552 (epub) |
ISBN 9780190059569 (OSO)
Subjects: LCSH: Child welfare—Decision making. | Child abuse—Decision making.
Classification: LCC HV713 .F58 2020 (print) | LCC HV713 (ebook) |
DDC 362.7—dc23
LC record available at https://lccn.loc.gov/2020005795
LC ebook record available at https://lccn.loc.gov/2020005796

9 8 7 6 5 4 3 2 1

Printed by Sheridan Books, Inc., United States of America

Cover image:
Hendrik Nicolaas WERKMAN (1882-1945)
Composition with Three Figures (1944)
Kunstmuseum De Haag, The Hague, the Netherlands

This book is dedicated to memory and the influences of Professors Leonard I. Dalgleish, University of Sterling, and Paul Durning, University of Paris Nanterre. While they both would have loved to have contributed to this volume, their contributions to our ideas and thinking continue to be a source of inspiration for this work.

Professionals working in child welfare and child protection are making decisions with crucial implications for children and families on a daily basis. The
types of judgments and decisions they make vary and include determining
whether to substantiate a child abuse allegation, whether a child is at risk of
significant harm by parents, and whether to remove a child from home or reunify a child with parents after some time in care. These decisions are intended
to help achieve the best interests of the child. Unfortunately, they can sometimes also doom children and families unnecessarily to many years of pain and
suffering.

Judgments and decisions in child welfare and protection are based to a large
extent on the formidable knowledge base on child abuse and neglect created
over the years to support this professional task. Nevertheless, making decisions
in complex and uncertain environments is fraught with many difficulties and
shortcomings. There are in fact many indications that decisions in this area
are not reliable and that many errors in judgment could be avoided had the
decision-makers relied on existing knowledge on decision-making under uncertainty and followed appropriate procedures. Much needs to be improved
on how these decisions are made by individual professionals and child welfare
agencies.

Surprisingly, despite the central role of judgments and decision-making in
professional practice and its deep impact on children and families, child welfare and protection training and research programs have paid little attention
to this crucial aspect of practice. Furthermore, although extensive knowledge
about professional judgment and decision-making has been accumulated in
relevant areas such as medicine, business administration, and economics, little
has been done to help transfer and translate this knowledge to the child welfare
and protection areas.

Fortunately, a growing awareness of the need to expand our knowledge and improve practice in this area has been recognized in recent years. For instance, the four editors of this book published, in 2015, the first-ever special issue on decision-making in child welfare and protection (*Child Abuse & Neglect*, Vol. 49, 2015). That special issue, "Decision-Making and Judgments in Child Maltreatment Prevention and Response" (Fluke et al., 2015), aimed at presenting research focused on how context and decision-maker behaviors impact child protection systems' decision-making and how such knowledge might lead to improvements in decision-making. Moreover, since 2016, the European Scientific Association on Residential and Family Care for Children and Adolescents (EUSARF) includes a special track for decision-making scholarship that has received in its last two iterations (2016 and 2018, as of this date) more paper applications than any other track proposed in this conference. Also, the DARE Symposia on Decisions, Assessment, Risk, and Evidence in Social Work, organized since 2010 by Ulster University (Belfast, Northern Ireland), and the Decisions, Assessment and Risk Special Interest Group (DARSIG) of the European Social Work Research Association, which has been formally established since 2014 (https://www.eswra.org/decisions_sig.php), are part of efforts to elevate interest and scholarship in this important area. Thus, although this area has not received enough attention in the past, our sense is that it is gaining increased awareness. In this sense, we believe that, in order to improve decision-making in the field of child welfare and protection, we have the important task to make accessible the recent knowledge gains to scholars, educators, practitioners, and policy-makers dedicated to protecting children and improving their well-being.

This book represents our aspiration to fill this critical gap in the child welfare and protection research agenda while providing an up-to-date resource for practitioners and policy-makers. It is our purpose to provide the reader with ideas, methods, and tools that will improve the reader's understanding of how context and decision-maker behaviors affect child welfare and protection decision-making and how such knowledge might lead to improvements in decision-making.

This book is thus intended for academic researchers and graduate students in social work, psychology, pedagogy, and related disciplines such as behavioral economics. Its development has already resulted in improvements to the academic programs and professional continuing education courses that some of its authors teach regularly at their respective universities. We hope that this book becomes a foundational resource for undergraduate and graduate courses at other universities worldwide. The fact that it provides context and insight from a range of authors from around the world whose work focuses on a range of child welfare systems might make it a more enriching teaching tool suitable for different contexts. From a professional perspective, we also hope that child welfare managers, administrators, and senior practitioners will find this book an excellent resource for reflecting on their decision-making processes at personal, organizational, and policy levels.

This book is organized into four major parts. Part I provides an introduction on frameworks and models in decision-making and judgment in child welfare and protection. It comprises two chapters. Chapter 1 lays out the key theoretical perspectives and historical overview of decision-making in child welfare and protection. Chapter 2 discusses the potential for using predictive analysis machine learning methods to support the complex and critical decisions professionals make on behalf of children and families.

Part II deals with the methodology for the study of decision-making in child welfare and protection. The empirical methods for studying decision-making in this field are the focus of Chapter 3. Chapter 4 presents a variety of instruments developed to understand the child protective services decision-making processes.

In Part III we present two ecological models of decision-making in child welfare and discuss research using both frameworks. Chapters 5 and 6 present, respectively, the Decision-Making Ecology (DME) model and the model of Judgments and Decisions Processes in Context (JUDPiC). Chapters 7 through 10 outline new research evidence explicated in the context of the DME domains.

Part IV focuses on the practice of decision-making in child welfare and protection. Chapter 11 provides an overview of the use and usability of decision-making theory in child welfare policy and practice. Chapter 12 looks more closely at the voice of the child in child protection decision-making through a comparison of policy and practice in three European countries. The experience of teaching and learning decision-making in child welfare and protection social work is the subject of Chapter 13.

Finally, in Chapter 14, the editors of this book reflect on the future of the field and provide a series of reflections for policy, practice, and research.

John D. Fluke, Mónica López López, Rami Benbenishty,

Erik J. Knorth, and Donald J. Baumann

REFERENCE

Fluke, J. D., López, M., Benbenishty, R., & Knorth, E. J. (Eds.). (2015). Decision-making and judgments in child maltreatment prevention and response. *Child Abuse and Neglect, 49*(special issue), 1–162. doi:10.1016/S0145-2134(15)00392-0

ACKNOWLEDGMENTS

As editors of this book, we would like to acknowledge several people for their support and contributions to this project. First and foremost, we would like to thank the chapter authors for the quality of their contributions and their commitment to the project. Our gratitude also goes to our editor, Dana Bliss, and the team at Oxford University Press for their support and patience during the course of the past 2 years as this project was becoming more ambitious and comprehensive (but also lengthy!). Thanks also to our students and colleagues in the field who have enriched our perspectives on child welfare and protection decision-making throughout many courses and training activities in various countries. Most importantly, we want to acknowledge the child protection and social care workers and supervisors throughout the world who are at the heart of decision making to protect children. We share your aspiration to make the difficult decisions your make daily on behalf of children and families best they can be. Thank you for your efforts and commitment to make better decisions for children and families! Finally, we would like to thank the significant others in our lives who have contributed their love, patience, and understanding to our work.

ABOUT THE AUTHORS

Kate Allan is a doctoral student at the Factor-Inwentash Faculty of Social Work and the Manager of the Vaccine Hesitancy Study. Her research interests focus on the intersection between social work and health, specifically the decision-making process of parents regarding routine childhood vaccination. She is also interested in the transition from pediatric to adult care for patients with rare diseases. Prior to beginning the PhD program, she was a site researcher for the Ontario Incidence Study of Reported Child Abuse and Neglect 2013. Kate has a keen interest in the interplay between psychosocial factors and physical health.

Helen Baldwin, MA, is Research Fellow at the University of York, with 10 years' experience conducting research in the areas of child protection and public health. Helen is currently completing her PhD thesis, which is examining social workers' responses to parental substance misuse. Other research projects that Helen has worked on include a study of outcomes for children in out-of-home care and a randomized controlled trial evaluating multisystemic therapy.

Cora Bartelink, PhD, is a researcher specializing in decision-making processes in child welfare and child protection. Recently, she worked as part of the research team "Transforming Youth Care" at the Hague University of Applied Sciences. Previously, she worked at the Netherlands Youth Institute, where she finished her PhD on decision-making in child maltreatment cases and contributed to guideline development on decision-making processes and out-of-home placement in child welfare and child protection.

Donald J. Baumann, PhD, holds a doctorate in social psychology and has more than 30 years of experience in designing and managing large-scale research projects as both a principal investigator and as a project director. He has been on the faculties of the University of Texas, Trinity University, and Saint Edwards University. He has directed numerous national multiyear research and evaluation projects over the years. He is retired from the Texas Department of Family and Protective Services where he was head of the Evaluation Section of Child Protective Services. He currently teaches at St. Edwards University. His areas of interest are decision-making, risk assessment, and disproportionality. He has written more than 75 reports, articles, and book chapters.

Rami Benbenishty, PhD is a professor (emeritus) at School of Social Work and Social Welfare at the Hebrew University of Jerusalem. Prof. Benbenishty has interests in several areas. He is interested in the safety, welfare and wellbeing of children around the world. He is studying children and youth both in community normative settings, such as schools, and in out of home placements, such as foster homes and residential care. He also investigates and tries to improve decision processes that lead to referral to protective services, removal of children from their biological families, and their reunification thereafter. He is also studying the decision making processes of child protection teams in hospitals which report children to community protective services. Prof. Benbenishty has developed a conceptual, methodological, and technological framework for monitoring processes and outcomes in human services. This framework was implemented in foster care services in the US and is being utilized to monitor school violence and climate in schools, districts, and at the national level. In all these area of research, Prof Benbenishty has conducted multiple international comparative studies, that aim to identify what is common and what is unique across contexts, including in child welfare decision making. He is consulting with governments and researchers in many places around the world.

Leonor Bettencourt Rodrigues, PhD, Postdoctoral researcher (DCT) at ICS-ULisboa, in Lisboa, Portugal. She graduated in Social Psychology in ISCTE/ IUL in 2004, and in 2013 completed an FCT funded PhD degree in Social, Environmental and Community Psychology in ISCTE/ IUL. Her research interests have been generically around social policy and intervention towards vulnerable groups. Her research interest on at- risk children and child protection began with an internship in a residential care setting, and then, as a research fellow in 2 international action- research projects (Dartington- i/ CIS-ISCTE) on the design and evaluation of new services, with the two major residential care institutions in Portugal (SCML and Casa Pia – one book chapter published). For her PhD she studied the psychosocial processes involved in out- of- home placement decisions, empirically demonstrating the role played by attitudes, norms, values, and emotions, as well as the complexity and ambivalence involved in those decisions, especially in child neglect cases. Between 2013 and 2017, she was a Postdoctoral Research Fellow in several research projects in ICS- ULisboa on the topic of social policies related to children, elderly people, families and parenthood, funded by Calouste Gulbenkian/ UNICEF Foundation, European Commission or EEA Grants.

Cindy Blackstock, PhD, is member of the Gitxsan First Nation, Cindy is the Executive Director of the First Nations Child and Family Caring Society of Canada and a Professor at the School of Social Work at McGill University. Her interdisciplinary work focuses on Indigenous children's rights and on culturally based equity for First Nations children in particular. She is best known for being a lead litigant in a successful human rights case alleging the Canadian government's inequitable funding of First Nations children's services was discriminatory. This ongoing case resulted in over $3 billion per year in additional services. She is frequently seen in the company of Spirit Bear, a very special stuffed bear, who engages children in reconciliation and education about the rich and distinct First Nations cultures, contexts and contributions.

Manuela Calheiros, PhD in Community Social Psychology, ISCTE (2003), is an Associate Professor at the Faculty of Psychology, University of Lisbon. Her research focuses on socio-cognitive processes covering the areas of self-development and well-being with children at-risk, parental abuse and neglect, social images of youth in residential care and decision making in child protection system. Her present projects articulate these processes in program design with abusive and neglectful families, institutionalized youth and CPS professionals. With a strong focus on socio-psychological intervention, Maria Manuela Calheiros has developed several research-based projects on programs that have been applied in different private and public institutions. She has a strong links to the community and has been working with the government (at the national level and the Council of Europe) in providing technical information to support the creation of regulations and guidelines (e.g., for preventing violence towards children), implementing changes in institutions and facilitating the national implementation of European politics. Her research has been published in several peer-reviewed journals.

Martin Chabot is responsible for consolidating and linking appropriate metadata using data matching, reduction, and restructuring techniques to create research-specific datasets. Martin is also responsible for the extraction of clinical-administrative data from partnering child protection organizations using SQL procedures and updating current datasets with annual extractions. Martin is also involved in the production of subdatasets based on project specifications, the development of data definition documents specific to each dataset and research initiative, the consolidation of multiple data sources (e.g., census data), supporting researchers and graduate students on matters concerning dataset management and manipulation, and discussions regarding the long-term sustainability of research initiatives.

Alan J. Dettlaff, PhD, is Dean of the Graduate College of Social Work at the University of Houston and the inaugural Maconda Brown O'Connor Endowed Dean's Chair. Prior to joining the University of Houston, Dean Dettlaff served on the faculty of the Jane Addams College of Social Work at the University of Illinois at Chicago. He received his bachelor's degree in social work from TCU, and master's in social work and PhD from the University of Texas at Arlington. Dean Dettlaff's research focuses on improving outcomes for children and youth in the child welfare system through examining the factors contributing to racial disparities and improving cultural responsiveness.

Rebecca Dillard, MSW, is a doctoral candidate in Ohio State University's College of Social Work. Rebecca received her BS in psychology and sociology from the University of Pittsburgh in 2015, and her MSW from Ohio State University in 2017. Rebecca's research is focused on developmental antecedents to adolescents engaging in sexual and nonsexual delinquent offending behaviors. She is particularly interested in the role of childhood trauma and maltreatment experiences as they contribute to the development of problematic sexual behaviors among youth.

Barbara A. Fallon, PhD, is a full Professor and holds a Canada Research Chair in Child Welfare. Her research focuses on the collection and sharing of reliable, valid national and provincial data to provide an evidence-based understanding of the trajectories of children and families in the child welfare system. She is currently the Scientific Director of The First Nations/Canadian Incidence Study of Reported Child Abuse and Neglect (FN/CIS) 2019 and the Ontario Incidence Study of Reported Child Abuse and Neglect (OIS) 2018. These studies provide a comprehensive description of the needs of children and families identified to the child welfare system allowing for evidence-based improvements to policy and practice. Other research interests include comparisons of child protection systems and the contribution of worker and organizational characteristics to child-welfare decision making. Dr. Fallon's past research has helped child welfare workers and policy-makers understand the use of risk assessments in child protection investigations and opportunities for early intervention and prevention for children at risk of maltreatment. Her research has also contributed to the implementation of key policy initiatives in child welfare including differential response models and specialized intimate partner violence teams.

John D. Fluke, PhD, is Professor and Associate Director for Systems Research and Evaluation at the Kempe Center in the Department of Paediatrics at the

University of Colorado School of Medicine. Prof. Fluke's is known internationally for his innovative research focused on developing and testing theoretical frameworks in child welfare decision making. In the area of child maltreatment epidemiology, he has been instrumental in developing and supporting sustainable child maltreatment data collection programs in the US and Internationally. His research extends to evaluations focused on improving the evidence base for child welfare and children's mental health interventions.

Sarah A. Font, PhD, is Assistant Professor at the Pennsylvania State University Department of Sociology and Criminology and a faculty member of the Child Maltreatment Solutions Network. Her research focuses on how the policies and practices of the child welfare system affect the experiences and outcomes of children exposed to maltreatment or related adversities. She earned a PhD in social welfare from the University of Wisconsin–Madison and a masters in social work from Western Michigan University.

Joel Gautschi has a master's degree in social work and is a PhD student and researcher at the University of Applied Sciences and Arts Northwestern Switzerland. His current research focus is on judgment and decision-making in child protection, client–professional working relationships, tacit knowledge, trust, and the factorial survey approach. He studies the professional practice of social workers in quantitative and qualitative research projects.

J. Christopher Graham, PhD, holds a master's degree and doctorate in social psychology from the University of Texas at Austin. He began his study of child welfare at the Texas Department of Protective and Regulatory Services, where he was statistician for the Texas Child Fatality Study. His research into maltreatment risk factors and CPS caseworker decision-making continued at the State of Washington's Office of Children's Administration Research, where he was co-investigator at the Seattle Site of Longitudinal Studies of Child Abuse and Neglect (LONGSCAN), as well as other studies, and then as a research scientist at the Child Welfare Research Group of the University of Washington's School of Social Work. He also has collaborated in this research with nonprofit organizations including the American Humane Association and Casey Family Programs. He specializes in decision support, program evaluation, and performance monitoring for agencies and caseworkers working with at-risk children, youth, and families and has for many years investigated racial disproportionality and disparity across decision points in the CPS system. He presently is a statistician and program evaluator at the Fetal Alcohol and Drug Unit (FADU) of the University of Washington's Alcohol and Drug Abuse Institute and is a researcher with the Washington State Department of Children, Youth, and Families (DCYF) Office of Innovation, Alignment, and Accountability (OIAA).

He is the author of numerous reports and scholarly articles in the field of child welfare.

Dana Hollinshead, MPA, PhD, is Assistant Research Professor with the Kempe Center for the Prevention and Treatment of Child Abuse and Neglect at the University of Colorado. She has over twenty years of experience conducting child welfare research, program evaluation, and policy analyses and is an expert in examining the influence of policies, practices, and participant demographics on child, family, and agency outcome measures. Her career has been devoted to designing, executing, and delivering consulting, evaluation, and oversight services for federal, state, and local child welfare agencies to foster enhanced performance management and system improvement. Dr. Hollinshead's primary focus is examining how agency, caseworker, and caregiver factors influence the engagement of families as well as their relationship to the implementation of and outcomes for child welfare interventions. Dr. Hollinshead received a bachelor's degree in psychology from Colby College, a master's in public administration from George Washington University, and a PhD in social policy from the Heller School at Brandeis University.

Joyce James, LMSW-AP, is President and lead racial equity consultant of Joyce James Consulting. She served as Assistant Commissioner of the Texas Child Protective Services and Associate Deputy Executive Commissioner of the Texas Center for Elimination of Disproportionality and Disparities. She is a recognized as a national expert in the field of child welfare. She is the originator of the Texas Model for Addressing Disproportionality and Disparities and the Groundwater Analysis of Racial Inequities. She holds an Honorary Doctorate of Humane Letters from University of St. Joseph's.

Erik J. Knorth, PhD, is a child psychologist and full professor (emeritus) at the Faculty of Social and Behavioral Sciences at the University of Groningen in the Netherlands. His research is focused on service and intervention characteristics that impact treatment outcomes for children and youth with severe emotional and behavioral problems. Related topics of interest are: evaluation of home-based and out-of-home care services, professional decision-making, child maltreatment, families experiencing multiple problems, children's participation in care, pedagogical work in residential and foster care, ethnic diversity and young refugees, and the transition of young care leavers to adulthood. Erik is a founding member and former vice-president of EUSARF and a member of the International Work Group on Therapeutic Residential Care. Most of his academic publications, including forty books and special issues, can be found at ResearchGate. In 2018 he was knighted by the King of the Netherlands as an Officer in the Order of Orange-Nassau.

Mónica López López, PhD, is an associate professor at the University of Groningen, the Netherlands. She teaches decision-making in child welfare at the master Youth, Society and Policy. Her research interests include disparities in child protection decisions and the participation of children and families in decision-making processes in the child protection system. She is a board member of the European Scientific Association on Residential and Family Care for Children and Adolescents (EUSARF). She has published a number of papers comparing policies and responses to child abuse and neglect in different countries.

Bruce MacLaurin is Assistant Professor at the Faculty of Social Work, University of Calgary. He was the co-investigator on the four cycles of the Canadian Incidence Study of Reported Child Abuse and Neglect, as well as the principal investigator for provincial studies in British Columbia, Alberta, Saskatchewan, and the Northwest Territories. His research and publications have focused on child maltreatment, child welfare service delivery and outcomes, foster care, youth at risk, and street-involved youth. He has more than 15 years of front-line and management experience in nonprofit child and family services in Alberta and Ontario.

Kathryn Maguire-Jack, PhD, is Associate Professor at the University of Michigan School of Social Work. Her research is focused on understanding the community context of parenting, child maltreatment prevention, and the effect of social welfare policies on child maltreatment. She has expertise in child welfare systems, maltreatment prevention, program evaluation, and policy analysis. She received a master of social work, master of public affairs, and a PhD in social welfare from the University of Wisconsin.

Cicero Pereira, PhD, is Full Professor of Social Psychology at the Federal University of Paraíba and an Associated Research at the Institute of Social Sciences of the University of Lisbon. His studies analyze how and in which conditions social actors in contemporary democratic societies legitimize their attitudes and actions supporting prejudiced and discriminatory policies against minority groups. He has published his research findings in several journal papers, such as Personality and Social Psychology Bulletin, Journal of Experimental Social Psychology, and European Journal of Social Psychology.

Jim Schwab is the Clara Pope Willoughby Centennial Professor Emeritus in Child Welfare at the University of Texas at Austin. He retired from the University of Texas at Austin after 40 years in teaching data analysis and computer applications.

Vandna Sinha is Associate Research Professor in the School of Education at the University of Colorado, Boulder, and Adjunct Professor in the School of Social Work at McGill University. She takes a mixed-methods interdisciplinary and community-engaged approach to exploring questions that are of interest to child welfare, health, social service, and child/youth advocacy organizations. Many of her recent projects have focused on understanding service disparities and the barriers to provision of appropriate services for First Nations children in Canada.

Natalie Sowinski joined the TACFS team in August 2018 as Associate Director of Training and Research and became Director of Special Projects in December 2018. Previously, she served as a member of the Applied Solutions Group at KaleidaCare Management Solutions, the consultation and customization department of the organization. While at KaleidaCare, she spent time in implementation before moving to serve as the product manager of the revenue management system. Most recently, her focus was around foster parent recruitment and retention. She has a master of science degree in social work from the University of Texas at Austin.

Kelly G. Stepura, PhD, is a licensed social worker and Vice President and Director of Research and Evaluation of the OmniCare Institute. Before joining the OmniCare Institute, she served as Executive Vice President of Applied Research and Solutions at KaleidaCare Solutions, Inc., for 19 years. Her background as a researcher for 7 years at Texas' Department of Family and Protective Services allowed for leadership roles in numerous multiyear, grant-funded research projects in child welfare related to child maltreatment, maltreatment-related fatalities, caseworker decision-making, and outcome measurement. She received her PhD in social work from the University of Texas at Austin in 2010 and has been a published author in the area of child maltreatment and foster care for more than 25 years.

Brian J. Taylor is Professor of Social Work at Ulster University in Northern Ireland where he leads the research cluster on Decision, Assessment, Risk and Evidence Studies and teaches these topics on qualifying and post-qualifying social work courses. He joined the University after 10 years' experience in practice and management and 15 years in training and organization development in health and social care. Brian is a Fellow of the UK Academy of Social Sciences; a Senior Fellow of the School for Social Care Research at the National Institute for Health Research, London; and a founding member of the Board of the European Social Work Research Association.

Ingrid J. Ten Berge received her PhD on decision-making in child protection from Utrecht University in 1998. Since then, she has worked as a researcher, program developer, and program leader on child welfare and child protection at the Netherlands Youth Institute. Currently, she is director of Expertise Centre William Schrikker, a national organization for child protection and juvenile rehabilitation in The Netherlands.

Stephanie Thorne received her Master of Science in Social Work with a concentration in Administration and Policy Practice from the University of Texas at Austin in August 2018. She has worked with children and families in diverse environments for several years, including providing equine therapy, volunteering at a crisis nursery, providing tutoring services, completing family assessments, and in social work case management. Additionally, Stephanie has experience in developmental psychology research and child welfare research. She is currently a Research Associate at Upbring, a child placement agency headquartered in Austin. Stephanie is pursuing her Doctor of Philosophy in Social Welfare at the University of California, Los Angeles beginning in the Fall 2019. Stephanie is a member of the National Association of Social Workers and the Eta Tau chapter of Phi Alpha, the Social Work Honor Society.

Tom A. van Yperen is senior expert at the Netherlands Youth Institute. He is also Special Professor in Monitoring and Innovating Youth Care at the University of Groningen. Much of his research is on the outcome of services in prevention, child and youth care, and special education. He helps many municipalities and institutions to further develop these services by using outcome monitoring as a tool to gradually improve the effectiveness of methods and interventions. He is chief editor of *Zicht op effectiviteit* ["A View on Effectiveness"] (Lemniscaat Rotterdam), which has become an important handbook for many researchers and practitioners in the field.

Susanne Witte, PhD, is a family psychologist; she received her PhD at the Ludwig Maximilian University of Munich. Currently she is working at the German Youth Institute, located in Munich. She is conducting studies covering a broad range of topics regarding child maltreatment. Her specific research interests are sibling relationships in the context of child maltreatment, training professionals to prevent child maltreatment, and international comparisons of child protections activities.

Kim Wittenstrom, PhD, has more than 15 years of experience in program evaluation and data analytics work in the field of Child Welfare. Her most recent work for the Texas Department of Family and Protective Services involves designing continuous quality improvement systems for the state's privatization initiative.

PART I

Frameworks and Models in Decision-Making and Judgment in Child Welfare and Protection

Frameworks and Models in Decision-Making and Judgment in Child Welfare and Protection

RAMI BENBENISHTY AND JOHN D. FLUKE ∎

The aim of this chapter is to provide the reader with an introduction to concepts, theoretical perspectives, and areas of scholarship that may serve as background for some of the complexities involved in understanding and improving decision-making in child welfare and protection. This is a very selective review of the many ideas, insights, and theoretical perspectives in this wide area of human inquiry. We will limit ourselves to some of the key concepts and models that we think are essential to begin navigating the vast terrain of decision-making in child welfare and protection.

Imagine a generous researcher who is interested in your decision-making processes presenting you with two envelopes. In the blue envelope there is a large amount of money, and in the yellow envelope there is half of that amount. Unfortunately, we cannot have them both; we have to *choose* between the envelopes. For (almost) all of us this will be a very easy choice. Imagine, though, that you are told that if you choose the blue envelope there is a 50% chance that you will receive $50 (and 50% that you get nothing); and if you choose the yellow envelope, you have a 25% chance of getting $100 (and 75% that you would come empty-handed). Which would you choose? For most of us this decision is

Rami Benbenishty and John D. Fluke, *Frameworks and Models in Decision-Making and Judgment in Child Welfare and Protection* In: *Decision-Making and Judgment in Child Welfare and Protection*. Edited by: John D. Fluke, Mónica López López, Rami Benbenishty, Erik J. Knorth, and Donald J. Baumann, Oxford University Press (2021). © Oxford University Press. DOI: 10.1093/oso/9780190059538.003.0001.

more difficult to make, requires some deliberation, and one might expect that not all of us make the same choice. The *uncertainty* of the outcomes made this choice more difficult.

A normative approach to decision-making—that is, a guide to how decisions *ought* to be made—suggests that one should compute the *expected value* of each alternative and choose the alternative with the highest expected value. The expected value is computed as:

(Probability of an outcome) × (Value of the outcome)
The expected value of the blue envelope—50% × \$50 = \$25
The expected value of the yellow envelope—25% × \$100 = \$25

These ideas are very relevant to decision-making in child welfare. Workers in child welfare are aware of the uncertainty of the outcomes of their decisions. When they deliberate between alternatives they know that when they choose the alternative of removing from home a child at risk for maltreatment they have to take into account that there is a certain probability that this would help keep the child safe from harm. They also are aware that there is a certain probability, a risk, that the outcome of this alternative may be further maltreatment or traumatization of the child in the child welfare system.

Note, however, that whereas in the envelope example decision-makers have all the relevant information required for their decision, this is not the case with child welfare decision-making. Practitioners rarely, if ever, know what the probability is of each possible outcome. This makes it even harder to make decisions that correspond with normative theory of choice under uncertainty. Uncertainty is a major characteristic of decision-making in child welfare and protection.

Social workers are also aware that while they weigh the probability that their choice may bring about a positive outcome, they also need to take into account the possibility that the consequences of their choice may be negative. In the envelope example, imagine that if you chose the blue envelope you had 50% chance of getting \$100 and 50% of paying a \$10 fine, and if you chose the yellow envelope you have a 25% chance of getting \$500 and 75% of paying a \$50 fine. The potential gain is higher if the yellow envelope is chosen, but so is the potential loss. How do you weigh the potential gains and losses?

Again, the normative approach is quite clear:

The expected value of the blue envelope—50% × \$50 + 50%(−\$10) = \$25 − \$5 = \$20
The expected value of the yellow envelope—20% × \$500 + 80%(−\$50) = \$100 − \$40 = \$60.

So, according to the normative approach, the answer may look quite obvious: choose the yellow envelope. Is it? Many of us would be very hesitant to select a course of action that carries such a high probability of loss and may prefer a lower expected value in order to avoid loss. In fact, Tversky and Kahaneman's *prospect theory* (1981) shows that decision-makers attach more significance to loss compared with an equivalent gain. Furthermore, a sure gain is favored over a probabilistic (higher) gain, and a probabilistic loss is preferred to a sure (smaller) loss. This is one of a very large number of examples that show that, in real life, decision-makers make choices that deviate from the expectations of the normative theory. This work had major impact on the area of behavioral economics and earned Kahneman the Nobel Prize in 2002 (a few years after Tversky's death).

One of the implications of these differences in weighing losses and gains is the vulnerability of decision-makers to the ways decisions are *framed*. The same decision situation could be framed in ways that emphasize the expected loss or in terms of the expected gains. Consider the following classic example.

Let us assume that we know of an approaching wave of extremely dangerous flu. A social worker is working in a home for the aged caring for 600 residents. The social worker needs to recommend one of two alternative treatments, A or B. There are two scenarios.

Scenario one: Using Treatment A, she will be able to save 200 lives; using Treatment B will produce a 33% chance of saving all 600 residents and a 66% chance of not saving any.
Scenario two: If she uses Treatment A, 400 will die; using Treatment B there is a 33% chance that no one will die and a 66% probability that all 600 will die.

From a normative perspective, these two scenarios, although framed differently, are equivalent. "Saving 200 lives for sure" is equivalent to "400 people will die," a 33% chance of saving all 600 is equivalent to a 33% chance that no resident will die, and saying that there is a 66% chance of not saving anyone is exactly the same as saying that there is a 66% probability that all will die.

Despite this clear equivalence, the actual responses to these two scenarios are drastically different. In the original experiment, 77% of those presented with the scenario in which Treatment A saves 200 lives chose this alternative, while only 22% selected this alternative when Treatment A was presented in terms of how many people will die.

This example and others drawn from prospect theory suggest that the way decisions are framed can influence the decisions of social workers in cases of alleged maltreatment. Presented in a positive light of how a particular alternative is expected to bring positive outcomes may (perhaps unintentionally) underplay the potential negative consequences of choosing this alternative, while a focus on the potential harm of an alternative may lead decision-makers to overlook the probability of good outcomes.

Fluke, Bauman, Dalgleish, and Kern (2014) presented to practitioners a decision problem, analogous to the one just discussed, in which they provided the probability of achieving reunification (that could be seen as a gain) and of remaining in placement (loss). They demonstrated that hypotheses derived from prospect theory were empirically supported and that how a decision has been framed made a significant difference in practitioners' responses to two equivalent cases.

VALUE VERSUS UTILITY

The normative theory of choice guides one to select the alternative with the highest product of probability and value. However, in real life, and especially in child welfare and protection, it is difficult to know the value of an outcome. When dealing with gambles that involve probabilities and sums of money, the choice may look straightforward: choose the alternative in which (Probability) × (Sum of Money) is greater. There are many indications, however, that this may not be the case. The *subjective* value may be more influential than the objective value. The subjective value of the same amount of $100 may be different for two people with different incomes, and a gain of $100 is much more subjectively significant when it is added to $500 compared to when it is added to $50,000. In another context, an outcome of adding 12 months to someone's life is probably valued much more by a person whose life expectancy is 24 months compared with the value of this extension to someone expecting to live 30 more years. Hence, it may be more relevant to examine the *subjective utility* of an outcome rather than its objective value.

Determining subjective utility of an outcome may be a difficult task. First, the relevant unit is not always clear. Dollar amount, number of lives saved, months added to life expectancy, number of products generated may all be fairly straightforward and possibly obvious measurements to assess the utility of outcomes in various contexts. In child welfare and protection, however, it is not clear what the natural units to assess the utility of outcomes are, even though concepts such as safety, well-being, healthy attachment, and a sense of belonging come to mind.

Even when the units are selected, one needs to "translate" potential outcomes to a utility construct. For example, what would be the value of prolonging the life of a terminal patent 3 months versus 6, 12, or 24 months? The utility may not be a linear function of the months added to someone's life, and a patient may see no utility in adding 3 more months to his or her life (given the excruciating pain involved in the experimental treatment) but may see a major increase in utility when the expected additional months of life expectancy is more than 1 year. Similar questions are raised when a practitioner attempts to weigh the relative utility of increased safety (e.g., through placement) versus maintaining familial bonds (e.g., through family perseveration).

Some ideas about ways to help child protection decision-makers assess the subjective utilities of child welfare outcomes could come from medicine, a discipline that has extensive experience in assessing the subjective utility of alternative health outcomes (e.g., Miyamoto, 2000). For example, Lee and colleagues (2018) used surveys to assess the utility of alternative health states of colorectal cancer-related health states. They indicate that in health-related issues a common metric to assess utility is the *quality-adjusted life-year* (QALY), a single index generated from combining disease mortality (deaths) and morbidity (disease), used as the official measurement scale in the United States and the United Kingdom. This index could be elicited from a representative sample of a given society (in Lee and colleagues' case, South Korea) or from groups of patients. There are several ways to elicit such indices, including visual analogue scale (VAS), time trade-off (TTO), and standard gamble (SG).

To illustrate, in one method, a VAS is presented to a participant, commonly as a single vertical line on a page with verbal (e.g., "best imaginable health state possible" and "worst imaginable health state possible") and numerical (e.g., 0 and 100) descriptors at each end. Participants (e.g., patients) are presented with a series of potential health states and are asked to rate the desirability of each using the scale. In another method the participant is asked for a tradeoff: How many years would the participant be willing to give up to maintain 10 years of current health (Attema, Edelaar-Peeters, Versteegh, & Stolk, 2013)? We are not aware of efforts to determine utility or to design a shared metric to assess the relative utility of child welfare outcomes.

MULTI-ATTRIBUTE UTILITY MODEL

To study basic processes of decision-making, many studies employ simplistic tasks that present the decision-maker with two alternatives, each with two potential consequences (e.g., win or lose). In real life, however, decision-makers often consider multiple alternative courses of actions, each with multiple potential consequences, and each of these consequences may have a different probability for each of the alternative courses of action. For instance, a social worker facing an adolescent with a history of self-harm may consider a range of alternatives from the least to most restrictive settings. The worker may focus on a rather small set of outcomes, such as being physically safe from self-harm, having a subjective sense of well-being, and being engaged in satisfying relationships with normative peers.

According to the normative approach, under these circumstances, the decision-maker is expected to employ a Multi-Attribute Utility Model (MAUT) to compute the utility of each of the alternative courses of action and select the option with the overall highest utility. As we saw earlier, to compute expected utility one needs to take into account both the probability that an outcome would happen and the utility of that outcome. To follow this approach, the decision-maker needs to assess how valuable an outcome is (its utility) and how likely this outcome is expected to occur in each of the alternatives. In this example, the social worker is expected to assess whether safety from self-harm is less likely when the most restrictive option is chosen and that the likelihood of self-harm would be higher for the least restrictive course of action. Similarly, the decision-maker may assess that if the adolescent was kept in a very restrictive environment, the probability of healthy engagement with peers may be less likely compared with being placed in a less restrictive placement. According to the model, these assessments of the likelihood of each outcome need to be weighted by the utility of each of these outcomes. The combination of the likelihood of a certain outcome and its utility will determine how attractive is the course of action.

BOUNDED RATIONALITY AND HEURISTICS

According to the normative theory of choice, a rational choice follows the steps just described to compute the expected utility. As may be evident from the preceding (quite simplified) example, finding the appropriate way to choose the optimal course of action involves extensive mental computations. However, given the limited human capacity to process information and the intractability of many choice problems, following the normative approach in the real-life decisions of both laypersons and experts may prove overwhelming if not impossible. Kahneman (2011) refers to physiological capacity in relation to decisions as *fast* and *slow thinking*, where fast thinking occurs through the use of heuristics, and slow thinking may utilize processes akin to MAUT. In fact, the shift in thinking with regard to our understanding of decision-making is that decision-making may not always be subject to a normative process and that there are patterns of decision-making behavior that do not reflect the normative framework. This discussion is often cast as the beginnings of an ongoing debate between proponents of *rational and irrational decision theory* (Wakker, 2010), an important but nuanced topic that is too complex to address thoroughly in this chapter.

This change in our perspectives regarding our view of decision-making had its origins in the work of Herbert Simon (1956) who is credited with coining the term "bounded rationality." His work in this area earned him the Nobel Prize for Economics. According to this framing of how human problem-solvers operate in real life, due to our inherent limitations in information processing, limited resources (e.g., of time), and the complexity of problems, humans (both laypersons and experts) function as *satisfiers* rather than optimizers of expected utility.

One of the more influential pioneering groups that emerged from this view, led by Tversky and Kahneman, explored how humans use simplified processes, shortcuts, rules of thumb, and *heuristics* to overcome their limitations. Although these scholars presented heuristics as useful mechanisms that could lead to accurate judgments in many decision contexts, much of this line of scholarship focused on the judgment errors caused by these heuristics. Over the years, there have been thousands of studies and publications describing a large number of heuristics. This body of evidence is relevant to child welfare decision-making because there is evidence to suggest that child welfare workers are not immune to heuristics and biases that can have negative consequences for the subjects of their decisions (e.g., Enosh & Bayer-Topilsky, 2015; Munro, 2011). We will not attempt to enumerate and describe them here, and we will only illustrate this topic with the example of the *base rate fallacy* and show how it could impact decisions in child protection.

Let us assume that a social worker has a very effective way of detecting incestuous relations in the family—so good, in fact, that in 99% of incest cases in the family, the social worker does not fail to realize the presence of incest, and only in 1% of the incestuous cases does she fail to see it. Let us also assume that this social worker is an excellent diagnostician, and, when there is no incest, she is able to notice that, and only says there is incest in a family in 1% of the cases when it has not happened. These may be highly inflated assessments of the accuracy of common diagnostic methods, but we will show that, even with these high figures, the problems associated with the heuristic are evident.

We now present a family to the social worker and ask for her opinion, and she concludes that this is a case of family incest. What is the probability that this is indeed an incest case? Most expert practitioners and layperson will say intuitively that, based on the social worker's high accuracy in identifying incest cases, the probability is close to 99% or slightly less. From a normative perspective, however, this intuitive estimate is a mistake. What makes this mistake very vivid is the fact that very few will notice that, to answer the question correctly, we need information that has not yet been presented. The essential (and missing so far) information is the base rate: What is the proportion of families with incestuous relationships in the caseload? Although it is not intuitive, the probability that the social worker is accurate in stating that this particular family has incestuous relationships depends on two factors: (1) how accurate is the social worker (or, stated in another form, to what extent this particular case is similar to a real incest family), and (2) unrelated to the specific case, to what extent incest is prevalent in the caseload (in other words, the base rate in the relevant population).

Assume, for instance, that the caseload consists of a 1,000 families and only 10 of them are involved in incest. In that case, and given the high accuracy of 99%, the social worker may identify about 1% by mistake as incestuous, which is 10 families out of 1,000. We do not know whether the family she named as incestuous comes from the 10 real cases of incest or from the 10 families with a mistaken label. It can be immediately seen that our confidence in her judgment needs to be attenuated considerably. In fact, even if she had 100% success in labeling correctly an incestuous family as such, we would still need to take into account that she may have named a family that is not involved in incest as such. The lower the base rate, the lower our confidence in the label and the greater the need for extra care in adding supporting evidence.

The importance of taking into account base rates when assessing the accuracy of prediction is demonstrated very clearly in Kearney's important work on predicting nonaccidental child death and the condemnation of protection workers who "failed" to predict accurately serious events of major harm to the child (Kearney, 2013). Given the very low base rate for the event of nonaccidental death among children formally subject to care plans (estimated at 0.025%), the limitations of predicting such rare events are enormous. Nonetheless, public inquires into nonaccidental deaths often end up by chastising child protection workers for not seeing the inevitable outcome.

This lack of understanding of the importance of base rate is compounded by another well-known heuristic: *hindsight bias* (Arkes, Faust, Guilmette, & Hart, 1988). That is, when humans know the outcomes of a decision, it impacts strongly their assessment of how predictable the outcomes of the event were. Consequently, review committees that are convened because the tragic outcomes are known find it extremely hard to put themselves in the shoes of a person who made the decision and examine the information known to the decision-maker before the outcomes were known.

As mentioned, in addition to the base rate fallacy and hindsight bias there are numerous studies that identify evidence for a range of human heuristics that may be useful in certain situations but lead to errors in others (see, e.g., reviews in Chapman & Sonnenberg, 2000). The reason to engage in understanding heuristics is not to dwell on human limitations, but to help decision-makers become aware of human limitations and try to reduce their negative impact on our judgments and decisions. For instance, extensive research has documented the tendency to form hypotheses early in the thinking process and then to move on to confirm them, searching only for information to support the hypotheses, not looking actively for disconfirming evidence and overlooking information that may go against the initial hypothesis. It is important to note that this *confirmation bias* (Nickerson, 1998) is not seen as a character flaw of decision-makers unwilling to admit a mistake. Instead, it is seen as a mechanism that reflects human information processing limitations, one that is used because it may lead to a correct answer with the investment of fewer resources of time and energy compared with other, more systematic and normative processes as described earlier, when considerable efforts are needed to calculate utility.

A series of studies suggested that laypersons and experts are often not aware of their reliance on heuristics in decision processes and limitations and are over-confident in their judgments (Garb, 1998). As an alternative view, Gigerenzer and Gaissmaier (2011) focuses on how simple shortcuts in decision processes may lead to better decisions than those based on formal optimal procedures. Another perspective has been the subject of research by Klein (2015) and is based on the concept of accumulated expertise over a very specific problem domain, where actions taken are based on a deep awareness of outcome patterns and immediate feedback to the decision-maker.

There are efforts to help decision-makers become aware of biases and build into their decision processes mechanisms that would attenuate this intuitive tendency to confirm hypotheses, as well as many other heuristics. In fact, the extensive literature in business and psychology on human information processing has been an essential part of *behavioral economics*. This field integrates the accumulating knowledge on how humans process information and are vulnerable to biases to understand economic behaviors and suggest ways of modifying less than optimal economic choices. Richard Thaler, a Nobel Prize laureate for his contribution to behavioral economics (2017) explains that because many of the biases are predictable, they could be prevented by using a range of ways to restructure the decision context in order to avert actions that biases might cause.

Efforts to address biases due to human error are also evident in psychology. For instance, the National Research Council (NRC) made a series of recommendations for improvements in all forensic sciences (NRC, 2009). Neal and Brodsky (2016) review the literature from the medical and forensic psychology fields on biases in judgment and corrective strategies to deal with these biases. They identified educational strategies that focus on making professionals aware of their biases and suggest ways of overcoming them, using workplace strategies that are procedural aspects of the decision-making process (e.g., requiring group consultation or slowing the process so that less pressure is exerted to use quick heuristics) and "forcing functions" that require professionals to use decision aids or requiring the satisfaction of certain criteria before some of the judgments could be made by the professional decision-maker.

In their qualitative study of expert forensic psychologists, Neal and Brodsky (2016) identified 25 corrective strategies, and, in a follow-up quantitative study, they asked experts to assess the effectiveness of these strategies. The findings indicate that experts tended to rate most of the strategies as effective, some of them with empirical support (e.g., educational interventions; see Nisbett, 2016), but some were already shown empirically to be ineffective (e.g., introspection).

Based on this awareness of the limitations of human decision-making in the uncertain environment of child protection, several scholars in the child welfare and protection field proposed ways of attending to these limitations, taking advantage of some effective heuristics (e.g., pattern recognition) and using critical thinking processes to overcome some intuitive biases (Gambrill & Gibbs, 2017; Munro, 2008). Brian Taylor suggested the concept of *psycho-social rationality* and proposed heuristic models of decision-making that take into account the limitations of human information processing and the complexity of real-life decision-making in child welfare (Taylor, 2013; van de Luitgaarden, 2011). Empirical studies with child protection professionals are important to create awareness of the limitations in their judgment processes and find ways of overcoming common pitfalls.

THE RELATIONSHIPS BETWEEN JUDGMENT AND CHOICE

In the area of child welfare and protection, the decision about what action one should choose (e.g., reunify a child with his or her family or continue placement) is based on a series of assessments and judgments (e.g., the risk of future maltreatment if the child returns home). Although choice and decisions are based on judgments, the relationships between judgment and decision are far from simple.

Consider a very simplified example in which a child protection worker who made a thorough risk assessment reaches the conclusion that the chances of further maltreatment at home, if returned, are not negligible but are still quite low. Perhaps, if pressed to provide a formal assessment, the worker may have assessed that the risk for maltreatment at home is 20%. What are the implications for the decision whether to recommend returning the child home? Is a 20% risk too high to take, and the worker should recommend continuing the placement or termination of parental rights? If a 20% chance of future maltreatment is considered a "reasonable" risk to take in order to promote long-term well-being, the worker may decide, based on this risk assessment, to return the child home.

The threshold of risk (the probability of further maltreatment if returned home in this example) that triggers a decision to reunify varies across practitioners (see Chapter 9 by Wittenstrom et al. and Chapter 6 by López and Benbenishty), and settings (see Chapter 6 by López and Benbenishty and Chapter 10 by Fallon et al.). Some social workers may not be willing to take almost any risk of further maltreatment, and their threshold may be much lower (e.g., no more than 5%), while others are so concerned with the potential negative consequences of continued placement or termination of parental rights that they would be willing to consider reunification even if the risk is considerably higher (e.g., 40%).

Expanding on the example, certain contexts that interact with potential risk are likely to influence strongly the worker's personal threshold (Dalgleish, 1988). Consider, for instance, a worker in an agency that is undergoing public scrutiny for making a decision to return a different child to her parents only to learn a week later that the parents severely abused the child. Under such circumstances, a practitioner in that agency would probably prefer a more cautious approach, a higher threshold of expected safety, before recommending reunification.

In our observations in child protection settings, we were struck by the fact that when there were disagreements in child welfare teams about the right decision, there was no clear separation between disagreement regarding the assessed risk and disagreements that stem from individual differences in thresholds. This is unfortunate. The issue of agreement on risk assessment can be addressed with more knowledge and shared learning, whereas thresholds carry with them personal values, attitudes, and organizational contexts. They require a different kind of deliberation process, one dealing with diversity in norms and values. We think that the literature in this area suggests that child protection teams need to discuss issues of differences in thresholds and find ways to arrive at a shared approach separately from agreeing on shared methods to assess risk. However, even with the advent of formal shared decision-making processes, we currently lack evidence that such processes are more effective in improving decision-making, and, in some situations, they may actually result in poor decision-making due to conformity and group influence (Salganik, Sheridan, & Watts, 2006; Sunstein, 2003).

THE RELATIONSHIPS BETWEEN WORKERS' PREDICTIONS AND ACTUAL OUTCOMES

When child welfare and protection practitioners face a new case, they use the case information to arrive at a judgment and to predict what might happen to the child and family. The worker takes into account an array of information cues available on this case and makes a judgment on whether the child is at risk for further maltreatment. The worker's prediction may be accurate, but it may also prove to be wrong.

Imagine a social worker who needs to make the decision whether to remove a child from home and then learns that the parents have already severely abused the child's sibling (who has been therefore removed from home). This piece of information has important diagnostic value as a potential indication of a propensity to abuse children, very similar to receiving a positive result on a diagnostic blood test. Still, we are aware that no single sign or test is perfect. Diagnostic tests may show positive results for cases that do not have the condition and may show negative results despite the fact that the condition exists. There are parents who have abused one of their children but who will not abuse any other child, and there are parents who have not abused any of their children but may abuse the next child they have (see Table 1.1).

There are several important lessons to be learned from presenting the common scenario of making judgment and prediction and then eventually finding out what actually happened. First, and perhaps the most important point, is that judgments about future events come with errors. Due to the uncertainty that is part of the real word and our imperfect knowledge of it, we will always make a certain amount of mistakes when we try to predict the future on the basis of information and knowledge we have acquired. One of the less intuitive consequences of this idea is that we should not rush to assess the quality of a decision by its outcomes. One may have done the best with the available information and knowledge, and still the outcome may be disappointing. Imagine you were given a choice between two lotteries: in one you have a 50% chance of getting $200 and in the other you have a 50% chance of getting $100. Which lottery would you choose? The rational and best decision you can make is to select the lottery with the possible outcome of $200. But, as we all know, you may still come up empty-handed. Does that mean that the decision was not the right one? Unfortunately, the public—and in many cases post-hoc investigations following disastrous outcomes—judge the prediction and decision by their outcomes rather than by the processes that led to the decision, which may have been faultless.

Table 1.1 POSITIVE AND NEGATIVE PREDICTIVE VALUES

	Actual behavior	
Prediction	Abuse	No abuse
Abuse	True positive	False positive
No abuse	False negative	True negative

Table 1.1 also shows that there are two types of errors: *false positive*, when we predicted that the child would be abused and she was not, and *false negative*, when we predicted that the child would not be abused and she was actually abused. It is important to realize that, in a given context and with particular knowledge, trying to minimize one type of error always is at the expense of increasing the other type of error. As we saw earlier in the discussion of thresholds, a decision-maker can decide to return a child home when the assessed safety is high. This preference would minimize those cases that a worker assessed that the child would be safe but the child was then maltreated (minimize false positives). However, by using a higher bar as a condition for returning home, the worker increases the chances that children who would have been safe in their family are not returned (increasing false negatives). On the other hand, if the bar is lowered and more children are reunified, the chances of a false negative result increase.

In this context it is useful to introduce two concepts that are mostly used when discussing diagnostic tests but are clearly relevant here. When a diagnostic test is developed (e.g., a blood test for hepatitis C), one is concerned that the test may show by mistake that a healthy person has the disease (a false positive). The degree to which the test is able to avoid this problem is called the test's *sensitivity*. The other concern, of the test failing to identify a person who is sick (a false negative) is called *specificity*. Test developers make judgments about the minimally acceptable levels of sensitivity and specificity. In some tests they may decide that they would rather have more patients misidentified as having the illness and suffer the consequences than have more patients misdiagnosed as not having the illness and have much more severe consequences. Hence, by deciding the *cutoff point*—the threshold—test developers determine the proportions of false positives and false negatives that are likely to occur. From our earlier discussion of the base rate heuristic, however, it is important recognize that variations in the number of persons reflected in these proportions may be quite different, especially if the base rate is low.

BRUNSWICK, HAMMOND, AND THE LENS MODEL

The preceding discussion on errors in judgment draws our attention to the question of how judgments are made and to what degree they are close to real-life outcomes. We think that the conceptual work laid by Egon Brunswik's *probabilistic functionalism* and expanded by Kenneth Hammond has contributed significantly to concepts, methods, and practical tools to improve decisions (e.g., Brunswik, 1966; Hammond, 1980). This work is best illustrated in Figure 1.1, the Lens Model.

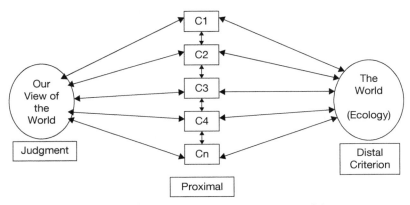

Figure 1.1 Brunswick's Probabilistic Functionalism Lens Model.

To understand the components of the model, consider that when a child protection worker receives a complaint about alleged maltreatment, she needs to
arrive at a judgment about whether the child's parents are likely to physically
abuse the child in the future. The model presents two sides of the lens. One side
is the real world (often called the "ecology" or "task environment"). It represents whether the child would actually be abused. The other side of the lens is
the decision-maker's cognitive system; that is, the decision-maker's judgment.
Unfortunately, the decision-maker cannot see the future. For her, whether the
child is abused in the future is a *distal* outcome. The decision-maker, however,
has access to a series of *proximal* information cues (such as physical signs of
abuse, information on previous referrals, parents' portrayal of their behavior,
observations made by teachers). Based on these cues the decision-maker forms
her judgment.

Having two sides of the lens, we can compare the judgment and the actual
outcome and ask to what extent the judgment was *accurate*. The Lens Model
draws attention to an important factor that is often overlooked: the predictability of an outcome in real life may be inherently low. There is a philosophical
issue in whether the limits of the predictability of certain phenomena are in-
herit in the phenomena (e.g., in quantum physics) or are a result of our limited
knowledge about the world. Regardless, it is clear that a decision-maker cannot
perform better than the limits set by how predictable the world is. Hence, when
we find that judgments in certain areas have low accuracy (i.e., they do not
match the real world), one reason we may fail to predict an outcome is the real-
life low predictability of the outcome. For the area of child protection, this may
be a sobering idea and a reason to have more realistic expectations about how
accurate it is possible to be in predicting outcomes such as future abuse, length
of stay in care, and a child's well-being.

The Lens Model has been used extensively to learn and improve the "cognitive side." Given that many decision-makers are not aware of their judgment process, the *Social Judgment Theory* (SJT; Hammond, McClelland, & Mumpower, 1980) uses decision analysis to "capture the policy" of decision-makers, modeling the ways they use information and then explicating them so that decision-makers can examine critically their own model. For instance, Unsworth, Harries, and Davies (2015) used SJT to examine how occupational therapists make decisions on fitness-to-drive by presenting them with 64 case scenarios. The authors were able to predict 87% of the variance in these decisions based on the driver characteristics. In child protection, Shapira and Benbenishty (1993) used 120 case vignettes to identify individual models for 28 child protection workers. Further analyses indicated that there were two "meta-models" for risk assessment, the major difference between the two clusters was that the participants in one meta-model put heavier weight on signs of abuse and neglect and on the child's socioemotional development, whereas the participants in the other put more weight on the mother's and father's relationships with the child.

In addition to the focus on the cognitive side, the Lens Model also offers ways to improve judgments by learning more about the real world, for instance, through studying to what extent cues exist that could predict the outcomes and how they could be put together to predict the outcome (Dalgleish, 1988). This information could be contrasted and compared with the cognitive side. Note that, in the model, cues are associated with *both* the judgment and the real-life outcome. That is, lines coming out of a cue (e.g., information on previous maltreatment) represent the weights that each cue has—on the one hand, with the decision-maker's judgment of the likelihood of future abuse, and, on the other hand, with the real-life outcome of actual abuse. Hence, if these respective weights are very different, we could target these differences and try to minimize them. By providing corrective "cognitive feedback" (i.e., informing the decision-maker about the mismatch between her use of the information and what is actually needed to be more accurate), we may be able to improve decision-making processes.

PREDICTIVE RISK MODELING

The idea that, by describing the "real-life" side of the Lens Model, we could improve the "judgment" side may be best captured by *predictive risk modeling* (PRM; Cuccaro-Alamin, Foust, Vaithianathan, & Putnam-Hornstein. 2017). PRM is defined as a statistical method of identifying characteristics that risk-stratify individuals in a population based on the likelihood that each individual will experience a specific outcome or event (Cuccaro-Alamin et al., 2017, p. 293). In this method, all available cues about children and families are examined to determine how these cues may be predicting the outcome of choice (e.g., recurrent maltreatment, child death, failed reunifications; Packard, 2016). With today's technology, these analyses are conducted on huge databases ("big data") and implemented using sophisticated mathematical algorithms that are able to model the complexity of patterns in the data and continuously change to reflect the dynamic nature of the relationships between information on children and families and their child protection–relevant outcomes.

It should be noted, however, that the analyses and the model's result from applying techniques such as machine learning are not accessible to the decision-makers (see Chapter 2 by Stepura et al.). In contrast to an approach like SJT, which involves a representation of a practitioner's decision model, predictive modeling in most cases does not exist as an understandable model that practitioners could review and adopt.

SIMPLE MODELS OR SIMPLE PROCESSES?

After presenting what we mean by simple and complex ways of using information, we can turn to this question: To what extent do experts compared with novices or laypersons use information in more complex and sophisticated ways that lead to better judgments? This question has been the subject of numerous empirical studies in multiple area. Most importantly for this chapter, the issue was studied in the area of helping professions. To summarize the studies in a nutshell, a highly cited paper in *The American Psychologist* claims that

> [i]t has been argued that psychotherapy is a profession without any expertise (Shanteau, 1992). We examine the validity of this claim, reviewing the literature on expertise, clinical decision-making, and psychotherapeutic outcome assessment, and find it a reasonable assessment. There is no demonstration of accuracy and skill that is associated with experience as a therapist. (Tracey, Wampold, Lichtenberg, & Goodyear, 2014, p. 218)

This assessment is based on a review of many studies of clinical judgment and decision-making (including psychotherapy and medicine) showing that laypersons and experts alike tend to be unreliable and inaccurate in many of their judgments and that simple statistical models outperform the clinicians from whose judgments these models were derived. Paul Meehl, a very prominent clinical psychologist, contrasted clinical judgment with *actuarial prediction* (based on simple statistical models) and concluded that statistical models outperform clinicians' judgments even when the statistical models were based on previous judgments made by clinicians (Dawes, Faust, & Meehl, 1989; Meehl, 1954).

CURRENT MODELS IN CHILD WELFARE DECISION-MAKING

A few descriptive child welfare decision-making theories in the literature are noteworthy. An early decision-making model was proposed by Stein and Rzepnicki (1984). This model included the goals of child welfare (e.g., safety and family preservation), pointing out some key processes that included decision-making along with important domains of information (e.g., family, others, agency, courts, law, etc.). The second is the Munro (2008) systems approach that takes human error as the starting point for understanding decision-making. It also takes into account individual factors (e.g., skills, knowledge), resources, and constraints (e.g., analytic vs. intuitive judgment), as well as the organizational context in which decisions are made (e.g., changes in thresholds). This model has been a major source of policy analysis and dialogue in the field (Munro, 2011).

In the past several decades two complementary descriptive theories of decision-making in child welfare have emerged: the Judgments and Decision Processes in Context (JUDPiC) Model (Benbenishty et al., 2015) and the Decision-Making Ecology (DME) Model (Baumann, Dalgleish, Fluke, & Kern, 2014; Baumann, Dalgleish, Fluke, & Kern, 2011; Baumann, Kern, & Fluke, 1997). Both models are intended to serve as a foundation for ongoing decision-making research, and, to that end, several studies covering a range of child welfare settings and decisions have applied these frameworks as a foundation, including several of the studies presented in this volume. The models are summarized in the following sections.

The Decision-making Ecology

The DME is a theoretical framework for organizing decision-making research in child welfare, and it places the topic squarely in the context of actual protective service operations in this field. The aim is to provide an understanding of both the context and process of decision-making, the goal of which is to predict behavioral thresholds for action. Decisions take place within an agency culture, where a systemic context combines with the case decisions made by the management and staff of the agency, listed below:

Case factors: Information related to the maltreatment incident and family circumstances

Organizational factors: Agency structure and functioning, management
   practices, staffing
External factors: Laws and policies informing appropriate decisions and
   subsequent responses, societal attitude toward child safety and family
   preservation
Decision-maker factors: Attitudes, knowledge, skill, and other characteristics
   of the worker making a decision

The context for decision-making includes a set of decision-making influences
displayed as ovals. They cover the range of case, external, organizational, and
individual factors that combine in various ways to influence decisions and
outcomes. These influences are divided into dimensions that represent their
important features, and decisions can be understood as a part of this entire
context. While the diagram indicates direct relationships to the decisions, many
of these factors operate as mediators in actual empirically tested analyses (see
Chapter 5 by Graham et al.).

According to the DME, three key features of decision-making in child
welfare are (1) the *range of decisions* made by the caseworker, referred to
as a *decision-making continuum*; (2) the psychological *process* of decision-
making; and (3) the outcomes, or consequences, of the decision. This latter
is represented by the rectangle on the right side of the Figure 1.2, with
arrows indicating that decision-making has consequences for children (e.g.,

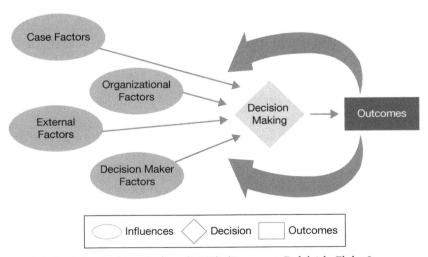

Figure 1.2 Decision-Making Ecology (DME); (Baumann, Dalgleish, Fluke &
Kern, 2011).

Brunswik, E. (1966). Reasoning as a universal behavior model and a functional differentiation between "perception" and "thinking." In K. R. Hammond (Ed.), *The psychology of Egon Brunswik* (pp. 487–494). New York: Holt, Rinehart and Winston. (Originally a paper presented at Montreal, 1954).

Chapman, G. B., & Sonnenberg, F. A. (Eds.). (2000). *Decision-making in health care: Theory, psychology, and applications.* Cambridge: Cambridge University Press.

Cuccaro-Alamin, S., Foust, R., Vaithianathan, R., & Putnam-Hornstein, E. (2017). Risk assessment and decision-making in child protective services: Predictive risk modeling in context. *Children and Youth Services Review, 79,* 291–298

Dalgleish, L. I. (1988). Decision-making in child abuse cases: Applications of social judgment theory and signal detection theory. In B. Brehmer & C. R. B. Joyce (Eds.), *Human judgment: The SJT view* (pp. 317–360). Amsterdam: Elsevier Science.

Dalgleish, L. I. (2003). Risk, needs and consequences. In M. C. Calder (Ed.), *Assessments in child care: A comprehensive guide to frameworks and their use.* (pp. 86–99). Dorset, UK: Russell House Publishing.

Dawes, R. M., Faust, D., & Meehl, P. E. (1989). Clinical versus actuarial judgment. *Science, 243*(4899), 1668–1674.

Enosh, G., & Bayer-Topilsky, T. (2015). Reasoning and bias: Heuristics in safety assessment and placement decisions for children at risk. *British Journal of Social Work, 45*(6), 1771–1787.

Fluke, J. D., Baumann, D. J., Dalgleish, L. I., & Kern, K. D. (2014). Decisions to protect children: A decision-making ecology. In J. Korbin & R. Krugman (Eds.), *Handbook of child maltreatment* (pp. 463–462). New York: Springer.

Gambrill, E., & Gibbs, L. (2017). *Critical thinking for helping professionals: A skills-based workbook.* New York: Oxford University Press.

Garb, H. N. (1998). *Studying the clinician: Judgment research and psychological assessment.* Washington, DC: American Psychological Association.

Gigerenzer, G., & Gaissmaier, W. (2011). Heuristic decision-making. *Annual Review of Psychology, 62,* 451–482.

Hammond, K. R. (1980). Introduction to Brunswikian theory and methods. *New Directions for Methodology of Social and Behavioral Science, 3,* 1–11.

Hammond, K. R., McClelland, G. H., & Mumpower, J. (1980). *Human judgment and decision-making: Theories, methods, and procedures.* Westport, CT: Praeger Publishers.

Kahneman, D. (2011). *Thinking, fast and slow.* New York: Farrar, Straus, and Giroux.

Kearney, J. (2013). Perceptions of non-accidental child deaths as preventable events: The impact of probability heuristics and biases on child protection work. *Health, Risk & Society, 15*(1), 51–66. doi:10.1080/13698575.2012.749451

Klein, G. (2015). A naturalistic decision-making perspective on studying intuitive decision-making. *Journal of Applied Research in Memory and Cognition, 4,* 164–168.

Lee, M. K., Park, S. Y., & Choi, G. S. (2018). Association of support from family and friends with self-leadership for making long-term lifestyle changes in patients with colorectal cancer. *European Journal of Cancer Care, 27*(3), e12846.

Meehl, P. E. (1954). *Clinical versus statistical prediction: A theoretical analysis and a review of the evidence.* Minneapolis: University of Minnesota.

Miyamoto, J. M. (2000). Utility assessment under expected utility and rank-dependent utility assumptions. In G. B. Chapman & F. A. Sonnenberg (Eds.), *Decision-making in health care: Theory, psychology, and applications* (pp. 65–109). New York: Cambridge University Press.

Munro, E. (2008). *Effective child protection*. Thousand Oaks, CA: Sage.

Munro, E. (2011). *The Munro review of child protection final report: A child-centred system*.

National Research Council. (2009). *Strengthening forensic science in the United States: A path forward*. Washington, DC: The National Academies Press.

Neal, T., & Brodsky, S. L. (2016). Forensic psychologists' perceptions of bias and potential correction strategies in forensic mental health evaluations. *Psychology, Public Policy, and Law, 22*(1), 58–76. https://doi.org/10.1037/law0000077

Nickerson, R. S. (1998). Confirmation bias: A ubiquitous phenomenon in many guises. *Review of General Psychology, 2*(2), 175–220.

Nisbett, R. E. (2016). Tools for smarter thinking. *Educational Leadership, 73*(6), 24–28.

Packard, T. (2016). *Literature review: Predictive analytics in human services*. San Diego, CA: Southern Area Consortium of Human Services.

Salganik, M., Sheridan, D., & Watts, J. (2006). Experimental study of inequality and unpredictability in an artificial culture. *Science, 311*, 854–856.

Shanteau, J. (1992). How much information does an expert use? Is it relevant? *Acta Psychologica, 81*(1), 75–86.

Shapira, M., & Benbenishty, R. (1993). Modeling judgments and decisions in cases of alleged child abuse and neglect. *Social Work Research and Abstracts, 29*(2), 14–19.

Simon, H. A. (1956). A comparison of game theory and learning theory. *Psychometrika, 21*(3), 267–272.

Stein, T. J., & Rzepnicki, T. L. (1984). *Decision-making in child welfare services: Intake and planning, Vol. 4*. Berlin: Springer Science & Business Media.

Sunstein, C. (2003). *Why societies need dissent*. Cambridge, MA: Harvard University Press.

Taylor, B. (2013). *Professional decision-making and risk in social work*. Exeter, UK: Learning Matters.

Thaler, R. H. (2017). Behavioral economics. *Journal of Political Economy, 125*(6), 1799–1805.

Tracey, T. J., Wampold, B. E., Lichtenberg, J. W., & Goodyear, R. K. (2014). Expertise in psychotherapy: An elusive goal? *American Psychologist, 69*(3), 218.

Tversky, A., & Kahneman, D. (1981). The framing of decisions and the psychology of choice. *Science, 211*(4481), 453–458.

Unsworth, C., Harries, P., & Davies, M. (2015). Using Social Judgment Theory method to examine how experienced occupational therapy driver assessors use information to make fitness-to-drive recommendations. *British Journal of Occupational Therapy, 78*(2), 109–120.

van de Luitgaarden, G. (2011). Contextualizing judgements and decisions in child protection practice at the point of first referral. *Journal of Social Intervention: Theory and Practice, 20*(3), 24–40.

Wakker, P. P. (2010). *Prospect theory: For risk and ambiguity*. Cambridge: Cambridge University Press.

Exploration in Predictive Analysis and Machine Learning

KELLY G. STEPURA, JIM SCHWAB, DONALD J. BAUMANN,
NATALIE SOWINSKI, AND STEPHANIE THORNE ■

INTRODUCTION

From the latter half of the 20th century through the present, the scientific liter-ature has strongly concluded that everyday decisions based on easily available data are fraught with human error, and the idea that humans are strictly rational decision-makers has come into question (cf., Kahneman, 2011; Kahneman & Tversky, 1973; Simon, 2010; Tversky & Kahneman, 1974, 1981). Moreover, mentally processing everyday information often involves more "efficient" fast thinking at the expense of more effortful slow thinking, resulting in the use of heuristics (mental rules of thumb) that frequently result in errors (Kahneman, 2011). Furthermore, the advent of large, complex systems has increased the likelihood of potential human errors in judgment due to the intricacies around extracting patterns from multifaceted data structures. We now know something about the ways in which scientists might assist decision-makers in extricating relevant patterns. One way is to inoculate decision-makers through training on the types of errors that are made in everyday decisions (though many are quite

Kelly G. Stepura, Jim Schwab, Donald J. Baumann, Natalie Sowinski, and Stephanie Thorne, *Exploration in Predictive Analysis and Machine Learning* In: *Decision-Making and Judgment in Child Welfare and Protection*. Edited by: John D. Fluke, Mónica López López, Rami Benbenishty, Erik J. Knorth, and Donald J. Baumann, Oxford University Press (2021). © Oxford University Press. DOI: 10.1093/oso/9780190059538.003.0002.

resistant; e.g., the tendency to confirm what you already believe). Another way is by developing actuarial instruments to assist decision-makers (e.g., Meehl, 1986). This chapter explores one other way of assisting decision-makers: machine learning. We begin our journey by discussing: (1) the task of prediction, (2) current practices and their limitations, and (3) the promise of these newer analytic techniques. As with many research enterprises, we did not come upon machine learning at the outset of our research. Instead, we exhausted more conventional practices first. Thus, our exploration in this chapter also involves describing how we arrived at our current destination.

THE TASK OF PREDICTION

Our work centers on an attempt to improve decision-making in child welfare through prediction. There are critical decisions being made every day on behalf of children, youth, and families in the foster care system. Decision-makers must ask themselves: If I place a child in this home or if I provide these services to a child, will they likely attain a permanent living situation when they leave my care? How long will it take? Our goal is to give decision-makers a way of thinking about the consequences of those placement and service provision decisions on relevant outcomes for children, youth, and families, such as whether permanency was attained and the length of time the child or youth remained in care. To be clear, our goal is not to create a system that makes the decisions for caseworkers. We endeavor to give caseworkers a reasonably accurate estimate of the likelihood that certain outcomes will occur, thus providing them with additional information to help them in their task, a piece of information that would not normally be available to them.

Traditionally, the way to make use of available data to assist decision-makers is to utilize techniques such as linear and logistic regression to determine whether the results produced sufficient accuracy to present a model to the field that would be helpful to use. In other words, a model would be created that estimates the likelihood of outcomes and achieves accuracy greater than that achievable by chance alone. In our journey, we attempted these more traditional approaches and were unable to approach an accuracy threshold that gave us the opportunity to confidently share a model with the field. Thus, we began searching for other techniques that we could employ to increase the accuracy of our models. In the course of that exploration, we encountered machine learning techniques, which in some respects build on traditional techniques and in other respects introduce new algorithms that enable us to approach our work in new ways.

Machine learning is a form of artificial intelligence that uses algorithms to build mathematical models of sample data (i.e., training data) to make predictions or decisions. Machine learning allows computer systems to perform tasks without explicit instructions, instead relying on models and inferences (Bishop, 2006). Machine learning is especially appropriate to the task of prediction because it focuses exclusively on future outcomes. Traditional approaches to prediction result in a static list of relevant variables and identified relationships between variables, promoting data reduction as much as possible before modeling. Machine learning has advantages over traditional approaches because it addresses the dynamic nature of child welfare by exploiting an abundance of data and adjusting as data changes over time. Rather than making a priori assumptions, machine learning enables systems to learn from data, based on the notion that these systems can identify patterns in data that are not obvious to humans and then use these patterns to improve decision-making. Machine learning can provide predictive feedback to help identify opportunities and avoid risks (Ayres, 2007; Boulesteix & Schmid, 2014; Breiman, 1997; Shmueli, 2010).

Machine learning is employed to create complex models and algorithms that aim to predict outcomes. The creation of these predictive models is known as *predictive analytics*. Predictive analytics use data to make predictions about future events. While predictive analytics and traditional historical forecasting are similar in that they both use historical data to predict the likelihood of future events, predictive analytics is different in that it leverages many replications of possible future outcomes to allow a deep understanding of risk, uncertainty, and confidence in results. Additionally, traditional prediction simplifies the nature of the inputs to the point where complex relationships may be obscured, both in terms of the number of cues considered and the nature of their relationship with the criterion; conversely, predictive analytics eliminates the need for over-simplification (Ayres, 2007; Boulesteix & Schmid, 2014; Breiman, 2001; Shmueli, 2010). This is an important consideration in child welfare, given the complexities inherent to the decisions being made in the field. An additional advantage of machine learning in child welfare is that it can create a process of prediction that continuously adjusts to changing contexts. In child welfare, the past often does not represent the future in a dynamic setting that must respond to new best practices, a younger and more inexperienced workforce, changing federal and state requirements, and a client population with constantly changing strengths, issues, and needs.

Despite persistent attention to controversial issues within the foster care system, the field struggles to consistently and accurately predict whether children and youth are likely to gain permanency, how long it will take, and what factors are relevant to these outcomes. To assist in this task, the task of prediction is to estimate the consequential future state of affairs based on caseworker decisions.

CURRENT PRACTICES AND THEIR LIMITATIONS

Overview

Machine learning algorithms are often used to apply complex mathematical calculations to large datasets to support decision-making. Machine learning models can analyze larger, more complex datasets with faster, more accurate results than traditional statistical approaches. In child welfare, the use of computer-based database systems such as Statewide Automated Child Welfare Information Systems (SACWIS) has expanded tremendously over the past 20 years, increasing the availability of large datasets for such purposes. Additionally, some groups, such as the Allegheny County Sharing Alliance for Health, are creating new opportunities to apply machine learning to complex multisector datasets, combining data that crosses various sectors, such as public health, human services, economic development, healthcare, and transportation (Allegheny County Sharing Alliance for Health, 2016).

The proliferation of computer-based data systems in child welfare and the availability of multisector datasets has resulted in a critical mass of data that can be used to address research questions using machine learning approaches. Most traditional statistical analyses are based on the notion of linearity. Results point to a specific number, and individuals lie above or below that number, so the task of prediction is to figure out on which side of the line individuals fall. This approach falls short when used for predictive purposes because of a lack of accuracy and specificity when the prediction is about an individual rather than a group. In addition, traditional linear models are sensitive to outliers, which can greatly affect the results of these traditional approaches. As we began our initial data analyses, these and other shortcomings of traditional methods hindered our ability to improve our predictions of the two important variables we will discuss below. The machine learning strategies described in this chapters methods section overcame these problems.

Permanency and Time in Care as Examples

We chose outcomes of importance to the field. In particular, the need for improvement in our current understanding of permanency and time in care for foster children and youth is apparent. Child welfare has acknowledged this issue and has focused on improving outcomes related to permanency and time in care. Though intended as a short-term, temporary solution, many children and youth languish in care awaiting a permanent home environment. It is commonly accepted that, while in care, the foster care system influences growth and development, sometimes with harmful results. Increased time in care is expensive and also increases the opportunity for children and youth to experience further changes to their familial and social networks, and those changes in living situation, school, neighborhood, and relationships are directly associated with negative outcomes (Fong, Schwab, & Armour, 2006). Previous research has documented negative outcomes associated with foster care on most aspects of foster children and youth lives, such as issues with education, attachment, development, behavior, mental health, and physical health, as well as the impact of foster care on their future as adults (Betz, 2010; Courtney et al., 2011; Cusick, Havlicek, & Courtney, 2012; Hook & Courtney, 2011; Jones, 2014; Pecora et al., 2006a, 2006b; White, O'Brien, Pecora, & Buher, 2015). For children and youth removed from their homes, the goal of all child welfare systems is to ultimately place them in a safe and permanent home environment as quickly as possible.

The optimal solution for concluding time in care is in finding a permanent home environment for children and youth. With more than 64,000 children and youth (15%) in care for 3 or more years, continued focus on finding a permanent home for children and youth is imperative. In fact, in 2015, more than 25,000 children and youth were emancipated from the foster care system as adults without attaining a permanent living situation, either through reunification, adoption, guardianship, or a placement with other relatives (US Department of Health and Human Services [USDHHS], 2016). For the majority of emancipating children and youth, prior research has documented a lack of employable skills, minimal education, inadequate preparation for independent adulthood, and limited social supports (Betz, 2010; Collins & Ward, 2011; Curry & Abrams, 2015; Jones, 2014). Long term, the likelihood of negative outcomes when transitioning to adulthood, such as unemployment, homelessness, lower incomes, economic hardships, poor health, educational deficits, and higher arrest rates, increase for emancipated children and youth compared to other young adults (Betz, 2010; Courtney, 2005; Courtney & Dworsky, 2006; Kushel, Yen, Gee, & Courtney, 2007; Paul-Ward, 2009; Perez & Romo, 2011; Raghavan, Shi, Aarons, Roesch, & McMillen, 2009).

There is limited information about what child or youth characteristics are associated with placement outcome and time in care. However, studies of the Child and Adolescent Needs and Strengths (CANS) instrument that have used particular CANS items or combinations of CANS items have found an association between CANS items and time in care for foster children and youth (Yampolskaya, Armstrong, & Vargo, 2007). CANS items have also been used to predict discharge placements for children and youth exiting residential care (Lyons, Uziel-Miller, Reyes, & Sokol, 2000). Additionally, a 2013 meta-analysis examining studies completed between 1971 and 2012 found primarily mixed results on the association of a variety of child and youth characteristics with placement outcomes. Age was found to play a role in placement outcomes, with about half of the studies concluding that younger children have more positive placement outcomes. One key characteristic related to placement outcomes appears to be mental health, while other potential characteristics requiring future study include attachment and youth substance use (Pritchett, Gillberg, & Minnis, 2013).

Published research regarding child and youth characteristics as predictors of time in foster care is scarcer. A 1986 study by Seaberg and Tolley found that child abandonment, physical or mental impairment, age, race, and sex all play a role in determining time in care. A more recent study examining time in care in relation to placement outcomes for boys found that mental health issues were associated with time in care when placement outcomes were reunification or transfer, while age and history of substance use were associated with quicker exits for boys who run away (Baker, Wulczyn, & Dale, 2005).

Recognizing the limitations of our ability to predict these critical outcomes for foster children and youth, there has been a trend in child welfare to improve care by shifting service provision and responsibility from public to private agencies through performance-based contracts (PBC). These contracts most often focus on whether providers meet goals set for permanency and time in care, and providers are rewarded or sanctioned based on whether they successfully attain these goals. The goals are often set through traditional methods and consensus among providers.

Predicting Performance-Based Contract Outcomes

The PBC that was in place when the data for this study were collected (children and youth entering care in fiscal year 2014 and 2015) evaluated each PBC provider by comparing their performance to the past performance of agencies in the same region of Tennessee. The objective was to incentivize agencies to improve performance outcomes to avoid costs associated with care as well as children and youth languishing in the foster care system (Tennessee Department of Children's Services, 2016).

Omni Visions Inc. (Omni), a multistate child placing agency, expressed an interest in making use of existing data relevant to PBC outcomes to identify foster children and youth who were likely to remain in care for long periods of time or who fail to achieve permanency on discharge. Thus, the current investigation sought to predict discharge outcomes relevant to Omni's PBC as early as possible in the child or youth's time in Omni's care.

Methods

DATA COLLECTION
When Omni receives a referral for an admission into their care, relevant data are passed from the State to an Omni caseworker. When possible, this generally includes demographic information, original removal details, placement history, and information from the CANS instrument. This admission information is entered by Omni staff into their agency's software system (KaleidaCare Management Solutions, Inc.), along with data related to case management, treatment planning, goals, services, and discharge, among others. For the purposes of this study, data were retrieved from this existing historical administrative dataset.

MEASURES
Initially, it was expected that the resulting models would determine which variables were most relevant, using only information that a worker would know on child/youth admission. With this strategy in mind, all items from the CANS at admission were included in the initial models. Additional admission information, such as child or youth demographics, referral information, and history with Child Protective Services, were also included as predictors (see Appendix A for a list of all variables).

Child and Adolescent Needs and Strengths
The CANS instrument is typically used to evaluate progress toward goals and to make recommendations for service planning based on "actionable treatment needs" (Lyons, 2009; Lyons, Weiner, & Lyons, 2004) for individual children and youth. Our study followed other research that used the CANS differently, examining the relationship between CANS results and youth outcomes (Fontanella, 2008; Kisiel, Fehrenbach, Small, & Lyons, 2009; Lyons, Griffin, Jenuwine, Shasha, & Quintenz, 2003; Lyons, Uziel-Miller, Reyes, & Sokol, 2000; McIntosh, Lyons, Weiner, & Jordan, 2010; Park, Mandell, & Lyons, 2009; Weiner, Leon, & Stiehl, 2011; Yampolskaya et al., 2007). The Tennessee version of the CANS used for this study (Version 3.15) was developed in 1999 and contains 10 domains and 66 items and is similar to more recent versions (John Praed Foundation, 2015).

Outcome Variables
Although reentry data were not available, data related to permanency and time in care were available, resulting in the two outcome variables used in this study: achievement of permanency and achievement of target care days. In parallel with the PBC contract, both variables were measured on discharge

from Omni's care for children and youth who remained discharged for at least 30 days. The Omni contract emphasized time in care, a general term specified in the contract based on a comparison of the actual number of days children and youth remained in Omni's care (i.e., "care days") and the number of days they were expected to remain in Omni's care (i.e., "target care days"). For the contract in effect when this study's admissions occurred, target care days for a specific child or youth differed based on the number of years they had been in care and were further specified based on age and adjudication. Agency reimbursements and financial penalties at the end of the contract were determined based on the overall difference between actual care days and target care days with adjustments for reentries and exits to permanency (Center for State Foster Care and Adoption Data, 2012; Children's Rights, 2011; Tennessee Department of Children's Services, 2016).

Achievement of permanency is defined based on whether the child or youth achieved permanency through adoption, reunification, kinship care, or guardianship when they left Omni's care. All other avenues for discharge (e.g., runaway, independent living, transfer to another agency, jail, hospitalization, or death) were considered to have resulted in not achieving permanency. Achievement of target care days was created based on whether each child or youth exceeded his or her established target care days. Thus, this study's two outcome variables parallel the Tennessee PBC outcomes to increase the practical utility of the results for Omni and help them better anticipate the performance outcomes identified for Tennessee's implementation of PBC.

PARTICIPANTS

The study's participants included Omni foster children and youth who were admitted under the PBC in Tennessee during the 2014 and 2015 fiscal years. Children and youth may have been placed in either treatment foster care or residential care and may have been admitted due to maltreatment or due to juvenile justice issues. Children and youth were not included if they were in care for less than 5 days, if they were already in care when the contract began, or if an admission CANS within 31 days of admission was not available. Additionally, Omni did not complete the CANS for children and youth who were less than 6 years of age, so these were excluded systematically. Finally, to ensure that children and youth had an equal chance of being discharged during the time frame of the study, those who were not discharged within 2 years of the last day of their admission fiscal year were also excluded. Participants may have been admitted into Omni's care more than once during the time frame of the study, and, per the PBC model, an exit from care resulting in a return to Omni within 30 days was considered a continuation of the prior admission. Otherwise, it was considered a new admission. These criteria resulted in a final dataset that included 915 admissions.

METHODOLOGICAL STRATEGY

Using historical, administrative data, this study attempted to predict the likelihood of two specific foster care outcomes: achievement of permanency and achievement of target care days. Initially, we attempted to analyze the admission data using traditional approaches. These methods included factor analysis, cluster analysis, and logistic regression. Each of these methods produced inadequate results. In particular, the logistic regression modeling attempts overfit the data for the training sample and failed to achieve an accuracy rate greater than what could be attained by chance alone for the test sample.

To investigate potential explanations for our failure to produce a viable model, the dataset was reexamined. It was recognized that issues of measurement are often associated with administrative data due to a lack of quality control and the possibility of missing information. We attempted to resolve these issues by reviewing data for accuracy and completing case readings to fill in missing data. Based on this analysis, additional reasons for our failure to produce results include issues with embedded subsamples (e.g., based on differences such as gender, placement type, and age), issues with multicollinearity, item multidimensionality, and issues related to the measurement of both the outcomes and predictors.

Following our review of the dataset, we re-ran analyses using traditional statistical methods. We remained unable to identify a model that had a predictive accuracy rate substantially above chance for a validation holdout sample. Our next step was to reexamine the relationship between each individual predictor and the outcome variable. The probability of a successful outcome was associated with individual scores on the different predictors. We then turned to an examination of pairs of predictors to understand their combined, or joint, pattern of success on the outcome variable.

To compute the joint probabilities for combinations of more than two variables, we searched for an efficient algorithm to compute these probabilities. This search resulted in the serendipitous discovery of the *naïve Bayes algorithm* for machine learning classification. The algorithm is based on Bayes' theorem, which is a mathematical equation used to calculate the probability of an event happening, given that it has a relationship to another event (ThoughtCo., 2017).

Experimenting with this technique using Scikit-learn (n.d.), a machine learning technique in Python (an open source programming language), we tested several variable combinations based on the "information gain calculation," which calculates the amount of information gained about a random

variable based on observation of another random variable. We also tested correlation matrices of variables to examine the "naïve" assumption of indepen-
dence between predictors. A model using four predictors was derived that met
the accuracy benchmark for 10-fold cross validation (see later discussion).

At this point, all potential predictors were included in the model, along with
multiple forms of the predictors. To test whether the inclusion of all possible
predictors was negatively affecting the model accuracy rate, we employed feature selection. *Feature selection* (also known as *variable selection*) is a technique
used in machine learning that reduces the number of variables used in a model
to lessen complexity, improve accuracy, and decrease overfitting. Additionally,
we examined each form of the predictors to determine which form most accurately predicted the outcome variables. For example, age at admission was
examined to determine whether a dichotomous variable would increase predictive accuracy over a continuous form of that variable, as well as which cutoff
point was best suited to dichotomize the variable. The selection of the cutoff
point is analogous to the split that is obtained in modeling a decision tree,
rather than a more traditional approach utilizing mean and median values. In
fact, all continuous variables were dichotomized due to distributional issues
and, when tested empirically, demonstrated improved accuracy in their dichotomous form. Similarly, various forms of each CANS item were created to determine which form would most accurately predict the outcome variables. The
potential forms of these variables included an ordinal scale utilizing all four
points (0, 1, 2, 3) on the CANS scale as well as dichotomous variables based
on combinations of the four points. It was found that the form that split the
CANS items dichotomously between scores of 0 and 1 and scores of 2 and 3
increased model accuracy more than other forms. Thus, this form of the CANS
items was utilized in the final models instead of using the entire ordinal scale.
This seemed especially appropriate given that it is recommended that CANS
items with a 2 or 3 be addressed in service and treatment planning. Thus, our
strategy altered from including all available admission information as predictors to including only those that were most relevant to the models in terms of
their ability to increase the accuracy of prediction.

Buoyed by this step forward, we explored other machine learning systems that
differed in capability and complexity such as WEKA (see https://www.cs.waikato.
ac.nz/ml/weka/) and the CARET (see http://topepo.github.io/caret/index.html)
package in R. Ultimately, we utilized the Machine Learning in R (MLR) package
because of its well-documented tutorial and common interface among the various machine learning algorithms which it encapsulates (Bischl et al., 2016).

The naïve Bayes analysis in MLR utilized a somewhat more rigorous validation strategy. First, the dataset was randomly divided into a 75% training
sample and a 25% validation sample, both stratified on the outcome variable.

The test sample was held out entirely from the analysis to test accuracy on a set of cases not included in model development.

The initial naïve Bayes model incorporated all the potential predictors, followed by variable importance calculations which identified the five variables that produced the highest accuracy rate for a 10-fold cross-validation model. In 10-fold cross-validation, the original sample is randomly partitioned into 10 equal-size subsamples to evaluate the predictive model by partitioning the original sample into a training set to train the model and a test set to evaluate it. The model with only five variables was computed to produce a cross-validated accuracy rate and applied to the test data.

Results

To exemplify the machine learning approach utilized in this study, the results of analyses of two naïve Bayes models are presented. In the first machine learning example, the model results are based on a technique using Python Scikit-learn (n.d.). In the second example, results are described for an analysis completed using MLR (Bischl et al., 2016).

MACHINE LEARNING EXAMPLE 1: PYTHON SCIKIT-LEARN

Achievement of Permanency

Model accuracy was computed using two strategies. First, the final naïve Bayes model predicted whether children and youth would or would not achieve permanency with a 73.5% classification accuracy rate for a test sample of 228 (25%) cases based on a training sample of 687 (75%) cases. Second, a 72.4% classification accuracy rate was based on a 10-fold hold-out of the 915 cases in the total sample. The strongest contributors to the model were age at admission, prior placements, siblings in care, and current runaway concerns as a CANS treatment need.

Age at admission. Age at admission was based on the child/youth's age when he or she was admitted into Omni's care. In its dichotomized form, this variable was categorized into children and youth aged 6–12 and children and youth aged 13 and older as the split that optimized the percentage of cases achieving permanency in the training sample.

Prior placements. Prior placements are placements that occurred before the child/youth's admission to Omni's care. These placements included non–foster care placements such as trial home visits, runaway events, and juvenile detention centers. The dichotomized form of this variable that optimized the percentage of cases achieving permanency in the training sample split the variable between zero to six prior placements and seven or more prior placements.

Table 2.1 MACHINE LEARNING EXAMPLE 1 CONFUSION MATRIX: PREDICTED AND
ACTUAL ACHIEVEMENT OF PERMANENCY

	Prediction		
Actual results	**Will not achieve permanency**	**Will achieve permanency**	Total
Did not achieve permanency	127	185	312
Did achieve permanency	64	539	603
Total	191	724	915

Siblings in care. Siblings in care refers to children and youth who have siblings who have been placed in Omni's care although they may or may not be placed in the same home.

Current runaway concerns as a treatment need. The CANS at admission was defined as the CANS nearest to the admission date that was within 31 days of the admission date. "Current runaway concern" is defined as a child/youth treatment need based on a score of 2 or 3 on the CANS runaway item.

The confusion matrix in Table 2.1 is used to describe the performance of the naïve Bayes model by allowing for visualization of algorithm performance. The overall model accuracy rate was 72.8%, with a prevalence rate of 65.9% of children and youth achieving permanency. In reviewing whether the model was equally accurate in predicting achievement permanency versus not, results indicated that the true-positive rate comparing predicted achievement with actual achievement was 89.4%, while the false-positive rate comparing those not predicted to achievement permanency with actual achievement was 59.3%. In terms of specificity, results indicated that the model accurately predicted that children and youth would not achieve permanency at a rate of 40.7% and accurately predicted permanency achievement at a rate of 74.5%.

Combinations of the four strongest contributors to the model were then reviewed in relation to how the presence or absence of each affected the likelihood that a child or youth with the given characteristics would achieve permanency. The number of cases and predicted probability of achieving permanency are presented in Table 2.2. When a combination of characteristics resulted in a predicted probability of permanency that was 50% or higher, the model predicted achievement of permanency. For combinations of characteristics where the predicted probability was less than 50%, the model predicted that children and youth would not achieve permanency. The process of reviewing this information can help to highlight combinations of characteristics and history that can further elucidate the relationship between the variables that are strong contributors to the model accuracy and the outcome variable.

Table 2.2 MACHINE LEARNING EXAMPLE 1: PREDICTED PROBABILITY OF PERMANENCY
FOR COMBINATIONS OF STRONG CONTRIBUTORS

	Adolescent	7 or more prior placements	Siblings in care	Current runaway concerns	Predicted probability of permanency	Number of cases
1	False	False	True	False	97%	166
2	False	False	True	True	90%	1
3	False	False	False	False	89%	83
4	True	False	True	False	86%	89
5	False	True	True	False	86%	4
6	False	False	False	True	69%	6
7	True	False	True	True	63%	10
8	False	True	False	False	60%	10
9	True	False	False	False	60%	346
10	True	True	True	False	53%	9
11	True	False	False	True	28%	72
12	True	True	True	True	23%	5
13	True	True	False	False	21%	80
14	True	True	False	True	7%	34

Achievement of Target Care Days

Overall, validation models attempting to predict whether children and youth would exceed the number of target care days applied by the state of Tennessee as part of performance-based contracting resulted in low accuracy rates. Further analyses using only those predictors that were strong contributors to models predicting permanency demonstrated that models attempting to predict achievement of target care days utilized different variables. Additional modeling is being conducted to better understand these variables in relation to the current results.

MACHINE LEARNING EXAMPLE 2: MLR

For the second machine learning example, achievement of permanency was examined as an outcome variable, but achievement of target care days was not, given our inability to produce a viable model for this outcome with the first machine learning example. Using MLR, the final naïve Bayes model predicted whether children and youth would or would not achieve permanency with a 68.9% accuracy rate for a hold-out test sample excluded from the training model and a 71.8% average accuracy rate for the 10-fold cross-validation training sample used to develop the model.

Table 2.3 MACHINE LEARNING EXAMPLE 2: PREDICTED AND ACTUAL
ACHIEVEMENT OF PERMANENCY

	Prediction		
Actual results	**Will not achieve permanency**	**Will achieve permanency**	Total
Did not achieve permanency	40	38	78
Did achieve permanency	33	117	150
Total	73	155	228

Table 2.3 describes the model's performance using a confusion matrix. For this machine learning example, the 915 cases were divided into a training sample of 687 cases (75%) and a test sample of 228 cases (25%) that were held out from the training process. The confusion matrix for example model 2 includes only the test cases, which allows for a more rigorous estimate of model accuracy for predicting unknown cases. The model accuracy rate was 68.9%, with a prevalence rate of 65.8% of children and youth achieving permanency. Results related to model accuracy for both achieving permanency and not achieving permanency indicated that the true-positive rate for achievement of permanency was 78.0%, while the false-positive rate for not achieving permanency was 48.7%. In terms of specificity, results indicated that the model accurately predicted that children and youth would not achieve permanency at a rate of 51.3% and accurately predicted that children and youth would achieve permanency at a rate of 75.5%.

The strongest contributors to the model were age at admission, prior placements, current runaway concerns as a CANS treatment need, the average child/youth risk behavior CANS domain score, and a factor based on CANS items, *externalizing behaviors*. Age at admission, prior placements, and current runaway concerns as a CANS treatment need were also strong contributors to the model described in Machine Learning Example 1, and specific definitions for those variables can be found in that section. The other two predictors, Child and Youth Risk Behaviors and Externalizing Behaviors, were not strong contributors to the model described in Machine Learning Example 1 and thus are defined here. It is noted that overlap exists between the variables that make up the strong contributors to the model. For example, current runaway concerns as a CANS treatment need is not only included in the model as a predictor but is also included in the creation of both the child/youth risk behaviors decrease much more after age 15. For the average domain score for child and youth risk behaviors, a negative linear curve is also exhibited. When the average score for child and youth risk behaviors is 0, the probability of achieving permanency is much higher than when the child or youth average score is 2. Prior placements exhibit a relatively dramatic negative linear curve, with the probability of achieving permanency evening out around 20 prior placements before admissions to Omni. Externalizing behaviors exhibits a negative linear curve, although less drastic than all of the others except age at admission.

While the accuracy rate for this model was lower than the accuracy rate for the initial four-variable model, the MLR package supports testing of alternative models and the development of ensemble models that combine the results of various machine learning algorithms (Bischl et al., 2016). The potential for ensemble models to improve the accuracy of machine learning models is addressed further in the "Discussion" section.

DISCUSSION

The relevance of this study is in offering a machine learning approach to predict foster child and youth outcomes and in the potential practical utility of the model itself. It has the potential for practical utility in that more accurate decisions hold the promise for more influence, efficiency, and accessibility. Although this work is not intended to advocate for decisions that are solely made based on machine learning models, machine learning approaches can be used to improve decision-making and lessen judgment inaccuracy due to human error. Using large datasets, machine learning techniques can uncover relationships that are not intuitive and are too complex for human processing.

Key Findings

MACHINE LEARNING EXAMPLE 1: PYTHON SCIKIT-LEARN

For the first machine learning example using Python Scikit-learn (n.d.), key findings in predicting permanency for foster children and youth in Omni's care included that age at admission, prior placements, siblings in care, and current runaway concerns as a CANS treatment need were the strongest contributors to a naïve Bayes model predicting permanency. Validation of models using whether children and youth were likely to exceed target care days as the outcome variable resulted in low accuracy rates.

MACHINE LEARNING EXAMPLE 2: MLR

A second machine learning example using MLR resulted in similar findings. Key findings were similar to the first example, such that age at admission, prior placements, and current runaway concerns as a CANS treatment need were included as strong contributors in both models predicting permanency. In the second example, whether the child or youth had siblings in Omni's care was not a strong contributor, while two additional variables were strong contributors. One of these was child and youth risk behaviors, a variable created using the average score for the CANS child and youth risk behavior domain. The second was created based on a principle components analysis that was conducted, resulting in two factors: internalizing behaviors and externalizing behaviors. Based on the inclusion of these additional variables in the analysis, the factor of externalizing behaviors was also included as a strong contributor in the second example.

Limitations

Limitations of the study include that the use of these machine learning approaches results in findings that are specific to the sample included in the modeling process and are inherently not generalizable. This differs from traditional social sciences approaches in that the results of this study are not necessarily representative of other foster children and youth populations. Additionally, the use of a historical administrative dataset presented some concerns related to data accuracy and missing data. These concerns were mitigated by case readings that involved searching case records for missing data and verifying accuracy through case readings.

Another limitation of the analyses is that the outcome variables used for the study represent the outcomes most relevant to performance-based contracting in Tennessee from the foster care agency's perspective and do not represent the child or youth's full experience while in care. Achievement of permanency as defined in this study does not take into account the child or youth's potential long-term permanency status or reentry into foster care. Similarly, time in care does not reflect their time in care either before or after their time in Omni's care.

By focusing on variable definitions relevant to Tennessee's performance-based contracting implementation, the study specifically defined whether the child or youth exceeded target care days based on targets established by the state. Thus, the results are dependent on the manner in which those targets were established.

can be a valuable alternative when traditional methods are unsuccessful, especially in situations where large datasets are available and complex decisions must be made. To further improve the accuracy rates of these models, *ensemble approaches* are particularly intriguing. An ensemble approach, which we intend to explore in the future, requires that multiple machine learning analyses be completed simultaneously so that the varying resulting models can be synthesized to combine results across models. For example, two ensemble methods are (1) result averaging, which is used with continuous data, and (2) majority voting, for classification of discrete data. This approach generally follows a supervised machine learning model training process and can ultimately be used to improve the accuracy of the final machine learning model. Ensemble approaches show great promise in improving the accuracy of machine learning models and thus can be highly beneficial in supporting the complex decisions that social workers make every day.

REFERENCES

Allegheny County Department of Human Services. (2017, April). Developing predictive risk models to support child maltreatment hotline screening decisions. Allegheny County Analytics: https://www.alleghenycountyanalytics.us/index.php/2017/04/17/developing-predictive-risk-models-support-child-maltreatment-hotline-screening-decisions/

Allegheny Sharing Alliance for Health. (2016). Data Across Sectors for Health (DASH) project profile. http://dashconnect.org/wp-content/uploads/2016/10/Allegheny-County.pdf

Ayres, I. (2007). *Super crunchers: Why thinking-by-numbers is the new way to be smart.* New York: Bantam.

Baker, A. J., Wulczyn, F., & Dale, N. (2005). Covariates of length of stay in residential treatment. *Child Welfare: Journal of Policy, Practice, and Program, 84*(3), 363–386.

Barth, R. P., Lloyd, E. C., Christ, S. L., Chapman, M. V., & Dickinson, N. S. (2008). Child welfare worker characteristics and job satisfaction: A national study. *Social Work, 53*(3), 199–209.

Baumann, D. J., Law, J. R., Sheets, J., Reid, G., & Graham, J. C. (2005). Evaluating the effectiveness of actuarial risk assessment models. *Children and Youth Services Review, 25*(5), 465–490.

Betz, C. L. (2010). Emancipation of youth in foster care: The dilemma. *Journal of Pediatric Nursing, 25*(4), 241–243.

Bischl, B., Lang, M., Kotthoff, L., Schiffner, J., Richter, J., Studerus, E., . . . Jones, Z. M. (2016). MLR: Machine Learning in R. *Journal of Machine Learning Research, 17*, 1–5.

Bishop, C. M. (2006). *Pattern recognition and machine learning.* New York: Springer.

Boulesteix, A.-L., & Schmid, M. (2014). Machine learning versus statistical modeling. *Biometrical Journal, 56*(4), 588–593.

Breiman, L. (1997). No Bayesians in foxholes. *IEEE Expert, 12*(6), 21–24.

Breiman, L. (2001). Statistical modeling: The two cultures. *Statistical Science, 16*(3), 199–215.

Center for State Foster Care and Adoption Data. (2012). Performance based contracting in Tennessee's Foster Care System. https://fcda.chapinhall.org/wp-content/uploads/2012/10/2012_TN-PBC-case-hx2.pdf

Children's Data Network. (n.d.). Assessing children's risk using administrative records: A proof of concept Predictive Risk Modeling (PRM) project. http://www.datanetwork.org/research/assessing-childrens-risk-using-administrative-records-a-proof-of-concept-predictive-risk-modeling-prm-project.

Children's Rights. (2011). What works in child welfare reform: Reducing reliance on congregate care in Tennessee. http://www.childrensrights.org/wp-content/uploads/2011/07/2011-07-25_what_works_reducing_reliance_on_congregate_care_in_tn_final-report.pdf

Collins, M. E., & Ward, R. L. (2011). Services and outcomes for transition age foster care youth: Youths' perspectives. *Vulnerable Children and Youth Studies: An International Interdisciplinary Journal for Research, Policy and Care, 6*(2), 157–165.

Courtney, M. E. (2005). *Youth aging out of foster care.* Philadelphia, PA: MacArthur Foundation Research Network on Transitions to Adulthood and Public Policy.

Courtney, M. E., & Dworsky, A. (2006). Early outcomes for young adults transitioning from out-of-home care in the USA. *Child & Family Social Work, 11*(3), 209–219.

Courtney, M. E., Dworsky, A., Brown, A., Cary, C., Love, K., & Vorhies, V. (2011). *Midwest evaluation of the adult functioning of former foster youth: Outcomes at age 26.* Chicago, IL: Chapin Hall at the University of Chicago.

Curry, S. R., & Abrams, L. S. (2015). Housing and social support for youth aging out of foster care: State of the research literature and directions for future inquiry. *Child and Adolescent Social Work Journal, 32*(2), 143–153.

Cusick, G. R., Havlicek, J. R., & Courtney, M. E. (2012). Risk for arrest: The role of social bonds in protecting foster youth making the transition into adulthood. *American Journal of Orthopsychiatry, 82*(1), 19–31.

Epstein, R. A., Bobo, W. V., Cull, M. J., & Gatlin, D. (2011). Sleep and school problems among children and adolescents in state custody. *Journal of Nervous and Mental Disease, 199*(4), 251–256.

Epstein, R. A., Schlueter, D., Gracey, K. A., Chandrasekhar, R., & Cull, M. J. (2015). Examining placement disruption in child welfare. *Residential Treatment for Children & Youth, 32*(3), 224–232.

Finkelstein, J., & Jeong, I. C. (2017). Machine learning approaches to personalize early prediction of asthma exacerbations. *Annals of the New York Academy of Sciences, 1387*(1); 153–165.

Fong, R., Schwab, J., & Armour, M. (2006). Continuity of activities and child well-being for foster care youth. *Children and Youth Services Review, 28*(11), 1359–1374.

Fontanella, C. A. (2008). The influence of clinical, treatment, and healthcare system characteristics on psychiatric readmission of adolescents. *American Journal of Orthopsychiatry, 78*(2), 187–198.

Funke, J. (1991). Solving complex problems: Exploration and control of complex systems. In R. J. Sternberg, & P. A. Frensch (Eds.), *Complex problem solving: Principles and mechanisms* (pp. 185–222). New York: Lawrence Erlbaum.

PART II

Methodology for the Study of Decision-Making in Child Welfare and Protection

3

Empirical Methods for Studying Decision-Making in Child Welfare and Protection

JOEL GAUTSCHI AND RAMI BENBENISHTY ■

INTRODUCTION

Professional decision-making and judgment in general, and in the area of child welfare and protection in particular, are complex processes. They are often described as a mixture of art and science, intuition and rational choice, and quick and slow processes. As can be seen in multiple chapters in this book, decisions in this area combine human judgment, prediction of future events under uncertainty, and choices made among alternatives, based on multiple factors, including case information, contextual factors, values, and policy directives. Given the importance of these decisions and their complexity, the challenges associated with studying them, with the aim of improvement, are formidable.

This chapter describes the current state of the art of the most prominent empirical methods used to study decision-making in child welfare and child protection and to identify empirical methods from other fields, with the potential to advance decision-making research in our domain. We describe these

Joel Gautschi and Rami Benbenishty, *Empirical Methods for Studying Decision-Making in Child Welfare and Protection* In: *Decision-Making and Judgment in Child Welfare and Protection.* Edited by: John D. Fluke, Mónica López López, Rami Benbenishty, Erik J. Knorth, and Donald J. Baumann, Oxford University Press (2021). © Oxford University Press. DOI: 10.1093/oso/9780190059538.003.0003.

methods critically to assess their advantages and limitations. We end with some ideas about future promising directions.

Our interest is in the whole range of judgments and decisions made in child welfare and child protection. As prototypical decision tasks, we considered two main challenges: using information about a case in order to arrive at a final judgment or choice (e.g., assessing whether a child is at risk and deciding whether to remove the child from home), and considering several alternative courses of action for a case (e.g., choosing a foster family from several available alternatives).

We follow the distinction made by Benbenishty (1992) between modeling the relationships between the input and output of the decision process without trying to model the processes that lead from input to output (a "black-box" approach) and modeling the decision processes leading from the input to the output. Each of these approaches has its strengths and limitations. For instance, while "input-output" analyses may provide more valid, reliable, replicable, and parsimonious models that could predict effectively outcomes of decision-making processes, process tracing may produce models that would help develop a theory of practice; these are more intuitively understood by practitioners and therefore could be translated into practice guidelines more easily. Because both these lines of research have the potential to contribute to our critical examination of decision-making and to improvement efforts in child protection, we will follow this basic classification and review them both.

INPUT-OUTPUT ANALYSIS

Many studies on decision-making in child protection investigate how input factors of interest (e.g., case factors) are related to an output (i.e., decision or judgment). We introduce common methods and designs for data collection in input-output studies. To analyze this type of data, different statistical models, like various types of regression analysis, ANOVA, or structural equation modeling, are used.

Input-output analyses differ in the extent to which they are based on existing real-life data or on data created for the purpose of research. We start our overview with methods based on using case files and administrative databases.

Collecting Existing Data: Case Files and Administrative Data

Most child protection practitioners maintain case files that are rich in information that could be most useful for research on decision-making. The information in these case files, however, is often unstructured, not standardized or consistent, across cases and practitioners. Some researchers have analyzed the content of such files to identify the statistical relationships between case characteristics and decisions.

Benbenishty and colleagues analyzed case files of child welfare decision-making committees in Israel charged with the mandate to decide on taking children out of their biological home in cases of confirmed abuse or neglect (Dolev, Benbenishty, & Timmer, 2001). The authors created coding instructions to transform the open-ended text to quantitative data and used regression equations to look for case factors associated with the decision to remove a child from home.

Inter- and intrarater reliability of case files coding can be achieved through training and practice. Still, due to the unstandardized nature of the case files, there are limitations on the quantitative data that could be extracted. First, it is unlikely that coders could assess reliably nuanced data using sensitive rating scales. Instead, one should expect more dichotomous coding ("Is there any indication on file that the child suffers medical neglect? Yes—No") rather than a rating scale from "not at all" to "a large extent").

Another major limitation is missing data. While a coding scheme addresses the whole range of data that were found in all files, most files contain only a subset of the potential data. Hence, when a case file does not contain information on parental mental health, it is not clear whether that means that there are no parental mental health issues (and this is why they were not reported), there is no available information on this topic, or perhaps that the practitioner neglected to report the information. This ambiguity reduces the validity of coding of existing files.

In the past few decades, many child welfare systems have introduced computerized administrative databases. Some of these systems contain mainly child and family background information and financial transactions related to the case, while others are much richer and contain important information on assessments, case processes, decisions, and outcomes over time that could be used for studying decision-making (e.g., Coohey, 2003; Rivaux et al., 2008). For a few child protection systems, nationwide administrative datasets are available (for an overview, see Krüger & Jud, 2015), like the US National Child Abuse and Neglect Data System (NCANDS) dataset that might be used for research on decision-making.

Using administrative data in research comes with certain major opportunities (Connelly, Playford, Gayle, & Dibben, 2016). (1) Given that actual decisions and real-world conditions are recorded in administrative data, the external validity of the findings for this specific context is high. (2) Most administrative databases include all relevant cases in a specific jurisdiction; this is a major advantage over surveys that typically employ only samples and struggle with significant levels of nonresponse. (3) The large number of cases accumulated by such administrative databases provides opportunities for complex statistical data analysis. (4) Databases that offer opportunities to examine different cohorts of cases over times may help address an important issue that is rarely addressed systematically: to what extent decision-making strategies change over time.

While computerized administrative databases offer significant opportunities, it is nonetheless crucial to take into account and address their challenges and limitations. Some of the major challenges are (Connelly et al., 2016) listed here

Content. Most administrative databases were developed to support management and financial transactions (e.g., paying providers). The content of these records may therefore lack information pertinent to decision-making, and, when it contains data on decisions, it is important to ascertain whether these decisions were carried out.

Data quality. The quality of the data maintained in administrative databases may not always be high enough to support valid research. There are multiple threats to record reliability and validity because there may not be—or has not been—enough opportunities to train for reliability within and between practitioners and due to regional or agency-based differences in reporting practices (Jud & Sedklak, 2015). Of special concern regarding validity is how practitioners' perceive the implications of their reports. Some administrative databases are used only for the purposes of management record keeping, while others serve as control and accountability devices. Practitioners' perceptions of the relevance of their reporting (e.g., only to satisfy managers demands and as having no consequences for inaccurate reporting), as well as the implications of what they choose to report, may create significant intentional or unintentional inaccuracies in reporting. All of these aspects must be carefully evaluated by researchers to ensure acceptable data quality.

Ethics issues. Because of the data's sensitive, personal nature at case level, legal and ethical issues like data security, confidentiality, permission, and appropriate use need to be clarified and complied with (Stiles & Boothroyd, 2015). This is especially true for linkage of administrative datasets with other datasets (e.g., child protection system data with mental health records, social security records, etc.; see, e.g., Bradt, Roets, Roose, Rosseel, & Bouverne-De Bie, 2015). While merging databases from different types of services offers the addition of important information, several legal and ethical issues arise in addition to technical issues.

Standardized Assessment Forms in Agency Surveys

In some studies, child protection workers use a standardized assessment form provided by researchers to document information about the child, family members, other involved actors, and the workers' judgments and decisions about each case. Questionnaires on case characteristics can be supplemented by questionnaires on workers and agency characteristics to study individual and context effects. These agency surveys allow researchers to define what measurements are used to collect the data. Lately, the World Health Organization provided a toolkit on agency standardized case assessments including recommendations on sampling procedures, obtaining agencies participation, data collection instrument construction, and statistical analysis (Jud, Jones, & Mikton, 2015). One of the major challenges is to obtain the participation of agencies and caseworkers in particular (Jud, AlBuhairan, Ntinapogias, & Nikolaidis, 2015). Caseworkers need to be motivated and supported to reliably complete the standardized assessment forms on their cases. To ensure that this additional effort required is not overwhelming, the length of the assessment forms is often reduced and hence limits the range of variables included in the study and how detailed they are when recorded. For instance, parent's mental health might be recorded in a dichotomous variable (mental health problem: yes/no) instead of through validated and detailed mental health scales. One way to make the implementation of standardized assessment forms acceptable to practitioners is to use existing administrative database and supplement them with standardized assessment forms. Combining agency surveys with administrative data reduces the caseworkers' workload.

In some countries, nationally representative standardized assessments agency surveys on child maltreatment incidences and agency responses have been conducted (Krüger & Jud, 2015). Some of these studies were primarily designed to conduct epidemiological research and therefore are not suitable to study child protection workers' decision-making. Other studies, however, show the potential of this approach to examine a large and representative sample of decisions. For example, data from the Canadian Incidence Study and related province-specific studies have been extensively used to study various types of decisions (Smith, Fluke, Fallon, Mishna, & Decker Pierce, 2018; Stoddart, Fallon, Trocmé, & Fluke, 2018; Tonmyr, Ouimet, & Ugnat, 2012).

Studies based on standardized case assessments have several limitations. One important limitation is that they do not provide opportunities to examine differences in agreement between workers (e.g., in different regions or countries) because cases differ between workers and contexts. Furthermore, with the observational designs used, it is methodologically and theoretically difficult to study the causal effect of case characteristics on child protection workers' decision-making. We do not know of any observational study on decision-making in child protection that made explicit use of methods and approaches for causal inferences. Doing this in the future would be a major advancement for knowledge in this area (see, e.g., Morgan & Winship, 2015).

An alternative to agency-based standardized forms are studies based on simulated cases constructed by researchers purposefully to answer specific research questions.

Simulated Cases: Vignette Studies

In child protection decision-making research, the most frequently used simulated-cases approach are brief descriptions of fictitious but realistic case situations, also called *vignettes*. These vignettes are presented to professionals with a request to make judgments and decisions as if they were assessing a real-life case.

Most vignettes studies are based on presenting text. There are, however, vignettes that are composed of other media, such as photographs, audio, and videos (Hillen, Van Vliet, Haes, & Smets, 2013). Depending on the real-world situation to be simulated, these other types of media might be more suitable than text. In one of the few studies using nontextual vignettes, Ards et al. (2012) showed photographs of a messy bedroom to caseworkers. Using photomontage, the pictures randomly varied with respect to whether a black baby, a white baby, or no baby was sitting on the bed in the very same bedroom, so that the judgments of caseworkers could be compared across pictures.

Constructing text vignettes and response questions that are suitable to answer specific research questions requires careful considerations of various methodological, theoretical, and practical aspects (Evans et al., 2015). Among other considerations, researchers need to balance between presenting a rich and realistic vignette that would resemble a real-life case decision and an attempt to generate shorter vignettes that do not require too much time from participants. Researchers may present the same vignette to multiple participants in order to assess similarities and differences between different decision-makers (e.g., experienced and inexperienced practitioners; Davidson-Arad & Benbenishty, 2016) and different contexts (e.g., different child welfare systems; Benbenishty et al., 2015; Berrick, Dickens, Pösö, & Skivenes, 2017). Vignettes were also used to test sociopsychological models of decision-making psychological theories explaining professionals' intentions in decision-making (Rodrigues, Calheiros, & Pereira, 2015).

In classical experimental vignette studies, respondents are presented with a randomly assigned version of a vignette. This allows assessing the causal impact of the varied attributes on respondents' vignette evaluation. For example, in a cross-national study, Benbenishty et al. (2015) used vignettes describing situations of potential child maltreatment. They randomly presented one of two versions that were identical except that in one the mother opposed strongly the removal of her child and in the other she did not. Comparing the responses to the two different vignettes the researchers could examine whether this case attribute had a causal impact on the caseworkers' risk assessment, substantiation decision, and intervention recommendation. In combination with the vignettes, respondents responded to questionnaires to describe their demographic characteristics and child protection attitudes. These data offered rich opportunities to investigate how the case variable (mother's wish), professional characteristics (child protection attitudes, demographic characteristics), and national child protection systems are associated with the rating of vignettes.

Researchers may want to examine the impact of more than one case factor. In such cases, multifactorial experimental designs like the factorial survey approach can be used (Auspurg & Hinz, 2015; Rossi & Anderson, 1982). Factorial surveys have become popular in social sciences to experimentally study human judgment in general (Wallander, 2009) and professionals' decision-making in particular (Taylor, 2006; Wallander, 2012). In factorial surveys, multiple attributes (factors) of a vignette are experimentally varied. This allows quantifying the causal effect of each of the factors and their interactions on vignette ratings. Stokes and Schmidt (2012), for example, varied eight attributes of a vignette describing situations of potential child maltreatment, such as housing, parental substance use, resources and support, and cooperation.

A full factorial design that allows the analysis of the effects of each of the factors and all of their possible interactions results in a large number of vignettes. For instance, a full factorial design with eight factors and three possible values per factor (e.g., high cooperation, ambivalent cooperation, low cooperation), requires 3^8 (6,561) vignettes. That is why factorial survey designs often do not use every vignette (*full factorial designs*) but instead choose a subsample of all possible vignettes (*fractionalized factorial design*) (Auspurg & Hinz, 2015).

In complex factorial experiments, it is often not feasible that each participant gets only one vignette (between-subject design) or that all participants get the same set of vignettes (within-subject design). The former often needs too many participants, the latter results in too many vignettes per participant. Factorial surveys with multiple factors, therefore, often use mixed designs where respondents get several vignettes (i.e., several combinations of factor levels), but not all of the respondents see the same set of vignettes (Atzmüller & Steiner, 2010). Having participants responding to several vignettes has the advantage of reducing the number of participants needed to respond to a given set of vignettes. In this type of design, however, respondents might become aware of the manipulations in the vignettes. This might result in possible biases for varying case factors with high social desirability, like race. For sensitive topics, some have therefore suggested using *between-subject designs* with only one vignette per participant (Beyer & Liebe, 2015) or *split-plot designs* (Goos & Jones, 2011). The latter allows keeping sensitive factors constant within persons, while the nonsensitive factors vary within persons (for a brief overview, see Auspurg, Hinz, Liebig, & Sauer, 2015). Split-plot designs seem to be a good compromise to avoid participants becoming aware of the experimental manipulation of sensitive factors while keeping the number of needed participants lower than in between-subject designs. Surprisingly, however, in a methodological study, a factorial survey without split-plot design was more capable of measuring the effect of a concrete sensitive factor than was a factorial survey with this sensitive factor held stable (Auspurg et al., 2015). In addition, making the experimental manipulation of factors even more transparent by showing two vignettes per screen to participants surprisingly showed less social desirability bias than showing only one vignette per page (Hainmueller, Hangartner, & Yamamoto, 2015). Nevertheless, the effects of different experimental survey designs are currently not understood well enough to make strong recommendations on which approach is least prone to social desirability bias. Finally, if it is intended that respondents make their judgments based on the comparison of different case situations and make tradeoffs, it is an advantage to assign not just one vignette (between-subject design), but multiple vignettes. It should be noted that if multiple vignettes are presented to each respondent, to avoid fatigue effects shorter (and less realistic) vignettes are used.

In a study that exemplifies a within-subject design, each of 28 child welfare practitioners responded to exactly the same set of 120 vignettes (Shapira & Benbenishty, 1993). These vignettes were very short and schematic, composed of 10 statements that varied based on a factorial design. Such short vignettes could not be seen as reasonable representations of real-life cases. The set of vignettes, however, helped to develop a personal model of each of the participants in the study based on their responses (using multiple regression) and to identify two clusters of practitioners that differed in their personal models.

Two related major critiques on vignette studies are (1) that vignettes are artificial and differ considerably from real-world situations and (2) that social desirability might be expected for sensitive issues and therefore cannot be generalized to real practice decisions. While it is true that vignettes cannot and are not intended to recreate real-world situations, the important question is whether vignettes cause cognitive and behavioral processes that approximate those processes in real life (Evans et al., 2015). There is a wide consensus based on theoretical reasoning and empirical studies that experimental designs using simulated cases, like vignettes, are significantly less prone to social desirability biases than simple direct survey questions (Armacost, Hosseini, Morris, & Rehbein, 1991; Beyer & Liebe, 2015; Evans et al., 2015). However, the question remains whether there is considerable bias of weighting factors in vignette studies compared to the significance of these factors in real-world behavior. On one side, there are studies showing deviation of respondents' weighting of factors in vignettes to giving weight to factors in real life (for social desirable behaviors, see, e.g., Pager & Quillian, 2016). On the other side, there are studies showing how responses to well-designed vignettes are reasonably good approximation to real-life behavior—even for sensitive issues (Hainmueller et al., 2015; for overviews, Auspurg & Hinz, 2015; Evans et al., 2015). Such studies are missing in child protection research.

STUDYING THE PROCESSES LEADING FROM INPUT TO OUTPUT

The goal of the preceding methods described is to analyze the relationships between input to the decision and the output: the decision. The aim of process-tracing studies is to explicate the systematic processes by which decision-makers look for information cues, weigh, and integrate them to reach their judgments and decisions. Due to space limitations we do not include in our review the important issue of *why*; that is, their rationale for employing these particular processes (e.g., Mosteiro, Beloki, Sobremonte, & Rodriguez, 2018; Osmo & Benbenishty, 2004).

Tracing the Process Through Decision-Maker Verbalization: Think-Aloud

We begin by exploring research methods that focus on what decision-makers say about their decision-making processes—*what* information cues they use to arrive at their judgments and decisions and *how* they process these cues. "Think-aloud" is a research method that has a long tradition in research on judgment and decision-making. Schulte-Mecklenbeck and associates (2017) noted that verbal protocols featured prominently in problem-solving research during the 1960s and 1970s. For instance, the early work on human problem solving conducted by Newell and Simon (1972), which culminated in a Nobel Prize to Simon in 1978, was based on participants verbalizing their thought processes as they were engaged in solving a problem presented by the researchers.

This research tradition relies to a large extent on the assumptions that decision-makers are aware of their decision processes and are able and willing to verbalize them accurately. This assumption may not be always valid. Professionals may be influenced by information cues of which they may not be aware or may find it unacceptable to verbalize their thought processes, such as when they are influenced by stigmatic views of certain client groups ("post hoc rationalization"; Königs, 2018). In such circumstances, professionals may provide less authentic and more rational and professionally acceptable reasoning, making this method vulnerable to social desirability especially with respect to what "good workers" should or should not take into account.

A review of the literature indicates that there are several variations in research methods in this domain. The differences among methods can be organized along several dimensions. We review these dimensions briefly so that researchers may consider their strengths and limitations in the context of their own future research.

In Vivo with Real Clients Versus in Vivo with Simulated Cases

In some studies, the researchers asked decision-makers to think aloud while making decisions in real life (e.g., Fisher & Fonteyn, 1995; Sendurur, 2018), whereas in other studies participants thought aloud while making decisions in simulated cases. Each of these approaches has its strengths and limitations. While thinking aloud in vivo about real clients has the advantage of authenticity, this method has its limitations as well. For instance, for ethical and practical reasons, it is unacceptable to verbalize decision processes while a child protection worker is interviewing a family to assess risk and make placement recommendation. Real-life cases, although representative, may also be limited in scope and do not provide enough opportunities to study "atypical" or "rare and difficult" cases that may yield important insights. Furthermore, given that real-life cases are not replicable, it is not possible to conduct comparisons between the same decision-makers over time, different types of decision-makers (e.g., novice vs. expert) and contexts (e.g., between agencies, child welfare systems, and so on).

An alternative to studying in vivo decision processes with real clients are studies conducted with simulated cases. Such simulations vary in their richness and how close to life they are. Many researchers have used text vignettes as stimuli, as presented earlier. While some text vignettes are much richer in content than others, they are still limited because they do not expose participants to visual and auditory cues which may have impact on decisions made with real-life clients.

Others use role-playing to enact the decision context. The richest simulated cases are being used in healthcare settings that employ trained actors simulating clients. Simulated cases involve actors using detailed and well-planned scripts enacted in a technology-rich environment that ensures reliable recording of both verbal and visual information (Prakash, Bihari, Need, Sprick, & Schuwirth, 2017). Under such circumstances, researchers can trace the thinking processes of a range of practitioners facing a well-planned range of cases. This line of research requires investments in the setting, technology, and actors. It should be noted that such settings already exist in some contexts and serve mainly for training and testing of students or novice practitioners (Asakura, Bogo, Good, & Power, 2018).

Concurrent Versus Retrospective

In some studies, the process of thinking aloud is conducted in vivo, concurrently when facing the decision-making task, either real or simulated. Compared with "thinking back" on a past case, this process has the potential to yield rich information because working memory is readily available and there is no significant memory loss due to difficulties in memory retrieval. Nonetheless, there are concerns that engaging concurrently in two tasks—thinking about a case and verbalizing the thinking process (in a way that would sound coherent to the observing researcher)—may interfere with professional performance and reduce the validity of the verbalization. This may diminish the ability to generalize from decision processes involving concurrent verbalization to decisions made in practice contexts.

Another approach is to ask decision-makers to return to past cases and reconstruct their decision-making process. For instance, Yates (2018) conducted retrospective interviews in order to study social workers' thinking processes in their practice. Such interviews may have limited validity due to memory loss and significant differences between interpretations and conclusions that were reached in real time compared with hindsight. This concern is especially valid when such delayed accounts of the decision-making considerations are "contaminated" by knowledge of decision outcomes unavailable at the time of the original decision. Aware of these limitations, Yates (2018) asked the participants "to prepare for interviews by reading through case files and preparing a chronology of events to assist their recall of key debates and dilemmas" (p. 179).

A more systematic approach is described as *chart simulated recall* (CSR), an offshoot of a procedure used to assess the competencies of physicians. In this procedure, physicians are interviewed on their decision-making process regarding a case, aided by the case's chart and case notes (Sinnott, Kelly, & Bradley, 2017). A recent scoping review concluded that, despite the empirical evidence that supports the acceptability, reliability, and validity of CSR, its use in decision-making research has been quite limited (Sinnott et al., 2017).

Interestingly, the main use of the CSR in research was to study the degree to which physicians' decision-making processes adhered to clinical guidelines. This line of research may be especially of interest in settings in which child protection practitioners are required to consult a risk assessment procedure or a decision aid. CSR may be used, for instance, in cases in which a practitioner may have reached a decision that was not recommended by the protocol. Reviewing the case and tracing the reasoning of the practitioner could help identify the need to modify the decision protocol and/or training.

AIDED AND UNAIDED ELICITATION

In all think-aloud studies there is a certain level of researcher involvement during the decision-making task, but in some research traditions this involvement is much more substantial and active. Ericsson and Simon (1993), for instance, minimized their involvement and intervened only when there was a silent period of at least 60 seconds, probing the participant to stay on task. Researchers used probes like "Please keep on talking," "What are you thinking?" or "What are you doing?" Others ask many more questions to make sure they retrieved detailed information on the thinking process. For instance, in a study of decision-making in nursing, nurses performed a simulation task involving actors as patients. During the task they were probed by the (simulated) patient (e.g., "What's wrong with me, doctor?"), and the supervising nurse: "What are you thinking? Why do you think so?" (Prakash et al., 2017).

In contrast, Abuzour, Lewis, and Tully (2018) refrained from asking any questions during the think-aloud process to allow uninterrupted thought processes, but they wrote down their queries. After completion of the unaided think-aloud session, the researchers conducted semi-structured interviews that incorporated their questions on observations during the think-aloud phase.

VARIATIONS IN METHODS OF ANALYSIS

Given the nature of the data elicited in the multiple forms of think-aloud methods, qualitative analyses are the central analytic tools. Our review indicates that researchers used a range of qualitative methods, varying in the specific techniques used and also in the degree to which the analysis used preconceived conceptual structures or more grounded approaches that tried to identify structures as an outcome of the analysis. For instance, Lundgren-Laine and Salantera (2010) applied *protocol analysis* designed specifically to study decision processes; this analysis consists of several phases, prescribed in advance. In another example, Ghanem, Kollar, Fischer, Lawson, and Pankofer (2018) conducted a micro-analysis of epistemic activities of social novice and expert social workers based on a model of scientific reasoning and argumentation. Based on this predetermined framework, the authors used the eight epistemic activities that underlie the decision process (such as problem identification, questioning, and evidence generation) to guide their analysis of the participants' verbalization (Fischer et al., 2014).

Other studies used approaches that were less predetermined, although some coding scheme may have been applied as a preliminary tool (e.g., Prakash et al., 2017). Researchers used a range of methods associated with inductive content analysis (Curran, Campbell, & Rugg, 2006) and other qualitative approaches, such as grounded theory, constant comparisons, mapping, and clustering (see, e.g., Yates, 2018).

Tracing the Process Through Decision-Makers' Behaviors: Information Acquisition

The previous sections described process-tracing methods that rely on decision-makers' verbalizations and their insights regarding their reasoning. Another approach does not rely on the decision-makers' awareness of their thought processes and on the validity and accuracy of their verbal description but instead traces information acquisition *behaviors and physical responses*. This approach tracks the information that decision-makers actively search and acquire and their physiological responses to that information, and then deducts from these behaviors the decision-making processes.

Schulte-Mecklenbeck and associates (2017) distinguished between three basic methods to trace information acquisition: *peripheral psychophysiology* (e.g., muscle tension tone or electromyogram [EMG] and facial muscle monitoring [fEMG]), neural techniques (e.g., electroencephalogram [EEG], functional magnetic resonance imaging [fMRI]), and movement-based methods (e.g., using eye movement tracking or a computer mouse to point and select information). Our reading of the literature did not find evidence that the first two methods could be informative for the purposes of this chapter; we therefore focus on movement-based methods—specifically, on eye movement and on information display boards.

TRACKING EYE MOVEMENT
There are multiple ways to study information acquisition. One technique used in behavioral economics, consumer research, and food choice is to trace eye movement. In this method, the researcher monitors eye movement and records *eye fixation*—where the eye is looking at a particular point for a certain amount of time. The main assumptions are that, in order to process information, participants need to look at the cue, and eye fixation is a sign that they are using that cue (the *utility effect*; cf. Meyerding, 2018). Eye movements are considered good indicators of visual attention and information acquisition, being closely related to higher order cognitive activity, and they are far less vulnerable to social desirability.

Eye-tracking technology has transformed from various head-mounted or contact lens devices to an infrared addition to the computer screen that tracks eye movements with no physical connection between the user and the computer. This technology is used extensively in the game industry and is implemented in areas such as neuroscience, cognitive psychology, marketing research, and behavioral econometrics. We could not find studies in child protection decision-making that have used this method.

INFORMATION DISPLAY BOARD/MATRIX

Variations of information display boards (IDB; Lehmann, Moore, & Churchill, 1980) or information display matrices (IDM; Aschemann-Witzel & Hamm, 2011) as they are also called, are by far the most common forms of studying information acquisition in decision tasks. In the basic process, the researcher reveals to the participant what categories of information are available to search (e.g., what child or foster family characteristics are available to acquire) and provides the participant with means to review the information they want to acquire, one piece of information at a time. The researcher records which cues are selected, in which order, and what was the final judgment/choice made by the participants. In many studies, the time that the participant takes to make the next choice is also recorded.

This procedure can be carried out manually. For instance, in a study comparing information search and decisions made by social work and business administration students, a fictive case was described with a series of cards. On one side of the card the information was presented and on the other side the category of information that the card contained (e.g., information on previous abuse). All cards were laid down so that only the category name was visible. The participants were given a few introductory sentences about the case and their task. They were then instructed to pick cards so that that they could make the required decision (e.g., what is the risk to the child depicted in the case and whether to recommend removing the child from home). They were told to select one card at a time in whatever order they wished and to stop the process whenever they thought they could make the decision. The researchers recorded the order in which cards were picked and after how many cards the process ended (Benbenishty, Segev, & Surkis, 2002).

Computerized IDBs have been used extensively in psychological and marketing research and have been described in detail (Aschemann-Witzel & Hamm, 2011). For instance, MouselabWEB, presents on the computer screen what categories of information are available, most often in a matrix form. The columns present several alternatives (e.g., available houses to rent), and the rows present the attributes of each of the alternatives (e.g., price, location). In the context of child protection decisions, the columns may be alternative placements (foster families A, B, C, D), and the rows may present the attributes of these placements (e.g., how many years of experience, previous complaints, is this a one-parent family, etc.). A "cell" in this matrix hides the information on the value of the attribute for the alternative (e.g., there were no complaints on this family). The participant uses the mouse to hover above the cell of interest to reveal the hidden information. She then moves to the next cell of interest, until making a choice. The computer program records the places that the participant visited and the time she spent after revealing a piece of information, the sequence of information search (e.g., moving from one alternative to the another alternative, or from one attribute of the alternative to another attribute of the same alternative). The reacquisition of information in a specific cell is also recorded, as this is an indication that the participant is considering the information as part of the process of integrating all information cues.

Most of the applications of computerized IDBs were designed to test alternative theories of information processing and choice and used as stimuli gambles or games. Others presented participants with information on a series of products and investigated how they search information on the attributes of each product to make choices between them (Dörnyei, Krystallis, & Chrysochou, 2017).

The extensive work using computerized information boards seems promising and may encourage scholars to explore the potential of adopting this method and technology in the area of child protection decision-making. The richness and depth of the information it provides could augment our understanding of how practitioners, both novices and experts, process information to arrive at their judgments and decisions. It can also provide insights on ways in which key pieces of information are incorporated into decision-making. For instance, whether, when, and how practitioners attend to information on the child's race; if they have a different decision strategy when they consider a girl versus boy; if they pay attention to parents' or children's preferences; or if these preferences make a difference in their thinking process and the acquisition of further information to reach a final decision.

Alongside the enthusiasm about the potential contribution of this line of research, our review also identified potential limitations that need to be considered. Traditionally, IDBs were designed to study decision-making processes that rely heavily on the processing of simple facts (e.g., the probability of winning is 0.70; the price of this cereal is $4) using working and short-term memory. Most of the decisions in child protection require processing large amounts of complex and often ambiguous information that require extensive deliberation.

Another limitation is the artificial nature of data acquisition using a mouse hovering over data labels, a situation far removed from practice. Similar concerns were also raised with regards to areas such as consumer choice behavior, in which the data acquisition process created in research seems too artificial and dissimilar to real-life situations (Aschemann-Witzel & Hamm, 2011). These authors argue, however, that technological changes in recent decades made the IDBs much more realistic, as many consumers are shopping online and are used to navigate between stores, products, and details about each product.

This argument may also be relevant to the child protection context. Many practitioners and supervisors are making recommendations and decisions based on case files stored in their word processors. It may be possible to develop an interface that helps the practitioner navigate easily among the various sections of the case file and display the information cues, while, unobtrusively in the background, the program records the information acquisition path of the practitioner. For instance, Benbenishty developed a case file menu that was used by practitioners to read through a computerized case file in a military mental health clinic while the program recorded the information that the practitioner was looking for in the case file (Benbenishty & Treistman, 1998).

Tracing the Complex Decision Process Through Ethnographies

Researchers are fully aware that real-life decisions are carried out in complex contexts and influenced by a myriad of factors, but they try to control some aspects of the task so that they can focus on and measure others. Therefore, much of the efforts of the process-tracing methods just described aim to focus on certain aspects of the process while controlling for others. In contrast, ethnographic studies embrace the complex nature of decisions in child protection and aim to capture rather than control them using a range of methods and techniques (Hammersley & Atkinson, 2007). These studies are based on participant observations in decision-makers' natural environments and recording their formal and informal verbal and nonverbal interactions around these decisions, often supplemented by studying case files, organizational documents, open-ended and semi-structured interviews, etc. Observations are recorded in field notes (Emerson, Fretz, & Shaw, 2011) and/or transcriptions of audio or video recordings.

To illustrate, despite the fact that much of decision-making in child protection takes place in interactions between practitioners who work in teams or refer the case to supervisors or colleagues with recommendations for decisions, much of the research in this area focuses on tracing the process of *individual* decision-makers. In contrast, ethnographic studies examine the multiple aspects involved in the collegial interactions that impact the decision. Helm (2016) and Whittaker (2018) used field notes on observations of practitioners' conversations in their naturalistic settings, such as meetings, phone calls, supervision sessions, and tea room talks. Natural and often informal conversations are an excellent source to get insights into practitioners' reasoning in decision-making. Helm's (2016) results show, for example, how social workers negotiated judgment responsibilities and how their use of different types of initial opening statements (e.g., emotional frames) in conversations established meaning about how a safeguarding situation is to be understood.

While field notes and observations are essential in such studies, they may also be supplemented by other techniques. For instance, in addition to field notes on observations in a stationary crisis intervention site, Pomey (2017) used transcripts of audio recordings of conversations between parents and professionals and interviews with professionals as well as parents as reliable data for a microanalysis of verbal sequences. This allowed in-depth insights into decision processes, where multiple actors, including family members, were directly involved. This work pointed out how practitioners made subtle informal assessments of the degree to which the parents were converging or deviating from an ideal picture of a family, and these assessments were an important decision heuristic.

Another example of the potential contribution of an ethnography to trace the processes that lead to judgments and decisions is the study of Freres, Bastian, and Schrödter (2019) on home visits. Information collected in home visits has a major impact on the workers' judgments and decisions. Freres and associates used field notes of observations made during home visits and additional data sources (e.g., interviews with workers and managers, case files, observations of case conferences, and court hearings) and described how caseworkers use a fast and frugal heuristic to make a decision about further interventions. In situations like home visits, field notes are sometimes the only feasible way to record observations ethically. Moreover, field notes provide rich information about different sensual experiences (e.g., smells), gestures, and movement through rooms. Freres et al. (2019), for example, described how a social worker discovered a sausage in a laundry basket during a home visit, what the family's reactions were, and how this affected the social workers' decision.

In recent years there has been growing interest in understanding how decision aids impact decision-making processes in child protection. Here, ethnographic studies that examined the real-life interactions of practitioners with decision aids, such as structured decision-making (SDM) tools, provide important insights (e.g., Bastian, 2017; Broadhurst et al., 2010; Gillingham & Humphreys, 2010). To study how practitioners use a structured decision-making tool, Gillingham and Humphreys (2010) observed caseworkers using this tool, conducted interviews, and audited case files in six sites for 2 weeks per site. Semi-structured interviews and informal private discussions, recorded as handwritten notes, were a major data source used to get a deeper understanding of the observed practices. Spending time at a site while observing and having private and confidential conversations allowed the researchers to get information about informal rules and practices. Their study revealed how the structured decision-making tool did not affect decisions; instead, the tool was "manipulated" by workers to get results matching workers' prior decisions. In-depth interviews indicated that workers' experience and knowledge, as well as contextual factors such as time constraints, had a stronger impact on decisions than the tool itself might have a direct effect on decisions.

Bastian's observations (2017) provide even deeper insight on the processes leading to recommendations on a case while working with a decision aid. Bastian (2017) observed a sequence in which a social worker used a standardized risk assessment tool in deciding if and how urgent a response is needed to a child protection report the social worker received from a school. The ethnographer described how the social worker oscillated with the mouse pointer between clicking or not clicking on a specific check box that would trigger a certain response, how she consulted a help tool with definitions, and what gestures and comments she made. These observations provided insights into how the social worker's judgments and intuitions needed to be negotiated with the standardized tool to lead to a certain judgment.

While ethnographic studies conducted in real-life contexts and employing a wide range of techniques could contribute significantly to tracing the processes leading from input to output, their limitations should not be overlooked. In ethnography, data collection and interpretive data analysis are not viewed as two subsequent steps, but rather as a dialectical, iterative process where data and ideas are in a constant interplay (Hammersley & Atkinson, 2007). This may raise concerns about the subjective and idiosyncratic nature of the interpretation. While ethnographers accept subjectivity as part of the method, this may be seen as a significant limitation by others.

Furthermore, although reactivity to the presence of a researcher is always a concern, it is especially pertinent in such ethnographies due to the intensive presence of the researcher. For instance, Bastian (2017) describes how the observed social worker looked at him and commented about her oscillation in deciding. It is hard to estimate how reactivity to the intense involvement of the researcher affected the process.

Finally, generalizability about a population is a significant concern. Ethnographic studies do not aim to be representative in their sampling, design, and interpretation. Therefore, it is not possible to estimate a phenomenon's frequencies in a population. However, ethnographic studies clearly aim to develop theories. Seeking to test these theories in other contexts and with other methodological approaches might prove fruitful. For example, other study designs we presented could be used to further test the decision-making heuristic discovered by Freres et al. (2019) and try to estimate its prevalence. Ethnography can be viewed as both a measure to develop theories and as a measure to further explore and challenge findings from studies using other methodologies.

CONCLUSION

Many decades ago, Hoffman (1960) noted that the same clinical judgment can be modeled in several different ways, all equally valid on their own terms. Our review shows that there are multiple methods to model the judgments and decisions of child welfare and protection professionals. Each of these methods can yield an informative model of judgments and decisions. It is therefore important to continue to expand the range of methods being used to study these complex issues. Yet, at the same time, the field could benefit from collaboration and integration of multiple methods, traditions, and disciplines.

Our review of process-tracing methods suggests that each of the existing methods has limitations and advantages. We think that integrating several methods may be most informative, as, for example, by entering all the relevant and known information about a real-life case into a version of an IDB. This board will provide practitioners with means to examine the case file while talking aloud about the case and the process of information search, as well as their conclusions based on the information they receive. All information search patterns and think-aloud statements will be recorded and analyzed.

Furthermore, input-output analysis and process tracing need to be employed jointly to gain a deeper understanding of both the statistical relationships between case characteristics and decisions and the ways practitioners reason about them. This is similar to calls to integrate actuarial and clinical methods (Mendoza, Rose, Geiger, & Cash, 2016). A dialog between researchers who analyze large databases to identify pattern of decision-making, scholars who investigate decision processes, and practitioners engaged in real-life decisions can help develop insights not only about how decisions are being made but also on how they could be improved based on multiple sources of knowledge.

Finally, this integration and collaboration should not be limited to the final stages of sharing findings from different strands of research. Instead, we think that it is essential that the collaboration among researchers, administrators, and practitioners starts in the foundational stage, when databases, information systems, and reporting requirements are being developed. Working together, a better foundation could be established for ongoing research on decision-making that could be integrated into practice and inform it based on multiple methods reviewed in this chapter.

REFERENCES

Abuzour, A. S., Lewis, P. J., & Tully, M. P. (2018). A qualitative study exploring how pharmacist and nurse independent prescribers make clinical decisions. *Journal of Advanced Nursing, 74*, 65–74. doi:10.1111/jan.13375

Ards, S. D., Myers, S. L., Jr., Ray, P., Kim, H.-E., Monroe, K., & Arteaga, I. (2012). Racialized perceptions and child neglect. *Children and Youth Services Review, 34*(8), 1480–1491. doi:10.1016/j.childyouth.2012.03.018

Armacost, R. L., Hosseini, J. C., Morris, S. A., & Rehbein, K. A. (1991). An empirical comparison of direct questioning, scenario, and randomized response methods for obtaining sensitive business information. *Decision Sciences, 22*(5), 1073–1090. doi:10.1111/j.1540-5915.1991.tb01907.x

Asakura, K., Bogo, M., Good, B., & Power, R. (2018). Teaching note—Social work serial: Using video-recorded simulated client sessions to teach social work practice. *Journal of Social Work Education, 54*, 397–404. doi:10.1080/10437797.2017.1404525

Aschemann-Witzel, J., & Hamm, U. (2011). Measuring consumers' information acquisition and decision behavior with the computer-based information-display-matrix. *Methodology, 7*, 1–10. doi:10.1027/1614-2241/a000018

Atzmüller, C., & Steiner, P. M. (2010). Experimental vignette studies in survey research. *Methodology: European Journal of Research Methods for the Behavioral and Social Sciences, 6*(3), 128–138. doi:10.1027/1614-2241/a000014

Auspurg, K., & Hinz, T. (2015). *Factorial survey experiments.* Thousand Oaks, CA: Sage Publications.

Auspurg, K., Hinz, T., Liebig, S., & Sauer, C. (2015). The factorial survey as a method for measuring sensitive issues. In U. Engel, B. Jann, P. Lynn, A. Scherpenzeel, & P. Sturgis (Eds.), *Improving survey methods: Lessons from recent research* (pp. 137–149). New York/Hove: Routledge.

Bastian, P. (2017). Negotiations with a risk assessment tool: Standardized decision-making in the United States and the deprofessionalization thesis. *Transnational Social Review, 30*, 1–13. doi:10.1080/21931674.2017.1313509

Benbenishty, R. (1992). An overview of methods to elicit and model expert clinical judgment and decision-making. *Social Service Review, 66*(4), 598–616. doi:10.1086/603950

Benbenishty, R., Davidson-Arad, B., López, M., Devaney, J., Spratt, T., Koopmans, C., . . . Hayes, D. (2015). Decision-making in child protection: An international comparative study on maltreatment substantiation, risk assessment and interventions recommendations, and the role of professionals' child welfare attitudes. *Child Abuse and Neglect, 49*, 63–75. doi:10.1016/j.chiabu.2015.03.015

Benbenishty, R., Segev, D., & Surkis, T. (2002). Information-search and decision-making by professionals and nonprofessionals in cases of alleged child abuse and maltreatment. *Journal of Social Service Research, 28*, 1–18. doi:10.1300/J079v28n03_01

Benbenishty, R., & Treistman, R. (1998). The development and evaluation of a hybrid decision support system for clinical decision-making: The case of discharge from the military. *Social Work Research, 22*(4), 195–204.

Berrick, J., Dickens, J., Pösö, T., & Skivenes, M. (2017). A cross-country comparison of child welfare systems and workers' responses to children appearing to be at risk or in need of help. *Child Abuse Review, 26*(4), 305–319. doi:10.1002/car.2485

Beyer, H., & Liebe, U. (2015). Three experimental approaches to measure the social context dependence of prejudice communication and discriminatory behavior. *Social Science Research, 49*, 343–355. doi:10.1016/j.ssresearch.2014.08.017

Bradt, L., Roets, G., Roose, R., Rosseel, Y., & Bouverne-De Bie, M. (2015). Poverty and decision-making in child welfare and protection: Deepening the bias–need debate. *British Journal of Social Work, 45*(7), 2161–2175. doi:10.1093/bjsw/bcu086

Broadhurst, K., Wastell, D., White, S., Hall, C., Peckover, S., Thompson, K., . . . Davey, D. (2010). Performing "initial assessment": Identifying the latent conditions for error at the front-door of local authority children's services. *British Journal of Social Work, 40*, 352–370. doi:10.1093/bjsw/bcn162

Connelly, R., Playford, C. J., Gayle, V., & Dibben, C. (2016). The role of administrative data in the big data revolution in social science research. *Social Science Research, 59*, 1–12. doi:10.1016/j.ssresearch.2016.04.015

Coohey, C. (2003). Making judgments about risk in substantiated cases of supervisory neglect. *Child Abuse and Neglect, 27*, 821–840. doi:10.1016/S0145-2134(03)00115-7

Curran, M. J., Campbell, J., & Rugg, G. (2006). An investigation into the clinical reasoning of both expert and novice podiatrists. *The Foot, 16*, 28–32. doi:10.1016/j.foot.2005.11.001

Davidson-Arad, B., & Benbenishty, R. (2016). Child welfare attitudes, risk assessments and intervention recommendations: The role of professional expertise. *British Journal of Social Work, 46*(1), 186–203. doi:10.1093/bjsw/bcu110

Dolev, T., Benbenishty, R., & Timmer, A. (2001). *Decision committees in Israel: Their organization, work processes, and outcomes.* Jerusalem: The Brookdale Institute. [Hebrew].

Dörnyei, K. R., Krystallis, A., & Chrysochou, P. (2017). The impact of product assortment size and attribute quantity on information searches. *Journal of Consumer Marketing, 34*, 191–201. doi:10.1108/JCM-10-2015-1594

Emerson, R. M., Fretz, R. I., & Shaw, L. L. (2011). *Writing ethnographic fieldnotes* (2nd ed.). Chicago: University of Chicago Press.

Ericsson, K. A., & Simon, H. A. (1993). *Protocol analysis: Verbal reports as data* (Rev. ed.). Cambridge, MA: MIT Press.

Evans, S. C., Roberts, M. C., Keeley, J. W., Blossom, J. B., Amaro, C. M., Garcia, A. M., . . . Reed, G. M. (2015). Vignette methodologies for studying clinicians' decision-making: Validity, utility, and application in ICD-11 field studies. *International Journal of Clinical and Health Psychology, 15*(2), 160–170. doi:10.1016/j.ijchp.2014.12.001

Fischer, F., Kollar, I., Ufer, S., Sodian, B., Hussmann, H., Pekrun, R., . . . Eberle, J. (2014). Scientific reasoning and argumentation: Advancing an interdisciplinary research agenda in education. *Frontline Learning Research, 5*, 28–45. doi:10.14786/flr.v2i2.96

Fisher, A., & Fonteyn, M. (1995). An innovative methodological approach for examining nurses' heuristics use in clinical practice. *Journal of Scholarly Inquiry, 9*, 263–276.

Freres, K., Bastian, P., & Schrödter, M. (2019). Jenseits von Fallverstehen und Prognose— wie Fachkräfte mit einer einfachen Heuristik verantwortbaren Kinderschutz betreiben: Internationaler Forschungsüberblick und Befunde einer ethnographischen Studie zu Hausbesuchen durch das Jugendamt. *Neue Praxis, 49,* 140–164.

Ghanem, C., Kollar, I., Fischer, F., Lawson, T. R., & Pankofer, S. (2018). How do social work novices and experts solve professional problems? A micro-analysis of epistemic activities and the use of evidence. *European Journal of Social Work, 21,* 3–19. doi:10.1080/13691457.2016.1255931

Gillingham, P., & Humphreys, C. (2010). Child protection practitioners and decision-making tools: Observations and reflections from the front line. *British Journal of Social Work, 40,* 2598–2616. doi:10.1093/bjsw/bcp155

Goos, P., & Jones, B. (2011). *Optimal design of experiments: A case study approach.* Hoboken, NJ: Wiley.

Hainmueller, J., Hangartner, D., & Yamamoto, T. (2015). Validating vignette and conjoint survey experiments against real-world behavior. *Proceedings of the National Academy of Sciences of the United States of America, 112*(8), 2395–2400. doi:10.1073/pnas.1416587112

Hammersley, M., & Atkinson, P. (2007). *Ethnography: Principles in practice* (3rd ed.). Hoboken, NJ: Taylor & Francis.

Helm, D. (2016). Sense-making in a social work office: An ethnographic study of safeguarding judgments. *Child & Family Social Work, 21*(1), 26–35. https://doi.org/10.1111/cfs.12101

Hillen, M. A., Van Vliet, L. M., De Haes, H. C. J. M., & Smets, E. M. A. (2013). Developing and administering scripted video vignettes for experimental research of patient-provider communication. *Patient Education and Counseling, 91*(3), 295–309. doi:10.1016/j.pec.2013.01.020

Hoffman, P. J. (1960). The paramorphic representation of clinical judgment. *Psychological Bulletin, 57,* 116–131.

Jud, A., AlBuhairan, F., Ntinapogias, A., & Nikolaidis, G. (2015). Obtaining agency participation. In A. Jud, L. M. Jones, & C. Mikton (Eds.), *Toolkit on mapping legal, health and social services response to child maltreatment* (pp. 55–62). Geneva: World Health Organization.

Jud, A., Jones, L. M., & Mikton, C. (Eds.). (2015). *Toolkit on mapping legal, health and social services response to child maltreatment.* Geneva: World Health Organization.

Jud, A., & Sedklak, A. J. (2015). Agency sampling. In A. Jud, L. M. Jones, & C. Mikton (Eds.), *Toolkit on mapping legal, health and social services response to child maltreatment* (pp. 20–28). Geneva: World Health Organization.

Königs, P. (2018). Two types of debunking arguments. *Philosophical Psychology, 31,* 383–402. doi:10.1080/09515089.2018.1426100

Krüger, P., & Jud, A. (2015). Overview of previous agency surveys and national administrative data sets. In A. Jud, L. M. Jones, & C. Mikton (Eds.), *Toolkit on mapping legal, health and social services response to child maltreatment* (pp. 4–9). Geneva: World Health Organization.

Lehmann, D. R., Moore, W. L., & Churchill, G. A. Jr. (1980). Validity of information display boards: An assessment using longitudinal data. *Journal of Marketing Research, 14,* 450–459. doi:10.1177/002224378001700404

Lundgren-Laine, H., & Salanter, S. (2010). Think-aloud technique and protocol analysis in clinical decision-making research. *Qualitative Health Research, 20*, 565–575. doi:10.1177/1049732309354278

Mendoza, N. S., Rose, R. A., Geiger, J. M., & Cash, S. J. (2016). Risk assessment with actuarial and clinical methods: Measurement and evidence-based practice. *Child Abuse and Neglect, 61*, 1–12. doi:10.1016/j.chiabu.2016.09.004

Meyerding, S. G. (2018). Combining eye-tracking and choice-based conjoint analysis in a bottom-up experiment. *Journal of Neuroscience, Psychology, and Economics, 11*, 28–44. doi:10.1037/npe0000084

Morgan, S. L., & Winship, C. (2015). *Counterfactuals and causal inference: Methods and principles for social research* (2nd ed.). New York: Cambridge University Press.

Mosteiro, A., Beloki, U., Sobremonte, E., & Rodriguez, A. (2018). Dimensions for argument and variability in child protection decision-making. *Journal of Social Work Practice, 32*, 169–187. doi:10.1080/02650533.2018.1439459

Newell, A., & Simon, H. A. (1972). *Human problem solving*. Oxford: Prentice-Hall.

Osmo, R., & Benbenishty, R. (2004). Children at risk: Rationales for risk assessments and interventions. *Children and Youth Services Review, 26*(12), 1155–1173. doi:10.1016/j.childyouth.2004.05.006

Pager, D., & Quillian, L. (2016). Walking the talk? What employers say versus what they do. *American Sociological Review, 70*(3), 355–380. doi:10.1177/000312240507000301

Pomey, M. (2017). *Vulnerabilität und Fremdunterbringung: Eine Studie zur Entscheidungspraxis bei Kindeswohlgefährdung*. Weinheim: Beltz Juventa.

Prakash, S., Bihari, S., Need, P., Sprick, C., & Schuwirth, L. (2017). Immersive high fidelity simulation of critically ill patients to study cognitive errors: A pilot study. *BMC Medical Education, 17*(1), 36. doi:10.1186/s12909-017-0871-x

Rivaux, S. L., James, J., Wittenstrom, K., Baumann, D., Sheets, J., Henry, J., & Jeffries, V. (2008). The intersection of race, poverty, and risk: Understanding the decision to provide services to clients and to remove children. *Child Welfare, 87*(2), 151–168.

Rodrigues, L., Calheiros, M., & Pereira, C. (2015). The decision of out-of-home placement in residential care after parental neglect: Empirically testing a psychosocial model. *Child Abuse and Neglect, 49*, 35–49. doi:10.1016/j.chiabu.2015.03.014

Rossi, P. H., & Anderson, A. B. (1982). The factorial survey approach: An introduction. In P. H. Rossi & S. L. Nock (Eds.), *Measuring social judgments: The factorial survey approach* (pp. 15–67). Beverly Hills, CA: Sage Publications.

Schulte-Mecklenbeck, M., Johnson, J. G., Böckenholt, U., Goldstein, D. G., Russo, J. E., . . . Willemsen, M. C. (2017). Process-tracing methods in decision-making: On growing up in the 70s. *Current Directions in Psychological Science, 26*, 442–450. doi:10.1177/0963721417708229

Sendurur, E. (2018). Students as information consumers: A focus on online decision-making process. *Education and Information Technologies, 23*(6), 3007–3027. doi:10.1007/s10639-018-9756-9

Shapira, M., & Benbenishty, R. (1993). Modeling judgments and decisions in cases of alleged child abuse and neglect. *Social Work Research & Abstracts, 29*(2), 14–19. doi:10.1093/swra/29.2.14

Sinnott, C., Kelly, M. A., & Bradley, C. P. (2017). A scoping review of the potential for chart stimulated recall as a clinical research method. *BMC Health Services Research*, *17*(1), 583. doi:10.1186/s12913-017-2539-y

Smith, C., Fluke, J. D., Fallon, B., Mishna, F., & Decker Pierce, B. (2018). Child welfare organizations: Do specialization and service integration impact placement decisions? *Child Abuse and Neglect*, *76*, 573–582. doi:10.1016/j.chiabu.2017.09.032

Stiles, P. G., & Boothroyd, R. A. (2015). Ethical use of administrative data for research purposes. In J. Fantuzzo & D. P. Culhane (Eds.), *Actionable intelligence: Using integrated data systems to achieve a more effective, efficient, and ethical government* (pp. 125–155). New York: Palgrave Macmillan.

Stoddart, J. K., Fallon, B., Trocmé, N., & Fluke, J. D. (2018). Substantiated child maltreatment: Which factors do workers focus on when making this critical decision? *Children and Youth Services Review*, *87*, 1–8. doi:10.1016/j.childyouth.2018.01.018

Stokes, J., & Schmidt, G. (2012). Child protection decision-making: A factorial analysis using case vignettes. *Social Work*, *57*, 83–90. doi:10.1093/sw/swr007

Taylor, B. J. (2006). Factorial surveys: Using vignettes to study professional judgment. *British Journal of Social Work*, *36*(7), 1187–1207. doi:10.1093/bjsw/bch345

Tonmyr, L., Ouimet, C., & Ugnat, A.-M. (2012). A review of findings from the Canadian Incidence Study of Reported Child Abuse and Neglect (CIS). *Canadian Journal of Public-Health Review*, *103*(2), 103–112. doi:10.17269/cjph.103.3008

Wallander, L. (2009). 25 years of factorial surveys in sociology: A review. *Social Science Research*, *38*, 505–520. doi:10.1016/j.ssresearch.2009.03.004

Wallander, L. (2012). Measuring social workers' judgments: Why and how to use the factorial survey approach in the study of professional judgments. *Journal of Social Work*, *12*(4), 364–384. doi:10.1177/1468017310387463

Whittaker, A. (2018). How do child-protection practitioners make decisions in real-life situations? Lessons from the psychology of decision-making. *British Journal of Social Work*, *48*, 1967–1984. doi:10.1093/bjsw/bcx145

Yates, P. (2018). "Siblings as better together": Social worker decision-making in cases involving sibling sexual behavior. *British Journal of Social Work*, *48*, 176–194. doi:10.1093/bjsw/bcx018.

Instrumentation to Understand the Child Protective Services Decision-Making Processes

ALAN J. DETTLAFF, DANA HOLLINSHEAD,
J. CHRISTOPHER GRAHAM, DONALD J. BAUMANN,
AND JOHN D. FLUKE ■

INTRODUCTION

When children come to the attention of the child welfare system, they become involved in a decision-making process in which decisions are made on their behalf that have a significant impact on their future and well-being. The decision to remove children from their families and place them into out-of-home care is particularly challenging and complex, but others, such as substantiating maltreatment, offering services or interventions, and reunifying children with their families, are equally complex and influence the trajectory a family's case may take. These and other decisions are often made under extremely difficult conditions in an environment characterized by uncertainty and ambiguity. The concepts of risk and safety, and guidelines for decision-making, are often vague and poorly defined, resulting in confusion among child welfare staff (Rycus & Hughes, 2008). Key information about the case may be lacking, and decisions must be made within very short time frames given the potential safety concerns facing children. Decision-makers are further challenged by the context of most child

Alan J. Dettlaff, Dana Hollinshead, J. Christopher Graham, Donald J. Baumann, and John D. Fluke, *Instrumentation to Understand the Child Protective Services Decision-Making Processes* In: *Decision-Making and Judgment in Child Welfare and Protection*. Edited by: John D. Fluke, Mónica López López, Rami Benbenishty, Erik J. Knorth, and Donald J. Baumann, Oxford University Press (2021). © Oxford University Press. DOI: 10.1093/oso/9780190059538.003.0004.

welfare agencies, which often is characterized by a lack of resources, high rates of staff turnover, and unreasonable workload demands (Dettlaff & Rycraft, 2008). In addition, decision-making may be further influenced by non–case-related factors such as caseworkers' personal values toward parenting and varying agency cultures and expectations regarding children. The result of these intersecting issues is a decision-making environment that is uncertain and vulnerable to error.

The removal decision is of particular importance due to the lifelong impacts this decision may have on children and families. Although removal is necessary in many instances to provide for children's safety, a body of research has documented the harmful effects that may result from out-of-home placement. Children placed in out-of-home care experience not only significant trauma but also are more likely than other children to experience a number of poor outcomes, including low educational attainment, homelessness, unemployment, economic hardship, unplanned pregnancies, mental health disorders, and involvement in the criminal justice system (Courtney et al., 2011; Pecora et al., 2005). Although these outcomes may at least partially be attributable to children's experiences of maltreatment prior to removal, the consistent evidence documenting poor outcomes for children who experience out-of-home care calls attention to the seriousness and lifelong consequences of this decision.

Yet despite the complexity and consequences of this and other decisions along the child welfare continuum, surprisingly little is understood about the process by which these decisions are made (Fluke, Baumann, Dalgleish, & Kern, 2014; Lindsey, 2004). While previous research has documented some (primarily case-related) factors that influence this process, there is little consensus on the criteria caseworkers use in arriving at these decisions and on which factors are most important in caseworkers' considerations (Lindsey, 2004). What is clear, however, is that decision-making is inconsistent (Gold, Benbenishty, & Osmo, 2001; Rossi, Schuerman, & Budde, 1999) and a great deal of the variability in caseworkers' decisions remains unexplained.

As a result, instrumentation has been developed and adapted over the past 20 years to further understand variations in child welfare outcomes that are decision-based, in particular concerning the removal decision, in order to provide a more thorough understanding of the intersecting factors that influence caseworker decisions. This effort is part of a larger program of research that seeks to better understand decision-making processes in child welfare systems in order to promote fairness, accuracy, and improved outcomes among children and families.

FACTORS THAT INFLUENCE THE DECISION-MAKING PROCESS

Although research has documented a number of factors that influence the decision-making process in child welfare, a challenge to understanding this process is that some of these factors may not be related to the case itself. This growing body of research has documented that, in addition to case-related factors, both personal factors of the decision-maker and organizational factors influence decisions, which may allow for subjectivity and bias to enter the decision-making process (Dettlaff et al., 2011; Lindsey, 1991; Rivaux et al., 2008). As a result, scholarship on the decision-making process has begun to embrace an ecological framework, whereby caseworkers are situated in and influenced by their environment, to better understand the multiple factors that play a role in child welfare decision-making throughout the decision-making continuum (Baumann, Dalgleish, Fluke, & Kern, 2011), including outcomes to the decision-maker such as burnout, turnover (Baumann, Kern, McFadden, & Law, 1997), and caseworker performance (Schultz, Law, Baumann, Kern, & Gober, 1997). In addition to case-related factors, these include individual factors, organizational factors, and external factors.

Case Factors

Case factors are the particular characteristics of the children and families involved in child welfare cases that influence decision-making regarding a case's trajectory through the child welfare system. Many studies have shown case factors to affect the decision to investigate, substantiate, provide services, and remove depending on the type of maltreatment (e.g., Schwab, Baumann, & Gober, 1997). Multiple studies have focused on the sociodemographic characteristics of the children and family members involved in child welfare cases, and research consistently has documented a relationship between these factors and the removal decision. For example, an early study by Phillips, Shyne, Sherman, and Haring (1971) identified as many as 43 child, parent, and family characteristics associated with the removal decision. Child characteristics include factors such as age, health, ethnicity, psychosocial functioning, and physical and mental abilities (DePanfilis, 1997; DePanfilis & Salus, 1992; Hibbard & Desch, 2007; Sullivan & Knutson, 2000). Parental characteristics include substance use, mental illness, and cognitive ability (Britner & Mossler, 2002; Davidson-Arad, Englechin-Segal, Wozner, & Arieli, 2005; Dorsey, Mustillo, Farmer, & Elbogen, 2008). A prior history of maltreatment of the parents themselves also is predictive of having their own children removed (Dixon, Browne, & Giachritsis, 2005; Fluke, Chabot, Fallon, MacLaurin, & Blackstock, 2010; Marshall & English, 1999). In a structural model Graham and his colleagues have shown the relationship between many of the case factors with each other and to their decision to remove (Graham, Dettlaff, Baumann & Fluke, 2015; also Chapter 5, this volume).

A growing body of research has also begun to document the impact of race and ethnicity on decision-making. For example, Baumann et al. (2010)

reported that the number of African American or Hispanic families in a worker's caseload was predictive of a reduction in racially disproportionate decisions to place the children of these families in out-of-home care in Texas. In another study of the Texas child welfare system, Rivaux et al. (2008) found that the race of children was predictive of the decision to remove children from their homes in lieu of receiving in-home services, with African American children significantly more likely than white children to be removed even after controlling for risk and other sociodemographic characteristics. In studies examining the impact of race on placement in out-of-home care, it has become important to also consider the role of poverty due to the strong relationship between poverty and maltreatment. For example, using county-level data, Wulczyn, Gibbons, Snowden, and Leary (2013) found that county-level poverty is associated with less of a disparity between black and white placement rates, suggesting that factors other than poverty and social disadvantage may account for the disparity that has been documented in many child welfare systems. Race and ethnicity also have been found to negatively impact the substantiation decision (Dettlaff et al., 2011) as well as the decision to reunify (Wittenstrom et al., Chapter 9, this volume), while taking other relevant factors into account.

In addition to these child and parent characteristics, the type of maltreatment and the severity of the most recent episode of maltreatment (in actual cases or in case vignettes) have been consistently identified as factors that influence the removal decision (Britner & Mossler, 2002; DePanfilis, 1997; Reid, Sigurdson, Christiannson-Wood, & Wright, 1995; Rossi, Schuerman, & Budde, 1999; Thompson & Wiley, 2008). Prior confirmed reports of maltreatment and the likelihood of recurrence have also consistently been associated with the decision to place children in out-of-home care (Britner & Mossler, 2002; Rossi et al., 1999).

Individual Factors

In addition to factors regarding the case, personal characteristics of the decision-makers may play a significant role, though studies focusing on these are rare. It has been demonstrated, by examining differences in placement rates by workers, that factors specific to caseworkers are important (Doyle, 2008) but what those factors are and how they are interrelated has not yet been sufficiently explained. However, though studies are few, some researchers have begun to give their attention to caseworker factors in particular. For example, Davidson-Arad and Benbenishty (2008) identified "pro-removal" and "anti-removal" groups of child protection workers based on a cluster analysis of their responses to a questionnaire; however, specific worker variables (i.e., demographic and professional characteristics) were not significantly associated with cluster membership. Similarly, Rossi et al. (1999) identified a group of child welfare experts who, in response to written summaries of child protection cases, were "risk averse" and who were more likely to decide they would take custody. But other than noting a geographical difference (that New York workers were more likely to take custody than those from Texas or Michigan) and that the female experts were more likely to take custody, the "risk averse" group was not further characterized. Similarly, Vanderloo (2017) found that female workers in Utah were more likely to place children in out-of-home care compared to their male counterparts.

Caseworker stress responses have been found to be significantly associated with risk assessment in maltreatment cases, which may influence decision-making. LeBlanc, Regehr, Shlonsky, and Bogo (2012) found that child protection caseworkers' stress responses are influenced by a parent's demeanor in simulated situations, with a confrontational scenario eliciting greater subjective anxiety among caseworkers than a nonconfrontational scenario. (All case factors were the same in each scenario, other than the parent's demeanor while being interviewed.) Risk assessment scores were higher in the confrontational scenario than in the nonconfrontational scenario.

Professional identification and experience, which may also encompass type and level of education, has also been linked to decision-making about out-of-home placement. Britner and Mossler (2002) found that different professional groups emphasize different information when making placement decisions. Mental healthcare providers and social workers focused on the severity of abuse and the parents' responses to prior services, while judges and guardians ad litem relied more strongly on the likelihood of recidivism, and Court Appointed Special Advocates (CASA) (volunteers appointed by the court to advocate for children's best interests) relied most strongly on information about family stability. Similarly, Mandel, Lehman, and Yuille (1995) compared social workers' and police officers' decision-making about the removal of children described in hypothetical cases of maltreatment and found that social workers were less likely than police officers to agree with a decision to remove. Individual factors such as caseworker skills can also affect caseworker's experience of empathic distress and thus burnout and turnover (Baumann, Kern, McFadden, & Law, 1997).

Organizational and External Factors

Although there is interest in the impact of organizational variables on child welfare outcomes (e.g., Glisson & Hemmelgarn, 1998; Yoo, 2002), few studies have explored the possibility of direct associations between organizational variables and decision-making, especially concerning removals. Cultural competence of the organization (Nybell & Gray, 2004), turnover (Baumann, Kern, McFadden, & Law, 1997; US Government Accountability Office, 2006), excessive caseloads (Mor Barak, Nissly, & Levin, 2001), job burnout (Anderson, 2000; Baumann, Kern, McFadden, & Law, 1997; Conrad & Kellar-Guenthar, 2006), and role ambiguity and adequate supervision (Baumann, Kern, McFadden, & Law, 1997) are all factors that have been found to impact caseworker performance, which may be indirectly related to decision-making.

Concern regarding personal liability resulting from decision-making has also been identified as a factor that may impact caseworkers' decisions (Dettlaff & Rycraft, 2008; Horowitz, 1984; Thoma, 2013). Those who have identified this issue have expressed the concern that negative publicity and liability fears will make caseworkers more likely to remove children to avoid a situation where a child is harmed following a decision to leave a child in the home. For example, in 2006, the Department of Children and Family Services (DCFS) in Illinois documented the considerable increase in the number of child removals following media reports on child fatalities in DCFS in the *Chicago Tribune* and *Chicago Suntimes* (Testa, 2006). Kanani, Regehr, and Bernstein (2002) refer to the tension between being forced to make a decision with minimal and often incomplete information while attempting to maintain parents' rights as the "personal liability paradox," which can create an atmosphere of fear and uncertainty during the decision-making process. This concern for liability may be further impacted by other organizational variables including supervisor support, adequacy of training, and the availability of resources (Dettlaff & Rycraft, 2008).

Wells, Fluke, and Brown (1995) found that the particular community within which an agency is situated impacts the decisions that are made, suggesting an organizational culture of decision-making that is specific to each community and influenced by its external environment. The availability of resources within communities is also a factor that has been identified as impacting the decisions that child welfare caseworkers make because the availability of community resources may impact the choices caseworkers perceive to be available to them when making decisions about the need for placement in lieu of a child remaining in the home (Baumann et al., 2010; Dettlaff & Rycraft, 2008). If necessary resources and services are unavailable for families in their communities, caseworkers may feel that removal is necessary to ensure safety.

By and large, the studies examining ecological factors and their association with caseworker decision-making have tended to focus on some but not all of the just-mentioned dimensions. In the only study we are aware of, Graham and his colleagues (Graham et al., 2015; Chapter 5, this volume) examined the intersection of case, caseworker, organizational, and external factors simultaneously. Their structural model found a complex relationship between and among these factors themselves, only some of which related to the decision to remove. Thus, we lack a robust understanding of the interplay of these potential influences on the outcomes studied. Still, in addition to underscoring the complexity of this decision-making process, this review highlights the need for continued and ongoing research into how decisions are made in order to facilitate positive outcomes for children involved in this system. The *Decision-Making Ecology* (DME) model (Baumann et al., 2011) provides a structure for understanding this process and a framework for conducting research to increase our understanding of this process.

THE DECISION-MAKING ECOLOGY

While much research has been done to understand the factors involved in decision-making, few child welfare–specific theories have been presented to explain the decision-making process. The DME integrates knowledge from the decision-making sciences to the field of child welfare, recognizing the unique environment of child welfare agencies (Baumann, Dalgleish, Fluke, & Kern, 2011; Baumann, Fluke, Dalgleish, & Kern, 2014; Baumann, Kern, & Fluke, 1997; Fluke et al., 2014). The DME examines the decision-making process holistically and considers the case factors, individual factors, organizational factors, and external factors that influence decision-making and that ultimately determine the outcome of those decisions. These outcomes may in turn influence the system as decision-making processes may change as a result of the consequences of those outcomes. The sequence of decision-making, which includes the decisions to report allegations of maltreatment, accept a case for investigation or assessment, substantiate allegations of maltreatment, provide services, place a child in out-of-home care, and enable a child to exit from out-of-home care, are referred to as the *decision-making continuum* (Figure 4.1).

A theoretical framework of the psychological process of decision-making is integrated into the DME and focuses on decision-making thresholds. Referred to as the General Assessment and Decision-Making Model (GADM; see Figure 4.2), this framework distinguishes between the assessment of a particular situation and the decision that results from the assessment (Dalgleish, 1988, 2003). In this framework, the factors that influence the assessment are likely different from those that impact the decision. Case factors are presumed to have the strongest influence on the assessment process, whereas other factors (e.g., individual, organizational) are presumed to have a stronger influence on the

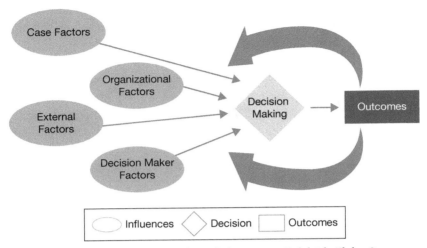

Figure 4.1 Decision-Making Ecology (DME); (Baumann, Dalgleish, Fluke, & Kern, 2011).

decision. This decision is influenced by the *decision-making threshold,* which is the point at which the decision-maker is willing to take action based on the information collected in the assessment process. For example, caseworkers may agree on the assessment of a particular case given the case factors but disagree on what action should be taken (i.e., removal vs. in-home services) given their individual and organizational contexts.

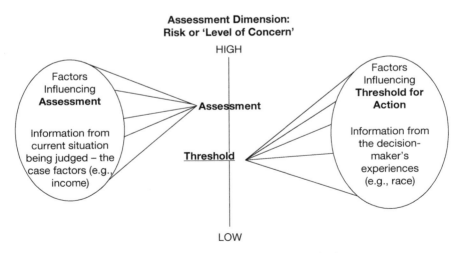

Figure 4.2 General Assessment and Decision-Making Model.

DEVELOPMENT, APPLICATION, AND VALIDATION
OF THE DME INSTRUMENT

The use of instrumentation to apply concepts of the DME began in the mid-1990s by Baumann, Fluke, and colleagues in studies examining caseworker characteristics related to decision-making in child maltreatment investigations as well as caseworker turnover and performance (Fluke et al., 2001; Baumann, Kern, & Fluke, 1997). Instruments were developed to assess case skills, empathy, motivation for doing casework (individual factors), supervisor adequacy, bureaucratic distractions, burnout, and turnover (organizational factors). These scales were factor analyzed and the variables used in structural modeling and regression. Item analyses were then used on a subset of these original instruments to shorten the scales, and these were later used in a study conducted in the state of Washington examining caseworker characteristics related to decision-making in unsubstantiated maltreatment investigations (English, Brummel, Graham, & Coghlan, 2002).

Development of a DME Instrument to Understand
Racial Disproportionality

In the mid-2000s, the DME framework was used as part of a statewide effort in Texas to understand the factors contributing to racial disproportionality, or the overrepresentation of children of color, particularly African American children, in that state's child welfare system. This began through a qualitative examination of the issue utilizing focus groups and interviews with child welfare–involved parents, caseworkers, administrators, and legal professionals in the Dallas/Fort Worth area to develop a preliminary understanding of the multiple factors contributing to disproportionality (Dettlaff & Rycraft, 2008). Findings from these focus groups suggested that disproportionate outcomes for African American children and families may result when caseworkers' decisions were influenced by factors including fear of liability, personal biases, cultural misconceptions, lack of empathy, difficulty engaging with hostile and uncooperative parents, and lack of availability of community resources.

Building on these results, an instrument (see Baumann et al., 2010, Appendix G) was developed for use with caseworkers to assess the influence of these and other factors on the decision-making process. The instrument retained two scales from prior studies—Caseworker Skills and Job Experiences (formerly bureaucratic distractions and additional scales)—and added five additional scales based on the results of this qualitative study. Thus, the final instrument included the following seven scales: (1) Caseworker Skills (items assessed caseworkers' interpersonal and case-related work skills), (2) Job Experiences (items assessed caseworkers' experiences with on-the-job conditions including workload, resources, supervision, and coworker support), (3) Removal Decisions (items evaluated caseworkers' attitudes about removals and factors associated with their willingness to remove), (4) Disposition Decisions (items evaluated considerations made by caseworkers when determining case dispositions), (5) Difficult Situations (items evaluated caseworkers' comfort level and skills when working with hostile or difficult clients), (6) Consensus over Liability (items assessed the extent to which caseworkers' concerns about liability impact decision-making and their perceptions of administrative support of their decisions), and (7) Community Services (items evaluated caseworkers' abilities to access available community resources). Items were rated on a 7-point Likert scale. While the instrument was developed for use at the caseworker level to examine individual and organizational factors related to decision-making, it was intended to be linked to administrative data to include case-related factors. The survey was administered electronically to all investigative caseworkers in Texas (approximately 1,620) during the period of August through December 2007, and 1,125 surveys (69%) were returned. Results regarding the properties of the scales are described next.

Principal Components Analysis of Removal Decisions Scale

Given the complexity of the removal decision, as described previously, we conducted a principal components (PC) analysis of the Removal Decisions scale to better understand the internal structure of this section and determine if it might be better broken up into multiple scales. PC analysis, similar to factor analysis, is a data reduction method that in effect defines one or more new scales based on distinctive mathematical weighting of the items that comprise them. The results are shown in what is called a *pattern matrix* (for rotated components, which means the scales may be correlated). For the purpose of scale construction, items were exclusively sorted to the one new scale on which they had the highest component loading, indicating that, of the two components, they were relatively most powerful in defining that scale and most characteristic of it.

The PC analysis resulted in the extraction of two components from the Removal Decisions section, as shown in the pattern matrix of Table 4.1, subsequently characterized as an External Reference and Internal Reference to decision-making. The items that were most strongly associated with an External Reference included, "I consider the short- and long-term impact of removal on the child before making this decision," "I believe that removal can cause significant trauma to a child and their parents," and "Before making the decision to remove, I try to consider how a family's culture affects their parenting decisions." In contrast, items that were most strongly associated with an Internal Reference included, "My beliefs about parenting can influence my decision to remove," and

Table 4.1 PATTERN MATRIX FOR THE TWO COMPONENTS EXTRACTED FROM THE REMOVAL DECISIONS SCALE

	Component	
	1 External	2 Internal
V39. I consider the short- and long-term impact of removal on the child before making this decision.	.736	-.196
V40. I believe that removal can cause significant trauma to a child and their parents.	.690	-.119
V52. Before making the decision to remove, I try to consider how a family's culture affects their parenting decisions.	.687	-.055
V51. Before making the decision to remove, I try to understand what the child and family are feeling.	.635	.119
V42. I understand how my personal and professional experiences can influence a decision to remove.	.604	.082
V41. I believe that in all but the most extreme cases the child is better off with their family than in substitute care.	.557	.066
V46. I consider that the consequences of removal may be more harmful than leaving the child with the family.	.557	.223
V44. My beliefs about appropriate parenting can influence my decision to remove.	.221	.701
V43. The way I was raised can influence my decision to remove.	.237	.681
V50. There are times it is necessary to remove before all the facts are gathered, so the family will understand the seriousness of the situation and will cooperate with the investigation.	-.163	.598
V47. The decision to remove is the only sure way to be compliant with agency policies and standards.	-.176	.581
V53. It is sometimes necessary to bend the rules and regulations to help a child or family.	.068	.508
V48. Even when the facts are clear, the decision to remove is hard for me.	.286	.391

"The way I was raised can influence my decision to remove." Thus, we concluded that caseworkers with an external reference were more likely to be influenced by the impact of their decisions on children and an understanding of families' feelings, while those with an internal reference were more likely to be influenced by their own beliefs and values about parenting. Yet, although this reflects a tendency, it should not be understood to imply that caseworkers having an internal reference are never influenced by the impact of their decisions or that those with an external reference are never influenced by their values and beliefs.

RELIABILITY ANALYSES

Reliability analyses were conducted for all sections to ascertain the level of internal consistency of the purported measures (i.e., how well each measures something in particular). Beyond Cronbach's alpha (α) for each measure as a whole, an initial analysis also resulted in item-level summary statistics, including information about what the alpha statistic would be if an item were deleted. Based on this, we dropped some items from certain sections, one at a time, to maximize the reliability of the scale as a whole. For the purpose of this study, and given the preliminary stages of the development of this instrument at that time, we retained scales with an alpha greater than 0.50.

Table 4.2 presents the reliability analyses of each section of the survey, including the number of items in each measure, the number of respondents, and Cronbach's α for each. From the Cronbach's α values, it can be seen that the pre-existing scales (Interpersonal Skills, Case Skills, Workload and Resources, and Supervision and Work Unit) all had good to excellent internal consistency (with alphas ranging from .86 for Interpersonal Skills to .95 for Case Skills). The scale related to Community Services, although composed of only three items, also had good reliability (α = .87). Of the two components of the Removal Decisions section, component 1 had the better reliability (α = .76), which is good, compared to component 2 (α = .66), which is acceptable. Reliability of the Difficult Situations scale also was acceptable (α = .65). Reliability of the Disposition scale was too low (α = .33) to be useful. Of the two Liability subscales, Support had good reliability (α = .72); reliability of the Worry scale was poor (α = .55) but may be useful for some purposes.

INTERCORRELATIONS AMONG SURVEY SCALES

Intercorrelations among the survey scales are presented in Table 4.3, which shows that the scales are more likely to be significantly correlated to some extent (positively or negatively) than not. The two Caseworker Skills subscales, Interpersonal Skills and Case Skills, were highly correlated (ρ = .69, $p < .01$). Other significant correlations included Worry and Workload and Resources (ρ = .32, $p < .01$) and Support and Case Skills (ρ = .43, $p < .01$). Responses to the Support scale were also significantly associated with the Services scale (ρ = .31, $p < .01$).

Table 4.2 SCALE RELIABILITY RESULTS

Scale/Subscale	N of items	N of respondents	Cronbach's alpha
Scale 1: Caseworker Skills			
1a: Interpersonal Skills	8	1,125	.862
1b: Case Skills	5	1,125	.946
Scale 2: Job Experiences			
2A: Workload and Resources	5	1,103	.925
2B: Supervision and Work Unit	9	1,103	.934
Scale 3: Removal Decisions			
3a (Pc1): External Reference	7	1,086	.764
3b (Pc2): Internal Reference	6	1,086	.661
Scale 4: Disposition Decisions			
4a: Disposition	3	1,083	.332
Scale 5: Difficult Situations			
5a: Difficult Situations	4	1,080	.653
Scale 6: Liability			
6a: Worry	3	1,073	.551
6b: Support	3	1,073	.720
Scale 7: Community Services			
7a: Services	3	1,070	.870

With regards to the two scales extracted from the PC analysis, External Reference was positively associated with Interpersonal Skills ($\rho = .17$, $p < .01$), whereas Internal Reference was negatively associated with that scale ($\rho = -.14$, $p < .01$). Internal Reference also was negatively associated with Case Skills ($\rho = -.21$, $p < .01$), whereas External Reference had no significant relation to it. Both the Internal and External Reference scales were directly associated with Workload and Resources ($\rho = .11$ and $\rho = .10$, respectively, $p < .05$), but, of the two, only Internal Reference was associated with Supervision and Work Unit ($\rho = .13$, $p < .01$). Both External and Internal Reference were associated with Difficult Situations (3A $\rho = .06$, $p < .05$ and $\rho = .35$, $p < .01$, respectively), though the strength of association was much higher for Internal Reference. Interestingly, Internal Reference was significantly associated with Worry ($\rho = .18$, $p < .01$) whereas External Reference was not, but External Reference was associated with Support ($\rho = .13$, $p < .01$), though Internal Reference was not. With regards to Services, there was a significant positive association between that scale and External Reference ($\rho = .14$, $p < .01$), but a significant negative association between Services and Internal Reference ($\rho = -.09$, $p < .01$). Thus we observed that there is considerable divergent validity supporting the idea that the two Removal Decisions scales are of very different character.

Table 4.3 SCALE INTERCORRELATIONS (SPEARMAN'S ρ)

Scale/Subscale	1A	1B	2A	2B	3A	3B	4A	5A	6A	6B	7A
1A: Interpersonal Skills	1.0	.69**	.10**	.06*	.17**	-.14**	.07*	-.15**	.02	.10**	.25**
1B: Case Skills	.69**	1.0	.08**	.03	.05	-.21**	.12**	-.20**	.05	.02	.20**
2A: Workload and Resources	.10**	.08**	1.0	-.15**	.11**	.10**	.14**	.12**	.32**	-.25**	-.15**
2B: Supervision and Work Unit	.06*	.03	-.15**	1.0	.13**	-.02	.03	-.02	-.11**	.43**	.20**
3A (PC1#): External Reference	.17**	.05	.11*	.13**	1.0	.35**	.28**	.06*	.06	.13**	.14**
3B (PC2#): Internal Reference	-.14**	-.21**	.10*	-.02	.35**	1.0	.17**	.35**	.18**	-.02	-.09**
4A: Disposition	.07*	.12**	.14**	.03	.23**	.17**	1.0	09**	.13**	.01	.06
5A: Difficult Situations	-.15**	-.20**	.12**	-.02	.06*	.35**	.09**	1.0.	.25**	-.08*	-.11**
6A: Worry	.02	.05	.32**	-.11**	.06	.18**	.13**	.25**	1.0	-.27**	-.11*
6B: Support	.10**	.02	-.25**	.43**	.13**	-.02	.01	-.08**	-.27**	1.0	.31**
7A: Services	.25**	.20**	-.15**	.20**	.14**	-.09**	.06	-.11**	-.11*	.31**	1.0

NOTE: Spearman's ρ is a nonparametric test, used due to the wide variety of scale distributions, most of which are non-normal.
*Correlation is significant at the 0.05 level (2-tailed).
**Correlation is significant at the 0.01 level (2-tailed).
#Unit weights.

Scale Replication and Instrument Expansion Efforts

Since the completion of the Texas disproportionality study, the staff survey instrument has been implemented in and adapted to incorporate factors of interest in various research settings. These include randomized control trial studies examining the efficacy of differential response interventions (QIC-DR, 2014), family group decision-making intervention research (Kempe Center & Casey Family Programs, 2015), and in Title IV-E Waiver research initiatives (Chapin Hall, 2017; SRI, 2016), among other initiatives.

The scales employed have demonstrated consistent results over time. For example, despite minor alterations to some scales (i.e., omission of a poorly performing item), findings from two rounds of survey implementation for frontline and supervisory staff associated with a Title IV-E Waiver evaluation (see Chapin Hall [2017] for more details) indicate parallel reliability results for the Interpersonal Skills, Case Skills, Workload and Resources, Supervision and Work Unit, and Community Services scales. Cronbach's α scores for each of these scales were within .01 to .06 of the scores presented in Table 4.2, indicating consistent performance despite smaller samples, geographic and agency differences, and a broader array of caseworker types in the studies' samples (e.g., out-of-home care and adoption staff).

Over time, the instrument has been expanded and adapted to the different study contexts and has employed an extended array of attitudinal scales. While some scales have been developed and tailored to the study context (e.g., examining attitudes about family group decision-making tenets, usefulness, etc.), others are applicable across study settings. Examples of cross-site/study scales include (8) Services Array (items assessed the degree of confidence staff had in specific services, such as mental health, substance abuse, domestic violence, etc.), (9) Administrative Leadership (items assessed perspectives about the quality of administrative leadership), (10) Shared Vision (items assessed the degree to which staff felt cohesion with other staff in their work unit), and (11) Job Satisfaction (items assessed degree to which staff indicated they were satisfied with their job).

Moreover, building on work exploring the role of caseworker bias and attitudes described elsewhere in this volume (Davidson-Arad & Benbenishty, 2008; Chapter 1, this volume), two subscales were used based on select items from Davidson-Arad and Benbenishty's original work (2008). These scales, (12A) Benbenishty Anti-Reunification and (12B) Benbenishty Pro-Removal, have been employed using items for staff to endorse the extent to which they would favor or be disinclined to support reunification or removal, depending on the nature of the maltreatment (e.g., physical abuse, neglect, etc.). For each of these scales, respondents were offered Likert-scale response options ranging from 1 to 7, with 1 = Strongly Disagree and 7 = Strongly Agree. Similarly, the instrument has incorporated a scale that measures staff proclivity toward

child safety versus family preservation beliefs. Called the (13) Dalgleish scale
(Dalgleish, 2010; Fluke, Corwin, Hollinshead, & Maher, 2016; Nikolova, Lwin,
& Fluke, 2017), this six-item scale employs forced choice responses (where
respondents must indicate their preference between a child safety or family
preservation statement) paired with a 5-point Likert scale that enables them
to indicate the strength of their endorsement (from very weak to very strong).
The resulting distribution identifies those with more centrist views as well as
those who tend to endorse more extreme preferences toward either child safety
or family preservation. Higher scores indicate a preference toward child safety
and lower toward family reunification. Results of reliability analyses of the new
scales included in the IV-E Waiver study are presented in Table 4.4.

INTERCORRELATION REPLICATION AND EXTENDED ANALYSES
Just as with the disproportionality placement study, correlational analyses have
been employed to examine the degree to which the scales measured distinct
caseworker and organizational factors. Table 4.5 presents the results of correlational analyses from the second wave of the IV-E Waiver study survey for both
the common and the extended set of scales that were employed.

Table 4.4 ADDITIONAL SCALE RELIABILITY RESULTS

Scale/Subscale	N of items	N of respondents	Cronbach's α
Scale 8: Services Array			
8a: Specific Services Array	8	273	0.872
Scale 9: Administrative Leadership			
9a: Administrative Leadership	15	269	0.948
Scale 10: Shared Vision			
10a: Shared Vision	6	269	0.807
Scale 11: Job Satisfaction			
11a: Job Satisfaction	9	269	0.864
Scale 12: Benbenishty			
12a: Benbenishty Pro-Removals	3	271	0.925
12b: Benbenishty Anti-Reunification	4	271	0.801
Scale 13: Dalgleish			
13a: Dalgleish	6	267	0.648

Table 4.5 CORRELATION REPLICATIONS AND ADDITIONS

	1A	1B	2A	2B	6A	6B	7A	8A	9A	10A	11A	12A	12B	13A
1A: Interpersonal Skills	1.0	.64**	0.00	0.00	-0.14	-0.06	0.12	0.12	-0.01	0.10	0.00	-0.03	-0.08	-0.07
1B: Case Skills	.64**	1.0	-.16*	0.06	-.27**	0.00	.19*	0.05	-0.01	0.09	.149*	-0.12	-0.11	-0.13
2A: Workload and Resources	0.00	-.16*	1.0	-.16*	.28**	-.34**	-.23**	-0.08	-.24**	-.38**	-.48**	0.00	-0.03	-0.06
2B: Supervision and Work Unit	0.00	0.06	-.16*	1.0	-.18*	.62**	.21**	0.14	.62**	.43**	.59**	.16*	-.18*	0.10
6A: Worry	-0.14	-.27**	.28**	-.18*	1.0	-.38**	-.17	-.19**	-.16*	-.18*	-.37**	0.08	0.13	0.03
6B: Support	-0.06	0.00	-.34**	.62**	-.38**	1.0	.22**	.18*	.63**	.41**	.56**	.14*	-0.11	0.07
7A: Services in General	0.12	.19*	-.23**	.21**	-.17	.22**	1.0	.55**	.25**	.25**	.20*	-0.08	-.18**	-.12*
8A: Confidence in Specific Services	0.12	0.05	-0.08	0.14	-.19**	.18*	.55**	1.0	.20**	.13*	0.11	0.03	-0.10	0.02
9A: Administrative Leadership	-0.01	-0.01	-.24**	.62**	-.16*	.63**	.25**	.20**	1.0	.50**	.51**	-0.02	-.12*	0.06
10A: Shared Vision	0.10	0.09	-.38**	.43**	-.18*	.41**	.25**	.13*	.50**	1.0	.47**	-0.10	-.30**	-0.10
11A: Job Satisfaction	0.00	.15*	-.48**	.59**	-.37**	.56**	.20*	0.11	.51**	.47**	1.0	0.00	-.19**	0.03
12A: Benbenishty Pro–Removal	-0.03	-0.12	0.00	.16*	0.08	.14*	-0.08	0.03	-0.02	-0.10	0.00	1.0	.33**	.27**
12B: Benbenishty Anti–Reunification	-0.08	-0.11	-0.03	-.18*	0.13	-0.11	-.18**	-0.10	-.12*	-.30**	-.19**	.33**	1.0	.22**
13A: Dalgleish	-0.07	-0.13	-0.06	0.10	0.03	0.07	-.12*	0.02	0.06	-0.10	0.03	.27**	.22**	1.0

**Correlation is significant at the 0.01 level (2-tailed).
*Correlation is significant at the 0.05 level (2-tailed).

When compared to the findings in Table 4.3, which are from the Texas disproportionality study, it appears that some findings are consistent while others diverge. Still, given the difference in sample sizes and in the roles of the staff involved in the two studies, differences found here could be due to inadequate power in the IV-E Waiver study (with a sample of fewer than 280 respondents [79% response rate] compared to more than 1,100 in the Texas disproportionality study), the presence of staff with a much broader array of functions (beyond investigations), or perhaps other factors such as a greater proportion of staff with less work experience in the current study.

Numerous findings regarding statistically significant correlations are consistent between the two studies. The relationship between the Casework Skills subscales, Interpersonal Skills and Case Skills, remains strong and statistically significant ($\rho = .64, p < .01$). Perspectives on Workload and Resources and Supervision and Work Unit also remained inversely correlated ($\rho = -.16, p < .05$); staff who felt more stress about their workload scored their supervision experience more negatively. Case Skills and more positive perspectives of Supervision and Work Unit were associated with greater confidence in Services ($\rho = .19, p < .05$ and $\rho = .21, p < .01$, respectively). Concerns about Workload and Resources were also inversely associated with general confidence in Services ($\rho = -.23, p < .01$), and Support ($\rho = -.34, p < .01$). Associations between Supervision and Work Unit and Support remained positive and particularly strong ($\rho = .62, p < .01$). Higher levels of Worry about liability concerns were inversely associated with Support ($\rho = -.38, p < .01$), Supervision and Work Unit ($\rho = -.18, p < .05$), and confidence in Services ($\rho = -.17, p < .05$), while moderately and positively associated with higher concerns about Workload ($\rho = .28, p < .01$). Staff who felt more Support also indicated greater confidence in Services ($\rho = .22, p < .01$).

CONTRARY OR DISPARATE FINDINGS

Despite the preceding consistencies, some results differed. Specifically, the associations between Interpersonal Skills and Workload and Resources, Supervision and Work Unit, Support, or general confidence in Services did not reach statistical significance in the much smaller Tennessee sample.

NEW FINDINGS

Of all the common scales between the two studies, only one statistically significant association was found in the Tennessee Title IV-E study that was not found in the Texas disproportionality study. Here, an inverse association was detected between Worry and self-perceptions of Case Skills ($\rho = -.27, p < .01$).

Still, as Table 4.5 reflects, seven additional scales were utilized in the Tennessee staff survey and these offer insights into an array of child welfare staff attitudes and concerns. Staff with more confidence in Specific Services in the community were associated with lower levels of Worry about liability ($\rho = -.19$, $p < .01$), higher levels of Support ($\rho = .18$, $p < .01$), more positive views of Administrative Leadership ($\rho = .20$, $p < .01$) and of Shared Vision or cohesion with their coworkers ($\rho = .13$, $p < .05$), as well as greater confidence in the general state of Services overall ($\rho = .55$, $p < .01$). Administrative Leadership was inversely associated with Workload ($\rho = -.24$, $p < .01$), Worry ($\rho = -.16$, $p < .01$), and Benbenishty Anti-Reunification ($\rho = -.12$, $p < .05$). On the other hand, Administrative Leadership was positively associated with Supervision and Work Unit ($\rho = .62$, $p < .01$), Support ($\rho = .63$, $p < .01$), Shared Vision ($\rho = .50$, $p < .01$), Job Satisfaction ($\rho = .51$, $p < .01$), and general confidence in Services ($\rho = .25$, $p < .01$). Relationships between Shared Vision and the variables associated with Administrative Leadership were parallel. Shared Vision was inversely associated with Workload ($\rho = -.38$, $p < .01$), Worry ($\rho = -.18$, $p < .05$), and Benbenishty Anti-Reunification ($\rho = -.30$, $p < .05$); that is, staff with greater shared vision/unit cohesion indicated a larger propensity to favor reunifying children with their families of origin. Positive associations were detected between Shared Vision and Supervision and Work Unit ($\rho = .43$, $p < .01$), Support ($\rho = .41$, $p < .01$), Services ($\rho = .25$, $p < .01$), and Specific Services ($\rho = .13$, $p < .05$), but, aside from the relationship with Administrative Leadership, the strongest correlation with this scale was with Job Satisfaction ($\rho = .47$, $p < .01$).

Scales assessing potential value biases also had statistically significant correlations. Benbenishty Pro-Removal was positively and moderately correlated with Benbenishty Anti-Reunification ($\rho = .33$, $p < .01$) and with Dalgleish ($\rho = .27$, $p < .01$). It was also associated with Supervision and Work Unit ($\rho = .16$, $p < .05$) and Support ($\rho = .14$, $p < .05$). Benbenishty Anti-Reunification had an inverse relationship Supervision and Work Unit ($\rho = -.18$, $p < .05$), Services ($\rho = -.18$, $p < .01$), and Job Satisfaction ($\rho = -.19$, $p < .01$) but a positive association with Dalgleish ($\rho = .22$, $p < .01$). Aside from the correlations with the Benbenishty subscales, Dalgleish was inversely correlated with Services ($\rho = -.12$, $p < .05$).

FINDINGS FROM APPLICATIONS OF THE DME INSTRUMENTS

Results from analyses employing the scales just reported have been promising and have illuminated the importance of caseworker, organizational, and external factors in relationship to an array of child welfare outcomes. In this section, we review a number of applications of the DME instrument in child welfare systems across the country to better understand their decision-making processes and to generate recommendations for improvements.

Factors That Influence the Decision Not to Substantiate a Child Protective Services Referral

This study, conducted between 1998 and 2000 in the state of Washington (English, Graham, Brummel, & Coghlan, 2002), gathered information from case record narratives, caseworkers, and caregivers to develop an understanding of the factors that led to determining that a case would be unsubstantiated. Most of the caseworker factors were measured using the DME instrument, which was also being used in parallel for the Dynamics of Unsubstantiation study described later. In addition to case and organizational factors, caseworker factors, experience, higher self-assessment of skills, and supportive relationships with peers were all associated with a greater likelihood to unsubstantiate an investigation.

Dynamics of Unsubstantiation Study

In a multistate study examining aspects of the DME and their relationship with child maltreatment report unsubstantiation and recurrence rates, analyses indicated that the perception and knowledge of the decision-maker regarding the organizational environment had an association with case decisions. Multiple regression analyses examining caseworker attitudes and rates suggested that the state in which one resides, perceptions of resources available for clients (an early version of Scale 7, Services), and perceptions of overwork and bureaucratic distractions (retitled Workload and Resources) were related to proportions of recurrence for their cases. Specifically, controlling for state, staff with poorer perceptions of the resources available to their clients had caseloads with higher recurrence rates (t = 2.50, p = .013) while those indicating they felt overworked were associated with lower recurrence rates (t = −2.359, p = .019; Fluke et al., 2001).

Texas Disproportionality Studies

Following a legislative mandate in 2005 to address the overrepresentation of African American children in the Texas child welfare system, DME instruments were administered to all investigative caseworkers in Texas to further understand how case, caseworker, and organizational factors influenced removals of African American children. The main outcome of interest was a disparity index calculated for each caseworker, which indicated whether the worker removed disproportionate numbers of African American children given the racial composition of children at the prior stage of decision-making (i.e., cases assigned to investigation). Findings indicated that the primary caseworker factor related to the disparity index was caseworkers' perceptions of their interpersonal skills. The higher they rated their interpersonal skills, the lower was their propensity to remove African American children. At the organizational level, the primary factor related to the index was the percentage of the worker's caseload that was African American. Higher percentages of African Americans on one's caseload were associated with lower disparity indices, suggesting that exposure to a greater number of African American families may reduce disproportionate removal decisions. At the case level, higher assessments of risk and having more low-income cases were significant predictors of removals (Baumann et al., 2010).

Family Group Conferencing Study

A more recent study examined staff survey data from a large urban child welfare jurisdiction consisting of two neighboring counties in an effort to identify reasons for significant variation in caseworkers' rates of referrals to Family Group Conferencing (FGC). The results indicate that time in current position and Supervision and Administrative Leadership were significantly associated with a worker's propensity to refer to FGC. Specifically, controlling for other organizational, attitudinal, and caseworker demographic factors, staff with fewer years in their current position and those who reported lower ratings on their Supervision and Work Unit or Administrative Leadership made a higher number of FGC referrals ($t = -2.31$, $p = 0.02$; $t = -2.08$, $p = 0.04$, respectively; Allan, Harlaar, Hollinshead, Drury, & Merkel-Holguin, 2017).

Title IV-E Waiver Studies

Related to the supplementary analyses of Tennessee IV-E Waiver staff survey results (presented earlier), an analyses of placement odds following an investigation or assessment response found that, controlling for case-level risk factors (e.g., child age, maltreatment allegation) and other worker demographics (e.g., years of experience in child welfare), workers who had a higher rating on the Support scale were less likely to place children in out-of-home care (odds ratio [OR]: 0.84; 95% confidence interval [CI]: 0.77, 0.92] per one-unit increase in scale above the mean). On the other hand, workers with higher ratings of Shared Vision within their teams were more likely to place children, after adjusting for covariates (OR: 1.25 [95% CI: 1.06, 1.46] per one-unit increase in scale above the mean).

Decision to Place and Recurrence rates: Utah IV-E

Another study conducted in Utah under the auspices of a Title IV-E Waiver evaluation linked data from 500 workers to more than 77,000 child protective service (CPS) records in an 8-year span. While no associations between race/ethnicity, the Benbenishty or Dalgleish scales, and removal decisions were detected, bivariate analyses found that, compared to women, men were less likely to place children in out-of-home care than women (OR: 0.77 [95% CI = 0.60, 0.98], $p <$ .05), staff with more tenure were more likely to place (OR: 2.45 [95% CI = 1.75, 3.43], $p <$ .001), and staff with higher adverse childhood experiences (ACEs) scores were less likely to place a child in out-of-home care (e.g., ACEs score of 4 [vs. 0] OR: 0.65 [95% CI = 0.43, 0.97], $p <$ .05; Vanderloo, 2017). Further analyses examining whether case recurrence rates are different for staff who remove more or fewer children found that, controlling for region, child age, child race/ethnicity, and number of prior substantiations, there was no association between the percent of child cases a worker removed and recurrence rates for cases on their caseload (OR: 1.02 [95% CI = 0.92, 1.12], $p =$ .75; Vanderloo, 2017).

Additional Applications and Current Studies

Still other studies conducted have found a relationship between the Dalgleish scale and self-reports on face-to-face contacts, where family preservation–oriented staff indicated making a lower frequency of in-person contacts (Price et al., 2016). Additional work examining relationships between staff perspectives and outcomes have occurred in Differential Response contexts (Nikolova et al., 2017) and are under way in studies examining the efficacy of parent advocates as additional supports for family group conferences and associations with the odds of planned permanent exits, as well as in other Title IV-E Waiver initiatives.

IMPLICATIONS

This line of research has an array of implications for child welfare practice, policy, and research. We believe one of the greatest strengths of the suite of DME instruments is the opportunity it provides to delve into questions about how staff-level factors may contribute to decisions on cases and, by extension, to the trajectories cases may take as well as agency performance on outcomes. The instruments also have value for improving the child welfare workforce and child welfare organizational settings. The instrument suite is adaptable to different research contexts, and scales can be supplemented with intervention, agency, or other environment-specific lines of inquiry pertinent to the goal of the research. Moreover, results from these studies have the potential to illuminate a myriad of areas where there may be opportunities for agencies to leverage change. The results may have implications for recruitment and hiring, unit or supervisor assignment, case assignment practices, training plans, supervision processes and quality, and agency culture and climate.

Despite this, there are limitations to the instruments. Lacking other objective sources, we are limited to staff perceptions of case skills, organizational culture and climate, etc. Still, as information systems become more advanced, we hope that efforts to triangulate data on some of these concepts using human resources and other worker performance data may enhance the robustness of our understanding of these factors. Furthermore, with few exceptions, the instrument has been employed largely in cross-sectional worker-focused studies. Opportunities to study and understand to what extent scales are measuring degree of decision-making variability at unit levels and over time in an agency's history or over time as a worker gains more experience remain largely untapped.

There is a vast, untapped potential for these instruments to assist in understanding why, how, and under what conditions staff are more or less likely to make certain types of case decisions and illuminate leverage points that agencies can address. It could further serve to enhance our ability to know when and how to intervene with a workforce that is beleaguered, often stressed, and prone to burnout and turnover.

While there have been many validation and promising outcomes analyses conducted to date, the instrument could be used in a variety of ways that have yet to be tested. For example, it is not clear if the same factors associated with an outcome such as placement decisions have a significant relationship with other decisions made by workers, such as substantiation, service provision, visitation frequency and quality, or case closure. Thus, more research on workers' decisions across their cases will help clarify what factors matter to what decisions and whether there are patterns across the myriad of outcomes that may be of interest. There should also be further exploration into DME factors that may function as mediators or moderators of workers' personal attributes on decisions made.

In keeping with the dynamic nature of research, this instrument should not be viewed as a static resource. Potential areas of further inquiry, whether for replication or exploration purposes should include worker ACEs, secondary trauma, shared adverse experiences within work units or offices (e.g., a child fatality or negative press about an active case), etc. We encourage use of the instrument with respect to different outcomes (e.g., turnover, child well-being, etc.) and similar work environments, such as juvenile justice and other social service settings. We look forward to seeing the results of these efforts in the years to come.

REFERENCES

Allan, H., Harlaar, N., Hollinshead, D., Drury, I., & Merkel-Holguin, L. (2017). The impact of worker and agency characteristics on FGC referrals in child welfare. *Children and Youth Services Review, 81*, 229–237. doi:10.1016/j.childyouth.2017.08.013

Anderson, D. G. (2000). Coping strategies and burnout among veteran child protection workers. *Child Abuse and Neglect, 24*, 839–848.

Baumann, D. J., Dalgleish, L., Fluke, J. D., & Kern, H. (2011). *The decision-making ecology.* Washington, DC: American Humane Association.

Baumann, D., Kern, H., McFadden, T., & Law, J. R. (1997). Individual and organizational factors in burnout and turnover: A decision making ecology approach. In H. Kern, D. J. Baumann, & J. D. Fluke. (Eds.), *Worker Improvements to the Decision and Outcome Model (WISDOM): The child welfare decision enhancement project* (pp. 15–29). Washington, DC: The Children's Bureau.

Baumann, D. J., Fluke, J. D., Graham, J. C., Wittenstrom, K., Hedderson, J., Rivaux, S., Dettlaff, A., Rycraft, J., Oritz, M. J., James, J., Kromrei, L., Craig, S., Capouch, D., Sheets, J., Ward, D., Breidenbach, R., Hardaway, A., Boudreau, B., & Brown, N. (2010). *Disproportionality in child protective services: The preliminary results of statewide reform efforts.* Austin, TX: Texas Department of Family and Protective Services.

Baumann, D. J., Fluke, J. D., Dalgleish, L., & Kern, H. (2014). The decision making ecology. In A. Shlonsky. A., & Benbenishty, R. (Eds.), *From evidence to outcomes in child welfare: An international reader* (pp. 24–38). Oxford: Oxford University Press.

Baumann, D. J., Kern, H. D., & Fluke, J. D. (1997). Foundations of the decision-making ecology and overview. In H. D. Kern, D. J. Baumann, & J. D. Fluke (Eds.), *WISDOM: The child welfare decision enhancement project.* Washington, DC: The Children's Bureau.

Britner, P. A., & Mossler, D. G. (2002). Professionals' decision-making about out-of-home placements following instances of child abuse. *Child Abuse and Neglect, 26*, 317–332.

Chapin Hall at the University of Chicago. (2017). *Tennessee's IV-E Waiver demonstration project interim evaluation report.* Chicago, IL: Chapin Hall.

Conrad, D., & Kellar-Guenther, Y. (2006). Compassion fatigue, burnout, and compassion satisfaction among Colorado child protection workers. *Child Abuse and Neglect. 30*, 1071–1080.

Courtney, M. E., Dworsky, A., Hook, J., Brown, A., Cary, C., Love, K., . . . Bost, N. (2011). *Midwest evaluation of the adult functioning of former foster youth.* Chicago, IL: Chapin Hall at the University of Chicago.

Dalgleish, L. (2010). *Balance of work focus in child welfare: Work practice and values scales for child protection.* Washington, DC: American Humane Association.

Dalgleish, L. I. (1988). Decision making in child abuse cases: Applications of Social Judgment Theory and Signal Detection Theory. In B. Brehmer & C. R. B. Joyce (Eds.), *Human judgment: The SJT view.* North Holland: Elsevier.

Dalgleish, L. I. (2003). Risk, needs and consequences. In M. C. Calder (Ed.), *Assessments in child care: A comprehensive guide to frameworks and their use.* (pp. 86–99). Dorset, UK: Russell House Publishing.

Davidson-Arad, B., & Benbenishty, R. (2008). The role of workers' attitudes and parent and child wishes in child protection workers' assessments and recommendation regarding removal and reunification. *Children and Youth Services Review, 30,* 107–121.

Davidson-Arad, B., Englechin-Segal, D., Wozner, Y., & Arieli, R. (2005). Social workers' decisions on removal: Predictions from their initial perceptions of the child's features, parents' features, and child's quality of life. *Journal of Social Service Research, 31,* 1–23.

DePanfilis, D. (1997). Is the child safe? How do we respond to safety concerns? In T. D. Morton & W. Holder (Eds.), *Decision making in child protective services: Advancing the state of the art* (pp. 86–102). Duluth, GA: National Resource Center for Child Maltreatment.

DePanfilis, D., & Salus, M. (1992). *Child protective services: A guide for caseworkers* (US Government Printing Office No.1992-625-670/60577). Washington, DC: National Center on Child Abuse and Neglect.

Dettlaff, A. J., Rivaux, S. R., Baumann, D. J., Fluke, J. D., Rycraft, J. R., & James, J. (2011). Disentangling substantiation: The influence of race, income, & risk on the substantiation decision in child welfare. *Children and Youth Services Review, 33,* 1630–1637.

Dettlaff, A. J., & Rycraft, J. R. (2008). Deconstructing disproportionality: Views from multiple stakeholders. *Child Welfare, 87*(2), 37–58.

Dixon, L., Browne, K., & Giachritsis, C. H. (2005). Risk factors of parents abused as children: A meditational analysis of the intergenerational continuity of child maltreatment (part I). *Journal of Child Psychology and Psychiatry, 46,* 47–57.

Dorsey, S., Mustillo, S. A., Farmer, E. M. Z., & Elbogen, E. (2008). Caseworker assessments of risk for recurrent maltreatment: Association with case-specific risk factors and re-reports. *Child Abuse and Neglect, 32,* 377–391.

Doyle, J. J., Jr. (2008). Child protection and adult crime: Using investigator assignment to estimate causal effects of foster care. *Journal of Political Economy, 116,* 746–770.

English, D. J., Brummel, S., Graham, J. C., & Coghlan, L. (2002). *Final report: Factors that influence the decision not to substantiate a CPS referral. Phase II.* Olympia, WA: DSHS, Children's Administration, OCAR.

Fluke, J. D., Baumann, D. J., Dalgleish, L., & Kern, H. (2014). Decisions to protect children: A decision making ecology. In Korbin, J. E., & Krugman, R. D. (Eds.), *Handbook of child maltreatment.* New York: Springer.

Fluke, J. D., Chabot, M., Fallon, B., MacLaurin, B., & Blackstock, C. (2010). Placement decisions and disparities among aboriginal groups: An application of the decision making ecology through multi-level analysis. *Child Abuse and Neglect, 34,* 57–69.

Fluke, J. D., Corwin, T. W., Hollinshead, D., & Maher, E. J. (2016). Family preservation or child safety? how experience and position shape child welfare workers' perspectives. *Children and Youth Services Review, 69,* 210–218.

Fluke, J. D., Parry, C., Shapiro, P., Hollinshead, D., Bollenbacher, V., Baumann, D., & Davis-Brown, K. (2001). *The dynamics of unsubstantiated reports: A multi-state study—final report.* Englewood, CO: American Humane Association.

Glisson, C., & Hemmelgarn, A. (1998). The effects of organizational climate and inter-organizational coordination on the quality and outcomes of children's service systems. *Child Abuse and Neglect, 5,* 401–421.

Gold, N., Benbenishty, R., & Osmo, R. (2001). A comparative study of risk assessments and recommended interventions in Canada and Israel. *Child Abuse and Neglect, 25,* 607–622.

Graham, J. C., Dettlaff, A., Baumann, D. J., & Fluke, J. D. (2015). The decision-making ecology of placing children in foster care: A structural equation model. In J. D. Fluke, M. Lopez Lopez, R. Benbenisty, & E. North (Eds.), *In Child Abuse and Neglect, 49,* 12–23.

Hibbard, R. A., & Desch, L. W. (2007). Maltreatment of children with disabilities. *Pediatrics, 119,* 1018–1025.

Horowitz, R. (1984). Improving the legal bases in child protection work: Let the worker beware. In W. Holder & K. Hayes (Eds.), *Malpractice and liability in child protective services* (pp. 17–27). Longmont, CO: Bookmakers Guild, Inc.

Kanani, K., Regehr, C., & Bernstein, M. M. (2002). Liability considerations in child welfare: Lessons from Canada. *Child Abuse and Neglect, 26,* 1029–43.

Kern, H. D., Baumann, D. J., & Fluke, J. D. (1997). *Worker's improvements to the structured decision and outcome model (WISDOM): The child welfare decision enhancement project.* Washington, DC: The Children's Bureau.

Kempe Center for the Prevention and Treatment of Child Abuse and Neglect, & Casey Family Programs. (2015). *No Place Like Home final progress report.* Aurora, CO: Kempe Center. USDHHS Grant 90F0051.

LeBlanc, V., Regehr, C., Shlonsky, A., & Bogo, M. (2012). Stress responses and decision making in child protection workers faced with high conflict situations. *Child Abuse and Neglect, 36,* 404–412.

Lindsey, D. (1991). Factors affecting the foster care placement of decision: An analysis of national survey data. *American Journal of Orthopsychiatry, 61,* 272–281.

Lindsey, D. (2004). *The welfare of children* (2nd Ed.). New York: Oxford University Press.

Mandel, D. R., Lehman, D. R., & Yuille, J. C. (1995). Reasoning about the removal of a child from home: A comparison of police officers and social workers. *Journal of Applied Social Psychology, 25,* 906–921.

Marshall, D. B., & English, D. J. (1999). Survival analysis of risk factors for recidivism in child abuse and neglect. *Child Maltreatment, 4,* 287–296.

Mor Barak, M. E., Nissly, J. A., & Levin, A. (2001). Antecedents to retention and turnover among child welfare, social work, and other human service employees: What can we learn from past research? A review and meta-analysis. *Social Service Review, 75,* 625–661.

Nikolova, K., Lwin, K., & Fluke, J. D. (2017). Attitudes on the responsibility for child safety: Key child protection worker characteristics. *Journal of Public Child Welfare, 3*(11) 318–338.

Nybell, L. M., & Gray, S. S. (2004). Race, place, space: Meanings of cultural competence in three child welfare agencies. *Social Work, 49,* 17–26.

Pecora, P. J., Kessler, R. C., Williams, J., O'Brien, K., Downs, A. C., English, D., & Holmes, K. (2005). *Improving family foster care: Findings from the Northwest Foster Care Alumni Study.* Seattle, WA: Casey Family Programs.

Phillips, M. H., Shyne, A. W., Sherman, E. A., & Haring, B. L. (1971). *Factors associated with placement decisions in child welfare.* New York: Child Welfare League of America.

Price, K., Feldman, S., Fluke, J. D., Hollinshead, D., & Wulczyn, F. (2016, September) *Attitudes and allocations: The relationship between workers' perspectives about their jobs and time spent on casework activities.* Presentation at the XIV International Conference EUSARF. Oveido Spain, 12–16 September.

Reid, G., Sigurdson, E., Christiannson-Wood, J., & Wright, A. (1995). *Basic issues concerning the assessment of risk in child welfare work.* Winnipeg: University of Manitoba.

Rivaux, S., James, J., Wittenstrom, K., Baumann, D., Sheets, J., Henry, J., & Jeffries, V. (2008). The intersection of race, poverty, and risk: Understanding the decision to provide services to clients and to remove children. *Child Welfare, 87,* 151–168.

Rossi, P. H, Schuerman, J., & Budde, S. (1999). Understanding decisions about child maltreatment. *Evaluation Review, 23,* 579–598.

Rycus, J. S., & Hughes, R. C. (2008). Assessing risk throughout the life of a child welfare case. In D. Lindsey & A. Shlonsky (Eds.), *Child welfare research: Advances for practice and policy* (pp. 201–213). New York: Oxford University Press.

Schultz, D. F., Law, J. R., Baumann, D., Kern, H., & Gober, K. (1997). Caseworker Studies of Individual and Organizational Measures Related to Performance. In D. J. Baumann, H. Kern, & J. D. Fluke. (Eds.), *Worker Improvements to the Decision and Outcome Model (WISDOM): The child welfare decision enhancement project* (pp. 31–51). Washington, DC: The Children's Bureau.

Schwab, J., Baumann, D. J., & Gober, K. (1997). Patterns of caseworker decision-making. In D. J. Baumann, H. Kern, & J. D. Fluke (Eds.), *Worker Improvements to the Decision and Outcome Model (WISDOM): The child welfare decision enhancement project.* Washington, DC: The Children's Bureau.

SRI. (2016). Utah Title IV-E Demonstration Project Interim Evaluation Report. Salt Lake City: Social Research Institute, College of Social Work, University of Utah. https://dcfs.utah.gov/wp-content/uploads/2017/11/Utah-Interim-Evaluation-Report-Final-June-2016.pdf

Sullivan, P. M., & Knutson, J. F. (2000). Maltreatment and disabilities: A population-based epidemiological study. *Child Abuse and Neglect, 24,* 1257–1274.

Testa, M. (2006). *Child Welfare and the Media. Advanced Child Welfare Lecture 5. Children and Family Research Center.* January.

Thoma, R. (2013). A critical look at the child welfare system: Defensive social work. http://www.liftingtheveil.org/defensive.htm.

Thompson, R., & Wiley, T. R. (2008). Predictors of re-referral to child protective services: A longitudinal follow-up of an urban cohort. *Child Maltreatment, 14,* 89–99.

US Government Accountability Office. (2006). *Improving social service program, training, and technical assistance would help address long-standing service-level and workforce challenges.* Washington, DC: US Government Printing Office.

Vanderloo, M. (2017). Caseworker factors that influence removal decisions in child welfare (doctoral dissertation). http://socialwork.utah.edu/wp-content/uploads/sites/4/
2017/08/Vanderloo-Mindy.pdf

Wells, S. J., Fluke, J. D., & Brown, C. H. (1995). The decision to investigate: Child protection practice in 12 local agencies. *Children and Youth Services Review, 17,* 523–535.

Wulczyn, F., Gibbons, R., Snowden, L., & Leary, B. (2013). Poverty, social disadvantage,
and the black/white placement gap. *Children and Youth Services Review, 35,* 65–74.

Yoo, J. (2002). The relationship between organizational variables and client outcomes: A
case study in child welfare. *Administration in Social Work, 26*(2), 39–61.

PART III

Ecological Models of Decision-Making in Child Welfare and Protection

The Decision-Making Ecology of Placing a Child into Foster Care

A Structural Equation Model

J. CHRISTOPHER GRAHAM, ALAN J. DETTLAFF,
DONALD J. BAUMANN, AND JOHN D. FLUKE ■

INTRODUCTION

Certain decisions made by human service professionals are especially "high-stakes," and the choice to remove a child from his or her home to be placed into foster care is one of them (Schwalbe, 2004). Placement is a characteristically difficult and consequential decision, but it is a decision surprisingly little understood by researchers. Placement decisions are part of a class of decision-making under uncertainty (Swets, 1992) and, as a consequence, are likely to be highly influenced by decision-making thresholds which are specific to the decision-maker (Dalgleish, 1988). It is demonstrable that characteristics of decision-makers (e.g., child protective services [CPS] caseworkers) have an influence, but the specifics of these have remained elusive. The aim of this chapter is to explore, at the worker level, the context of the placement decision, with the objective of providing a more detailed picture than has heretofore been available of the interrelationships among case, caseworker, and organizational factors. It is hoped that this endeavor will contribute both a framework for future

J. Christopher Graham, Alan J. Dettlaff, Donald J. Baumann, and John D. Fluke, *The Decision-Making Ecology of Placing a Child into Foster Care* In: *Decision-Making and Judgment in Child Welfare and Protection.* Edited by: John D. Fluke, Mónica López López, Rami Benbenishty, Erik J. Knorth, and Donald J. Baumann, Oxford University Press (2021). © Oxford University Press. DOI: 10.1093/oso/9780190059538.003.0005.

exploration as well as substantive knowledge about this challenging topic. This is part of a general program of research seeking to better understand placement decisions to support their fairness, accuracy, and consistency and, in so doing, to promote child well-being, family integrity when possible, and equal protection under the law.

According to data compiled by the US Department of Health and Human Services (2014), nationally, nearly 400,000 children were in out-of-home placement as of November 2012. With respect to entries into care (the subject of this study), 251,764 children entered into care in 2012. Although the decision to place children outside their home is necessary in many instances, the consequences of this decision to children are numerous. Studies have shown that children who are removed from their homes experience not only significant trauma but also are more likely than other children to experience negative outcomes as adults, including low educational attainment, homelessness, poverty, unemployment, mental health disorders, and criminal justice system involvement (Courtney, Dworsky, Lee, & Rapp, 2010; Pecora et al., 2003). Although it is unclear whether these outcomes can be attributed to children's placement in foster care or to their abusive family backgrounds, research by Doyle (2007) suggests that outcomes for children at the margin of placement (i.e., cases where there may be disagreement about the need for removal) are better for children who remain in their homes compared with children removed from their homes (who experience higher delinquency rates, higher teen birth rates, and lower earnings).

Limits of Knowledge

The decision to place a child into foster care has been much studied over the years but remains not well understood (Lindsey, 2004). Some researchers (Runyan, Gould, Trost, & Loda, 1981), finding little power in predicting removal of children based on social, family, and child characteristics, even went so far as to conclude "that assignment to foster care approximates *a random process* across a large population" (p. 710, emphasis added). Nonetheless, the placement decision is not entirely unpredictable (Rossi, Schuerman, & Budde, 1999), and, in fact, it has been demonstrated that a great many factors influence the decision-making process. For example, in early work, Phillips, Shyne, Sherman, and Haring (1971) identified 43 child, parent, and family characteristics associated with placement decisions, and other domains of influential factors have been identified as well (see Baumann, Schwab, & Schultz, 1997; Lindsey, 2004). However, as noted by Lindsey (2004), "early studies of the decision-making process revealed little consensus among caseworkers regarding criteria to use in deciding the future of children and families" (p. 163), and determining which factors are most important in caseworkers' considerations and how they are interrelated has remained an elusive goal. Whatever their basis, there seems to be little doubt that placement decisions are inconsistent (Gold, Benbenishty, & Osmo, 2001; Rossi et al., 1999), which is a major problem in view of each decision's "profound and potentially deleterious impact . . . on the child, the parents, and society" (Arad-Davidzon & Benbenishty, 2008, p. 108). As noted by Baumann, Schwab, et al. (1997) and Rossi et al. (1999), and as remains true today, a great deal of the variability in workers' decisions remains unexplained.

Increasingly, empirically validated risk assessment protocols such as actuarial models are being used in support of CPS decision-making to address these concerns (Ruscio, 1998; Shlonsky & Wagner, 2005), but with a few exceptions (Baumann, Grigsby, et al., 2011), these instruments are atheoretical (Schwalbe, 2004) and inconsistent, with varying levels of research support for the criteria used (DePanfilis & Scannapieco, 1994). Furthermore, they do little to shed light on the dynamics of decision-making (Baumann, Law, Sheets, Reid, & Graham, 2005). Consensus-based instruments, on the other hand, generally are not empirically validated and have not done well in comparison with actuarial measures when the aim is to predict recurrence (Baird & Wagner, 2000; Baird, Wagner, Healy, & Johnson, 1999). A synthetic view is that both actuarial instruments and clinical judgment have their place in evidence-based practice oriented toward meeting family needs (Shlonsky & Wagner, 2005). Regardless of what instruments (if any) are used, however, "decision-making involving out-of-home placements is often a difficult and confusing process for both the interested parties and the professionals. Identifying and understanding important dimensions of the underlying dynamic process is prerequisite to relieving some of this confusion" (Britner & Mossler, 2002, p. 328).

Influences on Caseworker Decision-Making

A large part of the difficulty in understanding the placement decision is that it is not simply a matter of determining what happened in the family and what is best for the child (Banach, 1998), difficult as those judgments can be. Additionally, factors not directly related to the case may play important roles, including the question of what constitutes abuse or neglect (Portwood, 1998), the lack of clear legal guidelines (Besharov, 1986), and uncertainty regarding what criteria should be used to make a decision (Gold et al., 2001; Lindsey, 2004). Furthermore, there are numerous possible extraneous influences on decision-making that have little or nothing to do with the specifics of a particular case, including the types of information that tend to be used by caseworkers (Britner & Mossler, 2002; Rossi et al., 1999) and their degree of professional experience (Gold et al., 2001; Rossi et al., 1999), as well as idiosyncrasies of professional judgment (Kominkiewicz, 2004; Stein & Rzepnicki, 1984), caseworker tendencies and decision-making thresholds (Dalgleish, 1988, 2006; Rossi et al., 1999), and reactions to issues of poverty, gender, and race, which have been shown to be important factors in decision-making (Dettlaff et al., 2011; Lindsey, 2004; Rivaux et al., 2008).

Generally speaking, social workers' role, their social, cultural, and political contexts, and their professional group membership may all affect their judgments (Arad-Davidzon & Benbenishty, 2008), as may their personal values (Benbenishty, Osmo, & Gold, 2003; Portwood, 1998), attitudes (Arad-Davidzon & Benbenishty, 2008), and beliefs about parenting (Daniel, 2000). There also are numerous other possible sources of bias, inconsistency, and error (Ruscio, 1998; Stein & Rzepnicki,1984). Given an historical lack of explicit decision-making rules, it is not surprising to learn that it has been a consistent finding "that workers exercise a great deal of personal discretion and . . . that personal values and idiosyncratic judgments exert a strong influence on decision-making in child welfare" (Stein & Rzepnicki, 1984, p. 11).

Caseworker factors historically have been somewhat neglected by researchers due to a focus instead on *case* factors. Yet there are many ways in which placement decisions can depend not just on case features, but also on factors influencing the *decision-maker*. What these factors are, however, how influential they are, and how they are interrelated has not yet been explicated. Portwood (1998) examined whether caseworkers' personal experiences with child-rearing and child maltreatment had effects on their assessments of abuse and neglect. However, she concluded that *none* of the final models that included demographic and professional factors adequately fit the data. Sullivan, Whitehead, Leschied, Chiodo, and Hurley (2008) looked at whether differences in severity ratings of risk for children differed depending on caseworkers' level of experience (they did not). Rolock and Testa (2005) examined the effect of caseworkers' race on substantiation of maltreatment, and found that white caseworkers were more likely to substantiate than were caseworkers of other races; however, they found no evidence of a relationship between caseworkers' race and the race of families in substantiated reports. Ryan, Garnier, Zyphur, and Zhai (2006) found that caseworker education and the racial match between caseworker and family were important to *other* child welfare outcomes (length of stay in care and reunification) but did not include the placement decision in their study. Baumann, Schwab, et al. (1997) found that, of the individual caseworker factors they included in their analyses, only empathy was related to investigator decisions, but marginally so. They concluded that "*case characteristics* explain the vast majority of the variance for both intake and investigation worker decisions" (p. 143, emphasis added).

Although to this point we have reviewed the literature in a way that may suggest that placement decisions are made by caseworkers acting independently, this is rarely, if ever, the case. For instance, Solnit, Nordhaus, and Lord (1992) remark in their casebook describing their work at the Connecticut Department of Children and Youth Services that "virtually every case discussed in this book involved group decision-making that included administrators, supervisors, social workers, and consultants" (p. ix). Hence, collaboration and consultation with others within the organization is an important aspect of the decision-making process. Regarding what organizational factors may be important to caseworker decision-making, workers participating in one of the first studies of the reliability of decision-making about foster care placement (Briar, 1963) commented that "practical realities, such as the availability of resources, strongly influenced their placement decisions" (Lindsey, 2004, p. 164, footnote). Baumann, Kern, and Fluke (1997) and Baumann, Schwab, et al. (1997) included organizational measures of role ambiguity, role conflict, and supervisor adequacy as organizational factors, and Yoo (2002) indicated the importance of job satisfaction, workplace support, and leadership to client outcomes. Yet while Yoo provided valuable descriptive texture of the organizational context of caseworker decisions, she did not address the placement decision in particular, nor did she empirically link the organizational factors to any client outcomes. A link has been demonstrated between certain organizational factors at the organizational level, including relatively high proportions of aboriginal children, specialized intake, and social work education, in placement decisions in Canada (Chabot et al., 2013; Fallon et al., 2013; Fluke, Chabot, Fallon, MacLaurin, & Blackstock, 2010), but although there is theoretical interest in the topic, few empirical studies have examined the possibility of direct connections between organizational variables in child welfare and actual client outcomes.

Although the studies reviewed here provide some insight into the influences on caseworker decision-making, it is important to note that almost all of these studies used the child or family as the unit of analysis. Few studies have used the worker as the unit of analysis, and none that we are aware of has done so in a study of placement decision-making involving actual placement decisions. It is arguable regarding vignette studies (e.g., Arad-Davidzon & Benbenishty, 2008) that a single vignette reflects a "worker" unit of analysis since there is a one-to-one correspondence between vignettes and (worker) respondents. Beyond such a limited approach, however, the purpose of this chapter is to examine the influences on the placement decision across many workers using the Decision-Making Ecology (DME) as an organizing framework, with the objective of providing at the worker level a more detailed picture than has heretofore been available of the interrelationships among case, caseworker, and organizational factors.

Overview of the Decision-Making Ecology

In thinking about placement decisions, it has been found helpful to consider them in a systematic context of caseworker decision-making; that is, a framework that includes more than the features of families (e.g., Munro, 2005; Ryan et al., 2006; Stein & Rzepnicki, 1984; Yoo, 2002). The DME (Baumann, Dalgleish, Fluke, & Kern, 2011; Baumann, Fluke, Dalgleish, & Kern, 2014; Baumann, Kern, et al., 1997; Fluke, Baumann, Dalgleish, & Kern, 2014) is one such framework that is theoretically and empirically based. In the DME model (Figure 5.1), case factors, individual factors, organizational factors, and external factors influence the decision-making process and jointly determine the outcome (i.e., what decision is made). The sequence of decisions made by agency staff as cases move through the system is referred to as a *decision-making continuum*. According to the DME, outcomes then may feed back into the system and decision-making thresholds may shift as a result of consequences of prior decisions.

Furthermore, a theoretical model of the *psychological process* of decision-making has been integrated into the DME, one that focuses on decision-making thresholds (i.e., the response criteria, in terms of signal detection theory). This is the General Assessment and Decision-Making (GADM) model (Dalgleish, 1988), which represents a synthesis of Social Judgment Theory (SJT) and Theory

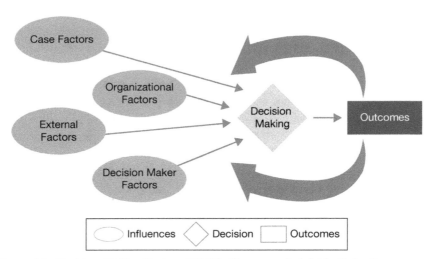

Figure 5.1 Decision-Making Ecology (DME); (Baumann, Dalgleish, Fluke, & Kern, 2011).

of Signal Detection (TSD) as applied to child protection. Its relevance to the present study is twofold: (1) the "environmental criterion variable" (in terms of the SJT Brunswick Lens model; Hammond, 1975) that Dalgleish studied was the "separation outcome," which is one outcome of the *placement decision* (in our terms); and (2) response bias (in TSD terminology) is a theoretical mechanism by which individual factors may be linked to variability across workers making placement decisions. In the present context, the idea is that individual differences (e.g., the relative degree of concern a worker has about negative consequences of either failing to remove a child at risk of harm or removing a child who may be safely maintained at home) may influence the threshold for action (i.e., the worker-specific criterion for removal that in part determines his or her decision). Another idea incorporated in the GADM is the distinction between judgment and decision (Baumann, Dalgleish, et al., 2011; Baumann et al., 2014; Fluke et al., 2014). In the context of child protection, the *judgment* involves determination of the facts of the case and assessment of risk to the child, whereas the *decision* is whether or not to take the action of removing the child. Case factors are presumed to influence the assessment process, whereas other factors in the DME influence the decision-making process.

The original DME model (Figure 5.1) did not postulate any connections between case factors, decision-maker (or worker) factors, and organization factors (other than the possibility of causal feedback from outcomes). Yet, as suggested previously, there may well be such connections. Though every type of connection is conceivable, we hypothesized, in terms of our present modeling process, specifically that there would be reciprocal influences between case factors and worker factors, and also reciprocal influences between worker factors and worker perceptions of organizational factors. We retained from the original DME model the hypothesized influences of case, worker, and organizational variables involved in the factors on the decision (percent of children removed and placed into foster care). Influences of case variables on organizational variables and vice versa were not a part of this model, though we did not exclude the possibility of these influences being incorporated in the course of the model-building process.

METHODS

Sample

The survey sample consisted of 1,103 CPS investigative caseworkers in Texas, electronically surveyed between August and December 2007, who also were successfully matched to administrative records (of the period described later) and who had made more than three placements in the course of their work. There were approximately 1,620 surveys sent to Investigators, of which 1,125 (69%) were returned. This sample of workers was 74% female, and about half white (49%), followed by 26% Hispanic, 22% African American, and about 1% each of Native American, Asian, and others. Age ranged from 21 to 68 years old, with a mean age of 35, and caseworker experience ranged from less than 1 year to 37 years (58% of caseworkers had no more than 1 year of experience, reflecting the high rate of turnover in the profession).

Measures and Procedures

Administrative Records. The administrative data included information from CPS records for the period September 2003 through the end of February 2008 (Baumann et al., 2010, p. 18). We also used administrative data from personnel records that included each worker's sex, age, years of experience with the agency, and race/ethnicity. These data were combined with aggregated information from the administrative case records about each worker's caseload (such as the racial distribution of clients, income levels of clients, results of risk assessments, number of investigations and removals). From these latter elements derived variables were computed, in particular the outcome variable (percent removed), which reflects the proportion of investigations conducted by a given worker during the designated period that resulted in a removal and placement of one or more children into foster care. For client income, the variable used to designate families with low income was the percent of alleged victims with an annual family income of less than $10,150.

Worker Survey. The history of the survey instrument on which this research is based began with an instrument developed by Kern, Baumann, Fluke, and colleagues in the course of various research projects (Fluke et al., 2001; Kern, Baumann, & Fluke, 1997). It later was extended as part of a study conducted in Washington state examining caseworker characteristics related to decision-making in unsubstantiated maltreatment investigations (English, Brummel, Graham, & Coghlan, 2002). The purpose of the measure from the beginning has been to examine caseworker characteristics as they may be related to decision-making in child maltreatment investigations. For the present study we retained items from two scales in this instrument: Caseworker Skills and Job Experiences. We then developed five additional scales based on a study that examined the factors contributing to the overrepresentation of children of color in Texas (derived from the qualitative research of Dettlaff and Rycraft [2008]) because this study resulted in the identification of multiple factors that influenced caseworker decision-making. The survey in its entirety is available in Baumann et al. (2010) and is further described in Dettlaff, Graham, Holzman, Baumann, and Fluke (2015).

Survey Scales

Online Table 5.1 includes the scales in the final investigation worker instrument, the number of items in each scale, and Cronbach's α on the scales and subscales. All items were rated using 7-point Likert scales. The table also includes the results of the reliability analysis (full details available in Baumann et al., 2010). As reflected in online Table 5.1, the instrument included seven scales: (1) Caseworker Skills (assesses caseworkers' interpersonal and case-related work skills), (2) Job Experiences (assesses caseworkers' perceptions of on-the-job conditions including workload, resources, supervision, and coworker support), (3) Removal Decisions (evaluates caseworkers' attitudes about removals and factors associated with their willingness to remove), (4) Disposition Decisions (evaluates considerations made by caseworkers when determining case disposition), (5) Difficult Situations (evaluates caseworkers' comfort level and skills when working with hostile or difficult clients), (6) Concerns over Liability (assesses the extent to which caseworkers' concerns about liability impact decision-making, and their perceptions of administrative support of their decisions), and (7) Community Services (evaluates caseworkers' abilities to access community resources).

A principal components analysis of the Removal Decisions items (Scale 3) resulted in two subscales subsequently characterized as *external reference* and *internal reference*. Caseworkers with an internal reference were more likely to be influenced by their personal beliefs about parenting and how they themselves were raised, while those with an external reference were more likely to be influenced by the impact of their decisions on children and an understanding of families' feelings. Intercorrelations of these scales demonstrated distinctly different types of associations with other scales, suggesting that they are measuring very different aspects of caseworker decision-making.

With one exception, we considered the scales reliable enough for further use (α of retained scales ranged from 0.55 to 0.95). Reliability of the Disposition Decisions scale (4A) was very low (α = 0.33) and the scale was dropped. However, we retained three items from it for inclusion in the analysis as single-item measures. These were the items, "I make my disposition decision based on my assessment that the child is at risk of abuse or neglect," (V56) "Collateral information from professionals is more reliable than collateral information from nonprofessionals such as family, friends, or neighbors," (V57) and, "I worry sometimes that CPS intervention in a child's life makes things worse for the child" (V58).

Within the framework of the DME, we used the following variables as the basis of modeling. Case Variables included the race/ethnicity of families as a proportion of caseload, low income (across cases), and risk assessment score (across cases). The risk assessment score is a composite score constructed by summing seven "Areas of Concern" reported by caseworkers that include child vulnerability, caregiver capability, quality of care, maltreatment pattern, home environment, social environment, and response to intervention. Each area is scored separately on a 5-point scale where 1 is rated "not at all a concern" and 5 is rated "an extreme concern." Worker Variables included gender, seniority, Interpersonal Skills (1A), Case Skills (1B), External Reference (3A), Internal Reference (3B), Difficult Situations (5A), Worry about Liability (6A), and the three items retained from the Disposition Decisions scale. Organizational Variables included Workload/Resources (2A), Supervision/Work Unit (2B), Support (6B), and Community Services (7A). The decision we focused on (i.e., the outcome) was Percent Removed by Worker (across cases). We ask the reader to bear in mind that, by design, the "organizational" variables under consideration reflect workers' *perceptions* of those factors rather than more objective measures.

Analysis

We conducted a worker-level analysis, allowing the closest possible look at worker decision-making processes, using Mplus Version 5.21 (Muthen & Muthen, 1998–2009). First, measurement models were defined for the risk latent variable and the latent survey factors by taking scale reliabilities into account. We then proceeded with model building empirically by first including the measurement models then adding structural paths and correlations. After developing an initial full model (setting some paths to zero as necessary for identification purposes), we followed a procedure in which we dropped patently nonsignificant paths, added paths and correlations based on modification indices, and iteratively refined the model through further reference to significance tests (likelihood-ratio tests). Race/ethnicity (i.e., proportions of African American and Hispanic families on workers' caseloads) was included subsequently as a follow-up analysis, which resulted in the final model presented here. As another follow-up analysis, we examined whether including race/ethnicity of workers led to a significantly better model. Model improvement was assessed by reference to standard absolute and incremental goodness of fit tests provided in the statistical package, including the root mean square error of approximation (RMSEA), standardized root-mean-square residual (SRMR), comparative fit index (CFI), Tucker–Lewis index (TLI), Akaike's information criterion (AIC), and Bayes information criterion (BIC) especially (for the nested models).

RESULTS

Descriptive statistics of the variables included in the analysis are presented in online Table 5.2, and a correlation matrix of the survey scales (Pearson's r) is presented in online Tables 5.3a,b,c. The main result of the analysis is presented in the structural equation diagram of Figure 5.2. As can be seen in Figure 5.2, the model is quite complex, and so we made certain accommodations to promote visual clarity. First, the measurement models and correlations are omitted from Figure 5.2 and are instead presented in online Tables 5.4a,b,c, Table 5.5, and online Figures 5.4 and 5.5. The "L" in the scale names in Figure 5.2 indicates the latent form of the variable, with reliability/ measurement error already taken into account. Furthermore, some of the exogenous variables (V57, V58, Male, Seniority, and PHisp) are shown in more

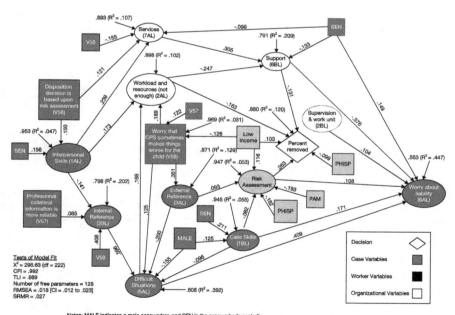

Figure 5.2 Structural diagram for child protective services investigation decision-making ($N = 1,103$).

than one place; it should be understood that conceptually these are singular and ideally would be shown in just one place with all the associated arrows leading into and out of them—the reader is asked to make this combination mentally. Please note that residuals and R^2 statistics (which correspond to the proportion of variance accounted for by the model) are given at the base of a short arrow leading into each endogenous variable (i.e., each variable that is "downstream" from any other variables in the model and hence has some proportion of its variance explained by it).

The model presented herein fits the observed data extremely well judging by the global fit statistics. The CFI and TLI (each ranging from 0 to 1) are both 0.99, the RMSEA is 0.018 ($p < 0.05$), and the SRMR is 0.027 (which is very low). In the remainder of this section we describe the model in terms of the latent variables and directional paths (represented by arrows) between them. We have organized the description of the structural model in terms of the DME, starting with influences on the outcome (Placement Decisions), and then consider other variables within each of the DME domains (specifically, Case, Organizational, and Individual domains). For each variable we describe what other variables in the model influence it and indicate the extent to which the variable was explained (or not) in total by other variables in the model. It is our hope that our description of these variables and their interrelationships, even those not directly related to the placement decision, will promote a better understanding of the placement decision by explicating its context in terms of the DME domains and their mutual influences.

Placement Decisions

We found five factors that significantly influenced the percent of cases that resulted in removal of a child and placement into foster care, though together they explained only a modest proportion of the decision's variance ($R^2 = 0.120$). *Case factors* even as aggregated to the worker level were of most importance: Percent Removed was increased in part by greater average Risk being assessed ($\beta = 0.263$) and more families on a worker's caseload being Low Income ($\beta = 0.103$). On the other hand, the placement percentage was decreased by higher proportions of Hispanic families on one's caseload ($\beta = -0.099$). Two *Organizational factors* were associated with lower percentages of removals: perceived organizational Support ($\beta = -0.131$) and Workload/Resources being perceived as unmanageable ($\beta = -0.163$). Another way to look at the negative coefficients is that placement rates were *increased* by lower proportions of Hispanic families on the caseload, as well as lower organizational support and a perception of manageable workload and sufficient resources. *Individual factors* (i.e., variables characterizing the caseworkers) were not found to directly influence the placement decision, including workers' own race/ethnicity.

Case Factors

Among case factors, only Risk Assessment was affected by other variables in the model, although it was not much explained by them (R^2 = .053). Low Income (β = 0.116) and caseworkers' External Reference (β = 0.093) influenced their risk assessments to be *higher* risk, whereas higher Case Skills (β = −0.082) and a greater proportion of African American (β = −0.193) or Hispanic (β = −0.182) families on the worker's caseload influenced their risk assessments to be *lower* risk.

Organizational Factors

Among *Organizational factors*, about a fifth of the variance (R^2 = .209) of Support was explained by the model. It was promoted by a perception of availability of Services (β = 0.305) and was detracted from by Seniority (β = −0.133) and by Workload being unmanageable (β = − 0.247). About 10% of the variance of Services was explained by the model (R^2 = .107). Interpersonal Skills (β = 0.239) and Disposition decision being based upon risk assessment (β = 0.121) increased perception that services were sufficiently available, whereas Worry that CPS sometimes makes things worse for the child (β = −0.155) and greater Seniority (β = −0.099) detracted from it. Also 10% of the variance of perceived Workload and Resources was explained by the model (R^2 = 0.102). Higher levels of Interpersonal Skills determined in part (β = 0.173) a perception that workload was too high and/or that resources were insufficient to adequately perform the job.

Caseworker Factors

The construct most fully explained by the model was Worry about Liability (R^2 = .447, which can be interpreted to indicate that nearly 45% of the latent construct's variance was determined by other variables in the model). Worry about Liability was directly influenced by Difficult Situations (β = 0.409) and indirectly by Support (β = −0.376). By way of illustration of how to interpret negative paths such as this, this latter finding can mean that the greater a worker's expectation of support by his or her supervisor if a child were to be harmed in one of the worker's cases, the less they tend to worry about the possible negative consequences to themselves that might happen due to such an event (e.g., getting disciplined or fired). Conversely, having less support causes more of this worry. The direct influence of Difficult Situations on Worry about Liability suggests that caseworkers who are uncomfortable working with hostile or difficult clients are more likely to be concerned about the personal consequences of their decisions. Workers also tended to be more worried about liability if they had more Seniority ($\beta = 0.149$), greater Case Skills ($\beta = 0.171$), and assessed their cases as being relatively risky ($\beta = 0.108$). Higher levels on the Supervision and Work Unit factor (which reflects caseworkers' perceptions of the quality of supervision they receive and support they receive from their coworkers) also were associated with more Worry about Liability ($\beta = 0.104$).

About 40% of the variance ($R^2 = .392$) of the latent construct Difficult Situations was explained by the model, which is directly affected by an Internal Reference orientation ($\beta = 0.596$), Workload and Resources being perceived as unmanageable ($\beta = 0.168$), and Worry that CPS makes things worse for the child ($\beta = 0.125$). On the other hand, Difficult Situations was lessened by the caseworker being male ($\beta = -0.155$), by having more of an External Reference orientation ($\beta = -0.200$), and by having a relatively high level of Case Skills ($\beta = -0.096$).

About a fifth of the variance ($R^2 = 0.202$) of Internal Reference was explained by the model, specifically by Worry that CPS sometimes makes things worse for the child ($\beta = 0.408$) and that Professional collateral information is more reliable ($\beta = 0.085$). Interpersonal Skills, however, negatively influenced Internal Reference ($\beta = -0.141$). Less of the variance of External Reference was explained by the model ($R^2 = 0.129$). However, it was similarly influenced by Worry that CPS sometimes makes things worse for the child ($\beta = 0.351$).

DISCUSSION

In our discussion of Figure 5.1 we hypothesized influences among domains of the DME; of these, we found empirical examples of all except those of *worker variables* on the outcome (see Figure 5.3). Both the evident lack of this particular relationship and the specifics we *did* find among other domains (and between those domains and the outcome) advance our understanding of both the process of caseworker decision-making and of the DME as an organizing framework. We consider some implications of these findings in the remainder of this section, along with an acknowledgment of limitations of the study and directions for future research.

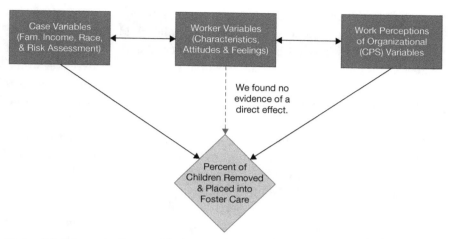

Figure 5.3 Schematic diagram of relations of Decision-Making Ecology (DME) domains involved in the placement decision.

As reported earlier, individual factors (i.e., variables characterizing the caseworkers) were *not* found to directly influence the placement decision. This is consistent with most of the previous research examining the effect of individual characteristics, with exceptions of Arad-Davidzon and Benbenishty (2008), in which respondent attitudes were found to impact decisions, and Chabot et al. (2013), who found that caseworker education may mediate aboriginal placements. Though it is possible that such connections were unobserved in our research due to limitations in our measuring of attitudes, this finding suggests the possibility of a more complex relationship between individual characteristics and the case and organizational variables also involved in decision-making, implying that, rather than individual characteristics having a direct influence on decision-making (which is often studied), it is the *context* within which decisions are made and the influence of caseworker characteristics on the perception of case and organizational variables that influence the decision.

In terms of the placement decision, we found five factors to significantly influence the percent of cases that resulted in placement into foster care; three of the five (risk assessment, family income, and proportion of Hispanic families on the caseload) reflect *case* features. In addition, two organizational variables (as perceived by the caseworkers), Support ($\beta = -0.131$) and Workload and Resources ($\beta = -0.163$), did affect placement rates of workers. These are findings that are of considerable substantive interest. At least in terms of caseworkers' perceptions of these variables, we found that placement rates were increased by *lower support* and also by manageable workloads and a perception of sufficient agency resources to manage their job responsibilities. Concerning lower support, the items related to this construct refer to caseworkers' perceptions of whether the agency would support them if a child was harmed on one of their cases following a decision to maintain a child in the home (rather than remove). This finding indicates that caseworkers who do not believe they would be supported if a child was harmed in one of their cases, that they themselves will be held responsible, are more likely to remove children to prevent this from occurring, hence possibly removing children due to concerns for their own liability rather than the best interests of the child. This raises the question as to whether the source of these concerns lies with workers or is an aspect of the organizational context—a matter of some importance and unfortunately one that the current study cannot directly address.

Concerning Workload and Resources, we found that caseworkers' perceptions of having a manageable caseload are associated with higher rates of removals. This may reflect that when caseworkers have enough time to adequately perform their job they are better able to spend the time necessary with families to identify risk factors warranting removal. If so, this finding is contrary to some studies that suggest that workers may be more likely to make the "safe" decision to *remove* children when they are overburdened with high caseloads and have less time to spend with families (Chibnall et al., 2003; US General Accounting Office, 2007). Our model, to the contrary, suggests that caseworkers having higher caseloads and unmanageable work demands may result in children who are in need of foster care remaining in unsafe environments because caseworkers do not have the time to adequately assess for risk and to do the tasks associated with making a removal and placement. Given the limits of structural equation modeling, however, other explanations are possible. For instance, it could be that a caseworker having a relatively high placement rate has the effect of minimizing the number of demanding cases on their caseload that require ongoing repeated visits over the long term. Or it could be that supervisors tend to assign the work-intensive cases most likely to involve placement to those caseworkers best able to manage the up-front burden of such work. Given that the model presented herein fits the data so well, the first explanation is the one to which we give emphasis in the following discussion. That said, further research is required to clarify the issue.

In terms of *case factors*, placement rates were *increased* by lower proportions of Hispanic families on one's caseload (correspondingly meaning that *higher* placement rates were found for workers with more families of *other* ethnic groups on their caseloads). This is consistent with several studies that have indicated strong protective factors among Hispanic families in child welfare cases that may lower their risk of placement (Drake et al., 2011; Putnam-Hornstein, Needell, King, & Johnson-Motoyama, 2013). Related to this finding, the model showed that having a greater proportion of either African American

($\beta = -0.193$) or Hispanic ($\beta = -0.182$) families on workers' caseloads influenced their risk assessments toward *lower* risk, possibly indicating that the more experience workers have with these groups the lower they tend to assess their risk. This raises the possibility that cultural competence resulting from greater exposure with families of color promotes a more appropriate assessment of risk and (in the case of Hispanic families) the need for placement. Alternatively, it may be that a different standard of comparison, resulting from greater experiences with these groups, affects decision-making thresholds such that risk is assessed lower than it should be and/or that Hispanic children are removed less often than they would be if consistent standards were applied across all cases.

Regarding *individual factors*, though we found no direct effects between decision-maker factors and the placement outcome, there remains the possibility of *mediated* effects of worker factors on the decision. As seen in Figure 5.3, worker factors could affect the placement decision via either *case factors* (e.g., assessment of risk) or through their perceptions of *organizational factors* (e.g., not having the resources to do their job). There are six examples of first-order mediated worker effects in our model, two operating through the case factor of Risk Assessment, and the remainder operating through organizational variables. Of the former, the worker factor of *external reference* ($\beta = 0.093$) was estimated to *raise* risk assessments (thus *increasing* the rate of placement, given the direct relationship between risk assessment and placement rate), while *case skills* ($\beta = -0.082$) was estimated to *lower* risk assessments (thereby *reducing* the number of placements). One important aspect of this finding is evidence that risk assessment results are influenced by caseworker characteristics, an issue that is commonly brought up to suggest that risk assessment is adjusted to be more consistent with caseworker decisions.

Mediated effects of worker variables on the placement decision through *organizational factors* include the influence of worker *seniority* on *perceptions of support*. The way this could work (given an inverse path of $\beta = -0.133$ between seniority and support) is either that more senior workers perceive less support, which *raises* their percent removed (given an inverse relationship between support and the outcome), and/or that less senior workers perceive more support, which *lowers* their percent removed. Additionally, three worker factors tend to increase the perception that workload is unmanageable and that there are not enough resources for them to do their jobs: Interpersonal Skills ($\beta = 0.173$), Difficult Situations ($\beta = 0.168$), and Worry that CPS makes things worse for the child ($\beta = 0.189$). The mediated effect would be that any or all of these factors could increase workers' perceptions of problems with workload and resources, which would *decrease* their rate of placement (given the inverse effect between perceived workload and resources and percent removed). Conversely, it could be that fewer interpersonal skills, fewer problems with difficult situations, and less worry that CPS may make things worse for the child could lead to workers feeling that their workload is relatively more manageable (and that their resources for doing their job are sufficient), which would tend to *increase* their placement rate.

Given an inverse effect between perceived Workload and Resources and Support ($\beta = -0.247$), a second-order mediated effect also is indicated. The net effect of this would be to mitigate the influences just described. For example, if Interpersonal Skills, Difficult Situations, and Worry that CPS makes things worse for the child are relatively high for some workers, hence increasing their perception of workload problems and tending to *lower* their placement rates, those workers also would tend to have lower perceptions of support, which would tend to *increase* their placement rate to an extent. This gives an idea of the ways in which the model illustrates how an exploration of complex sequences of mediation resulting in a network of influences could either dampen or amplify certain decision-making tendencies in complicated ways.

With regard to factors in the model other than the outcome, we observed that, in general, factors more related to worker's feelings (Difficult Situations, Support, External and Internal Reference) were far more explainable by the model than those related to skills (Interpersonal Skills, Case Skills), organizational factors (Supervision and Work Unit, Workload and Resources, Services), or case features (Risk Assessment).

Implications for Practice

This study provides new information to advance the understanding of the placement decision and raises several considerations for child welfare systems. For one, the finding that placement rates were increased by lower perceived support suggests that caseworkers need to operate in an environment in which they feel supported. In the event that a child is harmed through unforeseen circumstances, caseworkers should be able to trust that their decisions will be supported and that they will not face negative consequences as long as their casework has been conducted thoroughly and appropriately. Consistent with child welfare agencies demonstrating a commitment to maintaining children in their homes when assessment does not warrant a removal, caseworkers need to be able to trust that their decisions to do so will be supported.

Improvements may need to be made to the safety and risk assessment processes to minimize the possibility of ill-informed decisions, including advanced training on risk and safety assessment. This training needs to take into account the development of casework skills that may result in a more discerning assessment so that the level of assessed risk is more consistent. Ideally, individual characteristics should not influence worker's risk assessments, a condition that may prove challenging to achieve.

Furthermore, this study emphasizes the importance of policies and practices that facilitate an organizational environment in which caseworkers feel they have the time necessary to spend with families and the resources they need to do their jobs. Though our model showed that these factors increased placement rates, this suggests that when caseworkers perceive that they have the time and resources necessary to do their jobs thoroughly and effectively, they may have a greater ability to identify those families in need of intervention, which is the purpose of the child welfare system. If children in need of intervention are left in unsafe homes due to a perceived lack of time or resources, the system has failed to meet its mandate and the faith of the public in this system to protect children from abuse and neglect will deteriorate.

Limitations

The findings reported herein must be viewed with caution due to a modest response rate, use of self-report measures and agency administrative data (from a single state), and ambiguities of interpretation of the model (including direction of causality). However, given the study's novel approach of examining decision-making at the caseworker level within an organizational context, the study provides new information to build on our current understanding of the decision-making process.

Participation in the study was voluntary, and caseworkers' responses should be considered in that light. The response rate (69% for investigative workers) was lower than desired, and it is possible that those who did not complete it had relatively challenging or complex work demands, which may have influenced the results. There could be other differences as well between survey responders and nonresponders (and possibly their caseloads) that limit the generalizability of the findings.

Reliance on any single data source is limited, and this certainly applies to CPS administrative data, though, in particular, the record of removal of a child from the home and placement into foster care is a key data element for child protective agencies, of great legal import, and reported in the aggregate to the federal government; as such, we consider it an extremely reliable metric within the administrative data.

We also acknowledge that the study was based on one modest-sized sample in a single state and that, at the time of original publication of these results, the data already were 7 years old. We consider it unlikely that basic child welfare practices have changed significantly since then. Nonetheless, it is possible that policies and other factors have changed, and it should be apparent that Texas may not be representative of other states in important ways; if the study were conducted again, or elsewhere, the results might be different.

It is important to bear in mind that the analysis was conducted at the *worker* level, not the *case* level. The implication is that the study does not describe decisions made for a particular family. For instance, regarding risk assessment, though we found that in general workers with cases rated at relatively high risk are more likely to place children out of home, for individual workers some high risk cases will *not* be placed and some low risk cases *will* be placed.

Another limitation that should be recognized is that much of this research is based on self-report. For instance, when we report that caseworkers with greater seniority are associated with higher levels of Case Skills, the basis for this assessment is caseworkers' own reports of their degree of case skills. Improved survey scales with higher reliabilities would be desirable. Conclusions regarding Worry about Liability, in particular, should be tempered by an understanding that the scale reliability was not high.

As seen previously, interpretation of what we've represented as direct paths is not unproblematic in terms of causation. Direction of causality is uncertain, and it is possible that there are alternative models that fit the data equally well. At this exploratory stage of research, taking an empirical approach to model development as we did is perhaps a necessity, but this ambiguity regarding direction of causality is its drawback. One advantage of the approach, however, is that the results we've presented herein generally were not biased by theoretical preconceptions (given our framework, of course). Nonetheless, it is hoped that, with advances in this field, the specifics of research models will increasingly be guided by theoretical considerations. We see the present research, for all its shortcomings in this regard, as a modest step in that direction because it provides some empirical results that may serve as a basis for future theoretical developments and a modifiable framework that may promote hypothesis generation and possibly even inspirations for more controlled experimentation.

Directions for Future Research

First, the aim of the study was not to assess the accuracy of the placement decision post hoc; rather, it was to develop a basis for determining what and how the various DME factors were in play. When experts in the field are able to establish an acceptable criterion for "success," a "gold standard" for placement decisions, future research can begin to address the important consideration of which decisions qualify as "correct" (or "incorrect"), which we would expect to profoundly open up the field of research into directions for improvement in caseworker decision-making.

Several other directions for future research have become evident in the course of this work. For one, similar research within other geographical areas and with different CPS agencies would advance the field of investigation, given that some decision-making influences may be idiosyncratic or differ systematically across agencies or locales. Additional studies in other agencies and jurisdictions also would help to better understand the utility of the DME as an organizing framework. Future research may include objective ratings of case skills, and the same is true for organizational factors. For example, rather than relying on perceptions of workload and resources, actual workload and resources could be measured, though this would be a different type of design. Not only will studies that describe the association between subjective and objective aspects of organizations be important for further inquiry, it also will be important to discover whether objective or subjective organizational features are more influential with respect to decision-making. Also, it would be good for future research to include multiple types of informants, rather than just caseworkers, as recommended by Britner and Mossler (2002). Such a multimethod approach would have as one benefit increasing the reliability of measurement of latent constructs. Regarding another domain, *environmental* factors are posited by the DME to influence both case factors and organizational factors as well as decisions: How could study of these be incorporated into future research? Finally, the influences described here may be somewhat specific to the placement decision rather than to all points of the decision-making continuum, so extending this type of research to other CPS decisions would be an important advance.

ACKNOWLEDGMENTS

The authors thank both the Child Protection Research Center at the American Humane Association and Casey Family Programs for funding that supported a portion of this research. We also thank the Texas Department of Family and Protective Services and especially the caseworkers for their support. Finally, our appreciation goes to Pam Roth for preparing Figure 5.2 for publication.

This chapter was originally published as an article in *Child Abuse and Neglect* (2015, 49, 12–23) and is reprinted here with permission from that source.

REFERENCES

Arad-Davidzon, B., & Benbenishty, R. (2008). The role of workers' attitudes and parent and child wishes in child protection workers' assessments and recommendation regarding removal and reunification. *Children and Youth Services Review, 30*(1), 107–121.

Baird, C., & Wagner, D. (2000). The relative validity of actuarial and consensus-based risk assessment systems. *Children and Youth Services Review, 22*(11–12), 839–871.

Baird, C., Wagner, D., Healy, T., & Johnson, K. (1999). Risk assessment in child protective services: Consensus and actuarial model reliability. *Child Welfare, 78*(6), 723–748.

Banach, M. (1998). The best interests of the child: Decision-making factors. *Families in Society, 79*(3), 331–340.

Baumann, D. J., Dalgleish, L., Fluke, J. D., & Kern, H. (2011). *The decision-making ecology.* Washington, DC: American Humane Association.

Baumann, D. J., Fluke, J. D., Dalgleish, L., & Kern, H. (2014). The decision making ecology. In A. Shlonsky, & R. Benbenishty (Eds.), *From evidence to outcomes in child welfare: An international reader* (pp. 24–38). Oxford: Oxford University Press.

Baumann, D. J., Fluke, J. D., Graham, J. C., Wittenstrom, K., Hedderson, J., Rivaux, S., . . . Brown, N. (2010). *Disproportionality in child protective services: The preliminary results of statewide reform efforts.* Austin: Texas Department of Family and Protective Services.

Baumann, D. J., Grigsby, C., Sheets, J., Reid, G., Graham, J. C., Robinson, D., . . . Jeffries, V. (2011). Concept guided risk assessment: Promoting prediction and understanding. *Children and Youth Services Review, 33*(9), 1648–1657.

Baumann, D. J., Kern, H. D., & Fluke, J. D. (1997). Foundations of the decision-making ecology and overview. In H. D. Kern, D. J. Baumann, & J. D. Fluke (Eds.), *WISDOM: The child welfare decision enhancement project* (pp. 1–12). Washington, DC: The Children's Bureau.

Baumann, D. J., Law, J. R., Sheets, J., Reid, G., & Graham, J. C. (2005). Evaluating the effectiveness of actuarial risk assessment models. *Children and Youth Services Review, 27*(5), 465–490.

Baumann, D. J., Schwab, J., & Schultz, F. (1997). The influence of case, organizational and individual factors on the process of decision making. In H. Kern, D. J. Bauman, & J. D. Fluke (Eds.), *WISDOM: The child welfare decision enhancement project* (pp. 129–144). Austin, TX: Department of Protective and Regulatory Services.

Benbenishty, R., Osmo, J., & Gold, N. (2003). Rationales provided for risk assessment and recommended interventions: A comparison between Canadian and Israeli professionals. *British Journal of Social Work, 33*(2), 137–155.

Besharov, D. J. (1986). Child welfare liability: The need for immunity legislation. *Children Today, 15*, 17–20.

Briar, S. (1963). Clinical judgment in foster care placement. *Child Welfare, 42*(4), 161–169.

Britner, P. A., & Mossler, D. G. (2002). Professionals' decision-making about out-of-home placements following instances of child abuse. *Child Abuse and Neglect, 26*(4), 317–332.

Chabot, M., Fallon, B., Tonmyr, L., Maclaurin, B., Fluke, J. D., & Blackstock, C. (2013). Exploring alternate specifications to explain agency-level effects in placement decisions regarding aboriginal children: Further analysis of the Canadian Incidence Study of Reported Child Abuse and Neglect Part B. *Child Abuse and Neglect*, *37*(1), 61–76.

Chibnall, S., Dutch, N. M., Jones-Harden, B., Brown, A., Gourdine, R., Smith, J., & Snyder, S. (2003). *Children of color in the child welfare system: Perspectives from the child welfare community*. Washington, DC: US Department of Health and Human Services.

Courtney, M., Dworsky, A., Lee, J., & Rapp, M. (2010). *Midwest evaluation of the adult functioning of former foster youth: Outcomes at ages 23 and 24*. Chicago, IL: Chapin Hall at the University of Chicago.

Dalgleish, L. I. (1988). Decision making in child abuse cases: Applications of social judgment theory and signal detection theory. In B. Brehmer, & C. R. B. Joyce (Eds.), *Human judgment: The SJT view* (pp. 317–360). Amsterdam: Elsevier Science Publishers.

Dalgleish, L. I. (2006). Testing for the effects of decision bias on overrepresentation: Applying the GADM model. Paper presented at the 16th international congress of the International Society for Prevention of Child Abuse *and* Neglect (ISPCAN), York, England..

Daniel, B. (2000). Judgments about parenting: What do social workers think they are doing. *Child Abuse Review*, *9*(2), 91–107.

DePanfilis, D., & Scannapieco, M. (1994). Assessing the safety of children at risk of maltreatment: Decision-making models. *Child Welfare*, *73*(3), 229–245.

Dettlaff, A. J., Graham, J. C., Holzman, J., Baumann, D. J., & Fluke, J. D. (2015). Development of an instrument to understand the child protective services decision-making process, with a focus on placement decisions, *Child Abuse and Neglect*, *49*, 24–34.

Dettlaff, A. J., Rivaux, S. R., Baumann, D. J., Fluke, J. D., Rycraft, J. R., & James, J. (2011). Disentangling substantiation: The influence of race, income, & risk on the substantiation decision in child welfare. *Children and Youth Services Review*, *33*(9), 1630–1637.

Dettlaff, A. J., & Rycraft, J. R. (2008). Deconstructing disproportionality: Views from multiple stakeholders. *Child Welfare*, *87*(2), 37–58.

Doyle, J. J. (2007). Child protection and child outcomes: Measuring the effects of foster care. *The American Economic Review*, *97*(5), 1583–1610. 12

Drake, B., Jolley, J. M., Lanier, P., Fluke, J. D., Barth, R. P., & Jonson-Reid, M. (2011). Racial bias in child protection? A comparison of competing explanations using national data. *Pediatrics*, *127*(3), 471–478.

English, D. J., Brummel, S., Graham, J. C., & Coghlan, L. (2002). *Final report: Factors that influence the decision not to substantiate a CPS referral. Phase II*. Olympia, WA: DSHS, Children's Administration, OCAR.

Fallon, B., Chabot, M., Fluke, J. D., Blackstock, C., Maclaurin, B., & Tonmyr, L. (2013). Placement decisions and disparities among aboriginal children: Further analysis of the Canadian incidence study of reported child abuse and neglect part A: Comparisons of the 1998 and 2003 surveys. *Child Abuse and Neglect*, *37*(1), 47–60.

Fluke, J. D., Parry, C., Shapiro, P., Hollinshead, D., Bollenbacher, V., Baumann, D., & Davis-Brown, K. (2001). *The dynamics of unsubstantiated reports: A multi-state study—Final report.* Englewood, CO: American Humane Association.

Fluke, J. D., Baumann, D. J., Dalgleish, L. I., & Kern, H. (2014). Decisions to protect children: A Decision-Making Ecology. In J. E. Korbin, & R. D. Krugman (Eds.), *Handbook of child maltreatment.* New York: Springer.

Fluke, J. D., Chabot, M., Fallon, B., MacLaurin, B., & Blackstock, C. (2010). Placement decisions and disparities among aboriginal groups: An application of the Decision Making Ecology through multi-level analysis. *Child Abuse and Neglect, 34*(1), 57–69.

Gold, N., Benbenishty, R., & Osmo, R. (2001). A comparative study of risk assessments and recommended interventions in Canada and Israel. *Child Abuse and Neglect, 25*(5), 607–622.

Hammond, K. R. (1975). Social judgment theory: Its use in the study of psychiatric drugs. In K. R. Hammond, & C. R. B. Joyce (Eds.), *Psychoactive drugs and social judgment: Theory and research.* New York: John Wiley.

Kern, H. D., Baumann, D. J., & Fluke, J. D. (1997). *Workers improvements to the structured decision and outcome model (WISDOM): The child welfare decision enhancement project.* Washington, DC: The Children's Bureau.

Kominkiewicz, F. B. (2004). The relationship of child protection service caseworker discipline-specific education and definition of sibling abuse: An institutional hiring impact study. *Journal of Human Behavior in the Social Environment, 9*(1–2), 69–82.

Lindsey, D. (2004). *The welfare of children* (2nd ed.). Oxford: Oxford University Press.

Munro, E. (2005). Improving practice: Child protection as a systems problem. *Children and Youth Services Review, 27*(4), 375–391.

Muthen, B., & Muthen, L. (1998–2009). Mplus version 5.21. www.statmodel.com

Pecora, P., Williams, J., Kessler, R., Downs, C., O'Brien, K., Hiripi, E., & Morello, S. (2003). *Assessing the effects of foster care: Early results from the Casey National Alumni Study.* Seattle, WA: Casey Family Programs.

Phillips, M. H., Shyne, A. W., Sherman, E. A., & Haring, B. L. (1971). *Factors associated with placement decisions in child welfare.* New York: Child Welfare League of America.

Portwood, S. G. (1998). The impact of individuals' characteristics and experiences on their definitions of child maltreatment. *Child Abuse and Neglect, 22*(5), 437–452.

Putnam-Hornstein, E., Needell, B., King, B., & Johnson-Motoyama, M. (2013). Racial and ethnic disparities: A population-based examination of risk factors for involvement with child protective services. *Child Abuse and Neglect, 37*(1), 33–46.

Rivaux, S., James, J., Wittenstrom, K., Baumann, D., Sheets, J., Henry, J., & Jeffries, V. (2008). The intersection of race, poverty, and risk: Understanding the decision to provide services to clients and to remove children. *Child Welfare, 87*(2), 151–168.

Rolock, N., & Testa, M. (2005). Indicated child abuse and neglect reports: Is the investigation process racially biased? In D. Derezotes, M. Testa, & J. Poertner (Eds.), *Race matters in child welfare* (pp. 119–130). Washington, DC: CWLA Press.

Rossi, P. H., Schuerman, J., & Budde, S. (1999). Understanding decisions about child maltreatment. *Evaluation Review, 23*(6), 579–598.

Runyan, D., Gould, C., Trost, D., & Loda, F. (1981). Determinants of foster care placement for the maltreated child. *American Journal of Public Health, 71*, 706–711.

Ruscio, J. (1998). Information integration in child welfare cases: An introduction to statistical decision-making. *Child Maltreatment, 3*(2), 143–156.

Ryan, J. P., Garnier, P., Zyphur, M., & Zhai, F. (2006). Investigating the effects of caseworker characteristics in child welfare. *Children and Youth Services Review, 28,* 993–1006.

Schwalbe, C. (2004). Re-visioning risk assessment for human service decision making. *Children and Youth Services Review, 26*(6), 561–576.

Shlonsky, A., & Wagner, D. (2005). The next step: Integrating actuarial risk assessment and clinical judgment into an evidence-based practice framework in CPS case management. *Children and Youth Services Review, 27*(4), 409–427.

Solnit, A. J., Nordhaus, B. F., & Lord, R. (1992). *When home is no haven.* New Haven, CT: Yale University Press.

Stein, T. J., & Rzepnicki, T. L. (1984). *Decision making in child welfare services: Intake and planning.* Boston, MA: Kluwer-Nijhoff Publishing.

Sullivan, C., Whitehead, P. C., Leschied, A. W., Chiodo, D., & Hurley, D. (2008). Perception of risk among child protection workers. *Children and Youth Services Review, 30,* 699–704.

Swets, J. A. (1992). The science of choosing the right decision threshold in high-stakes diagnostics. *American Psychologist, 47*(4), 522–532.

US Department of Health and Human Services, Administration on Children, Youth and Families, Children's Bureau. (2014). Preliminary FY1 2012 estimates as of November 2013, no. 20. Washington, DC: US Department of Health and Human Services. http://www.acf.hhs.gov/sites/default/files/cb/afcarsreport20.pdf

US General Accounting Office (GAO). (2007). African American children in foster care: Additional HHS assistance needed to help states reduce the proportion in care. Washington, DC. http://www.gao.gov/new.items/d07816.pdf

Yoo, J. (2002). The relationship between organizational variables and client outcomes: A case study in child welfare. *Administration in Social Work, 26*(2), 39–61.

APPENDIX A

SUPPLEMENTARY DATA

Supplementary data associated with this chapter can be found with the online version of the original article, at https://dx.doi.org/10.1016/j.chiabu. 2015.02.020.

6

Lessons Learned from International Studies on Child Protection Decision-Making Employing the Model of Judgments and Decisions Processes in Context (JUDPiC)

MÓNICA LÓPEZ LÓPEZ AND RAMI BENBENISHTY ∎

This chapter draws on a variety of studies conducted using the model of Judgments and Decisions Processes in Context (JUDPiC; Benbenishty & Davidson-Arad, 2012) to compare judgments and decisions in cases of alleged maltreatment made by decision-makers in five countries: Israel, the Netherlands, Northern Ireland, Portugal, and Spain. The chapter begins with a brief overview of research on intercountry comparisons in the field of child protection decision-making. Next, we describe the JUDPiC model and present in some detail the first international comparison study conducted with this underlying model (Benbenishty et al., 2015). We offer next the subsequent developments of this research project

Mónica López López and Rami Benbenishty, *Lessons Learned from International Studies on Child Protection Decision-Making Employing the Model of Judgments and Decisions Processes in Context (JUDPiC)* In: *Decision-Making and Judgment in Child Welfare and Protection.* Edited by: John D. Fluke, Mónica López López, Rami Benbenishty, Erik J. Knorth, and Donald J. Baumann, Oxford University Press (2021). © Oxford University Press. DOI: 10.1093/oso/9780190059538.003.0006.

in the different countries involved. In the final section, we discuss some implications for child protection policy and practice and future research.

INTERCOUNTRY COMPARISONS IN THE FIELD OF CHILD PROTECTION DECISION-MAKING

Differences in child protection systems are tied to policy and administrative and judicial structures which determine how and when it is necessary to intervene in a family to protect a child (Gilbert, Parton, & Skivenes, 2011). These structures within the system are intimately connected to the social, economic, religious, and other wider contexts in which systems are situated. Consequently, child protection systems are not only different across contexts but are also subjected to constant change and adaptation as these contexts evolve (Wulczyn et al., 2010).

Child protection professionals are tasked with translating those structures into their daily practice through their assessments and decisions for children at risk. Deciding which families are going to be drawn into the child protection system, when a child should be placed out of home, or when a reunification is needed are some of the most difficult decisions facing professionals. Child protection professionals rely on different assessment tools and (implicit or explicit) decision-making frameworks depending on their country child welfare system and regimes, among other factors. Thus, child protection decision-making is expected to vary between countries while remaining relatively similar within a country (Berrick, Dickens, Pösö, & Skivenes, 2017b).

The study of intercountry variability of child protection decision-making has become an emerging research theme in the past decade. The most comprehensive set of studies comparing child welfare decision-making in different countries is being carried out by Berrick, Dickens, Pösö, and Skivenes. These researchers have carried out studies that compared aspects of child welfare decision-making in different countries that have different child welfare systems.

An early international vignette study focused on risk assessments made by child welfare workers in England, Norway, and California (Križ & Skivenes, 2013). Although certain issues were consistently considered important by workers across the three countries (e.g., mother cooperation, family isolation, and poverty), the authors reported systematic differences in levels of risk assessment and in the domains that these workers felt influenced their assessments (e.g., neglect, attachment, needs and history of child protection services). The authors interpreted the differences in risk assessment patterns as referring to differences in the child welfare regimes and the structure of services in the three countries studied.

More recently, the group of Berrick, Dickens, Pösö, and Skivenes have completed several international comparative studies of social work and legal decision-making in child protection in four countries (England, Finland, Norway, and the United States, represented by California). The authors examined how child protection workers involve children in decision-making regarding involuntary child removal (Berrick, Dickens, Pösö, & Skivenes, 2015). Based on a survey of 772 professionals responding to a hypothetical vignette, they found that child protection workers in all the participating countries were more likely to talk with older children, to provide and gather information, and to include them in the process when 11 compared to 5 years of age. The authors did not find consistent differences in the level of children's involvement in care order decision-making between the different regimes (family service and child protection) included in the study.

Berrick, Dickens, Pösö, and Skivenes (2017a) have explored as well the relation between parents' involvement in care order decision-making in cases of potential child removal and the child welfare orientation (family service and child protection) of the four countries studied. The findings, based on responses to a vignette of 768 child protection workers, do not show a consistent pattern of difference regarding parental involvement that align with the type of child welfare system in which the professional works.

The same group of authors has conducted a study examining child friendliness in judicial decision-making in child protection cases of the four legal systems (Berrick, Dickens, Pösö, & Skivenes, 2018). The findings, based on an online survey of 1,479 judicial decision-makers, show that the responses of these professionals are strongly influenced by their own country context, with important variations across countries. For instance, the judges from California were more positive about their courts being child friendly, while English judges perceived that their courts were not that responsive to the needs of children and that neither the environment nor language were child friendly.

Importantly, this group of authors has recognized that the similarities and differences between professionals in different countries found in their recent studies do not seem to align with the child welfare system orientations of the countries studied. This could suggest the need to reconsider whether the traditional classification of child welfare orientations developed by Gilbert and associates (2011) is at present useful in understanding variations between professionals in different countries. Furthermore, given that there are known variations among professionals *within* countries, there is a clear need for a more nuanced approach to understanding variations among child welfare professionals.

Another approach was evident in a set of studies that compared decisions made by Israeli and Canadian child welfare practitioners (Benbenishty, Osmo, & Gold, 2003; Gold, Benbenishty, & Osmo, 2001; Osmo & Benbenishty, 2004). This group tried to understand better not only the differences in decisions, but also the rationales provided by practitioners from the two countries. The authors presented the same case vignettes to professionals in both countries so

that similarities and differences could be identified. These comparisons provided important insights about professionals in these countries. For instance,
Israeli practitioners were more influenced in their judgments and decisions by
information on the mother's cooperativeness compared with their Canadian
colleagues. These studies led eventually to the development of the JUDPiC
model (Figure 6.1) that tried to systematize the factors that might impact judgment processes, including the contexts in which these decisions are being made.

According to the JUDPiC model proposed by Benbenishty and Davidson-
Arad (2012), and later expanded by Benbenishty (2019), child protection professionals make their judgments based on case information on the child and the
family. The way in which professionals interpret this information is influenced by
their own personal attributes as well as by the characteristics of the organizations
in which they work. This information search and processing leads to intermediate
judgments (e.g., substantiation of allegations, assessments of risk for further maltreatment). These judgments then lead to decisions aimed at protecting children.
According to the model, all these case-level considerations are embedded within

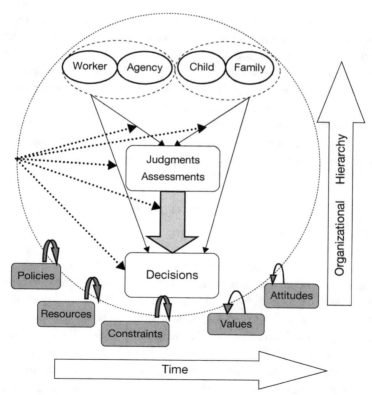

Figure 6.1 Judgments and Decision Processes in Context (JUDPiC) model
(Benbenishty, 2019).

broader contexts, such as the ecological context of the family, the organizational context of the decision-making agency, and wider contexts relating to the overall characteristics of the service system and the multiple cultural contexts in which these professionals operate. Hence, the links between the available information on the child and family and the judgments made by the professional, and the links between these judgments and the case decisions are moderated by a variety of factors, such as child protection policies, available knowledge and evidence about suitable interventions, existing resources, and values and attitudes about the rights of children and families. The model has recently been revised to include the time dimension (Benbenishty, 2019). Thus, the whole model is seen within "*evolving* contexts" (Astor & Benbenishty, 2019), emphasizing the dynamic and continuously changing aspects of the context in which child welfare decisions are being made. This can help explain, for instance, how decisions are influenced by major watershed events, such as child fatalities, or by major policy changes.

When this model is applied to comparative studies of judgments and decisions in child welfare and protection it offers a detailed and nuanced lens to predict, identify, and explain similarities and differences between judgments and decisions made in different child welfare systems. Moreover, it draws attention to variations *within* child welfare systems and *over time*. For instance, it helps understand why, within the same system, decisions may differ on the basis of the cultural context of the child and the agency or the resources differentially available to child welfare agencies within the same country. It could also help explain how decisions change following events such as the introduction of the United Nations Convention on the Rights of the Child to a child welfare system or changes in referral pattern after a policy change, such as a new policy forbidding the referral of young children to residential care (Silman, 2014; Zeijlmans, van Yperen, & López, 2020).

AN INTERNATIONAL STUDY OF CHILD PROTECTION DECISION-MAKING

The JUDPiC model was the basis for a large-scale international study comparing judgments and decision-making in cases of alleged maltreatment made by 828 decision-makers in four different countries (Benbenishty et al., 2015). The study employed a detailed vignette (a three-page description of a case) depicting a potential situation of child abuse (for a detailed description, see Benbenishty et al., 2015). Professionals filled out a Personal and Professional Background Questionnaire and the Child Welfare Attitudes Questionnaire. The attitudes questionnaire consists of 50 statements covering six content areas: (1) Against removal from home of children at risk, (2) Favors reunification and optimal duration of alternative care, (3) Favors children's participation in decisions, (4) Favors parents' participation in decisions, (5) Positive assessment of ability of foster care to promote children's development and well-being, and (6) Positive assessment of ability of residential care to promote children's development and well-being. In addition, after reading the case vignette, the participants provided their judgments of whether the allegations of physical, emotional, or sexual abuse were substantiated; their risk assessments of future emotional and physical maltreatment; and their intervention recommendation.

Placement Decisions

In an attempt to assess the impact of parent's wishes on judgments and decisions, the study presented two versions of the vignette to the professionals: the mother objected strongly to the idea of a placement versus the mother was willing to accept the placement. Surprisingly, mother's wishes toward the removal of the child did not have any impact on the judgments and decisions of professionals from any of the four countries. Although this is consistent with findings from previous studies (Davidson-Arad & Benbenishty, 2008), it is still an alarming result. Recent reforms of child protection policy in many countries indicate a shift from seeing parents as simple recipients of welfare benefits to considering them as service users and active agents in the decision-making processes (Biehal, 2019; López, Bouma, Grietens, & Knorth, 2019; Witte, Miehlbradt, van Santen, & Kindler, 2019). This finding could indicate that policy developments promoting parents' involvement might not be translating into more participatory practices straightaway.

In contrast, a follow-up study carried out in Portugal (Carvalho, Delgado, Benbenishty, Davidson-Arad, & Pinto, 2018) found that intervention recommendations were associated significantly with mother's wishes: while 61% recommended removal when the mother consented, 45% recommended removal when the mother was against it. This divergent finding suggests that between-country differences may exist even when child welfare systems are quite similar, as is the case with Portugal and Spain. There is a need for more in-depth exploration to understand these differences. One possible explanation is that the Portuguese study was carried out later than the international study, in a period in which there were many efforts made to reform the child protection systems of both Spain and Portugal. Therefore, the context might have changed over time.

When child welfare attitudes were explored among professionals across the four countries, the study found similarities and differences that seem to reflect both shared influences and between-countries variations. The smallest differences in professionals' attitudes between the four countries were with regard to the attitudes against removal of children from home. This seems to reflect the current shared ideology regarding the importance of family preservation and the prevention of removal, if possible (Al et al., 2012). The only country that deviated significantly from this approach was Spain.

Another case in point of both intercountry similarities and differences is the finding that, in three of the participating countries, attitudes toward foster care were much more positive than those toward residential care. This trend is very much along the current emphasis on children's rights (UNICEF, 2014), the superiority of family settings over residential care (e.g., Dozier et al., 2014), and the continued efforts to dismantle residential facilities in Europe, including massive closures of institutions in former Soviet Union countries, such as Romania (Nelson, Fox, & Zeanah, 2014). Within this global trend, Northern Ireland and the Netherlands stand out as more extreme cases, as negative attitudes regarding residential settings are fueled by media exposure to cruelties committed in residential settings in these countries (López et al., 2019).

In contrast to these attitudes shared by three of the countries, Israeli practitioners viewed residential care more favorably than other professionals and slightly more favorably than foster care. Hence, although Israeli practitioners are familiar with the literature on attachment and the importance of family settings (as indicated in this study by their reluctance to remove children from home), they had a positive view of residential care. This can be explained based on the historical context of the development of child welfare services in Israel that were influenced by the critical role that residential settings played in the Jewish tradition in providing a home for children during and following the Holocaust and in serving as a socializing context in the Zionist ideology that promoted collectivist settings (Dolev, Ben Rabi, & Zemach-Marom, 2009).

Spain presents another unique combination of attitudes to these placement alternatives. Attitudes toward residential care are not as negative as those of practitioners from Northern Ireland and the Netherlands, and, at the same time, their attitudes toward foster care are the most positive. This may reflect the recent developments in child protection in Spain that historically relied more on residential care. There is a gradual change in professional ideology, and intensive work has been carried out to convince professionals of the superiority of family-based interventions over residential placements. Moreover, program evaluations conducted in Spain have revealed a very positive picture of family foster care, with high placement stability (Del Valle, López, Montserrat, & Bravo, 2009; López, Del Valle, Montserrat, & Bravo, 2013) and a lower rate of placement breakdown (López, Del Valle, Montserrat, & Bravo, 2011). This positive portrait may have influenced the attitudes of professionals to accept family foster care as a good alternative.

Substantiation and Risk Assessment Decisions

When the substantiation and risk assessment judgments made by the practitioners were assessed, several patterns emerged. First, although there were some intercountry differences (Dutch professionals tended to substantiate alleged maltreatment significantly less than Israeli and Northern Ireland professionals), the within-country differences were quite substantial, indicating that being part of the same system (and judging the same case) does not guarantee agreement. Furthermore, personal attitudes of practitioners explained some of these variations in substantiation and risk assessment.

This study examined whether there were differences between practitioners from the participating countries in their recommendations with regard to intervention recommendations. Although we presented virtually the same vignette to all practitioners in the study (the manipulation did not have any impact), there was considerable variation in the interventions they recommended based on this case file. For instance, the number of practitioners in Spain who recommended removal (52%) was more than double the proportion in Israel (25%).

The lowest levels of removal recommendations by Israeli practitioners is consistent with previous studies (Benbenishty, Segev, Surkis, & Elias, 2002; Gold et al., 2001), and it could be explained by the ideological and professional stance in Israel that prioritizes that families be kept together, as well as by the current public criticism toward the intrusive response of child protection agencies in the lives of families. In contrast, Spanish practitioners present a much weaker stand against removal attitude and a low support for reunification and short optimal duration of placement. These findings could be associated with the prioritizing of residential care as the default child protection intervention in the Spanish system and the scarcity of family support programs aimed at preventing child abuse and neglect in families at risk.

Interestingly, the Carvalho et al. (2018) study mentioned earlier indicated that the pattern of attitudes in Portugal was more similar to the child welfare attitudes in Spain compared with the other countries. The Spanish and Portuguese systems share much in common, such as the prevalence of residential care and the late introduction of family support and family foster care programs. It seems that these similarities are also evident in the structure of child welfare attitudes among their practitioners. This may be an indication of how the child welfare system is translated into "on the ground decisions"—by internalized attitudes, rather than by mere directives.

As was the case with judgments, there were considerable variations between professionals within each country. Here again, personal child welfare attitudes explained some of this intracountry variations. Thus, for instance, while 22.2% of the practitioners with a strong "pro-removal" attitude recommended removal of the child even without parental consent, only 8.9% of the practitioners who were against removal recommended such removal.

CONTINUATION OF THE INTERNATIONAL DECISION-MAKING PROJECT

In the Netherlands, the project members have conducted further explorations of their country data in order to understand the role of reasoning, work experience, and attitudes in child protection decision-making (Bartelink et al., 2018). The Dutch team has conducted further analyses in a sample of 214 professionals and 381 students in order to investigate the rationales provided for an out-of-home placement decision and whether these rationales predict the decision, in addition to the decision-makers' risk assessment, work experience, and attitudes toward placement. The findings revealed that the mean number of rationales given by each respondent was low overall. The content of the reasoning was somehow superficial and missed core elements, such as references to the child's development or child abuse signs. Safety assessment and attitude toward placement predicted the placement decision: the higher the assessment of safety risk and the more positive respondents were about the out-of-home placement, the more likely it was that they would recommend placing the child in foster care.

Reasoning of the decision-makers was also studied by the team from Northern Ireland (Spratt, Devaney, & Hayes, 2015). One of the main contributions of Spratt and colleagues (2015) is the documentation of "confirmation bias" in the reasoning strategies of those social workers making decisions of removal and reunification. Their findings suggest that social workers are prone to selectively interpret the case information either positively or negatively to support their a priori assumptions about the case.

Seen together, these studies on reasoning suggest an important avenue for comparative research. They indicate that practitioners may differ not only in how they process available information, such as the information provided in the vignette or culled from case files. Their different professional perspectives may also influence what they look for and see in cases. There is a clear need for qualitative lens to supplement quantitative comparisons.

NEXT STEPS FOR THE FIELD OF INTERCOUNTRY COMPARISONS IN CHILD PROTECTION DECISION-MAKING

The series of international comparative studies presented in this chapter demonstrates the impact of the country context in child protection decision-making. Practitioners from the five countries studied diverged significantly in their maltreatment substantiation, risk assessments, and recommended interventions.

Furthermore, these studies indicated that one of the factors that can help explain within-country variations are the practitioners' child welfare attitudes. It seems therefore that the JUDPiC could be a valuable model to identify and understand similarities and differences between judgments and decisions made in different child welfare systems, as well as between practitioners within the same system.

From a theoretical point of view, we think the JUDPiC model needs to be developed further to help predict and improve decision processes, rather than just explain current findings. This theoretical additional work will need to expand much beyond the decision-making literature. It seems that there will be a need to integrate concepts and models from fields such as ecological, systems, and organizational theories that take into account the nestedness of the many contexts in which child welfare decision-makers are functioning. The theory work will be stronger if it takes into account that child welfare decision-making is a process that involves many players, some present in the room, such as the practitioner and the child-family, while others, such as the supervisor, the judge, and even the media, are "mentally present" in the mind of the practitioner. This more advanced theoretical work will help direct research in the future.

Given this state of theory, the comparative studies presented here were exploratory in nature and did not present many specific hypotheses. The JUDPiC model, however, provides opportunities to generate new directional hypotheses that could be tested with more sophisticated research methods to further expand our knowledge base on decision-making in child protection. For instance, a longitudinal approach could be useful to study the less-explored dimension of the impact of time (Benbenishty, 2019). Researchers can propose detailed hypotheses about how decisions in the child welfare system of a country would change gradually with the introduction of major policy changes, as is currently occurring in the Portuguese child protection system. Another set of hypotheses could address the role of resources on decision-makers. Hence, one could hypothesize that the relative abundance of a specific resource (e.g., residential care facilities or home preservation programs) in a country context would impact decision-makers. Moreover, hypotheses could be tested to explain within-country variations based on local variations in access to certain resources. These lines of research could benefit from advances in theory and could also help progress in our theoretical thinking.

From a practice point of view, one important implication of this series of studies is the need to make professionals and policy-makers more conscious and responsive of the impact of workers' attitudes and country context in judgments and decisions. It is of utmost importance that professionals be made more aware of the ways in which they bring their own values, beliefs, and attitudes into play when making decisions for children and families.

Likewise, understanding how decisions are shaped by the organizational and country cultures in which they operate should be prioritized in training and supervision, as well as be addressed in policy and organizational transformations. These issues have been traditionally neglected in curriculum development, textbooks, and professional training for child protection workers in favor of other subjects (e.g., the assessment of case characteristics in order to make accurate judgments and decisions). This narrow approach is being supplemented currently by research evidence, such as the one presented in this chapter, that illuminates how decision-maker or context characteristics impact decisions.

This research line suggests that there is still much to be learned from international comparisons of child protection decision-making. It can provide an important source of self-reflection and learning, and it might encourage changes in national policies and practices.

REFERENCES

Al, C. M., Stams, G. J., Bek, M. S., Damen, E. M., Asscher, J. J., & Van der Laan, P. H. (2012). A meta-analysis of intensive family preservation programs: Placement prevention. *Children and Youth Services Review, 34,* 1472–1479.

Astor, R. A., & Benbenishty, R. (2019). *Bullying, school violence, and climate in evolving contexts: Culture, organization and time.* New York: Oxford University Press.

Bartelink, C., Knorth, E. J., López, M., Koopmans, C., Ten Berge, I. J., Witteman, C. L. M., & Van Yperen, T. A. (2018). Reasons for placement decisions in a case of suspected child abuse: The role of reasoning, work experience and attitudes in decision-making. *Child Abuse and Neglect, 83,* 129–141.

Benbenishty, R. (2019, March). *Putting theory in context and putting context in theory.* Paper presented at the Andres Bello University, Santiago de Chile.

Benbenishty, R., & Davison-Arad, B. (2012, September). *A controlled study of placement and reunification decision in Israel.* Paper presented at the Conference of the European Scientific Association for Residential and Family Care of Children and Adolescents, Gasgow.

Benbenishty, R., Davidson-Arad, B., López, M., Devaney, J., Spratt, T., Koopmans, C., . . . Hayes, D. (2015). Decision-making in child protection: An international comparative study on maltreatment substantiation, risk assessment and intervention recommendations and the role of professionals' child welfare attitudes. *Child Abuse and Neglect, 49,* 63–75.

Benbenishty, R., Osmo, R., & Gold, N. (2003). Rationales provided for risk assessments and for recommended interventions: A comparison between Canadian and Israeli professionals. *British Journal of Social Work, 33*(2), 137–155.

Benbenishty, R., Segev, D., Surkis, T., & Elias, T. (2002). Information-search and decision-making by professionals and nonprofessionals in cases of alleged child-abuse and maltreatment. *Journal of Social Service Research, 28*(3), 1–18.

Berrick, J. D., Dickens, J., Pösö, T., & Skivenes, M. (2015). Children's involvement in care order decision-making: A cross-country analysis. *International Journal of Child Abuse and Neglect*. *49*, 128–141.

Berrick, J. D., Dickens, J., Pösö, T., & Skivenes, M. (2017a). A cross-country comparison of child welfare system responses to children appearing to be at risk or in need of help. *Child Abuse Review*, *26*(4), 305–319.

Berrick, J. D., Dickens, J., Pösö, T., & Skivenes, M. (2017b). Parents' involvement in care order decisions: A cross-country study of front-line practice. *Child & Family Social Work*, *22*, 626–637.

Berrick, J. D., Dickens, J., Pösö, T., & Skivenes, M. (2018). International Perspectives on Child-responsive Courts. *International Journal of Children's Rights*, *26*, 251–277.

Biehal, N. (2019). Balancing prevention and protection: Child protection in England. In R. D. Krugman, L. Merkel-Holguin, & J. D. Fluke (Eds.), *Child maltreatment series. Contemporary issues in research and policy* (pp. 51–74). New York: Springer.

Carvalho, J. M. S., Delgado, P., Benbenishty, R., Davidson-Arad, B., & Pinto, V. (2018). Professional judgements and decisions on placement in foster care and reunification in Portugal. *European Journal of Social Work*, *21*(2), 296–310.

Davidson-Arad, B., & Benbenishty, R. (2008). The role of workers' attitudes and parent and child wishes in child protection workers' assessments and recommendation regarding removal and reunification. *Children and Youth Services Review*, *30*, 107–121.

Del Valle, J. F., López, M., Montserrat, C., & Bravo, A. (2009). Twenty years of foster care in Spain: Profiles, patterns and outcomes. *Children and Youth Services Review*, *31*(8), 847–853.

Dolev, T., Ben Rabi, D., & Zemach-Marom, T. (2009). Residential care for children 'At Risk' in Israel: Current situation and future challenges. In M. E. Courtney, & D. Iwaniec (Eds.), *Residential care of children: Comparative perspectives* (pp. 72–87). London: Oxford University Press.

Dozier, M., Kaufman, J., Kobak, R., O'Connor, T. G., Sagi-Schwartz, A., Scott, S., . . . Zeanah, C. H. (2014). Consensus statement on group care for children and adolescents: A statement of policy of the American Orthopsychiatric Association. *American Journal of Orthopsychiatry*, *84*, 219–225.

Gilbert, N., Parton, N., & Skivenes, M. (2011). *Child protection systems: International trends and orientations*. Oxford: Oxford University Press.

Gold, N., Benbenishty, R., & Osmo, R. (2001). A comparative study of risk assessments and recommended interventions in Canada and Israel. *Child Abuse and Neglect*, *25*, 607–622.

Križ, K., & Skivenes, M. (2013). Systemic differences in views on risk: A comparative case vignette study of risk assessment in England, Norway and the United States (California). *Children and Youth Services Review*, *35*, 1862–1870.

López, M., Bouma, H., Grietens, H. (2019). The Dutch child protection system: Historical overview and recent transformations. In R. D. Krugman, L. Merkel-Holguin, & J. D. Fluke (Eds.), *Child maltreatment series. Contemporary issues in research and policy* (pp. 173–192). New York: Springer.

López, M., Del Valle, J. F., Montserrat, C., & Bravo, A. (2011). Factors affecting foster care breakdown in Spain. *Spanish Journal of Psychology*, *14*(1), 111–122.

López, M., Del Valle, J. F., Montserrat, C., & Bravo, A. (2013). Factors associated with family reunification for children in foster care. *Child and Family Social Work, 18*(2), 226–236.

Nelson, C. A., Fox, N. A., & Zeanah, C. H. (2014). *Romania's abandoned children: Deprivation, brain development and the struggle for recovery.* Cambridge, MA: Harvard University Press.

Osmo, R., & Benbenishty, R. (2004). Children at risk: Rationales for risk assessments and interventions. *Children and Youth Services Review, 26*, 1155–1173.

Silman, J. (2014). *A report of the committee to examine policies related to removal children from home and their visitation with their parents.* Jerusalem: Ministry of Welfare (Hebrew).

Spratt, T., Devaney, J., & Hayes, D. (2015). In and out of home care decisions: The influence of confirmation bias in developing decision supportive reasoning. *Child Abuse and Neglect 49*, 76–85.

UNICEF. (2014). Realising the rights of every child everywhere: Moving forward with the EU. Eurochild and UNICEF. http://www.eurochild.org/fileadmin/ThematicPriorities/ChildrensRights/Eurochild/EurochildUNICEFRealising-Childrens-Rights-EUFeb2014low-res.pdf

Witte, S., Miehlbradt, L., van Santen, E., & Kindler, H. (2019). Preventing child endangerment: Child protection in Germany. In R. D. Krugman, L. Merkel-Holguin, & J. D. Fluke (Eds.), *Child maltreatment series. Contemporary issues in research and policy* (pp. 93–114). New York: Springer.

Wulczyn, F., Daro D., Fluke J. D., Feldman S, Glodek C., & Lifada K. (2010). *Adapting a systems approach to child protection: Key concepts and considerations.* Working Paper. New York: United Nations Children's Fund (UNICEF).

Zeijlmans, K., van Yperen, T., & López, M. (2020). The level-headed approach on errors and mistakes in Dutch child protection: An individual duty or a shared responsibility? In K. Biesel, J. Masson, N. Parton, & T. Pösö (Eds.), *Errors and mistakes in child protection: International discourses, approaches, and strategies* (pp. 75–94). Bristol: Policy Press.

7

The Psychosocial Process Underlying Residential Care Placement Decisions

LEONOR BETTENCOURT RODRIGUES, MANUELA CALHEIROS, AND CÍCERO PEREIRA ■

INTRODUCTION

The modern family has been defined as paradoxical: on the one hand, there is a normative representation of infancy as a specific age category that is marked by vulnerability and a need for nurturing, care, and affection. On the other hand, there are too many instances of parental abuse and neglect (Almeida, Almeida, & André, 2002; Almeida, 2009). When such maltreatment does take place, official entities have to make a decision about whether to keep the child in the family or to place her in out-of-home placement: namely, to place the child in residential care (i.e., in an institutional facility). Both types of interventions try to assure protection and well-being to at-risk children, and they differ in terms of the level of restrictions imposed on parental responsibility/authority. Despite the legal framework of those intervention measures, the underlying decision is extremely complex and can appear a random process (Holland, 2001). Its complexity is evident in the multiplicity of factors, criteria, and constraints—legal, scientific, sociolegal, and cultural—that, in practice, support and determine decision-making in the context of child protection.

Leonor Bettencourt Rodrigues, Manuela Calheiros, and Cícero Pereira, *The Psychosocial Process Underlying Residential Care Placement Decisions* In: *Decision-Making and Judgment in Child Welfare and Protection.* Edited by: John D. Fluke, Mónica López López, Rami Benbenishty, Erik J. Knorth, and Donald J. Baumann, Oxford University Press (2021). © Oxford University Press. DOI: 10.1093/oso/9780190059538.003.0007.

Despite the legislative restructuring following the ratification of the Convention on the Rights of the Child, its implementation and operationalization have shown constraints summarized at three levels. On one level, the paradigmatic theoretical evolution observed in child protection social policies does not translate into the intervention undertaken, one marked by tensions, conflicts, and dilemmas (Dickens, 2007). On another level, laws are vague and lack definition of key concepts for case assessment and decision-making (Banach, 1998; Gold, Benbenishty, & Osmo, 2001; Wulczyn, 2004). On a third level, a set of limitations and inconsistencies in the available empirical data does not allow a great deal of support of various measures for every specific case (Azar, Benjet, Fuhrmann, & Cavallero, 1995; Davidson-Arad, Englechin-Segal, & Wozner, 2003).

Child protection intervention involves knowledge from multiple disciplines, such as psychology, social policy, and law, and, in this sense, it is a function of the contributions (and constraints) underlying the thinking about children and child protection in different disciplines. Those constraints underscore the lack of criteria—specific and action-oriented—that may determine the type of intervention required and, more specifically, if an out-of-home placement is needed (Mech, 1970). This decision is complex, ambiguous, and marked by errors and uncertainty (see Chapters 5 & 10 in this volume). Therefore, a process intended to be rational, lawful, and scientifically supported has been described as random—a stochastic model (Lindsey, 1994) dominated by ambiguities in the definition and application of concepts and criteria, by conflicts of values, and by dilemmas over the type of intervention to be developed (Dickens, 2007).

Furthermore, this uncertain and ambiguous decision-making context makes child protection caseworkers more aware and fearful of institutional and social judgment, leading them to adopt self-defensive decisions and to postpone interventions until a critical event occurs (Dickens, 2007). Therefore, there is a need to fully understand the decision-making process and study the role played by caseworkers' individual variables (Arad-Davidzon & Benbenishty, 2008; Summers, Gatowski, & Dobbin, 2012). In addition, although formal decision-making occurs within multidisciplinary teams, this formal process requires that each caseworker considers his or her own assessment, opinion, and proposal for action (Munro, 2005) and integrates those of other caseworkers in the intervention plan to be developed. In this sense, professional and individual-level decisions are, therefore, the most elementary unit of the system (Peters, 2001; Rodrigues, Calheiros, & Pereira, 2015).

One of the most well-known and applied theoretical frameworks of decision-making in the child protection field is the Decision-Makin Ecology (Baumann, Dalgleish, Fluke, & Kern, 2011; Baumann, Fluke, Dalgleish, & Kern, 2014; Fluke, Baumann, Dalgleish, & Kern, 2014). It determines how many different factors influence decision-making, from case-specific characteristics, to organizational factors, and external factors, as well as decision-maker factors. At this level, it integrates the General Model of Dalgleish (1988) which explains how the decision threshold operates for the decision-maker. For each specific decision in the decision-making continuum, each individual takes his or her own perspective and integrates other factors into the ecology to determine his or her own threshold—that line in the sand that defines how much evidence is enough to justify taking action. However, how that psychosocial process occurs, how the decision-maker integrates those multiple factors from the decision-making ecology is still empirically unclear.

In this chapter, we review the state of the art in the study of caseworkers' psychosocial processes underlying the out-of-home placement decision following instances of child maltreatment by integrating existing literature on both child protection and social psychology. This threefold chapter first attempts to review and summarize cues from empirical studies sustaining the role played by the psychosocial variables of caseworkers involved in out-of-home placement decisions. In the second part, we describe social-psychological decision-making models and present an overview of the main ideas from these models to apply to the study of decision-making in the area of child protection. In the third part of the chapter, we present the principal results of a recent empirically tested model of the residential care placement decision through which the caseworker integrates those multiple psychosocial factors in the decision process (Rodrigues, 2012; Rodrigues et al., 2015).

CUES SUSTAINING THE ROLE PLAYED BY CASEWORKERS' PSYCHOSOCIAL VARIABLES

The literature suggests that the largely studied child, family, and case characteristics (e.g., Atkinson & Butler, 1996; Dalgleish & Drew, 1989; Davidson-Arad, Englechin-Segal, Wozner, & Gabriel, 2003; Fialkov & Cohen, 1990; Festinger, 1996; Rossi, Schuerman, & Budde, 1999; Zuravin & DePanfilis, 1997) are only part of the decision-making equation (Baumann et al., 2011). Researchers have not been successful in fully determining the role played by individual variables involved in the out-of-home placement decision (see Chapter 5, this volume). There have been emerging cues pointing to the key role played, along with legal and theoretical guidelines, by individual variables, even if decisions are formally made collectively. Some of those cues highlight the role of caseworkers' risk perception and evaluation; others, the importance of their attitudes, values, and emotions or their previous experience and area of education. Still others implicate normative influences and barriers arising from institutional and broader social contexts—organizational and external factors—that frame the individual involved in the decision-making.

Legal and theoretical guidelines determine that judgment and decision-making in child protection ought to be a meticulous and rational assessment of the level of risk or danger involved to the child (Davidson-Arad, 2009). Theoretically, a child is at risk when he or she reveals, in comparison to other similar children, a higher probability of reaching an undesirable condition (Cicchetti & Rizley, 1981; Little, Axford, & Morpeth, 2004; Parton, 2010). Thus, the definition of an "at-risk child" implies both a time dimension and the likelihood of future consequences/damages to a child's development and well-being (Humphreys & Ramsey, 1993). In turn, a child is "in danger" if there is an imminent threat or if harm is already present and compromises child's well-being and integrity (Parton, 2010). Thus, "risk" and "danger" correspond to different levels of the same theoretical concept (Cicchetti & Rizley, 1981; Parton, 2010) and entail different levels of intervention: community-based intervention with preventive purposes or formal state intervention undertaken by official entities to change or control parental behavior and/or its impacts on child development (Davidson-Arad, 2009; Fallon, Tromé, & MacLaurin, 2011; Rossi et al., 1999).

However, there is a set of obstacles to the operationalization of risk assessment concepts. On the one hand, caseworkers struggle to not only aggregate and adequately weight the relevance of different risk and protection factors for each specific case, but also to identify and distinguish where to draw the line between risk and imminent danger. There is subjectivity and variability inherent in risk assessment and in the definition and conceptualization of the key concepts (e.g., children's needs) and child ecology subsystems underlying risk assessment (Camasso & Jagannathan, 1995; Doueck, English, DePanfilis, & Moote, 1993; English & Pecora, 1994; Lyons, Doueck, & Wodarski, 1996; Sullivan, Whitehead, Leschied, Chiado, & Hurley, 2008).

The literature in child protection also points out the importance of other informal and not always conscious evaluations made by caseworkers. Namely, how positively or negatively does the caseworker evaluate (i.e., his or her attitude toward) residential care placement? Arad-Davidzon and Benbenishty (2008) used the Child Welfare Questionnaire to access caseworkers' attitudes toward removal and reunification of at-risk children, with items related to different types of maltreatment, duration of out-of-home placement, and quality of residential care placement. The results revealed that caseworkers either have a pro-removal or an anti-removal attitude and that those who are against removal have more negative attitudes toward removal, more positive attitudes toward reunification, and especially can be differentiated from the pro-removal group for favoring shorter stays in out-of-home placement. Additionally, results showed an association between caseworkers' attitudes and their judgments and decisions: the more "pro-removal" they were, the more highly did they assess a child's risk at home and the more often did they proposed more intrusive interventions to protect the child. In a more recent study using that same questionnaire results indicate that, within out-of-home placement options, attitudes tend to be much more positive toward foster care than toward residential care (Benbenishty et al., 2015). Recent results suggest that, contrary to what is usually thought, caseworkers' attitudes, along with case information, influence decisions as well as judgments. This impact has been proven in different countries, thus supporting the subjectivity underlying child protection reasoning that might explain interprofessional inconsistencies (Benbenishty et al., 2015). This attitude-based inconsistency can be motivated by the different social values framing caseworkers.

Social values have long been considered relevant as a determinant of conceptual conflicts (Epstein, 1980), especially when referring to questions of social policy (Tetlock, 1986). In child protection, cultural values determine the perception of adequate parental practices, thus influencing the definition and judgment of abuse or neglect and the level of risk to the child. Their impact in child protection also seems to occur through their influence on institutional values that sustain services and practices (Gergen, Gloger-Tippelt, & Berkowitz, 1990) as well as overall social policy and the type of intervention implemented for child protection.

In the decision of residential care placement, the most emphasized conflict in the literature is that involving the presence of values that support the preservation of children's individual rights versus the presence of values that support the preservation of familial bonds and privacy (Besharov, 1985). This conflict results from the dilemma posed by the apparent impossibility of deciding on an intervention that, at the same time, safeguards the best interests of the child and the well-being of the family (Goldstein, Freud, & Solnit, 1980, Goldstein, Solnit, Goldstein, & Freud, 1996; Houston, 2003; Taylor, Beckett, & McKeigue, 2008). The presence of this conflict in judgment and decision-making is promoted by not only an informal social process of cultural socialization in which each individual is involved (Fernandez, 1996; Gergen et al., 1990; Portwood, 1998), but also by the coexistence, at least in some countries like Portugal, of two formal legal intervention principles: higher interest of the child and family preservation. Therefore, the decision apparently seems to encompass contradictory social values and legal principles (Dickens, 2007; Houston, 2003; Munro, 2005).

Although widely discussed in child protection literature, the impact of others and of social pressure on professional judgment has not yet been documented adequately (Goldstein et al., 1980; Munro, 1998, 2005; Rossi et al., 1999). It may occur through factors both external and internal to the decision-making context. Internally, decision-making in child protection, whether individually or collectively, occurs in the presence of peers and/or in the representation of a hierarchical superior. The strong presence of values related to family and child rights and the difficulty of initiating a formal, legal intervention in the private and informal matters associated with individual and universal rights opens the decision to publicity and social criticism and thus to the influence of external factors. Therefore, professional judgment has been described as being influenced by a fear of being blamed or judged (Kanani, Regehr, & Bernstein, 2002), not only by peers or superiors, but also by close (family and friends) and broad social contexts (public opinion/culture; Benbenishty et al., 2015).

In this sense, society plays a controlling role over the caseworker's action, a control that may lead to the adoption of defensive actions that safeguard against potential criticisms (Besharov, 1985, Dickens, 2007, Kanani et al., 2002, Lachman & Bernard, 2006; Munro, 2005). As a result, the adoption of defensive practices has direct implications in the efficacy of protecting at-risk children (Besharov, 1985; Dickens, 2007; Kanani et al., 2002; Lachman & Bernard, 2006; Munro, 2005).

The institutional/organizational dimension of the decision-making context refers to aspects of the formal state structures and entities responsible for the promotion and protection of child well-being. Despite the scarcity of studies that focus on this dimension, there is an emphasis on the importance of such structures' effectiveness in prevention, signaling, intervention, anticipation of reoccurrence, and risk assessment (Ben-Arieh, 2010; Ben-Arieh & Haj-Yahia, 2006; DePanfilis & Zuravin, 1999, 2002; Marks, McDonald, & Bessey, 1989; Parton, 2009; Taylor et al., 2008). Specific organizational characteristics and constraints frame caseworkers' judgment and decision-making (Munro, 2005): resources availability (in quantity and quality; Brosig & Kalichman, 1992; DePanfilis & Zuravin, 2001; Kenny, 2001; Zellman, 1990); bureaucracy and procedural volume (DePanfilis & Girvin, 2005; Munro, 2005; Rzepnicki & Johnson, 2005), and inter- and intra-institutional/disciplinary partnerships and cooperation (Beckett & McKeigue, 2003; Britner & Mossler, 2002; Dickens, 2007; Gambrill & Shlonsky, 2000; Gray, 2002; Knight & Oliver, 2007; Munro, 2002, 2005; Reder & Duncan, 2004).

The impact of institutional constraints on at-risk children, besides occurring directly through the quantity and quality of responses and services available—iatrogenic harm (Jones, 1991)—also occurs indirectly through its impact on professional judgment and as a mediator between judgment and decision-making: a judgments and decision processes in context model (Benbenishtiy et al., 2015).

The ambivalent nature attributed to out-of-home placement decisions explains that it is associated with a strong emotional component (Besharov,

1985; Conner & Sparks, 2005; Goldstein et al., 1980, 1996; Schwalbe, 1988; Taylor et al., 2008). The effect of a caseworker's emotions on these decisions was demonstrated by Summers and colleagues (2012), especially in caseworkers with low levels of experience. In this study, the focus of attention was on the effect of negative emotions experienced by the caseworker during the decision-making process—immediate emotions. However, the importance of anticipated emotions has been emphasized—those anticipated to be experienced after the decision has been made—as possibly explaining behavior, especially when negative consequences and feelings may result (Conner & Sparks, 2005).

Although there are no empirical studies clarifying what triggers such emotions, they are possibly linked to the impossibility of choosing an alternative that can respect and preserve the rights and interests of both the child and the family. Additionally, these emotions can be related to the potential (negative) impact of residential care on child development and the family (Bowlby, 1951; Tilbury & Osmond, 2006) or the fear of criticism and social and institutional recrimination that the misplacement of the child in a residential care setting may represent (Dickens, 2007; Kanani et al., 2002; Lachman & Bernard, 2006; Munro, 2005).

Therefore, the emotions that the caseworker anticipates after proposing an out-of-home placement decision can be related to consequences for the child he or she recommends for residential care placement. Similarly, the way the caseworker perceives institutional and social constraints and barriers, as well as the interests, opinions, and expectations of others—from both proximal and distal social and institutional contexts—can influence not only the consequences perceived for the child, but also the caseworker's anticipated emotions.

The implicit idea underlying the impact of previous experience in residential care placement decisions is that the contents, definitions, and perceptions that each individual brings to the decision process are a product of a self-construction process that results not only from a set of experiences with traditions, culture expectancies, and the media (Bronstein et al., 1996; Brooks-Gunn & Furstenburg, 1986; Goodnow, 1988; Goodnow & Collins, 1990; Mann, Pearl, & Behle, 2004; Runco & Johnson, 2002; Tamis-LeMonda, Shannon, & Spellmann, 2002), but also from life, parental, and professional experiences (Carugati & Mugny, 1985; Jagannathan & Camasso, 1996; LeVine, Miller, Richman, & LeVine, 1996; Vandenplas-Holper, 1987).

Although there is some inconsistency between studies (Sullivan et al., 2008), the predominant idea is that caseworkers with more years of experience in the field have a lower tendency to decide for an out-of-home measure (Cash, 2001; Davidson-Arad et al., 2003; Munro, 1999; Schuerman, Rossi, & Budde, 1999). Summers and colleagues' (2012) study constitutes good support for considering previous experience in the study of placement decision-making in child protection because it reveals the effect of practical professional knowledge previously acquired—regarding case assessment and other procedures involved in professional practice—in judgment and decision-making (Summers et al., 2012). Other hypotheses to explain a caseworker's experience effect in decision-making refer to the individual's beliefs about out-of-home placement, its constraints, and its consequences to the child (Davidson-Arad et al., 2003). Another possibility is related to the greater awareness of the caseworker about the impact that criticism and social and institutional pressures may have (Besharov, 1985; Dickens, 2007; Kanani et al., 2002; Lachman, & Bernard, 2006; Munro, 2005).

In addition to the variability that results from previous professional experience, both in terms of its contents and in terms of the number of years in the field, the literature also emphasizes the variability that comes from training and professional/discipline background (Arad-Davidzon & Benbenishty, 2008; Britner & Mossler, 2002, Mandel, Lehman, & Yuille, 1994). This individual variability explains the presence of, in addition to within-professional discrepancies, between-professional inconsistencies in risk assessment (Britner & Mossler, 2002).

SOCIAL PSYCHOLOGY DECISION-MAKING MODELS: THE THEORY OF PLANNED BEHAVIOR MODEL

When considering a rationalist perspective of behavioral decision-making, the main theoretical concept used in social psychology to understand the relationship between the psychological process that occurs in the individual and the behavior exhibited is the concept of *attitude*. Underlying the strong focus placed on attitudes since the first decades of the 20th century was the connection attributed to it in explaining, predicting, and changing behavior (Watson, 1925; Ajzen & Fishbein, 2005). This concept was initially defined as a process of individual consciousness that determines the individual's actual or potential activities in the social world (Ajzen & Fishbein, 2005) or as statements of self-descriptive behaviors considered equivalent to the statements that any outside observer could make about it (Bem, 1967). This strong and direct connection initially hypothesized between attitude and behavior was challenged by empirical findings (LaPierre, 1934) and criticisms from sociology (Blumer, 1955; Deutscher, 1966) and psychology (Campbell, 1963; Festinger, 1964) that encouraged disenchantment with this concept and the enormous discredit of it in the following decades.

While LaPierre's (1934) results were the first weak attitude–behavior empirical finding, Wicker's review of the empirical literature in 1969 was key for the dissemination of skepticism around attitudes by raising questions about its stability over time and, consequently, its utility in predicting explicit behavior (Armitage & Conner, 2001). The challenge to social psychologists was, then, how to improve the predictive power of attitude and attitude–behavior consistency (Ajzen & Fishbein, 2005; Armitage & Conner, 2001). This challenge motivated the work of Fishbein and Azjen and the development of more complex theoretical models in the explanation and prediction of human behavior (Olson & Zanna, 1993).

The *theory of reasoned action* (Fishbein & Ajzen, 1975) and the *theory of planned behavior* (TPB; Ajzen, 1985) models are the most applied and tested (Armitage & Conner, 2001; Conner & Sparks, 2005). These rational/deliberative theories have in common the proposition that the unobservable attitude and the observable behavior is mediated by *behavioral intention* (i.e., the individual's personal and conscious motivation). In these models attitude is understood as a "psychological tendency that is expressed in a favorable or unfavorable assessment of a specific entity." (Eagly & Chaiken, 1993, p. 1); that is, a kind of bias that predisposes the individual to make more positive or negative evaluations about an entity, "thing," or behavior—an *attitudinal object*.

These models also have in common the fact that the intention is predicted, not only by the attitude, but also by the *subjective norm*, which is defined as a psychological process that results from social influence and refers to the perception of how significant others perceive the behavior (Conner & Sparks, 2005). The inclusion of this variable is one of the great contributions of these models, reversing the prevailing tendency in the literature to value individual processes over social ones. This is especially relevant in theories applied to study decision-making processes in natural contexts, particularly when ethical decisions are at stake (Eagly & Chaiken, 1993).

What differentiates these two rational models is the fact that the TPB, in addition to motivational and informational factors, also includes *perceived behavior control* as a determinant of both behavior and behavioral intention (Ajzen, 1985; Armitage & Conner, 2001; Conner & Sparks, 2005; Eagly & Chaiken, 1993). The inclusion of this variable allows for the prediction of not only volitional behaviors—the ones the theory of reasoned action is directed to predict—but also behaviors that require the presence of specific skills, resources, or opportunities and therefore, do not solely depend on the will of the individual (Conner & Sparks, 2005; Fishbein, 1993).

The Theory of Planned Behavior

The model of behavioral prediction underlying the TPB (Azjen, 1985) states that, to predict a specific behavior, it is necessary to access the individual's

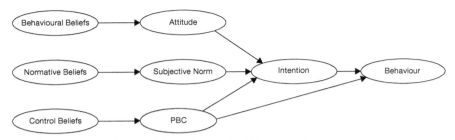

Figure 7.1 Theory of Planned Behavior Model (Ajzen, 1985).
SOURCE: Armitage & Conner (2001, p. 472).

behavioral intention, which is understood as a measure of how much a person wants to and is willing to make an effort to accomplish that behavior (Ajzen, 1991). Additionally, this model assumes that people tend to engage in behaviors that they not only feel motivated to, but also think are easy to achieve— *perceived behavior control* (PBC, see Figure 7.1).

As shown in Figure 7.1, the TPB model also stipulates the direct and indirect antecedents of behavioral intention. The direct antecedents are (1) the more or less favorable evaluation that the individual has on the behavior (*attitude*), (2) the individual's opinion on what relevant others think about the behavior (*subjective norm*), and (3) the individual's perception of the ease or difficulty of accomplishing the behavior (*perceived behavior control*, with both a direct and indirect effect on behavior).

Furthermore, the TPB model defines that each of those direct antecedents is determined by specific beliefs (Ajzen, 1991): *behavioral beliefs* (i.e., consequences one attributes to the behavior), *normative beliefs* (i.e., perception of what significant others think about the behavior), and *behavior control beliefs* (i.e., barriers and facilitators that determine motivation and behavior) (Figure 7.1). Each of these beliefs is measured by a multiplicative composite (Conner & Sparks, 2005) based on the summative model of attitudes: the strength and level of complacency of the individual in relation to each salient belief influencing the behavior (Ajzen, 2001; Conner & Armitage, 1998; Conner & Sparks, 2005; Eagly & Chaiken, 1993).

In the TPB model both direct and indirect antecedents correspond to different measures of the same construct; the first is a more subjective (direct/ global) measure and the former a more objective (indirect) one (Ajzen & Fishbein, 2005). The absence or relative weakness of predictive values in the relationship between the indirect cognitive-based measure (beliefs) and the direct measure of the behavioral intention's antecedents is attributed to the presence of different information processes underlying the decision of whether to take the behavior. Indirect measures that are accessed through beliefs are associated with a more deliberative processing, while direct/global measures are associated with a more automatic processing (Ajzen, 1991).

The TPB model has been applied to a variety of contexts and behaviors to study ethical decision-making, as in medical (Randall & Gibson, 1991) and financial contexts (Buchan, 2005). In general, the results support the validity of the TPB model in the prediction of behavioral intention and behavior, with an explained percentage of variance of around 39% and 27%, respectively (Ajzen, 1991; Armitage & Conner, 2001; Conner & Sparks, 2005).

However, recent criticism and discussion of the model underscores its purely rational perspective on predicting human behavior and its sole focus on the proximal determinants of behavior (Conner & Armitage, 1998; Conner & Sparks, 2005). In fact, if the contribution of the model is the description of the process through which variables such as attitude influence behavior, its gap is at the level of the processes through which other variables influence the components of the TPB model (Conner & Armitage, 1998). Its purely rational character is present in the consideration of antecedents of a cognitive nature and in the neglect of other noncognitive/irrational determinants of human behavior (Bagozzi, Lee, & Van Loo, 2001; Van der Pligt & De Vries, 1998). The discussion of these issues in the literature motivated proposals for the inclusion of new variables in the model that contribute, in particular, to a better understanding of the process of attitude formation—distal determinants of behavior—and to a more intuitive character and thus dualistic strand of explaining behavior (Conner & Armitage, 1998).

This criticism around the TPB model is additionally supported by the current understanding of attitude as a complex higher order construct that refers to the overall evaluation of behavior and that is the result of information obtained from cognitive but also affective, behavioral, and social influence processes (Ajzen, 2002; Bagozzi et al., 2001; Conner & Sparks, 2005; Hagger & Chatzisarantis, 2005). In this sense, there are suggestions for the extension of the model to include the presence of the affective and behavioral component of attitude in explaining the behavior (Conner & Sparks, 2005; Eagly & Chaiken, 1993). Thus, along with other variables pertinent to each specific behavior under study, two variables stand out in the literature as particularly relevant to the TPB model: emotions and previous behavior (Ajzen, 1991; Ajzen & Fishbein, 2005; Conner & Armitage, 1998; Conner & Sparks, 2005; Weber & Johnson, 2009). The inclusion of new variables is a possibility accepted and encouraged by the authors of TPB (Ajzen, 1991) and should occur when, after due theoretical support, there is empirical proof that, while controlling the effect of the components already considered in the model, their inclusion significantly adds to the explanation of the behavior (Ajzen, 1991; Conner & Armitage, 1998).

SOCIAL PSYCHOLOGY APPLIED TO CHILD PROTECTION: THE PSYCHOSOCIAL MODEL OF A RESIDENTIAL CARE PLACEMENT DECISION

When maltreatment takes place, a decision must be made about whether to keep the child in the family or move her to an out-of-home placement. That decision is complex, ambiguous, and marked by errors and uncertainty. The decision-making is even more difficult and uncertain for parental neglect cases, in which, although the long-term effects are detrimental (DePanfilis, 2006), the physical proofs are hard to obtain (Beckett, McKeigue, & Taylor, 2007; Dickens, 2007). Furthermore, this uncertain and ambiguous decision-making context makes child protection caseworkers more aware and fearful of institutional and social judgment, leading them to adopt self-defensive decisions and postpone intervention until a "catapult" event occurs (Dickens, 2007). Therefore, there is a need to fully understand the individual decision-making process and to do so while considering the role played by multiple factors of the decision-making ecology (Bauman et al., 2011) and based on theoretically designed and empirically tested models (Arad-Davidzon & Benbenishty, 2008).

Here, we present the main results of the empirical test of a residential care placement decision model that, based on a dual version of the TPB model, integrates those multiple psychosocial factors involved in the decision process (Rodrigues, 2012; Rodrigues et al., 2015).

Based on an online survey presenting a vignette of a 1-year-old neglected child (psychological and physical), caseworkers from different child and youth protection services in different regions of Portugal answered a questionnaire that operationalized the TPB variables plus risk assessment and emotional, experience and value-laden variables. A structural equation modeling analysis revealed that the caseworker's motivation (intention) to propose a residential care placement decision for a neglected child is highly explained by a positive evaluation of that behavior (Attitude), but also by significant others' approval of that behavior (Subjective Norm) and by how much relevance the worker attributes to the child's interests and protection (Value of Child; Figure 7.2). This model obtained an explained variance of 61%; it had good indexes of fit in terms of the ratio χ^2/df, comparative fit index (CFI), and standardized root mean square residual (RMR) value; and it was acceptable in terms of goodness of fit index (GFI), adjusted GFI (AGFI), and root mean square error of approximation (RMSEA) (Rodrigues et al., 2015).

Rational information processing was evident in the effect of caseworker's beliefs about consequences of residential care (e.g., "child protection," "parents' disregard for the child") and about the opinion of others from the professional context, personal networks, and broader social context. However, the effects

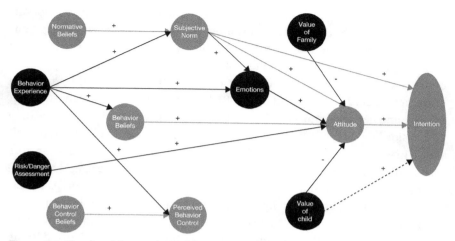

Figure 7.2 Results of the psychosocial process underlying the out-of-home placement in residential care decision-making for parental neglect.
--- Direct effects; — Mediation effects. Variables and arrows in gray correspond to the Theory of Planned Behavior (TPB) model; variables and arrows in black correspond to new variables and relations added to TPB' model.
Source: Adapted from Rodrigues et al. (2015).

of more value-laden, affective, and experiential variables, as well as behavior-specific variables, are also important.

The process differs for weighing the relative value to the child versus the value to the family and how each of those values relates to a caseworker's judgment and the level of conflict they bring. First, while the value of the family only has an indirect effect on intention, the value of the child has both a direct and an indirect effect (with opposite signs) on a caseworker's intention to propose the residential care placement of a neglected child. Second, unexpectedly, the conflict does not occur between the value of the child and the value of the family, as is usually thought (Besharov, 1985; Dickens, 2007; Goldstein et al., 1996), but rather within the value of the child; that is, there are two opposite forces at work in a caseworker's judgment related to a child's best interests (Rodrigues et al., 2015): one that favors residential care as an immediate response to parental neglect as a source of danger and thus avoiding/attenuating its developmental consequences on the child (DePanfilis, 2006), and another that focus on the pros and cons that a caseworker attributes to residential care as a social response (e.g., negative implications for the child; Johnson, Browne, & Hamilton-Giachritsis, 2006). Therefore, Rodrigues et al.'s (2015) study indicates the presence of a conflict in a caseworker's judgment and thus supports the presence of dilemmas and ambivalence that has been attributed to decision-making but, until now, without statistical confirmation (Beckett et al., 2007; Dickens, 2007).

The results of Rodrigues et al. (2015) also pointed out that positive emotions that the caseworker anticipates to experience following the decision (e.g., unconcerned; happy) are related to a favorable evaluation of that decision and with an intention to defend it. Thus, this result not only supports the presence of an emotional dimension within the decisional process in child protection (Summers et al., 2012; Taylor et al., 2008), but it also shows the specific effect of positive and negative emotions that are not immediately experienced at the time of decision-making, but that are anticipated to be experienced once the decision is made (Loewenstein, Weber, Hsee, & Welch, 2001). Regarding the factors that predict the caseworker's emotions, this study indicates the effects of socionormative and behavioral factors. That is, the feelings the caseworker anticipates experiencing are generally derived from past experience with this type of case and from the impact that social influence carries with the caseworker. One could think then that this result translates the idea, often discussed in the literature, that social pressure has a relevant impact on the caseworker and on his or her actions through fear that a wrong decision will cause recriminations and controversy at both organizational and social levels (Lachman & Bernard, 2006; Munro, 2005). A professional's experience in proposing the residential care placement of a neglected child positively affects caseworker's motivation to propose that decision through the mediation effect of the caseworker's positive evaluation about the implications of that social response. This result demonstrates that professional experience has an important role in decision-making in the child protection field (Davidson-Arad et al., 2003; Dickens, 2007), but it contradicts the idea that caseworkers with fewer years of experience are more likely to propose a residential care placement decision (Cash, 2001; Davidson-Arad et al., 2003; Munro, 1999; Schuerman et al., 1999).

Moreover, the results suggest that the effect of experience on a caseworker's evaluation and, in turn, on the intention to propose residential care, occurs through the effect of the caseworker's previous experience with the consequences of that social response to the child and through the feelings and emotions the caseworker experienced in the past after a residential care placement decision, as well as on the caseworker's previous perception about what people at work, family, and friends think of the residential care placement. This idea had already been hypothesized in the literature (Davidson-Arad et al., 2003; Dickens, 2007; Kanani et al., 2002; Lachman & Bernard, 2006; Munro, 2005), but only now has it received empirical support.

Concerning the role of risk assessment on a caseworker's decision, first, the effect of this variable not only confirms the application of legal and theoretical criteria on caseworker's judgment (Fallon et al., 2011), but it also shows that the level of risk/danger attributed to a neglect case was not consensual between participants and thus supports the complexity usually attributed to decision-making toward this type of maltreatment case (Beckett et al., 2007; Dickens, 2007). Second, it was demonstrated that, in decision-making concerning neglect cases, the risk assessment does not directly bear on the caseworker's intention to propose a residential care placement but is rather mediated by the caseworker's evaluation of that social response (i.e., attitude). Using Slovic et al.'s (Slovic, Peters, Finucane, & MacGregor, 2005) terms, the reaction of caseworkers to risk occurs more as an analysis and less as a kind of emotional reaction. More specifically, when the caseworker assesses the case as one of high risk/danger, the judgment involves the evaluation of residential care as a solution to the immediate protection of the child (Bullock, Little, & Millham, 1993; Kendrick, 2008) by keeping the child away from the danger source (i.e., parental neglect at home) and its impacts on the child's development (DePanfilis, 2006). When the case is considered as one of low risk/danger, the negative side of residential care placement—detrimental consequences to a child's physical, affective, and social development (Johnson et al., 2006)— becomes more prevalent in the caseworker's judgment.

CONCLUSION

This chapter made use of a social psychology theoretical model to empirically demonstrate the decision-making process in child protection and, more specifically, in residential care placement decisions.

Departing from the different cues highlighted in the extant literature, the first part of this chapter discussed the role played by individual factors that go beyond the largely studied child, family, and case characteristics as decision determinants (Davidson-Arad et al., 2003; Fialkov & Cohen, 1990; Zuravin & DePanfilis, 1997). The highlight here was on multiple professional factors that refer to individual but also contextual influences that are often understudied.

Based on a theoretical rational model from social psychology, applying the TPB theory (Ajzen,1985) to the residential care placement decision allows us to overcome the lack of theoretically designed and empirically tested models in child protection (Arad-Davidzon & Benbenishty, 2008). Furthermore, the test of the psychosocial model of the residential care placement decision empirically supported the complexity and effort involved in residential care placement decisions in the specific context of neglect cases (Beckett et al., 2007; Dickens, 2007). The complexity of residential care placement decisions was evident in the presence of multiple rational and intuitive factors involved in caseworkers' decisions (e.g., cognitive, emotional, value-laden, normative) and the presence of social processes affecting the emotional, attitudinal, and motivational components of caseworkers' judgments. The most striking result was the presence of values conflict in the decision-making process. These results not only sustain the view of decisions regarding neglect cases as effortful, but also bring attention to the implications that these varied forces and pressures might have in the caseworker's decisions. Moreover, it was possible to demonstrate that the caseworker is a preponderant factor in the decision-making process. This model can therefore be understood as a psychosocial "zoom lens" on the decision threshold involved in residential care placement (Baumann et al., 2011; Dalgleish, 1988). As the most elementary unit of the system, it is through the caseworker that all the problems, pressures, and ambiguities of the context are manifested. Judgment and decision-making in child protection involves understanding how the caseworker integrates and moderates the influences of multiple contexts and factors in determining his or her professional actions.

Without undermining these implications, some study limitations and unhypothesized effects must be accounted for; this in addition to other limitations related to sample and quality of measures discussed elsewhere (Rodrigues et al., 2015; e.g., the inability to prove the influence of external barriers [perceived behavior control] on the caseworker's psychosocial decision-making process).

Although acknowledging these limitations, the results of this study represent one further step in formulating empirical evidence that can have both practical and theoretical implications. In turn this contributes cues to a rethinking of the child protection system and future research in this field.

Therefore, it becomes urgent to develop training programs specifically focused on the multiple factors (e.g., social norms, emotions, cultural values, and personal and professional experience) influencing judgment and decision-making in child protection. Caseworkers should be made aware of those factors that may be unconsciously influencing their decisions and should be incited to examine themselves regarding the attitudes, values, and beliefs that sustain their assessments and decisions. Recognizing the factors and pressures involved might prevent biases and defensive practices (Besharov, 1985; Dickens, 2007; Kanani et al., 2002; Lachman & Bernard, 2006; Munro, 2005), as well as their consequences for the child (i.e., iatrogenic harm; Jones, 1991). To control the influence of individual attitudes, beliefs, and values, the decision-making process has to become increasingly more collective. To assure that those decisions are a product of different professional and personal perspectives, caseworkers must feel comfortable to express freely their opinions and concerns. The influence of others on caseworkers' decisions was quite evident in this study, thus pointing to the need to promote more democratic institutional and organizational work environments. Additionally, because social influence comes not only from close and direct relations with others (e.g., coworkers and superiors) but also from public opinion in general—namely through the media—it is important to promote a positive image of child protection services at the community level, which would increase the social recognition of state interventions in the family as a mechanism that intends to promote and protect child well-being and integrity. This could, in turn, promote a better understanding of child protection and decrease the level of social criticism that exists regarding child protection caseworkers (Dickens, 2007; Kanani et al., 2002; Lachman, & Bernard, 2006; Munro, 2005).

Other practical implication of this study should be to rethink some of the conflicts underlying decision-making in child protection because some of them may be fed by institutional and organizational issues like the quality of services/intervention provided at home and the quality of residential care. In this study, conflict in the decision-making process was related to the coexistence of an automatic response that considers residential care as the least detrimental alternative to immediately protect the child and a more weighted response that includes one's perceptions and knowledge of that social response and its long-term impacts on the child. The first response leads the caseworker to defend the residential care placement of the child, and the second leads to the opposite scenario. Therefore, it is important to ensure, at the institutional and political level, a redesign of child protection social responses in Portugal. The improvement in services and institutions (in residential care, foster care, and at-home interventions) could therefore prevent out-of-home placement, promote parents' rehabilitation and behavioral change, change the impact of the child protection system on children, and increase caseworkers' options when taking a decision. These improvements would likely change caseworkers' experiences regarding residential care placement, and that, as suggested by these results, could have an emotional and cognitive effect on caseworkers' future decisions. Also, group sessions for child protection caseworkers might be an opportunity to discuss and exchange experiences and perceptions, to deconstruct or resolve bad experiences, and also could promote a greater consistency of responses given to similar cases.

There is a need to promote this new perspective in the study of decision-making in child protection that not only considers the role of multiple determinant factors influencing decision-making, but also benefits from theoretical and empirical knowledge on key disciplines and on the more general decision-making topic. Additionally, further studies should focus on conflict that might explain ambivalence in residential care placement decisions and, more specifically, on the determinants, experiences, and conditions that induce conflict and ambivalence toward the decision. Furthermore, the psychological and mere quantitative approach of this work failed to assess the influence of political, legal, and organizational barriers to decision-making. Therefore, adding a qualitative approach and multilevel methods might be one way forward.

Finally, new studies are needed not only to prove the replicability of the model for abuse cases in other cultural and social policy contexts (cross-country) but also to test it with different target children (e.g., younger/older children), maltreatment cases (abuse), and other social responses (e.g., foster care).

REFERENCES

Ajzen, I. (1985). From intentions to actions: A theory of planned behavior. In J. Kuhi & J. Beckmann (Eds.), *Action control: From cognition to behavior* (pp. 11–39). Heidelberg: Springer.

Ajzen, I. (1991). The theory of planned behavior. *Organizational Behavior and Human Decision Processes, 50*, 179–211.

Ajzen, I. (2001). Nature and operation of attitudes. *Annual Review of Psychology, 52*, 27–58.

Ajzen, I. (2002). Perceived behavioral control, self-efficacy, locus of control, and the theory of planned behavior. *Journal of Applied Social Psychology, 32*, 665–683.

Ajzen, I., & Fishbein, M. (2005). The influence of attitudes on behavior. In D. Albarracin, T. J. Blair, & M. P. Zanna (Eds.), *The handbook of attitudes* (pp. 173–221). New Jersey: Lawrence Erlbaum Associates, Inc.

Almeida, A. N. (2009). *Para uma Sociologia da Infância—Jogos de Olhares, Pistas para a Investigação*. Lisboa: Imprensa de Ciências Sociais.

Almeida, A. N., Almeida, H., & André, I. M. (2002). Os maus tratos à criança na família. *Acta Médica Portuguesa, 15*(4), 257–267.

Arad-Davidzon, B., & Benbenishty. R. (2008). The role of workers' attitudes and parent and child wishes in child protection workers' assessments and recommendation regarding removal and reunification. *Children and Youth Services Review, 30*(1), 107–121.

Armitage, C. J., & Conner, M. (2001). Efficacy of the theory of planned behaviour: A meta-analytic review. *British Journal of Social Psychology, 40*, 471–499.

Atkinson, L., & Butler, S. (1996). Court-ordered assessment: The impact of parental compliance on clinical recommendations. *Child Abuse and Neglect, 20*, 185–190.

Azar, S. T., Benjet, C. L., Fuhrmann, G. S., & Cavallero, L. (1995). Child maltreatment and termination of parental rights: Can behavioral research help Solomon? *Behavior Therapy, 26*, 599-623.

Bagozzi, R. P., Lee, K-H., & Van Loo, M. F. (2001). Decisions to donate bone marrow: The role of attitudes and subjective norms across cultures. *Psychology and Health, 16*, 29–56.

Banach, M. (1998). The best interests of the child: Decision-making factors. *Families in Society, 79*(3), 331–340.

Baumann, D. J., Dalgleish, L., Fluke, J. D., & Kern, H. (2011). *The decision-making ecology*. Washington, DC: American Humane Association.

Baumann, D. J., Fluke, J. D., Dalgleish, L., & Kern, K. (2014). The decision making ecology. In A. Shlonsky & R. Benbenishty (Eds.), *From evidence to outcomes in child welfare: An international reader* (pp. 24–40). New York: Oxford University Press.

Beckett, C., & McKeigue, B. (2003). Children in limbo: Case where care proceedings have taken two years or more. *Adoption and Fostering, 27*, 31–40.

Beckett, C., McKeigue, B., & Taylor, H. (2007). Coming to conclusions: Social workers' perceptions of the decision-making process in care proceedings. *Child & Family Social Work, 12*(1), 54–63.

Bem, D. J. (1967). Self-perception: An alternative interpretation of cognitive dissonance phenomena. *Psychological Review, 74*, 183–200.

Ben-Arieh, A. (2010). Localities, social services and child abuse: The role of community characteristics in social services allocation and child abuse reporting. *Children and Youth Services Review, 32*(4), 536–543.

Ben-Arieh, A., & Haj-Yahia, M. M. (2006). The "geography" of child maltreatment in Israel: Findings from a national data set of cases reported to the social services. *Child Abuse and Neglect, 30*, 991–1003.

Benbenishty, R., Davidson-Arad, B., López, M., Devaney, J., Spratt, T.,…Hayes, D. (2015). Decision making in child protection: An international comparative study on maltreatment substantiation, risk assessment and interventions recommendations, and the role of professionals' child welfare attitudes. *Child Abuse and Neglect, 49*, 63–75. doi:10.1016/j.chiabu.2015.03.015

Besharov, D. J. (1985). Right vs. rights: The dilemma of child protection. *Public Welfare, 43*, 19–27.

Blumer, H. (1955). Attitudes and the social act. In H. Blumer (Ed.), *Symbolic interaction: Perspective and method* (pp. 90–100). Englewood Cliffs, NJ: Prentice Hall.

Bowlby, J. (1951). Maternal care and mental health. *World Health Organization Monograph Series* (No. 2).

Britner, P. A., & Mossler, D. G. (2002). Professionals' decision-making about out-of-home placements following instances of child abuse. *Child Abuse and Neglect, 26*, 317–332.

Bronstein, P., Duncan, P., D'Ari, A., Pieniadz, J., Fitzgerald, M., Abrams, C. L., . . . Oh Cha, S. (1996). Family and parenting behaviors predicting middle school adjustment: A longitudinal study. *Family Relations, 45*, 415–425.

Brooks-Gunn, J., & Furstenberg, F. F. (1986). The children of adolescent mothers: Physical, academic, and psychological outcomes. *Developmental Review, 6*, 224–251.

Brosig, C. L., & Kalichman, S. C. (1992). Child abuse reporting decisions: Effects of statutory wording of reporting requirements. *Professional Psychology: Research and Practice, 23*, 486–492.

Buchan, H. F. (2005). Ethical decision making in the public accounting profession: An extension of Ajzen's theory of planned behavior. *Journal of Business Ethics, 61*, 165–181.

Bullock, R., Little, M., & Millham, S. (1993). *Residential care for children: A review of the research.* London: HMSO.

Camasso, M. J., & Jagannathan, R. (1995). Prediction accuracy of the Washington and Illinois risk assessment instruments: An application of receiver operating characteristics curve analysis. *Social Work Research, 19*(3), 174–183.

Campbell, D. T. (1963). Social attitudes and other acquired behavioral dispositions. In S. Koch (Ed.), *Psychology: A study of a science, Vol. 6* (pp. 94–172). New York: McGraw-Hill.

Carugati, F., & Mugny, G. (1985). La théorie du conflit sociocognitif. In G. Mugny (Ed.), *Psychologie sociale du développement cognitif* (pp. 57–70). Berne: Peter Lang.

Cash, S. J. (2001). Risk assessment in child welfare: The art and science. *Children and Youth Services Review, 23*, 811–830.

Cicchetti, D., & Rizley, R. (1981). Developmental perspectives on the etiology, intergerational transmissions, and sequele of child maltreatment. *New Directions for Child Development, 11*, 31–55.

Conner, M., & Armitage, J. (1998). Extending the theory of planned behavior. *Journal of Applied Social Psychology, 28*, 1429–1464.

Conner, M., & Sparks, P. (2005). Theory of planned behaviour and health behaviour. In M. Conner & P. Sparks (Eds.), *Predicting health behaviour: Research and practice with social cognition models* (2nd ed.). (pp 170–222). Mainhead: Open University Press.

Dagleish, L., & Drew, E. (1989). The relationship of child abuse indicators to the assessment of perceived risk and the decision to separate. *Child Abuse and Neglect, 13*, 491–506.

Dalgleish, L. I. (1988). Decision-making in child abuse cases: Applications of social judgment theory and signal detection theory. In B. Brehmer & C. R. B. Joyce (Eds.), *Human judgment: The SJT view*. North Holland: Elsevier.

Davidson-Arad, B. (2009). Four perspectives on the quality of life of children at risk kept at home and removed from home in Israel. *British Journal of Social Work, 40*(6), 1719–1735. doi:10.1093/bjsw/bcp099

Davidson-Arad, B., Englechin-Segal, D., & Wozner, Y. (2003). Short-term follow-up of children at risk: Comparison of the quality of life of children removed from home and children remaining at home. *Child Abuse and Neglect, 27*, 733–750. doi:10.1016/S0145-2134(03)00113-3.

Davidson-Arad, B., Englechin-Segal, D., Wozner, Y., & Gabriel, R. (2003). Why social workers do not implement decisions to remove children at risk from home. *Child Abuse & Neglect, 27*(6), 687–697. doi:10.1016/S0145-2134(03)00106-6.

DePanfilis, D. (2006). *Child neglect: A guide for prevention, assessment, and intervention.* Washington, DC: US Department of Health and Human Services, Administration on Children and Families, Administration for Children, Youth, and Families, Children's Bureau, Office on Child Abuse and Neglect.

DePanfilis, D., & Girvin, H. (2005). Investigating child maltreatment in out-of-home care: Barriers to effective decision-making. *Children and Youth Services Review, 27*(4), 353–374. doi:10.1016/j.childyouth.2004.11.010

DePanfilis, D., & Zuravin, S. J. (1999). Predicting child maltreatment recurrences during treatment. *Child Abuse and Neglect, 23*(8), 729–743.

DePanfilis, D., & Zuravin, S. J. (2001). Assessing risk to determine the need for services. *Children and Youth Services Review, 23*(1), 3–20.

DePanfilis, D., & Zuravin, S. J. (2002). The effect of services on the recurrence of child maltreatment. *Child Abuse and Neglect, 26*(2), 187–205.

Deutscher, I. (1966). Words and deeds. *Social Problems, 13*, 235–254.

Dickens, J. (2007). Child neglect and the law: Catapults, thresholds and delay. *Child Abuse Review, 16*, 77–92.

Doueck, H. J., English, D. J., DePanfilis, D., & Moote, G. T. (1993). Decision-making in child protective services: A comparison of selected risk-assessment systems. *Child Welfare, 72*, 441–452.

Eagly, A. H., & Chaiken, S. (1993). *The psychology of attitudes*. Fort Worth, TX: Harcourt Brace Jovanovich College Publishers.

English, D. J., & Pecora, P. J. (1994). Risk assessment as a practice method in child protective services. *Child Welfare, 73*(5), 451–473.

Epstein, A. S. (1980). New insights into problems of adolescent parenthood. *Bulletin of High/Scope Educational Research Foundation, 5*, 6–8.

Fallon, B., Trocmé, N., & MacLaurin, B. (2011). Should child protection services respond differently to maltreatment, risk of maltreatment, and risk of harm? *Child Abuse and Neglect, 35*(4), 236-239. doi:10.1016/j.chiabu.2011.03.001

Fernandez, E. (1996). *Significant harm: Unravelling child protection decisions and subsequent care careers of children*. Avebury, UK: Ashgate Publishing.

Festinger, L. (1964). *Conflict, decision, and dissonance*. Stanford, CA: Stanford University Press.

Festinger, T. (1996). Going home and returning to foster care. *Children and Youth Services Review, 18*, 383–402.

Fialkov, M. J., & Cohen, E. (1990). The mental health professional, the legal process, and the child in out-of-home care. In P. V. Grabe (Ed.), *Adoption resources for mental health professionals* (pp. 189–202). New Brunswick, NJ: Transaction Publishers.

Fishbein, M. (1993). Introduction. In D. J. Terry, C. Gallois & M. McCamish (Eds.), *The theory of reasoned action: Its application to AIDS-preventive behaviour* (pp. xv–xxv). Oxford: Pergamon.

Fishbein, M., & Ajzen, I. (1975). *Belief, attitude, intention and behaviour: An introduction to theory and research*. Reading, MA: Addison-Wesley.

Fluke, J. D., Baumann, D. J., Dalgleish, L. I., & Kern, H. D. (2014). Decisions to protect children: A decision making ecology. In J. Korbin & R. Krugman (Eds.), *Handbook of child maltreatment. Contemporary Issues in Research and Policy, vol. 2*. Dordrecht: Springer.

Gambrill, E., & Shlonsky, A. (2000). Assessing risk in child maltreatment. Risk assessment in context. *Children and Youth Services Review, 22*(11/12), 813–837.

Gergen, K. J., Gloger-Tippelt, G., & Berkowitz, P. (1990). The cultural construction of the developing child. In G. R. Semin & K. J. Gergen (Eds.), *Everyday Understanding* (pp. 108–129). London: Sage.

Gold, N., Benbenishty, R., & Osmo, J. (2001). A comparative study of risk assessment and recommended interventions in Canada and Israel. *Child Abuse and Neglect, 25*(5), 607–622.

Goldstein, J., Freud, A., & Solnit, A. (1980). *Beyond the best interest of the child*. New York: Free Press.

Goldstein, J., Solnit, A., Goldstein, S., & Freud, A. (1996). *The best interest of the child*. New York: Free Press.

Goodnow, J. (1988). Parents' ideas, actions, and feelings: Models and methods from developmental and social psychology. *Child Development, 59*, 286–320.

Goodnow, J. J., & Collins, W. A. (1990). *Development according to parents: The nature, sources and consequences of parents' ideas*. Hove, UK: Lawrence Erlbaum.

Gray, J. (2002). National policy on the assessment of children in need and their families. In H. Ward & W. Rose (Eds.), *Approaches to needs assessment in children's services* (pp. 169–194). London: Jessica Kingsley.

Hagger, M. S., & Chatzisarantis, N. (2005). *The social psychology of exercise and sport.* Buckingham, UK: Open University Press.

Holland, S. (2001). Representing children in child protection assessments. *Childhood, 8*(3), 322–339. doi:10.1177/0907568201008003002.

Houston, S. (2003). Moral consciousness and decision-making in child and family social work. *Social Work, 27*(3), 61–70.

Humphreys, J., & Ramsey, A. (1993). Child abuse. In J. Campbell & J. Humphreys (Eds.), *Nursing care of survivors of family violence* (2nd ed.). St. Louis: Mosby.

Jagannathan, R., & Camasso, M. J. (1996). Risk assessment in child protective services: A canonical analysis of the case management function. *Child Abuse and Neglect, 20*, 599–612.

Johnson, R., Browne, K., & Hamilton-Giachritsis, C. (2006). Young children in institutional care at risk of harm. *Trauma, Violence, and Abuse, 7*(1), 34–60.

Jones, D. P. (1991). Professional and clinical challengers to protection of children. *Child Abuse and Neglect, 15*, 57–66.

Kanani, K., Regehr, C., & Bernstein, M. M. (2002). Liability considerations in child welfare: Lessons from Canada. *Child Abuse and Neglect, 26*, 1029–1043.

Kendrick, A. (Ed.). (2008). *Residential child care: Prospects and challenges.* Research Highlights Series. London: Jessica Kingsley.

Kenny, M. C. (2001). Child abuse reporting: Teachers' perceived deterrents. *Child Abuse and Neglect, 25*, 81–92.

Knight, A., & Oliver, C. (2007). Advocacy for disabled children and young people: Benefits and dilemmas. *Child & Family Social Work, 12*(4), 417–425. doi:10.1111/j.1365-2206.2007.00500.x

Lachman, P., & Bernard, C. (2006). Moving from blame to quality: How to respond to failures in child protective services. *Child Abuse and Neglect, 30*, 963–968.

LaPiere, R. T. (1934). Attitudes vs. actions. *Social Forces, 13*(2), 230–237

LeVine, R. A., Miller, P. M., Richman, A. L., & LeVine, S. (1996). Education and mother–infant interaction: A Mexican case study. In S. Harkness & C.M Super (Eds.), *Parents' cultural belief systems: Their origins, expressions, and consequences* (pp. 254–269). New York: Guilford.

Lindsey, D. (1994). *The welfare of children.* New York: Oxford University Press.

Little, M., Axford, N., & Morpeth, L. (2004). Risk and protection in the context of services for children in need. *Child and Family Social Work, 9*(1), 105–118.

Loewenstein, G., Weber, E. U., Hsee, C. K., & Welch, N. (2001). Risk as feelings. *Psychological Bulletin, 127*, 267–286.

Lyons, P., Doueck, H. J., & Wodarski, J. S. (1996). CPSrisk assessment: A review of the empirical literature on instrument performance. *Social Work Research, 20*, 143–155.

Mandel, D. R., Lehman, D. R., & Yuille, J. C. (1994). Should this child be removed from home? Hypothesis generation and information seeking as predictors of case decisions. *Child Abuse and Neglect, 18*, 1051–1062.

Mann, M. B., Pearl, P. T., & Behle, P. D. (2004). Effects of parent education on knowledge and attitudes. *Adolescence, 39*, 154, 355–360.

Marks, J., McDonald, T., & Bessey, W. (1989). *Risk factors assessed by instrument-based models.* Portland, ME: National Child Welfare Resource Center for Management and Administration.

Mech, E. (1970). Decision analysis in foster care practice. In H. D. Stone (Ed.). *Foster care in question* (pp. 26–51). New York: Child Welfare League of America.

Munro, E. (1998). *Understanding social work: An empirical approach.* London: Continuum Press.

Munro, E. (1999). Common errors of reasoning in child protection. *Child Abuse and Neglect, 23,* 745–758.

Munro, E. (2002). *Effective child protection.* London: Sage.

Munro, E. (2005). Improving practice: Child protection as a systems problem. *Children and Youth Services Review, 27,* 375–391.

Olson, J. M., & Zanna, M. P. (1993). Attitudes and attitude change. *Annual Review of Psychology, 44,* 117–154.

Parton, N (2009). From Seebohm to Think Family: Reflections on 40 years of policy change of statutory children's social work in England. *Child & Family Social Work, 14*(1), 68–78.

Parton, N. (2010). From dangerousness to risk: The growing importance of screening and surveillance systems for safeguarding and promoting the well-being of children in England. *Health, Risk & Society, 12*(1), 51–64.

Peters, D. F. (2001). Examining child sexual abuse evaluations: The types of information affecting expert judgment. *Child Abuse and Neglect, 25,* 149–178.

Portwood, S. G. (1998). The impact of individuals' characteristics and experiences on their definitions of child maltreatment. *Child Abuse and Neglect, 22,* 437–452.

Randall, D. M., & Gibson, A. M. (1991). Ethical decision making in the medical profession: An application of the theory of planned behavior. *Journal of Business Ethics, 10,* 111–122.

Reder, P., & Duncan, S. (2004). Making the most of the Victoria Climbié inquiry report. In N. Stanley & J. Manthorpe (Eds.), *The age of inquiry: Learning and blaming in health and social care.* London, Routledge.

Rodrigues, L. (2012). *The application of promotion and protection measures to at-risk-danger children: Psychosocial Context of Decision-Making* (Unpublished Doctoral diss., University Institute of Lisbon; ISCTE, Lisbon).

Rodrigues, L., Calheiros, M., & Pereira, C. (2015). The decision of out-of-home placement in residential care after parental neglect: Empirically testing a psychosocial model. *Child Abuse and Neglect, 49.* 35–49. doi:10.1016/j.chiabu.2015.03.14.

Rossi, P. H., Schuerman, J., & Budde, S. (1999). Understanding decisions about child maltreatment. *Evaluation Review, 23*(6), 579–98.

Runco, M. A., & Johnson, D. J. (2002). Parent's and teacher's implicit theories of children's creativity: A cross-cultural perspective. *Creativity Research Journal, 14*(3/4), 427–438.

Rzepnicki, T. L., & Johnson, P. R. (2005). Examining decision errors in child protection: A new application of root cause analysis. *Children and Youth Services Review, 27*(4), 393–407.

Schuerman, J., Rossi, P. H., & Budde, S. (1999). Decision on placement and family preservation. *Evaluation Review, 23*(6), 599–618.

Schwalbe, M. L. (1988). Role taking reconsidered: Linking competence and performance to social structure. *Journal for the Theory of Social Behaviour, 18,* 411–436.

Slovic, P., Peters, E., Finucane, M. L., & MacGregor, D. G. (2005). Affect, risk, and decision making. *Health Psychology, 24*(4), S35–S40.

Sullivan, C., Whitehead, P. C., Leschied, A. W., Chiodo, D., & Hurley, D. (2008). Perception of risk among child protection workers. *Children and Youth Services Review, 30*(7), 699–704.

Summers, A., Gatowski, S., & Dobbin, S. (2012.). Terminating parental rights : The relation of judicial experience and expectancy-related factors to risk perceptions in child protection cases. *Psychology, Crime and Law, 18*(1), 95–112.

Tamis-LeMonda, C. S., Shannon, J., & Spellmann, M. (2002). Low-income adolescent mothers' knowledge about domains of child development. *Infant Mental Health Journal, 23*, 88–103.

Taylor, H., Beckett, C., & McKeigue, B. (2008). Judgments of Solomon: Anxieties and defences of social workers involved in care proceedings. *Child and Family Social Work, 13*, 23–31.

Tetlock, P. E. (1986). Integrative complexity of policy reasoning. In S. Kraus & R. Perloff (Eds.), *Mass media and political thought* (pp. 267–289). Beverly Hills, CA: Sage.

Tilbury, C., & Osmond, J. (2006). Permanency planning in foster care: A research review and guidelines for practitioners. *Australian Social Work, 59*(3), 265–280.

Van der Pligt, J., & De Vries, N. K. (1998). Expectancy-value models of health behavior: The role of salience and anticipated affect. *Psychology and Health, 13*, 289–305.

Vandenplas-Holper, C. (1987). Les théories implicites du développement et de l'éducation. *European Journal of Psychology of Education, 2*, 17–39.

Watson, J. B. (1925). *Behaviorism*. New York: People's Institute Publishing Company.

Weber, E. U., & Johnson, E. J. (2009). Mindful judgment and decision-making. *Annual Review of Psychology, 60*, 53–85.

Wulczyn, F. (2004). Family reunification. *The Future of Children, 14*(1), 95–113.

Zellman, G. L. (1990). Child abuse reporting and failure to report among mandated reporters: Prevalence, incidence and reasons. *Journal of Interpersonal Violence, 5*(1), 3–22.

Zuravin, S. J., & DePanfilis, D. (1997). Factors affecting foster care placement of children receiving child protective services. *Social Work Research, 21*, 34–42.

8

The Decision to Substantiate Allegations of Child Maltreatment

SARAH A. FONT, KATHRYN MAGUIRE-JACK, AND REBECCA DILLARD ■

INTRODUCTION

The child protective services (CPS) system is charged with receiving and investigating suspected child maltreatment. Investigations are typically carried out within 30–60 days by a caseworker employed within a county CPS agency. At the conclusion of the investigation, the caseworker (often with supervisory input) makes a determination of whether maltreatment occurred; this decision is referred to as *substantiation*. In 2016, more than 3.4 million US children were investigated as possible victims of maltreatment; yet, for fewer than 700,000 children were the allegations substantiated (US Department of Health and Human Services, 2017). Similarly, the cumulative incidence of investigated maltreatment for US children is approximately 37.4% (Kim, Wildeman, Jonson-Reid, & Drake, 2017), but only 12.5% for substantiated maltreatment (Wildeman et al., 2014). These values highlight that the vast majority of investigated allegations of maltreatment are concluded by the investigating caseworkers to be false or unverifiable due to insufficient evidence. The low rate of substantiated allegations has raised the question of whether the decision to substantiate is a meaningful or objective characterization of the facts of a case: answering this question is critical to ensure that families are treated fairly and in

Sarah A. Font, Kathryn Maguire-Jack, and Rebecca Dillard, *The Decision to Substantiate Allegations of Child Maltreatment* In: *Decision-Making and Judgment in Child Welfare and Protection.* Edited by: John D. Fluke, Mónica López López, Rami Benbenishty, Erik J. Knorth, and Donald J. Baumann, Oxford University Press (2021). © Oxford University Press. DOI: 10.1093/oso/9780190059538.003.0008.

accordance with their needs and to inform the use of substantiated allegations as a measure of maltreatment in research.

In this chapter, we first explain why the substantiation decision warrants empirical inquiry. We then review two bodies of research that provide insight into the meaning and utility of substantiation: one examines whether substantiation differentiates subsequent child and family trajectories and the other examines how factors unrelated to the veracity of allegations influences the substantiation decision. Third, we describe the variability in substantiation rates (per investigated child) across the United States and over time. Fourth, we examine case, caseworker, agency, and county characteristics associated with the decision to substantiate in a national sample of CPS investigations. Last, we discuss new directions in how substantiation is used and potential further reforms.

WHY SUBSTANTIATION MATTERS

A clear understanding of the decision to substantiate is important for several reasons. First, substantiation is closely linked with the probability of receiving post-investigative services. The following statistics, from the *Child Maltreatment 2016* report (US Department of Health and Human Services, 2017), illustrate this point. Nationally, it is reported that 61% of children whose cases were substantiated received services versus 30% of children with unsubstantiated allegations. Yet, in many states, the differences are much starker: in at least 18 states, the rate of service provision among those with substantiated allegations was at least five times higher than the rate among those with unsubstantiated allegations. Moreover, whereas about 22% of children with substantiated allegations are placed in out-of-home care, only 2% of children with unsubstantial allegations are placed. Whether intervention constitutes a positive (children are protected and families receive help for maltreatment-related risks) or a negative (the state separates families or coerces families into complying with unwanted services) is beyond the scope of this chapter. Nevertheless, the decision to substantiate is highly predictive of the probability of receiving an intervention and the intensity of that intervention. Of course, the temporal ordering is ambiguous: although substantiation may inform subsequent decisions about the need and scope of intervention, it is equally possible that substantiation (or unsubstantiation) is used to justify a decision to intervene (or not intervene).

In addition to the importance of substantiation as a pathway to (or perhaps pretext for) providing services to investigated families, substantiation can also carry penalties. The majority of states, in policy or regulation, uses central registries to track individuals who are substantiated as perpetrators of child maltreatment (Child Welfare Information Gateway, 2014). The ability to track perpetrators is important for child safety; it allows caseworkers to evaluate allegations as part of a potential pattern of behavior. Tracking data on the risks and needs of families who have perpetrated maltreatment can inform the creation and implementation of preventive services. Tracking perpetrators also aids system reform by allowing for research to evaluate the effects of CPS interventions or services on recidivism. However, it can also hold significant long-term consequences in ways akin to criminal records. Although CPS records are granted a higher degree of confidentiality than criminal justice records under federal law, at least 32 states and the District of Columbia permit certain employers to check whether prospective employees have been substantiated as perpetrators of maltreatment (Child Welfare Information Gateway, 2017). Consequently, the decision to substantiate can have meaningful and long-term impacts on the accused perpetrators. This is largely, though not entirely, limited to persons applying for positions that involve regular access to children, such as work at daycare facilities, schools, or healthcare agencies, or to persons applying to foster or adopt children.

Last, many research studies of causes or effects of maltreatment rely on substantiated maltreatment or similar case-level determinations as their primary outcome or explanatory measure (Mersky & Reynolds, 2007; Noll & Shenk, 2013; Palusci, 2011; Sidebotham, Golding, & Team, 2001; Widom, Czaja, Bentley, & Johnson, 2012), and the number of substantiated victims of child maltreatment is often cited as a measure of maltreatment incidence. The use of CPS involvement to identify maltreatment is, by definition, limited to cases that are reported to authorities. Differences across groups or populations in the probability of CPS involvement, conditional on maltreatment having occurred, can introduce bias to estimates of the effects of maltreatment. The use of a substantiated CPS report to measure maltreatment introduces an additional layer of complexity in that substantiation determinations are made by caseworkers whose decisions are difficult to evaluate because such evaluations rely on the information presented by the decision-makers themselves (Prottas, 1978). If substantiation is a poor indicator of the presence of maltreatment, then much of what research shows about the incidence, causes, and consequences of maltreatment may be affected by opaque (or even biased) decision-making processes.

IS SUBSTANTIATION A VALID INDICATOR OF MALTREATMENT?

Whereas studies of maltreatment effects often compare children with substantiated maltreatment to the general child population, efforts to determine whether substantiation is a valid or meaningful indicator of maltreatment have focused on comparisons between children or families with substantiated and unsubstantiated investigations. First, several studies have examined whether substantiated and unsubstantiated cases differ in terms of recidivism—the premise here being that families who have perpetrated maltreatment should be more likely to perpetrate maltreatment in the future than those who have not perpetrated maltreatment, and, if substantiation is a valid indicator, then substantiated families should have higher rates of future CPS involvement than unsubstantiated cases. These studies have found that rates of recidivism did not significantly differ for those who were substantiated versus unsubstantiated during their initial CPS contact (Kohl, Jonson-Reid, & Drake, 2009) with unsubstantiated cases often having similar levels of recidivism risk as substantiated cases (Drake, Jonson-Reid, Way, & Chung, 2003). Importantly, this body of work does not inform the meaningfulness of substantiation if it is the case that substantiation leads to services that effectively reduce risk. In other words, although it is clear that families with unsubstantiated cases are re-reported with subsequent unsubstantiated and substantiated allegations at high rates (Jedwab et al., 2015), it is possible that the rates of recurrent involvement among substantiated cases would have been higher if not for substantiation itself.

Second, researchers have examined whether substantiated and unsubstantiated cases differ in terms of children's future well-being. The premise of such studies is thus: if it is true that maltreatment is harmful to children and that substantiation is a valid way to distinguish those who were maltreated from those who were not, then children with substantiated cases should be at higher risk for negative life outcomes than children with unsubstantiated cases. Findings from these studies have not consistently supported this premise. Multiple studies have found no differences in the effects of substantiated versus unsubstantiated maltreatment on measures of later academic and behavioral problems, with both groups experiencing elevated rates of developmental concerns (Fantuzzo, Perlman, & Dobbins, 2011; Hussey et al., 2005). Both substantiated and unsubstantiated youth who have come into contact with CPS have exhibited lowered levels of school readiness, though substantiated youth experienced additional social and emotional development problems above and beyond the diminished school readiness outcomes (Bell, Bayliss, Glauert, & Ohan, 2018). Delinquency is a notable negative outcome associated with maltreatment history. Similar delinquency subtypes have emerged across substantiated and unsubstantiated youth, with unsubstantiated youth having a higher likelihood of stealing and shoplifting behaviors or attacking someone with a weapon, whereas substantiated youth are at greater risk for carrying hidden weapons (Snyder & Smith, 2015). Substantiated youth had slightly more severe delinquency group proportions compared with unsubstantiated youth (Snyder & Smith, 2015), and relative risk for juvenile arrest is higher among substantiated youth compared with unsubstantiated youth who have similar maltreatment allegations (Chiu, Ryan, & Herz, 2011). The evidence suggests that contact with CPS puts children at greater risk for negative outcomes regardless of their substantiation status, but whether substantiation is associated with worse outcomes is inconclusive. Again, however, these studies do not directly address the potential for substantiation (through the provision of services, monitoring, or other interventions) to directly reduce risk.

Last, a large body of work has focused on factors that are predictive of the substantiation decision and, in particular, whether factors unrelated to the veracity of allegations are significantly correlated with substantiation. Official child maltreatment occurrences lie at the intersection of both a behavior by a caregiver and the decision of a CPS caseworker or supervisor. CPS workers are tasked with making difficult decisions with limited time, resources, and information. These decisions are "high stakes": decision-making errors that avoid intervention can expose vulnerable children to additional harm, whereas decision-making that errs consistently in favor of intervening can unnecessarily intrude on families' lives and inefficiently target scarce public funding.

This research typically draws on the Decision-Making Ecology (DME) framework (Baumann, Dalgleish, Fluke, & Kern, 2011). The DME framework consists of three separate components: the factors that influence decisions, the decision-making process itself, and the outcomes of the decision. The model stipulates that there are multiple influences for CPS decisions, including factors related to the individual case, the specific CPS agency (their policies and procedures, time and resource constraints, caseload size, and organizational culture), the CPS caseworker (education, background, personal experiences, and attitudes), and external forces (laws, public attitudes, community norms, and resources) (Baumann et al., 2011). In the DME framework, all these factors influence decision-making, both by informing the range of possible decisions to be made and through the psychological process of decision-making (Baumann et al., 2011; Fluke, Baumann, Dalgleish, & Kern, 2014). Despite the fact that the standard of evidence required for substantiation is set at the state level, it is posited that individual CPS workers apply individualized thresholds for determining substantiation, in part because they may weight evidence differently (Dalgleish, 1988). Caseworkers' thresholds for substantiation may change over time in response to different influences, such as a policy that specifies an age requirement for cases that must be accepted (organizational factor) or the experience level of the worker (Baumann et al., 2011; Fluke et al., 2014). In this chapter, we review some of the many potential influences on decision-making.

Child Protective Service Agency Characteristics

Organizational factors refer to characteristics of an overseeing child welfare agency, such as structure, culture, hierarchy, and policies. These factors exert influence over the decision-making process for caseworkers by constraining their options, setting expectations, and providing oversight of their decisions. An example of an organizational policy that may influence decision-making is the standard of proof for maltreatment substantiation that is set at the state level. Most states use a preponderance standard (roughly interpreted as *more likely than not*), but a few states use lower standards and one state (Kansas) currently uses a higher standard. Higher standards of proof are associated with lower rates of substantiation and provision of services (Kahn, Gupta-Kagan, & Hansen, 2017). In addition, CPS agencies that have implemented differential response programs (which often do not require a decision to be made about whether maltreatment occurred) have lower investigation and substantiation rates compared with counties without differential response programming (Janczewski, 2015).

For several decades, states and counties have experienced lawsuits pertaining to the actions or inactions of their CPS systems (Child Welfare League of America, 2005). These lawsuits often result in consent decrees, under which states or counties are monitored by the courts to ensure compliance with specific reforms. These lawsuits and consequent consent decrees generally emerge from well-publicized tragedies, such as a child's death, which contributes to a culture of fear of liability (Gluck Mezey, 1998; Smith & Donovan, 2003). Hence, workers in agencies who are under a consent decree may be more likely to substantiate maltreatment: fear of liability may lead to lower thresholds for substantiation in an attempt to eliminate the possibility of a false negative (not intervening when intervention is necessary) (Camasso & Jagannathan, 2013; Fluke et al., 2014).

Time. Through the federal Child and Family Services Review, CPS agencies are required to meet a number of benchmarks related to the timing of individual cases. These include timelines for assessments, termination of parental rights, reunification, and adoption. However, federal standards still allow for flexibility to set shorter or longer timelines for the conclusion of an investigation. Additional time to gather information may lead to more substantiations, but the evidence is unclear (Child Welfare Information Gateway, 2003).

Service accessibility. Caseworkers must rely on existing community structures to provide needed services to clients. The presence of high-quality, voluntary services in the community may prevent the need for removal or ongoing case monitoring. Maguire-Jack and Byers (2013) found that having maltreatment prevention services within the county may influence CPS workers' decisions to substantiate maltreatment and provide ongoing services, with some workers providing more services when community services were not available and others being more likely to substantiate services when families would not voluntary take up community services. However, caseworkers face many barriers to aiding clients, with service availability and accessibility limited, and even when services are available, agencies may lack the funding to pay for needed services or the staffing needed to provide adequate attention to each case (Geen & Tumlin, 1999).

Decision-making tools. Despite the proliferation of decision-making tools for CPS in recent decades, there remains a great deal of subjectivity in maltreatment screening, investigation, and substantiation decisions (DePanfilis & Girvin, 2005; Wells, Lyons, Doueck, Brown, & Thomas, 2004). CPS workers and supervisors must make a maltreatment determination based on the limited information they are able to gather during the investigation process, using statutory definitions of maltreatment that may be vague and overarching. Often, structured decision-making and other standardized assessment tools have been used in an effort to reduce errors and improve consistency in decision-making, but there is limited evidence to suggest that such efforts are successful. An ethnographic study suggests that caseworkers do not use the tools to inform their decisions to the extent intended and that the tools undermine development of critical assessment skills (Gillingham & Humphreys, 2010).

County Characteristics

CPS agencies are typically organized at the county level; hence, characteristics of the county population may affect the decision-making context. Although several studies have examined linkages between neighborhood or local context and child maltreatment (Maguire-Jack, 2014), the effects of county context on the decision to substantiate are potentially quite different. For example, whereas local poverty rates are associated with an increased risk of maltreatment in the general population, these rates could reduce the risk of substantiation by raising the threshold for intervention. In other words, counties with a high prevalence of risk factors for maltreatment may strain the capacities of CPS agencies and thus reduce the proportion of families for whom substantiation (and/or additional intervention) is deemed necessary. Few prior studies that have examined individual-level decision-making have also considered the county context. However, a multilevel study using county as the geographic unit of interest found that the availability of maltreatment prevention services was associated with substantiations, but the study did not find support for an association between county-level disadvantage or residential instability and substantiations (Maguire-Jack, 2014).

State overhead spending is another example of a recently examined macro factor. McLaughlin and Jonson-Reid (2017) found that when states decreased spending on child welfare, the proportion of cases that are substantiated likewise decreases. Funding can be a source of pressure exerted, and its impacts can be seen in the context of decision-making. Even factors at a national level may have an effect on caseworker-level decision-making. Variance in decision-making can be impacted by the institutional structure of child welfare, conceptualizations of risk and abuse, definitions of evidence, and handlings of poverty at the national level (Keddell, 2014). Similarly, international contexts cannot be discounted. One study examining child welfare settings across different countries found that nation-level factors influenced worker perceptions of institutional support, turnaround times for decision-making, and confidence in decisions (Berrick, Dickens, Pösö, & Skivenes, 2016). Recent literature indicates that factors at all of these levels of the decision-making ecology—as well as the interaction between factors at different levels—can be helpful in explaining variability in child welfare decision-making.

Caseworker Characteristics

Assignment of cases to caseworkers generally occurs on a rotation and thus is generally not a function of the family's characteristics. Hence, the probability of a given outcome would be approximately equal across caseworkers (within a given agency) if there were no unmeasured tendencies of caseworkers themselves. Yet it is generally understood that caseworkers' decision-making falls on a spectrum, with some caseworkers having a higher or lower propensity for intervening (Child Welfare Information Gateway, 2003; Doyle, 2007). The characteristics of caseworkers that inform their decision-making have only been examined in a few studies that suggest that caseworkers with more experience, higher self-perceived skills, and supportive coworker relationships substantiate less, whereas the role of workload and other factors are less clearly elucidated (Child Welfare Information Gateway, 2003). Large caseloads may impede caseworkers from meeting time requirements for case disposition and thereby result in "tunnel vision," in which the worker considers only a narrow range of options to save time and effort (Munro, 2008).

Studies investigating decisions other than substantiation may also be informative. Some research indicates that workers who have been employed by child welfare longer were more oriented toward family preservation efforts, whereas newer caseworkers were more likely to exhibit a child safety orientation (Fluke,

Corwin, Hollinshead, & Maher, 2016). Effects of caseworker education on various case outcomes has been the focus of several studies, with mixed results (Dhooper, Royse, & Wolfe, 1990; Perry, 2006a, 2006b; Ryan, Garnier, Zyphur, & Zhai, 2006). However, higher caseworker education may increase the risk of substantiation by producing more observant caseworkers who are better able to collect information.

Child and Family Characteristics

Most studies using substantiated maltreatment as an outcome are focused on the prediction of maltreatment and typically do not use unsubstantiated maltreatment as the counterfactual condition. As with county characteristics, child and family factors that are associated with the risk of substantiated maltreatment generally may not differentiate substantiated and unsubstantiated maltreatment investigations. Of work that has focused specifically on the decision to substantiate among investigated cases, it has been found that prior incidence of maltreatment, substance abuse, domestic violence, and mental illness are associated with substantiation (Child Welfare Information Gateway, 2003; Freisthler, Kepple, Wolf, Curry, & Gregoire, 2017; Victor, Grogan-Kaylor, Ryan, Perron, & Gilbert, 2018). These factors are typically identified by CPS workers in risk assessments completed during an investigation. One child characteristic that appears to be important is child age, with young children (0–2) and teenagers at higher risk for substantiation than other age groups (Child Welfare Information Gateway, 2003). The decision to substantiate cases of maltreatment is also influenced by factors related to caregiver risk. Parents who were unwilling to cooperate, reports for older children in the family, and the presence of emotional or mental health concerns for the child in question also influence substantiation (Stoddart, Fallon, Trocmé, & Fluke, 2018).

Decades of research documents racial and ethnic disproportionality in the child welfare system, but the evidence about whether race affects the decision to substantiate an investigation is far more controversial. Some studies have found no association between race and substantiation (Font, Berger, & Slack, 2012) and others found that black children are more likely to have their cases substantiated (Dettlaff et al., 2011). One literature review culminated in the development of a flexible conceptual framework that takes into consideration many of the previously discussed factors that influence decision-making (e.g., organizational structure, biased and inconsistent decision thresholds, individual factors, community characteristics, etc.) and may place African American children and families at increased risk for disproportional representation in the child welfare system (Boyd, 2014). Importantly, researchers have highlighted that a large degree (though not all) of the differences in national substantiation rates by race are attributable to geographic differences in where black and white children live and the practices of those counties. In other words, there is far less evidence of racial disparities within counties than in aggregated state or national data (Ards, Myers, Malkis, Sugrue, & Zhou, 2003; Krase, 2015; Maguire-Jack, Font, & Dillard, 2018). Studies of disparities for Native American and Hispanic populations are less common due to the geographic clustering of these populations and, in the case of Native American children, their comparatively small population numbers. However, existing data indicate overrepresentation among substantiated investigations for Native American and Hispanic children (Maguire-Jack et al., 2018).

VARIATION IN SUBSTANTIATION DECISIONS ACROSS THE UNITED STATES

Using an extended version of the National Child Abuse and Neglect Data System (NCANDS) provided by the National Data Archive on Child Abuse and Neglect (NDACAN), we plotted the substantiation rate for 2013–2015 by county. We used a broad definition of substantiation that, in addition to traditional substantiation determinations, includes cases that are listed as indicated or an alternative response victim determination (both designations are only used in a handful of states). By aggregating multiple years of data, we reduce the risk of calculating outlier values in counties with very few annual investigations. The map of these values is shown in Figure 8.1. Unsurprisingly,

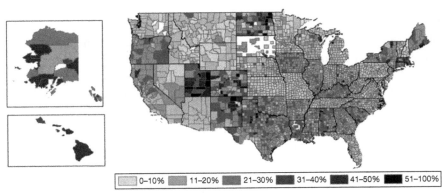

Figure 8.1 Substantiation rates by county, 2013–2015. Data based on data from the National Child Abuse and Neglect Data System, provided by the National Data Archives on Child Abuse and Neglect. Substantiation rates include reports investigated in 2013 through 2015 and include alternative response victim determinations, indicated reports, and traditional substantiations. White space indicates data not available.

there is substantial variability across states, which may reflect any number of factors, including differences in the standards of evidence for substantiation, use of alternative response programs, how reports are screened for investigation, or statutory definitions of maltreatment. Differences within states are less easily explained, but screening of calls for investigation still occurs at the county level in many states, which may play an important—though not well-understood—role. Notably, overall substantiation rates are low: nearly half of counties substantiate 20% or less of their investigations, and a substantive majority of counties substantiate 30% or less.

FACTORS ASSOCIATED WITH SUBSTANTIATION IN A NATIONAL SAMPLE

Data from the second cohort of the National Survey of Child and Adolescent Well-Being (NSCAW II) were used to examine predictors of substantiation at the case, caseworker, agency, and county levels. NSCAW II, when weighted, comprises a nationally representative sample of CPS investigations. Data for the baseline survey (Wave 1) of NSCAW II began in 2008 and 2009 and included 5,873 investigations that were closed with a 15-month period (for a more in-depth overview of the sample design, refer to Dolan, Smith, Casanueva, & Ringeisen, 2011). These investigations were located throughout 88 agencies in 83 counties. Although follow-up interviews were conducted, this study used data from Wave 1 because that was when substantiation consequent to the index investigation was measured. We made no exclusions to the original sample. Missing data were multiply imputed using chained equations. Due to multiple levels of measurement, individual level data were imputed separately from agency level data, and these sets were merged post-imputation (Gelman & Hill, 2007).

Measures

The outcome, substantiation, was a dichotomous indicator with 1 indicating yes and 0 otherwise. Three groups of independent variables were included: agency-level variables, county characteristics, and child and family factors. Agency-level variables included three time-related measures, five service accessibility measures, and three decision-making measures. All agency-level variables were reported by the local agency director.

Time. The length of time allotted for investigations was measured as 0 = 30 days and 1 = more than 30 days. The time allotted between removal and an initial court hearing was measure as 0 = 3 or fewer days, 1 = more than three days. Increased workload was equal to 1 if the agency reported any increase in the number of cases over the past 12 months relative to prior years. Together these three items approximated whether caseworkers have adequate time to thoroughly investigate each case.

Service accessibility. Variables in this group included service availability, collaboration, services for unsubstantiated cases, presence of a system of care, and funding cuts. A scale of 17 items was used to approximate service availability (indicating whether specific types of services are present in the area, such as domestic violence or transportation services), and a scale of six items was used to approximate how much agencies collaborate with other social institutions (e.g., "What types of collaborations does your agency have with family courts?"). Both scales were created based on the average across included items. Service availability was intended to capture the breadth of services that are offered in the area; whereas collaboration focused on the degree of cooperation between the CPS agency and other relevant institutions like schools, law enforcement, and courts. Services for unsubstantiated cases were measured with a single dichotomous item indicating whether services are able to be offered when an investigation is unsubstantiated. The fourth item was a dichotomous indicator of whether the agency director reported that there was a system of care in the community in which the agency was set. Last, there was an indicator equal to 1 if the agency lost more than one-quarter of its funding in the past 12 months and 0 otherwise.

Decision-making. The third set of agency factors was decision-making constraints. Specifically, we included two dichotomous measures—whether the agency (1) operated under a consent decree and (2) used a structured decision-making model—as well as a count measure of the number of standardized assessment tools an agency used during investigations.

County characteristics. We included five county factors. First, a measure of logged county population (in 2008) was used to assess population density. Second, to identify disadvantaged communities, we included measures of child poverty (the percent of children falling under the federal poverty line) and crime (arrest rate per 100,000), both dichotomized as equal to 1 if the community falls in the top quintile of the distribution. These were dichotomized due to a non-normal distribution of values. Finally, ethnic heterogeneity was measured using two variables: percent of the county population that was black and percent that was Hispanic.

Caseworker characteristics. We considered four caseworker variables. Education was measured with two indicators: whether the caseworker has (1) a social work degree or (2) an advanced degree (i.e., masters or higher). Years of experience in child welfare was measured as a discrete count, and workload was equal to caseworkers' report of the average number of new investigations per months over the past 3 months.

Family risk factors and child demographics. Family risk factors were five dichotomous indicators as assessed by the caseworker at the time of the investigation: history of CPS involvement, mental health or substance abuse problems, domestic violence, poor parenting skills, economic hardship, and child safety/special needs. Child demographics were age (years) and race (black, Hispanic, or other race: reference white).

Analytic Approach

We used hierarchical linear modeling (HLM) to estimate the associations of agency, county, child, and family characteristics with substantiation. HLM is the approach of choice with nested data; in this case, investigations (level 1) were nested within agencies and counties (level 2). Notably, NSCAW II sampled primarily one agency per county (81 of the 83 counties were represented by a single agency). Thus, we considered agency and county to occur at the same level of estimation, although in reality some counties have multiple agencies. Similarly, despite instances where there were multiple cases assigned to a single caseworker, there were more than 5,000 caseworkers sampled in Wave 1 (Dolan et al., 2011) indicating that very few cases involved the same caseworker. Thus, caseworker variables were considered as level 1 variables. HLM assumes that the level 2 units have their own intercept; meaning that, net of all other characteristics, the probability of substantiation will differ by agency and county.

The model was weighted using multilevel weights (separate weights for the agency and case levels) that were provided to us by the parties responsible for the NSCAW study at our request. The weighted sample constitutes a nationally representative sample of investigations; weights adjust for factors such as the oversampling of infants and children/families receiving services and nonresponse. This analysis was conducted in Stata Version 13, using the mixed-effects model commands for multiply imputed data. Last, given our use of multiply imputed data, which results in larger standard errors, we note coefficients at significance levels up to .10. Although we are less confident in estimates with p values between .05 and .10, we consider these results to be marginally significant and believe they warrant additional examination. Given our relatively large sample, particularly of level 2 units, we do not believe statistical power is substantially hindering our analyses. (Note: A more complete set of models can be found in the original article from which this chapter was derived [Font & Maguire-Jack, 2015].)

Results

Approximately 25% of cases were substantiated in our sample. Results of our HLM estimates predicting substantiation are found in Table 8.1. We found no

Table 8.1 REGRESSION OF SUBSTANTIATION ON AGENCY, COUNTY, CASEWORKER AND CASE CHARACTERISTICS

	B	SE
TIME CONSTRAINTS		
Allows more than 30 days to complete investigation	.069	.073
Allows 3+ between removal and initial hearing	−.018	.045
Increase in agency workload	−.001	.050
SERVICE ACCESSIBILITY CONSTRAINTS		
Collaboration with other social institutions	−.155**	.050
Can provide services for unsubstantiated cases	−.199*	.078
Service availability	.093	.079
Community has system of care	−.005	.092
Agency lost 25% or more of funding in last 12 months	.158	.132
DECISION-MAKING CONSTRAINTS		
Consent decree	.138	.086
Structural decision-making model	−.200**	.064
Number standardized assessments used	.021+	.012
COUNTY CHARACTERISTICS		
% of county black 2008	.002	.002
% of county Hispanic 2008	−.007*	.003
County population 2008	.003	.031
High arrest rate	−.033	.090
High poverty rate	−.044	.052
CASEWORKER CHARACTERISTICS		
Social work degree	−.002	.030
Advanced degree	.056*	.023
Years of experience	.001	.002
Average number of new investigations—Past 3M	−.000	.001
FAMILY RISK FACTORS		
CPS history	−.003	.019
Caregiver mental health/substance abuse problems	.227***	.035
Domestic violence	.195***	.041
Poor parenting skills	.186***	.040
Economic hardship	.055	.053
Child safety/Child has special needs	.101***	.022

Table 8.1 CONTINUED

	B	SE
CHILD DEMOGRAPHICS		
Black	.029	.026
Hispanic	.047	.037
Other race	.015	.037
Age	-.000	.002

NOTES: Models estimated using multilevel sampling weights. Cases = 5,872. Agencies = 85. Counties = 83.
+ p<.10 * p<.05 ** p<.01 *** p<.001.

statistically significant associations between time factors and substantiation. However, for service availability, we found that two factors—collaboration and ability to provide services for unsubstantiated cases—were associated with a significantly lower probability of substantiation even after controlling for county, family and child characteristics. These factors predicted a 16 (collaboration) and 20 (services for unsubstantiated cases) percentage point (PP) lower probability of substantiation. For decision-making factors, use of a structural decision-making model predicted a large decrease in the probability of substantiation, whereas each additional standardized assessment used predicted a (marginally significant) 2.1 PP increase in the probability of substantiation. Agency under a consent decree was not a statistically significant predictor. Joint significance tests confirmed that decision-making and service accessibility factors were both important sets of predictors for substantiation. One county characteristic was associated with substantiation risk: a 1% increase in the proportion of Hispanic residents predicted a 0.7 PP decrease in the probability of substantiation.

Caseworker factors were largely insignificant, with the exception of advanced degree, which predicted a 5.6 PP increase in substantiation. Family risk factors were the strongest predictors of substantiation, with all risk factors except economic problems and CPS history predicting increased probability of substantiation. Neither child age nor child race predicted substantiation.

DISCUSSION

The decision to substantiate an allegation of child maltreatment can inform the services and interventions families receive and whether those interventions are voluntary or court-ordered. It can also determine whether the records of those cases are expunged or maintained in databases that are used to screen for certain forms of employment. Outside of potential effects of the substantiation decision on vulnerable children and families, the use of substantiation as a research metric means that decision-making practices also influence how researchers estimate the incidence and prevalence of maltreatment and measure its effects. In turn, this research may be used to inform government funding levels, targeted programs, and other decisions that can also affect vulnerable children.

This chapter highlights potential problems with the use of substantiation, including substantial geographic variability in the probability that an investigation is substantiated, and the seeming influence of agency and county factors on decision-making. The extent to which substantiation may be conditional on which side of a county line one lives suggests that reliance on substantiated maltreatment to screen prospective employees or foster and adoptive parents may inappropriately disqualify candidates while also failing to keep children safe from maltreating adults. Little research has examined the role of central registries either in restricting adults' employment options or in improving child safety: given the concerns raised by prior work and highlights in this chapter, such studies are long overdue.

Increasingly, states and counties are turning to predictive analytics to address concerns about erroneous decision-making. A recent literature review concluded that use of predictive risk modeling technologies with current child welfare data can improve caseworker decision-making by supplementing current assessment approaches (Cuccaro-Alamin, Foust, Vaithianathan, & Putnam-Hornstein, 2017). Though beyond the scope of this chapter, we note that scholars have also raised concerns about the ethics of predictive analytics and their potential to perpetuate human biases (for further information, see Capatosto, 2017). We raise another concern: namely, that these models largely predict risk of future harm. Thus, while predictive analytics models are adept at identifying families in need of services or intervention, they cannot compose an evidentiary basis for determining whether maltreatment allegations are true. Through the use of alternative response and similar programs that avoid the use of substantiation altogether, some states have moved toward decoupling substantiation and services receipt. Predictive analytics can be used to identify which families need to be assessed for risk and to whom services should be offered. In combination with a complete separation of the decision to provide services from the decision to substantiate, this may eliminate the influence of certain factors, like resources or service availability, on substantiation. However, because courts rely on evidentiary standards to impose court-order services or place or maintain a child in foster care, predictive analytics cannot replace the need for investigation and evidence gathering that culminates in a determination of whether maltreatment occurred.

Nevertheless, there are possible ways to improve the objectivity and consistency of substantiation decisions. One option would be to limit child maltreatment clearances for employment to only cases that were adjudicated by a family court, rather than all cases in which a caseworker made a determination of substantiation. This could place a greater burden on the court system if caseworkers were compelled to take more cases to court to ensure the perpetrator was tracked. Alternatively, forms of group decision-making that currently are used in child welfare for a variety of decisions could be used to weigh the evidence to arrive at a substantiation determination. By incorporating multiple perspectives and relying on a consensus decision, the substantiation determination would be more transparent and decision-making errors or biases may be prevented. Moreover, by subjecting one's work to a form of peer review, caseworkers may be motivated to improve the quality of their investigative practices and documentation. Again, such a practice would place a time and staffing burden on child welfare agencies, many of which are already struggling with burgeoning caseloads and high turnover. Moving forward, researcher–agency partnerships may be useful to develop and test practice reforms targeting evidentiary decision-making.

REFERENCES

Ards, S. D., Myers, S. L., Malkis, A., Sugrue, E., & Zhou, L. (2003). Racial disproportionality in reported and substantiated child abuse and neglect: An examination of systematic bias. *Children and Youth Services Review, 25*(5/6), 375–392. doi:10.1016/S0190-7409(03)00027-6

Baumann, D. J., Dalgleish, L., Fluke, J. D., & Kern, H. (2011). *Decision Making Ecology.* Washington, DC: American Humane Association. http://www.americanhumane.org/assets/pdfs/children/cprc-dme-monograph.pdf

Bell, M. F., Bayliss, D. M., Glauert, R., & Ohan, J. L. (2018). School readiness of maltreated children: Associations of timing, type, and chronicity of maltreatment. *Child Abuse and Neglect, 76,* 426–439. doi:10.1016/j.chiabu.2017.12.001

Berrick, J., Dickens, J., Pösö, T., & Skivenes, M. (2016). Time, institutional support, and quality of decision making in child protection: A cross-country analysis. *Human Service Organizations: Management, Leadership & Governance, 40*(5), 451–468. doi:10.1080/23303131.2016.1159637

Boyd, R. (2014). African American disproportionality and disparity in child welfare: Toward a comprehensive conceptual framework. *Children and Youth Services Review, 37,* 15–27.

Camasso, M. J., & Jagannathan, R. (2013). Decision making in child protective services: A risky business? *Risk Analysis, 33*(9), 1636–1649. doi:10.1111/j.1539-6924.2012.01931.x

Capatosto, K. (2017). *Foretelling the future: A critical perspective on the use of predictive analytics in child welfare.* Columbus: Ohio State University, Kirwin Institute. http://kirwaninstitute.osu.edu/wp-content/uploads/2017/05/ki-predictive-analytics.pdf

Child Welfare Information Gateway. (2003). *Decision-making in unsubstantiated child protective services cases: Synthesis of recent research.* Washington, DC: US Department of Health and Human Services. https://www.childwelfare.gov/pubPDFs/decision-making.pdf

Child Welfare Information Gateway. (2014). *Establishment and maintenance of central registries for child abuse reports.* Washington, DC: US Department of Health and Human Services, Children's Bureau. https://www.childwelfare.gov/systemwide/laws_policies/statutes/centreg.cfm

Child Welfare Information Gateway. (2017). *Disclosure of confidential child abuse and neglect records.* Washington, DC: US Department of Health and Human Services, Children's Bureau. https://www.childwelfare.gov/topics/systemwide/laws-policies/statutes/confide/

Child Welfare League of America. (2005). *Child welfare consent decrees: Analysis of thirty-five court actions from 1995 to 2005.* Washington, DC: Author/American Bar Association Center on Children and the Law. http://www.cwla.org/advocacy/consentdecrees.pdf

Chiu, Y.-L., Ryan, J. P., & Herz, D. C. (2011). Allegations of maltreatment and delinquency: Does risk of juvenile arrest vary substantiation status? *Children and Youth Services Review, 33*(6), 855–860. doi:10.1016/j.childyouth.2010.12.007

Cuccaro-Alamin, S., Foust, R., Vaithianathan, R., & Putnam-Hornstein, E. (2017). Risk assessment and decision making in child protective services: Predictive risk modeling in context. *Children and Youth Services Review, 79,* 291–298. doi:10.1016/j.childyouth.2017.06.027

Dalgleish, L. I. (1988). Decision making in child abuse cases: Applications of social judgment theory and signal detection theory. *Advances in Psychology, 54,* 317–360. doi:10.1016/S0166-4115(08)62178-0

DePanfilis, D., & Girvin, H. (2005). Investigating child maltreatment in out-of-home care: Barriers to effective decision-making. *Children and Youth Services Review, 27*(4), 353–374. doi:10.1016/j.childyouth.2004.11.010

Dettlaff, A. J., Rivaux, S. L., Baumann, D. J., Fluke, J. D., Rycraft, J. R., & James, J. (2011). Disentangling substantiation: The influence of race, income, and risk on the substantiation decision in child welfare. *Children and Youth Services Review, 33*(9), 1630–1637. doi:10.1016/j.childyouth.2011.04.005

Dhooper, S. S., Royse, D. D., & Wolfe, L. C. (1990). Does social work education make a difference? *Social Work, 35*(1), 57–61. doi:10.1093/sw/35.1.57

Dolan, M., Smith, K., Casanueva, C., & Ringeisen, H. (2011). *NSCAW II Baseline Report: Introduction to NSCAW II Final Report OPRE Report 2011-27a.* Washington, DC: Office of Planning, Research and Evaluation, Administration for Children and Families, US Department of Health and Human Services.

Doyle, J. J. J. (2007). Child protection and child outcomes: Measuring the effects of foster care. *American Economic Review, 97*(5), 1583–1610. doi:10.1257/aer.97.5.1583

Drake, B., Jonson-Reid, M., Way, I., & Chung, S. (2003). Substantiation and recidivism. *Child Maltreatment, 8*(4), 248–260. doi:10.1177/1077559503258930

Fantuzzo, J. W., Perlman, S. M., & Dobbins, E. K. (2011). Types and timing of child maltreatment and early school success: A population-based investigation. *Maltreatment of Infants and Toddlers, 33*(8), 1404–1411. doi:10.1016/j.childyouth.2011.04.010

Fluke, J. D., Baumann, D. J., Dalgleish, L., & Kern, K. (2014). Decisions to protect children: A decision making ecology. In J. Korbin & R. Krugman (Eds.), *Handbook of child maltreatment* (pp. 462–463). New York: Springer. doi:10.1007/978-94-007-7208-3_25

Fluke, J. D., Corwin, T. W., Hollinshead, D. M., & Maher, E. J. (2016). Family preservation or child safety? Associations between child welfare workers' experience, position, and perspectives. *Children and Youth Services Review, 69*, 210–218. doi:10.1016/j.childyouth.2016.08.012

Font, S. A., Berger, L. M., & Slack, K. S. (2012). Examining racial disproportionality in child protective services case decisions. *Children and Youth Services Review, 34*(11), 2188–2200. doi:10.1016/j.childyouth.2012.07.012

Font, S. A., & Maguire-Jack, K. (2015). Decision-making in child protective services: Influences at multiple levels of the social ecology. *Child Abuse & Neglect, 49*, 50–62. doi:10.1016/j.chiabu.2015.02.005

Freisthler, B., Kepple, N. J., Wolf, J. P., Curry, S. R., & Gregoire, T. (2017). Substance use behaviors by parents and the decision to substantiate child physical abuse and neglect by caseworkers. *Children and Youth Services Review, 79*, 576–583. doi:10.1016/j.childyouth.2017.07.014

Geen, R., & Tumlin, K. C. (1999). *State efforts to remake child welfare: Responses to new challenges and increased scrutiny.* Washington, DC: Urban Institute.

Gelman, A., & Hill, J. (2007). *Data analysis using regression and multilevel/hierarchical models.* New York: Cambridge University Press.

Gillingham, P., & Humphreys, C. (2010). Child protection practitioners and decision-making tools: Observations and reflections from the front line. *British Journal of Social Work, 40*(8), 2598–2616. doi:10.1093/bjsw/bcp155

Gluck Mezey, S. (1998). Systemic reform litigation and child welfare policy: The case of Illinois. *Law and Policy, 20*(2), 203–230. doi:10.1111/1467-9930.00048

Hussey, J. M., Marshall, J. M., English, D. J., Knight, E. D., Lau, A. S., Dubowitz, H., & Kotch, J. B. (2005). Defining maltreatment according to substantiation: Distinction without a difference? *Child Abuse and Neglect, 29*(5), 479–492. doi:10.1016/j.chiabu.2003.12.005

Janczewski, C. E. (2015). The influence of differential response on decision-making in child protective service agencies. *Child Abuse and Neglect, 39*, 50–60. doi:10.1016/j.chiabu.2014.06.006

Jedwab, M., Benbenishty, R., Chen, W., Glasser, S., Siegal, G., & Lerner-Geva, L. (2015). Child protection decisions to substantiate hospital child protection teams' reports of suspected maltreatment. *Child Abuse and Neglect, 40*, 132–141. doi:10.1016/j.chiabu.2014.11.006

Kahn, N. E., Gupta-Kagan, J., & Hansen, M. E. (2017). The standard of proof in the substantiation of child abuse and neglect. *Journal of Empirical Legal Studies*, 14(2), 333–369. doi:10.1111/jels.12149

Keddell, E. (2014). Current debates on variability in child welfare decision-making: A selected literature review. *Social Sciences*, 3(4), 916–940. doi:10.3390/socsci3040916

Kim, H., Wildeman, C., Jonson-Reid, M., & Drake, B. (2017). Lifetime prevalence of investigating child maltreatment among US children. *American Journal of Public Health*, 107(2), 274–280. doi:10.2105/AJPH.2016.303545

Kohl, P. L., Jonson-Reid, M., & Drake, B. (2009). Time to leave substantiation behind: Findings from a national probability study. *Child Maltreatment*, 14(1), 17–26. doi:10.1177/1077559508326030

Krase, K. S. (2015). Child maltreatment reporting by educational personnel: Implications for racial disproportionality in the child welfare system. *Children and Schools*, 37(2), 89–99. doi:10.1093/cs/cdv005

Maguire-Jack, K. (2014). Multilevel investigation into the community context of child maltreatment. *Journal of Aggression, Maltreatment and Trauma*, 23(3), 229–248. doi:10.1080/10926771.2014.881950

Maguire-Jack, K., & Byers, K. (2013). The impact of prevention programs on decisions in Child Protective Services. *Child Welfare*, 92(5), 59–86.

Maguire-Jack, K., Font, S. A., & Dillard, R. (2018). Child protectives services decision-making: The role of children's race and county context. Unpublished manuscript.

McLaughlin, M., & Jonson-Reid, M. (2017). The relationship between child welfare financing, screening, and substantiation. *Children and Youth Services Review*, 82, 407–412. doi:10.1016/j.childyouth.2017.10.013

Mersky, J. P., & Reynolds, A. J. (2007). Child maltreatment and violent delinquency: Disentangling main effects and subgroup effects. *Child Maltreatment*, 12(3), 246–258. doi:10.1177/1077559507301842

Munro, E. (2008). Lessons from research on decision making. In D. Lindsey, & A. Shlonsky (Eds.), *Child welfare research: Advances for practice and policy* (pp. 194–200). Oxford: Oxford University Press.

Noll, J. G., & Shenk, C. E. (2013). Teen birth rates in sexually abused and neglected females. *Pediatrics*, 131(4), e1181–e1187. doi:10.1542/peds.2012-3072

Palusci, V. J. (2011). Risk factors and services for child maltreatment among infants and young children. *Children and Youth Services Review*, 33(8), 1374–1382. doi:10.1016/j.childyouth.2011.04.025

Perry, R. E. (2006a). Do social workers make better child welfare workers than non-social workers? *Research on Social Work Practice*, 16(4), 392–405. doi:10.1177/1049731505279292

Perry, R. E. (2006b). Education and child welfare supervisor performance: Does a social work degree matter? *Research on Social Work Practice*, 16(6), 591–604. doi:10.1177/1049731506290548

Prottas, J. M. (1978). The power of the street-level bureaucrat in public service bureaucracies. *Urban Affairs Quarterly*, 13(3), 285–312. doi:10.1177/107808747801300302

Ryan, J. P., Garnier, P., Zyphur, M., & Zhai, F. (2006). Investigating the effects of case-worker characteristics in child welfare. *Children and Youth Services Review, 28*(9), 993–1006. doi:10.1016/j.childyouth.2005.10.013

Sidebotham, P., Golding, J., & Team, A. S. (2001). Child maltreatment in the "Children of the Nineties": A longitudinal study of parental risk factors. *Child Abuse and Neglect, 25*(9), 1177–1200. doi:10.1016/S0145-2134(01)00261-7

Smith, B. D., & Donovan, S. E. F. (2003). Child welfare practice in organizational and institutional context. *Social Service Review, 77*(4), 541–563. doi:10.1086/378328

Snyder, S. M., & Smith, R. E. (2015). Do youth with substantiated child maltreatment investigations have distinct patterns of delinquent behaviors? *Children and Youth Services Review, 58*, 82–89. doi:10.1016/j.childyouth.2015.09.008

Stoddart, J. K., Fallon, B., Trocmé, N., & Fluke, J. D. (2018). Substantiated child maltreatment: Which factors do workers focus on when making this critical decision? *Children and Youth Services Review, 87*, 1–8. doi:10.1016/j.childyouth.2018.01.018

US Department of Health and Human Services. (2017). *Child maltreatment 2016.* Washington, DC: Author, Administration for Children and Families, Administration on Children, Youth and Families, Children's Bureau. https://www.acf.hhs.gov/sites/default/files/cb/cm2016.pdf

Victor, B. G., Grogan-Kaylor, A., Ryan, J. P., Perron, B. E., & Gilbert, T. T. (2018). Domestic violence, parental substance misuse and the decision to substantiate child maltreatment. *Child Abuse and Neglect, 79*, 31–41. doi:10.1016/j.chiabu.2018.01.030

Wells, S. J., Lyons, P., Doueck, H. J., Brown, C. H., & Thomas, J. (2004). Ecological factors and screening in child protective services. *Children and Youth Services Review, 26*(10), 981–997. doi:10.1016/j.childyouth.2004.05.002

Widom, C. S., Czaja, S. J., Bentley, T., & Johnson, M. S. (2012). A prospective investigation of physical health outcomes in abused and neglected children: New findings from a 30-year follow-up. *American Journal of Public Health, 102*(6), 1135–1144. doi:10.2105/AJPH.2011.300636

Wildeman, C., Emanuel, N., Leventhal, J. M., Putnam-Hornstein, E., Waldfogel, J., & Lee, H. (2014). The prevalence of confirmed maltreatment among US children, 2004 to 2011. *JAMA Pediatrics, 168*(8), 706–713. doi:10.1001/jamapediatrics.2014.410

9

The Impact of Drugs, Infants, Single Mothers, and Relatives on Reunification

A Decision-Making Ecology Approach

KIM WITTENSTROM, DONALD J. BAUMANN,
JOHN D. FLUKE, J. CHRISTOPHER GRAHAM,
AND JOYCE JAMES ■

INTRODUCTION

Decisions regarding when and whether to return a child in placement to their home of origin are among the most challenging in child welfare. Such decisions have implications for child safety, child well-being, and for child welfare costs. Given the centrality of the reunification decision, it is important to research how context may influence workers' decision-making processes.

The Decision-Making Ecology (DME) framework (Baumann, Kern, & Fluke, 1997; Baumann, Dalgleish, Fluke, & Kern, 2011; Baumann, Fluke, Dalgleish, & Kern, 2014; Fluke, Baumann, Dalgleish, & Kern, 2014) is one way to theoretically incorporate context into decision-making research. The DME framework suggests the evaluation of how case, organizational, external, and individual decision-maker factors affect both independently and interactively the decision-making process. In child welfare, the DME has been successfully applied to the

Kim Wittenstrom, Donald J. Baumann, John D. Fluke, J. Christopher Graham, and Joyce James, *The Impact of Drugs, Infants, Single Mothers, and Relatives on Reunification* In: *Decision-Making and Judgment in Child Welfare and Protection*. Edited by: John D. Fluke, Mónica López López, Rami Benbenishty, Erik J. Knorth, and Donald J. Baumann, Oxford University Press (2021). © Oxford University Press. DOI: 10.1093/oso/9780190059538.003.0009.

substantiation decision (Dettlaff et al., 2011; Fluke et al., 2001), the decision to place children into care (Chabot et al., 2013; Fallon et al., 2013; Fluke, Chabot, Fallon, MacLaurin, & Blackstock, 2010; Graham, Dettlaff, Baumann, & Fluke, 2015), maltreatment recurrence (Maguire-Jack & Font, 2014), and burnout and turnover (Baumann, Kern, McFadden, & Law, 1997). This study uses the DME to examine potential sources of disproportionality in the reunification decision.

In 2005, the Texas Department of Family & Protective Services began an initiative to identify and reduce the disproportionality of African American children in the state foster care population. A comprehensive evaluation of the initiative found that African American children exited to reunification more slowly than Caucasian children (Baumann et al., 2010). The present study grew out of the desire to more precisely identify the contexts in which a race differential was occurring, with the goal of better targeting remediation efforts. This research focus raises interesting methodological challenges.

Numerous studies, mostly using proportional hazards models, have added race to their models as a main effect and shown that, similarly to Texas, African American children are reunified with their parents from foster care more slowly than Anglo children (Connell, Katz, Saunders, & Tebes, 2006; Courtney, 1994; Courtney, Piliavin, & Wright, 1997; Courtney & Wong, 1996; Goerge & Bilaver, 2005; Harris & Courtney, 2003; Hill, 2005; Lu et al., 2004; McMurtry & Lie, 1992; Wells & Guo, 1999; Wulczyn, Brunner, & Goerge, 2000; Wulczyn, Chen, & Oriebek, 2009). This general finding can be described as, averaging across all different case types, African Americans will leave care to parents more slowly than Anglo children.

While it is important to know that race is a factor in decision-making, the DME suggests that case, organizational, and external factors might affect the magnitude of the race effect in different ways. In fact studies have crossed race with a single case factor such as child age, parent's marital status or drug problems, or the external factor geography and shown that the race effect is not equal across all covariates (Baumann et al., 2010; Goerge, 1990; Harris & Courtney, 2003; Wells & Guo, 1999). For example, Wells and Guo show that African American children of married parents exit to reunification at similar levels to Anglos, while children of single African American parents exit much more slowly.

This study adds to the literature by attempting to identify how the magnitude of the African American/Anglo race effect can vary based on the presence or absence of four interrelated factors: drugs, infants, and single mothers (case characteristics), and relative placements (an organizational characteristic), while holding other case, organizational, and external characteristics constant. This is equivalent to adding multiple interaction terms to a model. We believe that the lack of attention in the literature to understanding variability in a race effect is due to the difficulties involved in introducing complex interaction terms into proportional hazards models, as well as to the absence of theoretical models that support the notion of multiple decision-making influences on decisions that produce disparities.

Our analytic approach is as follows: (1) we use a proportional hazards model to identify significant main-effect variables on the rate at which children exit to reunification; (2) we develop a profile variable that allows for the exploration of the five-way interactions among drugs, infants, marital status, relative placements, and race; and (3) we develop a model with a race interaction term. (This term identifies differential race effects for each of our profile cases.) Our underlying hypothesis is that models that try to unpack complex interactions between factors will serve to better illuminate the underlying dynamics of disproportionality than will single-factor models.

Prior Research on Reunification

A METHODOLOGICAL NOTE

For the most part research on reunification has relied on proportional hazards models to identify the factors that are associated with the speed at which children leaving substitute care will be reunified with their parents. *Proportional hazards models* analyze variables in relation to time to an event. The model hazards ratio describes how individuals with a particular characteristic are more or less likely to experience the event per unit of time compared to a base group. Proportional hazard models make two assumptions that are important to take into account. One is that censored observations are independent of the event of interest (in the current study, the exit to reunification). The second is that the risk of exiting during time for a particular explanatory variable is the same across all time periods. If the hazard ratio is proportional across time, those children who are exiting more slowly to reunification will also be those who, in the end, have been less likely to be reunified.

Certain methodological advancements are being made in the field to address deviations from these assumptions when modeling exits from foster care. For example, competing risk models have been used to address the dependence of exits from foster care. If a child exits to reunification, he or she is no longer at risk of exiting to adoption or to guardianship during the same foster care episode (Akin, 2011; Connell et al., 2006; Courtney & Hook, 2012; McDonald, Poertner, & Jennings, 2007). Hence, in child welfare, exit events are not independent. Discrete time hazards and the inclusion of time interaction variables have been used to model change in hazards across time (Akin, 2011; Wulczyn, Chen, & Courtney, 2010). Multilevel or hierarchical models have been used to give better estimates when there is non-independence of explanatory factors, as occurs when children are nested within counties and county-level indicators are added to the model (Wulczyn et al., 2010). As of yet there has been little attention given to methodological issues associated with possible complex interactions among models' explanatory variables.

KEY EXPLANATORY VARIABLES FOR REUNIFICATION OUTCOMES

From a DME perspective the most common model explanatory factors used in the reunification literature have been case factors such as the child's race, marital status of mother, age of child, the presence of siblings in care, parental drug involvement, poverty, and child disabilities. The most common organizational factor was placement with kin while in foster care. The most common external factor was geographically based (e.g., urban vs. rural, administrative units such as counties, etc.). In the remainder of this section we detail the findings associated with these types of factors, first as they have been studied as main effects and then as they have been studied in interaction with other factors.

Most studies have found that race does affect the speed at which children are reunified, with African American children returning home more slowly than Anglo children, and Hispanic children having comparable hazard ratios for reunification with respect to Anglo children (Baumann et al., 2010; Courtney, 1994; Courtney et al., 1997; Courtney & Wong, 1996; Goerge & Bilaver, 2005; Hill, 2005; Lu et al., 2004; McMurtry & Lie, 1992; Wells & Guo, 1999; Wulczyn et al., 2000, 2009, 2010). In studies using the more complete competing risks approach to exits from foster care, Courtney and Hook (2012) and Connell et al. (2006) showed African American children exiting more slowly to reunification, while the models of Akin (2011) and McDonald et al. (2007) did not. Since most studies, like the current one, are derived from data from a single county or state child welfare system, contrary findings may have to do with contextual differences in the child welfare systems from which the data are drawn. An additional explanation may be that factors are more or less significant depending on how they combine with other factors.

Understanding how the age of the child affects reunification has been complicated by variability in how age is operationalized in models. For example, McDonald et al. (2007) added age as a continuous variable and found child's age was not a factor in reunification hazard rates. However, studies that separate out infants of less than 1 year old at entry have consistently shown young infants to have lower reunification hazard rates than children aged 1–12 (Akin, 2011; Baumann et al., 2010; Connell et al., 2006; Courtney & Wong, 1996; Grella, Needell, Shi, & Hser, 2009; Harris & Courtney, 2003; Shaw, 2010). Teens also generally have lower reunification hazard rates than children 1–12 (Baumann et al., 2010; Harris & Courtney, 2003; Hayward & DePanfilis, 2007; Wulczyn, 2004).

There have been only limited studies examining how family problems, considered a case characteristic in the DME, affect reunification. Some studies have used the case characteristic allegation type as a proxy indicator for the types of problems families are experiencing. Studies have found that children removed for reasons of neglect return home more slowly than children placed for other reasons (Courtney et al., 1997; Fernandez, 1999; Goerge, 1990; Wells & Guo, 1999). A few studies have tried to narrow the definition of family problem(s). These studies have differentiated cases with and without the case characteristic of drug problems and found that drug use decreases the hazard rate of children returning to their families (Baumann et al., 2010; McDonald et al., 2007; Rosenberg & Robinson, 2004; Shaw, 2010). Courtney and Hook (2012), however, did not find a significant relation between parent drug use and the timing of exits to reunification. Studies have also found that the case characteristic of poverty decreases reunification hazard rates (Baumann et al., 2010; Courtney & Wong, 1996; Shaw, 2010).

Additionally studies have added child problems to their models. Children with disabilities have been found to have lower reunification hazard rates than other children (Courtney, 1994; Courtney et al., 1997; Rosenberg & Robinson, 2004; Wells & Guo, 1999; Wulczyn, 2004). Akin (2011) also found that a child's disability or mental health problems slowed his or her rate of exit to reunification but that this effect disappeared over time.

More commonly, the case characteristic of family structure has been included in the statistical models. Such studies have found that children return home more quickly to two-parent families than to single parents or other relatives (Baumann et al., 2010; Courtney et al., 1997; Fernandez, 1999; Glisson, Bailey, & Post, 2000; Harris & Courtney, 2003; McDonald et al., 2007; Shaw, 2010; Wells & Guo, 1999). Courtney and Wong (1996) found no difference, but they combined exits to kin, guardians, and parents in their model, which might be expected to mask a family structure effect. Studies also have examined the effect of having siblings in care. Wulczyn et al. (2009) found that the presence of siblings in care decreased the hazard rate of reunification, while both Shaw (2010) and Baumann et al. (2010) found that siblings being in care increased the reunification hazard rate. Akin (2011) found that children placed all together and children with no siblings in care exited more quickly to reunification than children with siblings in separate placements. Hence Akin combines case and organizational factors in her model. The important factor is not presence of siblings or not, but how a sibling factor and a placement factor combine. Being placed in kinship foster care, an organizational characteristic, has in general been found to slow the speed at which children leave care to return to parents (Baumann et al., 2010; Berrick, Barth, & Needell, 1994; Connell et al., 2006; Courtney, 1994; Courtney et al., 1997; Courtney & Wong, 1996; Grella et al., 2009; Harris & Courtney, 2003; Shaw, 2010; Wulczyn et al., 2009). Koh and Testa (2008), however, suggest that this finding may be due to differences in the type of children in kinship care rather than kinship care itself. In their study they use a propensity matching score methodology to equalize the age, race, and child disabilities between kin and non-kin samples. When they do this, they find kinship placement has no significant effect on reunification rates. In a 2010 article, Wulczyn, Chen, and Courtney noted a reduction in the importance of kin placement to reunification outcomes. They attributed this to possible policy changes around kin placements. Akin (2011) found that children placed initially in kin placements exited more quickly to reunification than children initially place in foster homes.

Last, studies have found that geography, an external characteristic, affects the speed at which children return home. Children return home more slowly from urban counties, counties with more female-headed households, and larger percentages of African Americans (Courtney, 1994; Goerge, 1990; Wulczyn et al., 2010). In Texas, the different legal/administrative systems under which a child lives, an organizational characteristic, in part determines how quickly a child returns home (Baumann et al., 2010).

INTERACTION TERMS WITH RACE
While the preceding studies describe significant main effects on the hazard rates of reunification, the following few studies include interaction terms in their models. (Another way to put this is that they examined the possibility that the race effect is *moderated* by other variables in the DME.) Harris and Courtney (2003) suggest that racial differences in reunification hazard rates do not exist among married couples, only in cases with single mothers (case variable). The Baumann et al. (2010) study suggests that racial effects are more prominent in families with drug and housing problems. African American children coming from families without these problems showed no difference from Anglo children. Wells and Guo (1999) showed the race effect to be more pronounced in younger children, especially children under 1 year old at entry, compared to all other case characteristics.

In a less direct manner, Koh and Testa's work (2008) also suggests that there exists an interaction between kinship placement, race, and reunification outcomes. Koh and Testa argued that kinship placements in and of themselves did not lower rates of exits to reunification. They suggested that it was difference in the type of children in kinship placements (i.e., the greater numbers of African American children in kinship care that caused the effect). Hence, they suggest that placement type can possibly modulate the magnitude of a race effect.

GAPS IN THE LITERATURE AND FOCUS OF STUDY
In this study we focus on the four-way interactions among marital status, drug use, single infant removals, and kinship placement. The preceding literature

review suggests that each of these factors individually interacts with race to create disparities in children's reunification hazards rate. In most cases adding the interaction term increased the size of the race effect for some African American children and decreased the size for others. These interactions did not, however, necessarily eliminate race as a main effect. This suggests that either there is an undifferentiated contribution of race across all types of cases or that some important interactions affecting outcomes by race have yet to be included in these models. In this study we hypothesize that adding a more complex interaction term to the model can help to clarify the race effect by better localizing a constellation of factors that might elicit a racially differentiated response from decision-makers.

Methods

Consistent with prior research, proportional hazard models in SPSS Statistics 22 were used to measure the contribution of explanatory variables to the speed at which children exited to reunification. Also consistent with other research, the analysis was conducted using an administrative dataset drawn from a census of children placed in foster care. The dependent variable in the model is time to exit via reunification, and we code children exiting care to other exits as "right censored." To assure that making these assumptions does not change our main findings, we checked our analyses by performing additional discrete time, competing risk models in M Plus version 7.3 (Muthen & Muthen, 1998–2014) with respect to the placement outcomes adoption and permanent kin placement. The results of the competing risks analyses disclosed only minor differences in the parameter estimates from our original findings.

For each group of explanatory variables in the models, one category was chosen as the reference group. The rate of children exiting to reunification per unit of time is measured with reference to this reference category. For example, a hazard ratio of 0.6 indicates a 40% lower speed, or rate of exit to reunification, than the reference category (1–0.6).

Since the purpose of the study was to explore how combinations of variables (i.e., a particular case profile) affect outcomes rather than how independent variables individually affect outcomes, it was necessary to consider how to add complex interaction terms to the model. Given the difficulties of interpreting complex interactions terms, a categorical variable reflecting mutually exclusive profiles of cases drawn from the literature was formulated. This categorical variable is then combined with race in a two-way interaction term. The hazard rate of the interaction term in combination with the hazards of the main effects provides a disparity measure for how race may affect the speed at which children exit to reunification among the different case profiles. The profiles were then applied to cases involving African American and Anglo families with young children who were removed due to neglect or physical abuse.

Two multivariate models were run, each successively adding terms to the models. Model 1 (the *Main Effects Model*) includes the main factors (case, organizational, and external) of interest as dichotomous main effects. Model 2 (*Profiles in Interaction with Race Model*) examines whether there is variability in the race effect depending on case characteristics. It does this by adding a profile main effect, a race main effect, and a profile-by-race interaction term. This allows the assessment of how a constellation of case characteristics can affect the speed of reunification for Anglos and African Americans separately. Hence, it can provide a more nuanced picture of racial disparities in exits to reunification.

The data used were Texas Department of Family and Protective Services child welfare administrative data from FY 2004–2006 (September 1, 2003–August 31, 2006), for 44,874 children who entered foster care for the first time in Texas. The dataset analyzed consisted only of African American and Anglo (white, non-Hispanic) children with allegation types of neglect, physical abuse, or multiple abuse types who were either under 13 or over 13 but part of a family grouping that included children under 13. Excluded cases were sex abuse cases (1.1%), cases involving a sole adolescent (3.8%), and cases involving Hispanic children (38%) or other races (2.2%). The resulting study population of 21,763 children accounted for 48.5% of the total CPS population during the time selected, and 78.2% of the population of African American and Anglo children. Children were followed until May 6, 2008, a follow-up of from 20 to 51 months. By the end of the study 83% of the sample had exited care, and 31.9% of the sample had been reunified.

EXPLANATORY VARIABLES

Table 9.1 outlines the explanatory variables that were used in the model. Each is classified by its DME characteristic *Risk Level*. Risk in Texas is measured during an investigation on seven factors, each with a scale of 1–5. The sum of these factors (ranging from a low of 7 to a high of 35) were combined and then divided into low, medium, and high risk categories. Based on the distribution of the summed risk score, low risk was defined as a sum score of 18.5 and under, medium risk was 19–22. A score of 22–35 was defined as high risk. Risk levels for the children removed during an in-home services case, called a *family-based safety services* (FBSS) case, were taken from the investigation that led to the opening of the FBSS case.

Income. Families with incomes of less than $10,150 were coded at 1. Families with incomes of $10,150 or more were coded as 0.

Table 9.1 CASE, ORGANIZATIONAL, AND EXTERNAL
CHARACTERISTICS VARIABLES USED IN THE MODEL AND
DECISION-MAKING ECOLOGY (DME) CLASSIFICATION

Name	DME type
Race	Case
Risk assessment level	Case
Income	Case
Drugs	Case
Marital status	Case
Case with single infant	Case
Kin placement	Organizational
Removal stage of service	Organizational
Geographic location	External
Population density	External

Drugs. Cases where parental use of drugs such as methamphetamines, co-caine, etc. or drug manufacturing was indicated as a factor in the removal deci-sion were coded as 1. If drugs were not indicated, the case was coded as 0.

Martial status of parent. The case was coded as 1 if the parents were married and 0 if the child came from a single-parent household.

Case with single infant. Cases were coded as a 1 if the case involved a single child under the age of 1. All other case types were coded as 0.

Kin placement. Cases were coded as 1 if the child spent half or more of his or her time in foster care in the home of kin. All other scenarios were coded 0.

Removal state of service. Children removed during the investigation stage (INV) were coded as 0 and during the FBSS stage as 1.

Geographic location. Texas has 11 administrative regions. The smaller geo-graphically connected regions were combined to make a total of eight different geographical locations. Region 3 Dallas/Fort Worth, with the largest number of children in care, was chosen as the reference group.

Population density. Families were coded as 1 if they come from an urban county (i.e., the county had a population greater than 1,000 people per square mile). All others were coded 0.

SELECTION OF PROFILES

The four mutually exclusive profiles constructed for the analysis include all caregivers who are *both* single and use drugs; the profiles differ in whether or not the case involves a sole infant and whether or not the children have lived with relatives for the majority of their foster care career. (Table 9.2 shows the

Table 9.2 CHARACTERIZATION OF MUTUALLY EXCLUSIVE ANALYSIS PROFILES

Type of profile	Profiles	Description	Single	Drug	Kin	Infant	Total $N = 21,763$
Distinct profiles (all single parent with drug use)	1	Not living with kin Has infant	Yes	Yes	No	Yes	Percent (4.6%)
	2	Not living with kin Doesn't have infant	Yes	Yes	No	No	Percent (14.9%)
	3	Living with kin Doesn't have infant	Yes	Yes	Yes	No	Percent (19%)
	4	Living with kin Has infant	Yes	Yes	Yes	Yes	Percent (3%)
Combined into single reference profile	5	Single parent No drugs	Yes	No	All Combinations		
	6	Not single parent With drugs	No	Yes			Percent (58%)
	7	Not single parent No drugs	No	No			

four combinations that are represented in profiles 1–4.) The rest of the cases are put into the reference profile. Note that the reference profile (cells 5–16 combined) includes those caregivers who are single or use drugs *but not both*. Hence our focus is on a particular *constellation of factors* present in the case and not on the presence or absence of the factor at the individual level. These profiles were chosen based on the relatively consistent large effect size of each of these variables on reunification hazard ratios at the bivariate level.

Results

Results in this section describe the distributions of the variables analyzed and, for the various models, structure the findings associated with the main effects, the case profiles, and the interactions of the profiles with race.

DESCRIPTIVE STATISTICS

Table 9.3 shows that more than half of the children in the sample who entered care came from just two regions. These were Region 3 (where Dallas/Fort Worth is located) and Region 6 (where Houston is located). Fifty-seven percent of the cases indicated drug use as a removal reason. Two-thirds of the children came from a single-parent home, and 61.1% of the families had an annual income of less than $10,150. Many of the children (43.4%) stayed with relatives for more than half of their foster care stay. A total of 31.9% of the children were reunified, although this descriptive statistic is not adjusted for time in care.

Table 9.3 also shows some important differences between the Anglo and African American samples. Notably, 63.4% of the African American children came from high-density urban areas compared to 28.5% of the Anglos children. Also 43.5% of the Anglo children came from two-parent families compared to only 21.4% of the African American children. Last, 36.2% of the Anglo children were reunified during the time period compared to 27.8% of African Americans.

MULTIVARIATE FINDINGS

In line with previous studies, Model 1 in Table 9.4 indicates that all but one of the main effect variables significantly influence the rate at which children exit to reunification per unit of time. For example, the model suggests that the presence of drugs lowers the speed at which children exit to reunification by 26.1%. An income of less than $10,150 slows a child's exit to reunification by 40.1%. Children from two-parent households will be reunified 18.2% faster than children from single-parent households. A lone infant will leave care to reunification 39.5% more slowly than other types of children. Also the model shows that, when all the other variables are controlled for, African American

Table 9.3 DEMOGRAPHICS OF STUDY CASES

	Total sample population (N = 21,763)		Anglos* N = 12,260 (56.3%)	African American N = 9,503 (43.7%)
Region 3	6798	31.2%	29.8%	33%
Region 6	5092	23.4%	17.9%	30.4%
Region 7	3028	13.9%	15.1%	12.5%
Region 8	1478	6.8%	5.9%	8%
Region 2, 9	1245	5.7%	8%	2.8%
Region 1, 10	1227	5.6%	7.1%	3.8%
Region 11	454	2.1%	2.6%	1.6%
Density high county	9498	43.6%	28.5%	63.4%
Density other	12245	56.3%	71.5%	36.6%
Risk level low	8019	36.8%	35.3%	39.8%
Risk level medium	5694	26.2%	27.2%	24.8%
Risk level high	8051	37.0%	37.5%	35.4%
Removed during FBSS stage	2699	12.4%	12.9%	14.6%
Removed during INV stage	19056	87.6%	87.1%	85.4%
Drugs present	12432	57.1%	60%	53.4%
No drugs	9331	42.9%	40%	46.6%
Income <$10,150	13295	61.1%	55.9%	67%
Income ≥$10,150	8468	38.9%	44.1%	33%
Single infant	3371	15.5%	14.3%	16.5%
Family or single child 1–12 yrs	18392	84.5%	85.7%	83.5%
Originating caregiver married	7369	33.9%	43.5%	21.4%
Originating caregiver single	14394	66.1%	56.5%	78.6%
Relative care (> 50% of time in care)	9450	43.4%	42.4%	44.4%
Other out-of-home care	12313	56.6%	57.6%	55.6%
Profiles Reference profile	13225	58.3%	64%	56.6%

(*continued*)

Table 9.3 CONTINUED

	Total sample population (N = 21,763)		Anglos* N = 12,260 (56.3%)	African American N = 9,503 (43.7%)
Single, drugs, no relative, infant	1053	4.6%	4.4%	5.4%
Single, drugs, no relative, no infant	3384	14.9%	14.9%	16.4%
Single, drugs, relative, no infant	4351	19.1%	14%	18.2%
Single, drugs, relative, infant	650	2.8%	2.7%	3.4%
Total reunified	6950	31.9%	36.2%	27.8%

*Anglo and African American populations differed significantly on all factors at p <.01/.

children exit to reunification 11.6% slower than Anglo children. Interestingly, averaging across all case types, the model does not show relative placement to affect the timing of exit to reunification. This is different from prior results but is in line with recent questions about the need for more research on the role of kin care in child reunification (Koh & Testa, 2008; Wulczyn et al., 2010).

By adding an interaction and profile term, Model 2 changes the meaning of the main effects for the race and profile variables. The main effect *profile* variable shows how the combined characteristics of single parent, drug involvement, kin care, and single infants affect the speed at which Anglos return home vis-à-vis Anglos in the reference group. The main effect for race identifies differences between races in the profile reference group only. The main effect profile variable in combination with the interaction term shows how the combined characteristics affect the speed at which African Americans return home compared to African Americans in the reference group. Last, the hazard ratios for the main race effect combined with the interaction term give the race effect between Anglos and African Americans for each profile group. These within-race and cross-race hazards ratios are displayed in Table 9.5.

The cross-race hazards in column 2 of Table 9.5 present five, not one, race effects on speed to reunification. Contrary to Model 1, the main effect for race in Model 2 is not significant. This demonstrates that there is not a statistical

Table 9.4 FINDINGS FOR THE MAIN EFFECT MODEL AND THE PROFILES IN INTERACTION
WITH RACE MODEL

	Model 1 hazards	CI lower	CI upper	Model 2 hazards	CI lower	CI upper
Region 1, 10	.738**	.659	.814	.749**	.670	.828
Region 2, 9	.819**	.737	.910	.817**	.736	.909
Region 4, 5	.846**	.766	.913	.859**	.787	.938
Region 6	.702**	.652	.750	.714**	.666	.766
Region 7	.881**	.810	.942	.885**	.820	.954
Region 8	.861**	.774	.950	.887*	.801	.983
Region 11	1.609**	1.387	1.847	1.677**	1.454	1.935
Region 3 (ref)						
Density other	1.435**	1.350	1.526	.1.433**	1.348	1.523
Density high						
Risk high	.687**	. 646	. 725	.689**	.650	.730
Medium	.847**	.797	.899	.850**	.801	.903
Low (ref)						
2006	1.04	.976	1.104	1.033	.971	1.099
2005	1.07 *	1.012	1.142	1.065*	1.002	1.131
2004 (ref)						
Income < 10,500	.599**	.571	.630	.576**	.549	.604
Income ≥ 10,500						
Removed FBSS	.691**	.637	.751	.704**	.649	.765
Removed INV						
African Am	.884**	.838	.932	1.01	.952	1.074
Anglos (ref)						
Drugs present	.739**	.706	.778			
No drugs (ref)						
Single infant	.605**	.556	.657			
All others (ref)						
Married	1.182**	1.125	1.243			
Single (ref)						
Kin care	.981	.934	1.034			
Other care (ref)						
Reference profile				.853**	.784	.929
No infant, no kin				.537**	.443	.651
Infant, no kin				.908	.823	1.01
No infant, kin				.679**	.531	.868
Infant, kin						

(*continued*)

Table 9.4 CONTINUED

	Model 1 hazards	CI lower	CI upper	Model 2 hazards	CI lower	CI upper
Profile*race No infant, no kin Infant, no kin No infant, kin Infant, kin				.823** .614** .469** .309**	.719 .444 .395 .188	.942 .848 .556 .506
-2Log Like	130,173			130,181		

* p<.05, **p<.01.

difference in the speed at which Anglo and African Americans in the profile reference group are reunified. Hence, a full 56% of cases involving African Americans showed no statistically significant racial difference from Anglos in their speed of exiting to reunification. However results in the first column of Table 9.5 (*Effects of Race Within Profiles*) do demonstrate race effects. When no relative and no sole infant is involved in a single-parent drug case, African Americans exit 17% more slowly to reunification than similarly placed Anglos. When an infant is not placed with kin in a single-mother drug case, African Americans exit 38% more slowly. When a kin placement is made without an infant, African American children's rate of reunification is 53% less than Anglos.

Table 9.5 PROFILE RACE INTERACTION HAZARD RATIOS

	Effect of race within profiles hazard ratio	Effect of profile within Anglos hazard ratio	Effect of profile within African Americans hazard ratio
Reference cases	1.01 (NS)		
Profiles: Single parent with drug issues			
1) No infant, no kin	.83**	.85**	.70**
2) Infant, no kin	.62**	.54**	.33**
3) No Infant, kin	.47**	.91 (NS)	.43**
4) Infant, kin	.32**	.68**	.21**

** p< .01.

When an infant is placed in a kin placement, African American children exit to reunification 68% more slowly than similarly placed Anglo children. Looking at the within-race hazards offers additional information with respect to Anglo children. Column 2 in Table 9.5 shows that, for Anglos, there is no statistical difference in speed to reunification between a single-parent drug case with a relative placement and no infant and the reference group. Furthermore, when there is a sole infant case, the child will exit to reunification faster when there is a relative placement than with a non-relative placement. The infants in relative placements exit 32% slower than reference group, while the infants placed with a non-relative exit 47% slower than the reference group. In contrast, with African Americans, when a kin placement is made in a single-parent drug case without an infant, the child will exit to reunification 57% more slowly than African American children in the reference group. If the relative placement involves a sole infant, the infant exits 79% more slowly than African American children in the reference group. Hence, Model 2 shows that kinship placements play out very differently in African American and Anglo cases involving single parents and drugs. This difference by race in the role of kin placements in speed of reunification may explain why kin as a main effect was not significant in Model 1. There may have been directional cancellation of effect. Model 2 also demonstrates substantial variability in race effects across the different profile cases.

Discussion

The reunification literature suggests that there is a race effect in reunification outcomes among Anglos and African Americans, with African American children exiting more slowly to reunification than Anglos (Baumann et al., 2010; Connell et al., 2006; Courtney, 1994; Courtney et al., 1997; Courtney & Wong, 1996; Goerge & Bilaver, 2005; Harris & Courtney, 2003; Hill, 2005; Lu et al., 2004; McMurtry & Lie, 1992; Wells & Guo, 1999; Wulczyn et al., 2000, 2009). However, the literature to date does not offer a clear leverage point to consider where policy and practice changes would have the most impact. The hypothesis of this study was that perhaps the significant but persistent and subtle race effect size found in these studies is due to the fact that race makes more of a difference in some types of cases and places than in others. Systematically identifying factors associated with larger race effects could help focus intervention and research efforts.

In methodological terms, the research focused on multifactor interaction effects. The approach of the analysis was to take a similar type of family presenting problems and examine how the constellation of people involved in the case may change the case decision-making for Anglo versus African American children. The features of interest were kin, the marital status of the parents, and whether or not the case involved a single infant. The presenting problem was neglect/physical abuse with and without drug involvement.

A key finding from the study is that the amount of racial disparity in reunification decisions varies greatly depending on the particular combination of case and external factors present in a case. In other words, the presence of drugs in a case, in and of itself, may not lead to a disparity, but rather may only lead to a disparity when other factors are present (such as single parenthood and kin placements). Hence, the study was successful in demonstrating the limitation of main-effects-only models. Furthermore, the findings contradict the assertion by Bartholet (2009) that the more factors controlled for the less likely one is to find effects for racial bias. This study added a complex interaction variable and still found significant race effects. Last, the study was successful in suggesting possible types of cases to target in disproportionality remediation efforts. The findings specifically emphasize the need to better understand the role of kin placements in reunification decision-making.

LIMITATIONS

That said, the study's emphasis on certain variable clusters and not others does have a number of important limitations. First, the study does not examine all different types of child abuse and neglect cases. It purposely does not include cases involving sexual abuse and abandonment or cases involving single teens. Hence the results cannot be generalized to these populations. Second, the study cannot say whether greater disparities exist with the combination of kin placement, marital status, drug history, and infants due to worker biases or to lack of services in African American communities. Additional qualitative studies or case reviews by quality assurance teams will have to be done. Third, the study does not offer a systematic, statistical method for determining which of the many possible potential interactions are the best to include in the model. For example, the important combination of case characteristics that led to large racial disparity rates in this study may change if they are also combined with a geography variable. For instance, the combination of characteristics that lead to disparity differences in rural areas may be very different from those in urban areas. These limitations point to some important future directions for work in the field.

IMPLICATIONS

Developing a clear and actionable understanding of disparities in child welfare is a complex undertaking that requires methodological improvements and attention to the Decision-Making Ecology. While some have argued that racial inequities in the child welfare system are primarily a function of poverty (Drake et al., 2011), this is not necessarily a complete explanation, particularly once families have engaged in the child welfare system for some period of time and where the population of Anglo families is comparable. This study suggests that when the decision to reunify is made, differences appear in the trajectories of African American and Anglo children. The study directs us to the combination of a kin placement, drug history, single parenthood, and infants as a place where the causal relationships associated with racially disparate reunification decision-making can occur.

Practice implications might include the need for special staffings, worker training, and/or greater cross-institutional collaboration. First, special staffing can be done in the delayed reunifications with this combination of DME factors to determine the reasons for the delay. These staffings may uncover a potential bias in how workers evaluate the risk to children of drug use among African American mothers relative to Anglo mothers. For instance, workers may view African American mothers as more likely to relapse than Anglo mothers, thus causing delays in reunification. Staffings may also uncover differences in worker assumptions about the role of kin in African American and Anglo families. For example, workers may see Anglo kin placements as temporary and African American kin placements as equivalent to a return home. If biases are found, extra worker training may be needed. Staffings may also find structural and institutional factors such as the absence of adequate housing or drug abuse treatment services in predominately African American communities. Workers may be reluctant to reunify in the absence of proper housing or mothers may move in with kin after treatment, thus making reunification seem unnecessary. Finding these issues would point to the need for greater cross-systems collaborations in efforts to reunify these families. Any or all of these factors can impact decision-making and should be considered.

ACKNOWLEDGMENTS

The authors thank both the Child Protection Research Center at the American Humane Association and Casey Family Programs for the funding that supported a portion of this research. We also thank the Texas Department of Family and Protective Services and the caseworkers for their support.

This chapter was originally published as an article in *Child Abuse and Neglect* (2015), *49*, 86–96, and is reprinted here with permission from Child Abuse and Neglect.

REFERENCES

Akin, B. (2011). Predictors of foster care exits to permanency: A competing risks analysis of reunification, guardianship, and adoption. *Children and Youth Services Review, 34*, 999–1011.

Bartholet, E. (2009). The racial disproportionality movement in child welfare: False facts and dangerous directions. *Arizona Law Review, 51*, 871–932.

Baumann, D. J., Dalgleish, L., Fluke, J. D., & Kern, H. (2011). *The decision-making ecology.* Washington, DC: American Humane Association.

Baumann, D. J., Fluke, J. D., Dalgleish, L., & Kern, H. (2014). The decision-making ecology. In A. Shlonsky, & R. Benbenishty (Eds.), *From evidence to outcomes in child welfare: An international reader* (pp. 24–40). New York: Oxford University Press.

Baumann, D. J., Fluke, J. D., Graham, J. C., Wittenstrom, K., Hedderson, J., Riveau, S., … Brown, N. (2010). *Disproportionality in child protective services: The preliminary results of statewide reform efforts.* Austin: Texas Department of Family and Protective Services.

Baumann, D., Kern, H., & Fluke, J. D. (1997). Foundations of the Decision-Making Ecology and overview. In H. Kern, D. J. Baumann, & J. D. Fluke (Eds.), *Worker Improvements to the Decision and Outcome Model (WISDOM): The child welfare decision enhancement project* (pp. 1–12). Washington, DC: The Children's Bureau.

Baumann, D., Kern, H., McFadden, T., & Law, J. R. (1997). Individual and organizational factors in burnout and turnover: A decision-making ecology approach. In H. Kern, D. J. Baumann, & J. D. Fluke (Eds.), *Worker Improvements to the Decision and Outcome Model (WISDOM): The child welfare decision enhancement project* (pp. 15–29). Washington, DC: The Children's Bureau.

Berrick, J., Barth, R. P., & Needell, B. (1994). A comparison of kinship foster homes and foster family homes: Implications for kinship foster care as family preservation. *Children and Youth Services Review, 16*(1/2), 33–64.

Chabot, M., Fallon, B., Tonmyr, L., Maclaurin, B., Fluke, J. D., & Blackstock, C. (2013). Exploring alternate specifications to explain agency-level effects in placement decisions regarding aboriginal children: Further analysis of the Canadian incidence study of reported child abuse and neglect part B. *Child Abuse and Neglect, 37*(1), 61–76.

Connell, C. M., Katz, K. H., Saunders, L., & Tebes, J. K. (2006). Leaving foster care: The influence of child and case characteristics on foster care exit rates. *Children and Youth Services Review, 28*(7), 780–798.

Courtney, M. E. (1994). Factors associated with the reunification of foster children and their families. *Social Service Review, 68*, 81–108.

Courtney, M. E., & Hook, J. (2012). Evaluation of the impact of enhanced parental legal representation on the timing of permanency outcomes for children in foster care. *Children and Youth Services Review, 34*, 1337–1343.

Courtney, M. E., Piliavin, I., & Wright, B. R. E. (1997). Transitions from and returns to out-of-home care. *Social Service Review, 71*, 652–667.

Courtney, M. E., & Wong, Y. I. (1996). Comparing the timing of exits from substitute care. *Children and Youth Services Review, 18*(4–5), 307–334.

Dettlaff, A., Rivaux, S., Baumann, D. J., Fluke, J. D., Rycraft, J., & James, J. (2011). Disentangling substantiation: The influence of race, risk and poverty on the substantiation decision in child welfare. *Children and Youth Services Review, 33*(9), 1630–1637.

Drake, B., Jolley, J. M., Lanier, P., Fluke, J. D., Barth, R. P., & Jonson-Reid, M. (2011). Racial bias in child protection? A comparison of competing explanations using national data. *Pediatrics, 127*(3), 471–478.

Fallon, B., Chabot, M., Fluke, J. D., Blackstock, C., Maclaurin, B., & Tonmyr, L. (2013). Placement decisions and disparities among Aboriginal children: Further analysis of the Canadian incidence study of reported child abuse and neglect part A: Comparisons of the 1998 and 2003 surveys. *Child Abuse and Neglect, 37*(1), 47–60.

Fernandez, E. (1999). Pathways in substitute care: Representation of placement careers of children using event history analysis. *Children and Youth Services Review, 21*(3), 177–218.

Fluke, J. D., Baumann, D. J., Dalgleish, L., & Kern, H. (2014). Decisions to protect children: A Decision-making Ecology. In J. E. Korbin, & R. D. Krugman (Eds.), *Handbook of Child Maltreatment* (pp. 464–476). New York: Springer.

Fluke, J. D., Chabot, M., Fallon, B., MacLaurin, B., & Blackstock, C. (2010). Placement decisions and disparities among aboriginal groups: An application of the Decision-Making Ecology through multi-level analysis. *Child Abuse and Neglect, 34*, 57–69.

Fluke, J. D., Parry, C., Shapiro, P., Hollinshead, D., Bollenbacher, V., Baumann, D., & Davis-Brown, K. (2001). *The dynamics of unsubstantiated reports: A multi-state study: Fnal report*. Denver, CO: American Humane Association.

Glisson, C., Bailey, J., & Post, J. A. (2000). Predicting the time children spend in state custody. *Social Service Review, 73*, 253–280.

Goerge, R. M. (1990). The reunification process in substitute care. *Social Service Review, 64*, 422–457.

Goerge, R. M., & Bilaver, L. M. (2005). The effect of race on reunification from substitute care in Illinois. In D. M. Derezotes, J. Poertner, & M. F. Testa (Eds.), *Race matters in child welfare* (pp. 201–214). Washington, DC: Child Welfare League of America.

Graham, J. C., Dettlaff, A., Baumann, D. J., & Fluke, J. D. (2015). The decision-making ecology of placing children in foster care: A structural equation model. *Child Abuse and Neglect, 49*, 12–23

Grella, C. E., Needell, B., Shi, Y., & Hser, I. (2009). Do drug treatment services predict reunification outcomes of mother and their children in child welfare? *Journal of Substance Abuse Treatment, 36*(3), 278–293.

Harris, M. S., & Courtney, M. E. (2003). The interaction of race, ethnicity, and family structure with respect to the timing of family reunification. *Children and Youth Services Review, 25*, 409–429.

Hayward, A., & DePanfilis, D. (2007). Foster children with an incarcerated parent: Predictors of reunification. *Children and Youth Services Review, 29*(10), 1320–1334.

Hill, R. B. (2005). The role of race in parental reunification. In D. Derezotes, J. Poertner, & M. Testa (Eds.), *Race matters in child welfare* (pp. 215–229). Washington, DC: Child Welfare League of America.

Koh, E., & Testa, M. (2008). Propensity score matching of children in kinship and nonkinship foster care: Do permanency outcomes still differ? *Social Work Research*, 32(2), 105–116.

Lu, Y. E., Landsverk, J., Ellis-Macleod, E., Newton, R., Ganger, W., & Johnson, I. (2004). Race, ethnicity, and case outcomes in child protective services. *Children and Youth Services Review*, 26(5), 447–461.

Maguire-Jack, K., & Font, S. A. (2014). Predicting recurrent maltreatment among high-risk families: Applying the decision-making ecology framework. *Children and Youth Services Review*. http://dx.doi.org/10.1016/j.childyouth.2014.04.014

McDonald, T. P., Poertner, J., & Jennings, M. A. (2007). Permanency for children in foster care: A competing risks analysis. *Journal of Social Service Research*, 33(4), 45–56.

McMurtry, S. L., & Lie, G. (1992). Differential exit rates of minority children in foster care [Electronic version]. *Social Work Research & Abstracts*, 28(1), 42–48.

Muthen, B., & Muthen, L. (1998–2014). Mplus Version 7.3. www.statmodel.com

Rosenberg, S. A., & Robinson, C. C. (2004). Out-of-home placement for young children with developmental and medical conditions. *Children and Youth Services Review, 26*, 711–723.

Shaw, T. (2010). Reunification from foster care: Informing measures over time. *Children and Youth Services Review*, 32(4), 475–481.

Wells, K., & Guo, S. (1999). Reunification and reentry of foster children. *Children and Youth Services Review*, 21(4), 273–294.

Wulczyn, F. (2004). Family reunification. *Future of Children, 14*, 95–113.

Wulczyn, R., Brunner, K., & Goerge, R. (2000). *An update from the Multistate Foster Care Data Archive: Foster care dynamics 1983–1998*. Chicago: Chapin Hall Center for Children at the University of Chicago.

Wulczyn, F., Chen, L., & Courtney, M. (2010). Family reunification in a social structural context. *Children and Youth Services Review, 33*, 424–430.

Wulczyn, F., Chen, L., & Oriebek, B. (2009). Evaluating contract agency performance in achieving reunification. *Children and Youth Services Review, 31*, 506–512.

10

Exploring Alternate Explanations for Agency-Level Effects in Placement Decisions Regarding Aboriginal Children

BARBARA A. FALLON, JOHN D. FLUKE, MARTIN CHABOT,
CINDY BLACKSTOCK, VANDNA SINHA, KATE ALLAN,
AND BRUCE MACLAURIN ■

INTRODUCTION

This chapter summarizes a series of papers published in the journal *Child Abuse and Neglect* that used data from the Canadian Incidence Study of Reported Child Abuse and Neglect (CIS) to explore the influence of case and organizational characteristics on the decision to place Aboriginal children in out-of-home placements at the conclusion of child maltreatment investigations. The premise of the analyses was that these influences were consistent with the framework of the Decision-Making Ecology (DME; Baumann, Dalgleish, Fluke, & Kern, 2011). The CIS is a cross-sectional cyclical survey that captures information on the characteristics of alleged maltreatment, the characteristics of investigated children and families, the qualification of workers, and characteristics of the child welfare organizations for which they work. The papers

Barbara A. Fallon, John D. Fluke, Martin Chabot, Cindy Blackstock, Vandna Sinha, Kate Allan, and Bruce MacLaurin,
Exploring Alternate Explanations for Agency-Level Effects in Placement Decisions Regarding Aboriginal Children In:
Decision-Making and Judgment in Child Welfare and Protection. Edited by: John D. Fluke, Mónica López López, Rami
Benbenishty, Erik J. Knorth, and Donald J. Baumann, Oxford University Press (2021). © Oxford University Press.
DOI: 10.1093/oso/9780190059538.003.0010.

used multilevel statistical models to analyze the influence of clinical and organizational variables on the placement decision. The proportion of investigations conducted by the child welfare agency involving Aboriginal children was a key agency-level predictor of the placement decision in each of the papers. Specifically, the higher the proportion of investigations of Aboriginal children, the more likely placement was to occur for any child. It was our hypothesis that the proportion of Aboriginal investigations acted as a proxy for a number of contextual factors, but few of these contextual factors were significant in the models that were developed.

INTRODUCTION: LITERATURE REVIEW

Overrepresentation of Aboriginal Children in Canadian Child Welfare

In Canada, Aboriginal children are overrepresented at all points of child welfare decision-making: investigation, substantiation, and placement in out-of-home care (Auditor General of Canada, 2008; Blackstock, Prakash, Loxley, & Wein, 2005; McKenzie, 1997; Royal Commission on Aboriginal Peoples, 1996; Trocmé, Knoke, & Blackstock, 2004). The most reliable source of data on Aboriginal children in the Canadian child welfare system comes from the Canadian Incidence Study of Reported Child Abuse and Neglect, CIS (Public Health Agency of Canada, 2010; Trocmé et al., 2001, 2005). This cross-sectional study is conducted in 5-year cycles and includes data on initial child protection investigations in Canada, including key service decisions and dispositions (i.e., substantiation, transfer to ongoing services, referrals to internal/external support services, out-of-home placement). The CIS also includes measures of the Aboriginal status of children identified to the child welfare system, disaggregated by the three major cultural groups of Aboriginal people recognized by the Canadian constitution: Métis, Inuit, and First Nations.

In Canada, Aboriginal children comprise 40% of all children in out-of-home care (Sinha, 2014). Based on national census data for 2008, while 6% of children in Canada were Aboriginal, Aboriginal children made up 22% of substantiated reports of child maltreatment in Canada (Trocmé et al., 2010). The significantly higher rate of substantiation for investigations involving First Nations children was fully explained by case characteristics, with the majority of difference being accounted for by caregiver characteristics (Sinha, Ellenbogen, & Trocmé, 2013). Lone parenthood and housing problems increased the odds of substantiation for investigations involving First Nations children but not for investigations involving non-First Nations children, suggesting that associations between specific case factors and substantiation may vary across ethno-racial groups (Sinha et al., 2013). In 2008, First Nations children living in the geographic areas served by sampled agencies were 4.2 times more likely than non-Aboriginal children to be reported for maltreatment-related concerns (Sinha et al., 2013). First Nations children also had a greater percentage of reports from nonprofessional referral sources, which may indicate disparities in access to professional support services.

The overrepresentation of Aboriginal children is particularly striking in investigations involving neglect as the sole concern (Trocmé et al., 2013). While Aboriginal children comprise a small proportion of the child population in Canada, 26% of neglect investigations involved Aboriginal children (Trocmé et al., 2013). Investigations in which neglect was the sole concern typically involved a more complex constellation of family-level risk factors (Trocmé et al., 2013). Poverty and housing problems were more often noted in these cases compared to cases involving other forms of maltreatment (Trocmé et al., 2013).

Research from the CIS suggests that certain case characteristics such as maltreatment type, child functioning concerns, and physical or emotional harm do not account for the significant overrepresentation of Aboriginal children in out-of-home placements. Case factors accounting for the overrepresentation of Aboriginal children at all service points in the child welfare system include poverty, poor housing, and substance misuse (Trocmé et al., 2004, 2005). It seems that these factors, when coupled with inequitable resources for First Nations children residing on reserves, have resulted in the overrepresentation of Aboriginal children in the Canadian child welfare system (Auditor General of Canada, 2008, 2011; Standing Committee on Public Accounts, 2009). The long history of oppression caused by assimilation policies in Canada, including residential schools, led to an accumulation of disadvantages including high rates of infant mortality and disease, low levels of school performance, high dropout rates, and other health, economic, and social disadvantages for First Nations families (Filbert & Flynn, 2010). Aboriginal families are more likely to live in poverty and have inadequate housing than other Canadians, which likely contributes to the importance of these factors for Aboriginal children who come into contact with the child welfare system (Loppie-Reading & Wien, 2009; National Council on Welfare, 2008).

Overrepresentation of Aboriginal Children Outside of Canada

Despite the fact that the National Child Abuse and Neglect Data System (NCANDS) and the Adoption and Foster Care Analysis and Reporting System do not include data collected from American Indian and Alaskan Native child welfare programs operated by tribal agencies in the United States, there is emerging evidence that American Indian and Alaskan Native children are overrepresented in the American child welfare system at the point of reporting, substantiation, and placement (Carter, 2010). Carter (2010) found that urban Native American children comprise twice as large a proportion of the foster care population as would be expected based on their proportion of the urban child population. In the United States, Native American families are more likely to be identified as having caregiver functioning issues like substance use and mental health issues as compared to non-Native American families. However, even in cases where non-Native families present with greater substance use issues, Native American children are more likely to be placed in out-of-home care (Carter, 2010). A study by Olesnavage, Preston, Sorrells, and Tadgerson (2010) noted that the American child welfare system fails to identify vulnerable families early enough, provide culturally appropriate services, and promote family reunification and connection with American Indian and Alaskan Native leaders. Research conducted by Filbert and Flynn (2010) suggests that these failures may result in missed opportunities to foster resilience and other capacities, which were found to be attributable to the possession of developmental and cultural resources. According to this research, cultural assets are protective in the development of behavioral difficulties and include self-government and community control over health, educational, and social services (Filbert & Flynn, 2010).

Data analysis indicates that factors including poverty, poor housing, multigenerational impacts of colonization, and inequitable resource distribution drive the interactions of families with the child welfare system in Australia as well as in Canada and the United States (Blackstock, 2009).

In Australia, Aboriginal and Torres Strait Islander children are three times more likely to be reported to child welfare, four times more likely to be investigated and substantiated for maltreatment, six times more likely to receive a court order, and seven times more likely to enter out-of-home placements (Tilbury, 2009). Out-of-home placement disproportionality is driven by domestic violence, substance abuse, and caregiver mental health (Zhou & Chilvers, 2010). Macro-level factors driving child welfare involvement with this population include the influences of colonization, immigration, and racism, which impact agency-level factors such as institutional racism, culturally appropriate services, discriminatory practices, and potential biases in decision-making (Sullivan & Charles, 2010; Tilbury & Thoburn, 2009). Aboriginal and Torres Strait Islander youth are also overrepresented in the youth detention system (Doolan, Najman, Mills, Cherney, & Stratheran, 2013). Doolan et al. (2013) found that social disadvantage and a history of substantiated child abuse and/or neglect did not fully explain the overrepresentation of Aboriginal and Torres Strait Islanders in the youth detention system. Systemic discrimination, which may also impact child welfare decision-making, is another possible explanation for this overrepresentation of Aboriginal youth in detention (Doolan et al., 2013). Overall, placement decisions for this population were driven by poverty, child age, unemployment, and caregiver risk factors (Bowman, Hofer, O'Rourke, & Read, 2009; Sullivan & Charles, 2010; Tilbury & Thoburn, 2009).

Impact of Organizational and Worker Factors on Child Welfare Decisions

Given the diversity among workers and child welfare organizations, there is an implicit assumption that worker and organizational characteristics influence child welfare decision-making (Fallon et al., 2013). However, empirical evidence has been slow to accumulate due to a number of measurement issues including challenges associated with isolating specific worker characteristics, the use of case vignettes as opposed to child welfare administrative data, and difficulties in delineating and clarifying organizational factors (Ashton, 2007; Drasgow & Schmitt, 2002; Grasso & Epstein, 1988; Hoagwood, 1997; Hollingsworth, Bybee, Johnson, & Swick, 2010; Yoo, 2002).

There is debate within the literature as to whether race and racial bias have an impact on child welfare decision-making, with some studies suggesting that worker ethnicity impacts the decision to place a child in out-of-home care and the type of care arrangement selected (Ryan, Garnier, Zyphur, & Zhai, 2006; Smith, 2006). Other studies suggest that risk, particularly poverty, is a greater driver of child welfare decision-making compared to race and racial bias (Drake et al., 2011; Howell, 2008). Similarly, there is no consensus in the literature about whether worker education or professional orientation strongly impact caseworkers' decisions. While some differences in decision-making have been noted with regard to placement, definitions of maltreatment, level of risk, family reunification, and sibling maltreatment by workers with different educational backgrounds, other research suggests that professional status and education do not directly impact worker decisions (Benbenishty, Segev, & Surkis, 2002; Britner & Mossler, 2002; Howell, 2008; Schuerman, Rossi, & Budde, 1999; Shdaimah, 2009; Smith, 2006). Additional research suggests that professional experience and worker age may influence decision-making. Though the mechanisms through which they may exert influence are still unclear, it has been suggested that these differences may be attributable to reduced anxiety related to agency processes and differences in the assessment of risk (Csiernik, Smith, Dewar, Dromgole, & O'Neill, 2010; Drury-Hudson, 1999; Lazar, 2006; Rossi, Schuerman, & Budde, 1999). A qualitative study examining Aboriginal child welfare workers' perception of the best interests of the child principle indicated that the Aboriginal worldview involves a holistic approach to the assessment of risk and protective factors and an emphasis on cultural identity and the multitude of factors that can influence child-rearing practices (Long & Sephton, 2011). These findings highlight the impact that a worker's approach to risk assessment may have on child welfare decision-making at all points of service delivery.

Organizational variables have been found to influence reporting to child welfare including the presence of an expressed mandate to report, worker involvement in decision-making, and the combination of an expressed mandate and negative sanctions for failing to report; however, agency size was not found to impact reporting (Ashton, 2007). There is conflicting evidence about whether organizational factors impact workers' assessment of risk or decisions regarding intervention (Darlington, Healy, & Feeney, 2010; Hollingsworth et al., 2010). While there is evidence to suggest that intervention standards may be impacted by the national, regional, and jurisdictional context in which organizations operate, few studies have been able to account for organizational factors when examining service decisions because of a failure to control for differences in the population served and all clinical factors (Giovannoni & Becerra, 1979; Grinde, 2007; Johnson & L'Esperance, 1984; Rossi et al., 1999; Schuerman et al., 1999; Wolock, 1982). Exceptions to this are the study by Graham et al. (Chapter 5, this volume), which found factors such as workload, strong supervision, and organizational support influenced placement decisions even in the presence of risk. The decision to provide ongoing services and respond to the needs of vulnerable families, particularly overrepresented populations, is an important service decision with significant resource implications (Blackstock, 2009; Chabot et al., 2013).

Our overarching theoretical framework for the study is the DME (Baumann et al., 2011). The DME describes case, individual (e.g., caseworker), organizational, and external factors that operate in a complex way to result in the pattern of decision-making over time that describes the characteristics of a service delivery system. Case factors are thought to influence the assessment of individual cases that describe the level of concern, and the other factors influence the thresholds for action of the decision-maker actors in the system (Dalgleish & Drew, 1989). For this study we examine case characteristics and organizational factors in a multilevel context, where we hypothesize that children are more likely to be placed out of home in agencies that serve a relatively high proportion of Aboriginal children. For this study, data limitations prevent including decision-maker factors, and consequently it is not a test of the range of influences that are a part of the DME. Furthermore, we suppose that there are other organizational factors operating, as we discovered in our prior analysis (Chabot et al., 2103), that may help to explain placement likelihood.

METHODS

The primary objective of the CIS is to produce a Canadian estimate of the incidence of child maltreatment in the year the study takes place. Using a multistage sampling design, a representative sample of agencies was first selected from the complete list of child welfare organizations in Canada. The second sampling stage involved selecting cases opened in the study sites during the 3-month period from October 1 to December 31, 2008. Screened-in investigations were evaluated to ensure that they met the study definitions of maltreatment. Investigations where child maltreatment was alleged/suspected or the possibility of future maltreatment was assessed during the investigation were included in the sample. These procedures yielded a final unweighted sample of children aged 0–15 years who were investigated because of maltreatment-related concerns.

To further investigate the role of proportion of Aboriginal investigations in placement decisions, a secondary analysis of the CIS datasets was conducted. The datasets contain information about key clinical factors collected during the course of child maltreatment investigations. In addition, characteristics of the workers who conducted the investigation and of the organization from which the investigation originated are also available.

Data Collection Instruments

The information was collected using a three-page data collection instrument consisting of an Intake Face Sheet, a Household Information Sheet, and a Child Information Sheet. Data collected by this instrument included type of abuse and neglect investigated, level of substantiation and duration of maltreatment, physical and emotional harm to the child, functioning concerns for the children and their caregivers; housing information, and information about short-term service dispositions. Child welfare workers were also asked to complete a self-reporting questionnaire that included questions about their age, caseload size, academic credentials, years of experience in social services and child protection, and if they had received additional training in the course of their child protection experience. In addition, information on organizational size and location was collected for the participating sites. Sites completed an Organizational Questionnaire that included questions about the structure of the organization, minimum qualifications for caseworkers, worker morale, computerization of case file information system, and workplace overcrowding.

A subsample of investigations is used in the present analyses. Only investigations in which maltreatment is substantiated and the case remained open for ongoing services are included in order to examine predictors of placement in out-of-home care. To allow comparability with previous CIS cycles, cases from Quebec and cases investigated for exposure to domestic violence were excluded from this analysis.

Variables Included in Present Analysis

Key clinical and organizational variables were included in the model to reflect an ecological approach to understanding child maltreatment and child welfare service decisions. This approach allows for an understanding of the relative contribution of clinical variables and variables that, in principle, should be extraneous to the case disposition (specifically, worker and organizational variables).

OUTCOME VARIABLE
Workers were asked to indicate whether the child subject of the investigation was placed in out-of-home child welfare care at the conclusion of the initial investigation. The variable used in this analysis is dichotomous (formal placement, no placement).

LEVEL 1: CLINICAL VARIABLES
Clinical variables were selected based on literature that identifies the key clinical factors associated with child maltreatment and risk of future child maltreatment. Comparability with our previous analyses was also a determining factor (see Table 10.1).

LEVEL 2: ORGANIZATIONAL VARIABLES
Organizational variables were selected based on the theoretical literature that has explored the influence of organizational factors on child welfare service provision. For this analysis, organizational variables were available that were not included in previous cycles: structure of the agency, nature of services offered, presence of differential/alternate response to investigations, whether there is the possibility of an alternative dispute resolution process other than judicial procedures, and the availability of on-reserve services for Aboriginal populations (see Table 10.2). (Differential response in the Canadian context refers to a process of assessing case situations that are considered low risk for maltreatment concerns.)

Analysis Plan

Multilevel logistic regression was used to analyze the subsample of CIS-2008 investigations. Multilevel statistical models allow for analysis of the influence of clinical and organizational variables on placement decisions. Mplus software was used to produce model estimates. Mplus allows for dichotomous outcome variables, which are more reflective of decision-making in child welfare and

Table 10.1 LEVEL 1 CLINICAL MEASURES

Measures	Definition	Coding
Physical harm	Defined as no harm, or at least one of: bruises/cuts/ scrapes, burns and scalds, broken bones, head trauma, other health conditions.	1, some type of physical harm noted 0, no harm
Mental/ emotional harm	Defined as mental or emotional harm caused by the investigated maltreatment. The child harmed by the action/ inaction of caregiver.	1, some type of emotional harm noted 0, no harm
Cooperation level	The level of cooperation with the investigation by the caregivers. If one caregiver was deemed not cooperative then the household level of cooperation was not cooperative.	1, cooperative 0, not cooperative
Ethnicity	Ethno-racial categories developed by Statistics Canada for the 2006 Canadian Census.	1, Aboriginal (Métis and Inuit excluded) 0, non-Aboriginal

facilitate the specific use of the logistic link function for binary outcome variables under maximum likelihood estimation using multiple imputation to correct bias due to missing data.

After fitting the same single first-level regression, Level 2 predictors were each added individually. All models were fitted on 50 multiple imputation datasets using Mplus 7.1 (Muthén & Muthén, 1998–2012).

RESULTS

Table 10.3 presents descriptive statistics for the variables included in the multilevel analysis using the subsample of 1,710 substantiated maltreatment investigations opened to ongoing child welfare services used in this contribution. More than one-quarter (28%) of these investigations originated from agencies where 45% or more of the total investigations involved Aboriginal children. Slightly more than half (55%) of these investigations originated from an agency

Table 10.2 LEVEL 2 ORGANIZATIONAL MEASURES

Measures	Definition	Coding
Proportion of aboriginal investigations	The proportion of all investigations agencies conduct which involve Aboriginal children	1, agencies with 45% or more investigations involving Aboriginal children 0, agencies with less than 45% of investigations involving Aboriginal children
Government-run	Whether the agency is administered by the provincial government or by a community agency that receives provincial funding	1, government-run 0, community-run
Array of services	Whether the agency provides a range of social services or strictly provides child protection services	1, array of services 0, child protection only
Differential response	The agency operates a Differential/Alternate Response as well as an Investigation Response	1, yes 0, no
Alternative resolution	Office uses Alternative Dispute Resolution approach with families	1, yes 0, no
On reserve	Agency services Aboriginals on reserve	1, yes 0, no
Remoteness	The geographic remoteness of the agency based on census data	1, yes 0, no

that was government-run. The majority (69%) originated from agencies that utilized differential response, and more than 60% (62%) of substantiated investigations originated from agencies located on First Nations' reserves.

Fourteen percent of all investigations were substantiated and referred for ongoing services. Of these investigations, physical and mental/emotional harm was noted in almost half of the cases (44%). Most investigating workers described the caregivers as cooperative (80%). Overall, approximately one-third (33%) of investigations involved Aboriginal children.

Prior to the parametric modeling, a descriptive analysis of the multi-level structure is conducted where the proportion of agency placement and

Table 10.3 CHARACTERISTICS OF VARIABLES IN THE ANALYSIS ($N = 1,710$)

Measures				
Dependent variable: Placement	**Frequency**	**%**	**Frequency**	**%**
Level 1 variables	Yes		No	
Physical harm noted	238	13.92	1472	86.08
Mental/emotional harm noted	757	44.27	953	55.73
Caregivers cooperative	1,376	80.47	334	19.53
Aboriginal identity child	559	32.66	1151	67.31
Level 2 variables	**Frequency**	**%**	**Frequency**	**%**
Proportion of Aboriginal investigations (>45% of investigations)	478	27.95	1232	72.05
Government-run	938	54.85	772	45.15
Array of services	847	49.53	520	30.41
Differential response	1177	68.83	510	29.82
Alternative dispute resolution	1061	62.05	473	27.66
On reserve	537	27.66	1125	62.05
Remoteness	782	45.73	786	45.96

a continuous version of our principal independent variable (proportion of Aboriginal investigations) are crossed with four of the five other organizational predictors, giving the means of the two continuous indicators within both presence and absence of each of the four agency-level factors. The four organizational variables distribute themselves in a similar fashion across the placement and the principal predictor. Correlations for these four data points are 0.92 for the presence category and 0.96 for the absence category. This in itself is indicative of a relevant pool of variables, again strongly supporting the centrality of proportion of Aboriginal investigations, and lends credibility to these organizational indicators as possible contextual factors that may clarify the role of the proportion of Aboriginal investigations variable.

For the inferential models, ordering regressions by the absolute t-value of the coefficient of first-level variable Aboriginal status, we find that the models' result set is divided in two, with the first half including a term for proportion of Aboriginal investigations. Disproportionality of the decision to place Aboriginal children is the main focus for these series of studies, and this finding

Table 10.4 COEFFICIENTS ASSOCIATED WITH PLACEMENT LIKELIHOOD: LEVEL 1 AND
LEVEL INDEPENDENT VARIABLES (CIS-2008)

	Model 4 full	Beta	S.e.	T-value	p value
Level 1 variables (case)	Emotional harm	0.350	0.121	2.884	0.004
	Physical harm	0.261	0.166	1.570	0.116
	Family cooperation	−0.732	0.143	−5.116	0.000
	Child Aboriginal status	−0.003	0.157	−0.021	0.983
Level 2 variables (organizational)	Proportion of Aboriginal investigations	1.210	0.402	3.010	0.003
	Provincial government-run agency	1.033	0.296	3.490	0.000
	Proportion of Aboriginal investigations *government-run	−0.543	0.538	−1.009	0.313

reinforces the conclusion from the previous analyses (Fallon et al., 2013; Fluke et al., 2010) about the centrality of that indicator.

The final and statistically best-fitted model is presented in Table 10.4. Models 1 and 2 include proportion of Aboriginal investigations and government-run agency governance, respectively, and Models 3 and 4 consist of these combined together with their interaction. It appears that there are additive effects from Models 1 and 2 to Model 3, but Model 4 clearly prevents it from being of linear form.

DISCUSSION

The present analysis of CIS-2008 data is consistent with findings exploring the role of organizational variables in previous cycles of the study (Chabot et al., 2013; Fallon et al., 2013; Fluke et al., 2010). Investigations are more likely to result in out-of-home placements in agencies serving large proportions of Aboriginal children (45% or more of investigations at agency involve Aboriginal children). Based on our previous work (Chabot et al., 2013), we hypothesized that contextual factors (i.e., at the organizational level) may explain the disparate placement decision-making. In the present analysis, we incorporated additional factors at the organizational level to explore this hypothesis. After performing multiple tests of these other factors, the proportion of Aboriginal investigations remains an important main organizational level effect in our models.

That said, our analysis tested other organizational-level factors to see if they substitute for or operate in conjunction with the proportion of Aboriginal investigations. According to the statistical models presented earlier, the most important of these is whether the provincial government operates the child welfare agency. As with the proportion of Aboriginal children on the caseload, the risk of a child being placed is greater in government-run agencies compared to agencies operated by private agencies.

Interestingly there tends to be higher Aboriginal caseloads and higher than average placement rates in situations where the provincial government directly provides child welfare services, compared to when such services are provided by community-based organizations. From other studies, disparities in aggregate rates of placement at the provincial level for First Nations compared to non-Aboriginal children are very large, approaching differences of 10 to 1 in provinces that operate child welfare agencies (Sinha, 2014).

However, when government-run and Aboriginal caseload variables are both included in the models, both are statistically significant. Part of the explanation appears to be the disparate use of placement in provincially run agencies. This is also the case from our models where First Nations agencies are excluded as well. It remains unclear how policy differences in governmentally versus non-governmentally operated agencies result in these disparities and precisely how these interact with the proportion of Aboriginal investigations. However, we return to earlier observations regarding the possible difficulties of funding services that might prevent out-of-home placement in agencies that serve a relatively large proportion of indigenous children (Blackstock, 2009). In addition, the results for provincially operated agencies may reflect difficulties in developing broad-based and culturally appropriate community supports for families and the possible challenges this may present for governmental agencies in contrast to community-based agencies. Of course, from our results, this may be especially problematic for provincial agencies that serve relatively large Aboriginal caseloads.

The analysis is also interesting in that other organizational factors that we thought might be explanatory of placement risk in the presences of Aboriginal caseload and government-operated agencies were not. This is especially true of our composite for remoteness, which we hypothesized might be indicative of the difficulties of making support services available in more rural areas, given that the lack of such services was one explanation we thought might be involved (Fallon et al., 2013; Fluke et al., 2010). Thus, the capacity of child welfare services to provide a wider array and more appropriate services may be the larger challenge compared to remoteness. Interestingly, the use of alternative dispute resolution and differential response, while not attaining statistical significance in the presence of our other factors, were explanatory on their own, were associated with lower placement risk, and were less common in agencies with high Aboriginal caseloads and government-run services. This suggests that structural practices and policies like these may have some potential to reduce placement risk more generally if operationalized in agencies with larger Aboriginal caseloads.

Strength and Limitations

The CIS is an excellent source of information for this type of analysis since it reflects data on placement decisions from the investigating worker and it captures data on children at the initial investigation stage. However, limitations of this study should be considered since we did not control for the non-independence of siblings in the sample, and the data are cross-sectional.

In this study, we chose to capture only the primary form of child maltreatment, which represents the child protection workers' overriding concerns. However, co-occurrence of different types of maltreatment may also increase the likelihood of placement.

Limitations of CIS Dataset/Differences Between 1998 and 2003 and 2008

Workers who were primarily responsible for conducting the child maltreatment investigation completed the data collection instrument at the conclusion of the investigation. These ratings were not independently verified, including the type of maltreatment investigated and the level of substantiation. It is possible that this could influence the variables examined in the analysis. Workers could first make decisions about the case and then complete the data collection instrument to justify their judgments; for instance, by endorsing various risk factors to justify the decision to place a child in out-of-home care (or, conversely, failing to endorse risk factors to justify discontinuing service to the family) (cf., Bartelink et al., 2018).

The conclusions made about the investigation as represented in the dataset usually reflected a time period of 30 days. Child functioning issues, caregiver functioning problems, and other key risk factors may not have been known to the investigating worker at the time the data collection instrument was completed. The non-Aboriginal group includes children who may be ethnically and racially diverse (approximately 10% of sample is not white or Aboriginal).

Cases that were screened out by a child welfare authority or investigated only by the police were not included in the study. Cases that were known to a community member or maltreatment that was known only to the child were also not included in the dataset. These findings cannot be generalized to Québec because data from this province were not included in the analyses due to differences in data collection procedures in this province.

The primary objective of the CIS-2008 was to provide a reliable estimate of the incidence of child maltreatment in Canada. Although information was collected about workers and agencies, these variables were collected to provide context with respect to the primary objective. Thus, key concepts in the literature related to human resources, such as worker stress, worker burnout, and levels of social support, were not measured. These factors are theorized in the literature as having influence in the delivery of child welfare services. The study was not designed to collect precise organizational measures, and therefore the proportion of Aboriginal investigations is likely a proxy for a number of constructs, including a lack of services and resources. More research is needed to develop more precise organizational measures that are able to deconstruct this contribution. Similarly, the measure used to assess organizational culture was the rating assigned to the agency by research staff responsible for data collection. It did not reflect an organizational-level self-reported rating of organizational culture and therefore may be inadequate.

Implications

There is clear evidence that Aboriginal children are overrepresented in the Canadian child welfare system and that both case- and organizational-level factors influence the placement decision. Consistent with the CIS-1998 and 2003 analyses, a higher proportion of Aboriginal families served by an agency is associated with an increased likelihood of placement in the presence of clinical variables. Further analysis needs to be conducted to fully understand individual- and organizational-level variables that may influence decisions regarding placement of Aboriginal children. There is also a need for research that is sensitive to differences among Métis, Inuit, and First Nations populations on and off reserve communities. The legacy of colonialism has left Aboriginal peoples disproportionately ranked among the poorest people in Canada, living in the worst housing conditions (Wilson & Macdonald, 2010). Special attention should be given to exploring and addressing the multigenerational impacts of colonialism and discrimination through the First Nations residential schools programs that operated through the mid-1900s and the child welfare system as well (Blackstock &

Trocmé, 2005) and to remedying outstanding inequities in child welfare resources (Auditor General of Canada, 2008, 2011; Standing Committee on Public Accounts, 2009).

REFERENCES

Ashton, V. (2007). The impact of organizational environment on the likelihood that social workers will report child maltreatment. *Journal of Aggression, Maltreatment & Trauma, 15*(1), 1–18.

Auditor General of Canada. (2008). First Nations Child and Family Services Program-Indian and Northern Affairs Canada. 2008 May: Report of the Auditor General of Canada. https://www.afn.ca/uploads/Social_Development/Report%20of%20the%20Auditor%20General%20-%20Chapter%204_en.pdf

Auditor General of Canada. (2011). Programs for First Nations on reserve. June 2011 Status Report of the Auditor General of Canada. http://www.oag-bvg.gc.ca/internet/English/parl_oag_201106_04_e_35372.html

Bartelink, C., Knorth, E. J., López López, M., Koopmans, C., Ten Berge, I. J., Witteman, C. L. M., & Van Yperen, T. A. (2018). Reasons for placement decisions in a case of suspected child abuse: The role of reasoning, work experience and attitudes in decision-making. *Child Abuse and Neglect, 83*, 129–141. doi:10.1016/j.chiabu.2018.06.013

Baumann, D. J., Dalgleish, L., Fluke, J. D., & Kern, H. (2011). *The decision-making ecology*. Washington, DC: American Humane Association.

Benbenishty, R., Segev, D., & Surkis, T. (2002). Information-search and decision-making by professionals and nonprofessionals in cases of alleged child-abuse and maltreatment. *Journal of Social Service Research, 28*(3), 1–18.

Blackstock, C. (2009). After the apology why are so many First Nations children still in foster care? A summary of the research on ethnic overrepresentation and structural bias. *Children Australia, 34*(1), 22–31.

Blackstock, C., Prakash, T., Loxley, J., & Wein, F. (2005). Summary of findings. In FNCFCS (Ed.), *Wein:de: We are coming to the light of day* (pp. 13–59). Ottawa: First Nations Child and Family Caring Society of Canada.

Blackstock C., & Trocmé, N. (2005). Community-based child welfare for Aboriginal children: Supporting resilience through structural change. *Social Policy Journal of New Zealand, 24*(12), 12–33.

Bowman, A., Hofer, L., O'Rourke, C., & Read, L. (2009). *Racial disproportionality in Wisconsin's child welfare system*. Madison, Wisconsin: University of Wisconsin–Madison, Department of Children and Families.

Britner, P. A., & Mossler, D. G. (2002). Professionals' decision-making about out-of-home placements following instances of child abuse. *Child Abuse and Neglect, 26*(4), 317–326.

Carter, V. B. (2010). Factors predicting placement of urban American Indian/Alaskan Natives into out-of-home care. *Children and Youth Services Review, 32*(5), 657–663.

Chabot, M., Fallon, B., Tonmyr, L., MacLaurin, B., Fluke, J. D., & Blackstock, C. (2013). Exploring alternate specifications to explain agency-level effects in placement decisions regarding Aboriginal children: Further analysis of the Canadian Incidence Study of Reported Child Abuse and Neglect Part B. *Child Abuse and Neglect, 37*, 61–76.

Csiernik, R., Smith, C., Dewar, J., Dromgole, L., & O'Neill, A. (2010). Supporting new workers in a child welfare agency: An exploratory study. *Journal of Workplace Behavioral Health, 25*(3), 218–232.

Dagleish, L., & Drew, E. (1989). The relationship of child abuse indicators to the assessment of perceived risk and the decision to separate. *Child Abuse and Neglect, 13*, 491–506.

Darlington, Y., Healy, K., & Feeney, J. A. (2010). Approaches to assessment and intervention across four types of child and family welfare services. *Children and Youth Services Review, 32*, 356–364.

Doolan, I., Najman, J., Mills, R., Cherney, A., & Strathearn, L. (2013). Does child abuse and neglect explain the overrepresentation of Aboriginal and Torres Strait Islander young people in youth detention? Findings from a birth cohort study. *Child Abuse and Neglect, 37*, 303–309.

Drake, B., Jolley, J. M., Lanier, P., Fluke, J. D., Barth, R. P., & Jonson-Reid, M. (2011). Racial bias in child protection? A comparison of competing explanations using national data. *Pediatrics, 127*(3), 471–478.

Drasgow, F., & Schmitt, N. (Eds.). (2002). *Measuring and analyzing behaviour in organizations.* San Francisco, CA: Jossey-Bass.

Drury-Hudson, J. (1999). Decision making in child protection: The use of theoretical, empirical, and procedural knowledge by novices and experts and implications for fieldwork placement. *British Journal of Social Work, 29*, 147–169.

Fallon, B., Chabot, M., Fluke, J. D., Blackstock, C., MacLaurin, B., & Tonmyr, L. (2013). Placement decisions and disparities among Aboriginal children: Further analysis of the Canadian Incidence Study of Reported Child Abuse and Neglect Part A: Comparisons of the 1998 and 2003 surveys. *Child Abuse and Neglect, 37*(1), 47–60.

Filbert, K., & Flynn, R. J. (2010). Developmental and cultural assets and resilient outcomes in First Nations young people in care: An initial test of an explanatory model. *Children and Youth Services Review, 32*, 560–564.

Fluke, J. D., Chabot, M., Fallon, B., MacLaurin, B., & Blackstock, C. (2010). Placement decisions and disparities among Aboriginal groups: An application of the decision making ecology through multi-level analysis. *Child Abuse and Neglect, 34*(1), 57–69.

Giovannoni, J., & Becerra, R. (1979). *Defining child abuse.* New York: Free Press.

Grasso, A., & Epstein, I. (1988). Management by measurement: Organizational dilemmas and opportunities. *Administration in Social Work, 11*(3/4), 89–100.

Grinde, T. V. (2007). Nordic child welfare services: Variations in norms, attitudes and practice. *Journal of Children's Services, 2*(4), 44–58.

Hoagwood, K. (1997). Interpreting nullity: The Fort Bragg experiment—a comparative success or failure? *American Psychologist, 52*, 546–550.

Hollingsworth, L. D., Bybee, D., Johnson, E. I., & Swick, D. C. (2010). A comparison of caseworker characteristics in public and private foster care agencies. *Children and Youth Services Review, 32,* 578–584.

Howell, M. L. (2008). Decisions with good intentions: Substance use allegations and child protective services screening decisions. *Journal of Public Child Welfare, 2*(3), 293–316.

Johnson, W., & L'Esperance, J. (1984). Predicting the recurrence of child abuse. *Social Work Research and Abstracts, 20*(2), 21–26.

Lazar, A. (2006). Determinants of child protection officers' decisions in emergency situations: An experimental study. *Child and Youth Care Forum, 35,* 263–276.

Long, M., & Sephton, R. (2011). Rethinking the "best interests" of the child: Voices from Aboriginal child and family welfare practitioners. *Australian Social Work, 64*(1), 96–112.

Loppie-Reading, C., & Wien, F. (2009). *Health inequalities and social determinants of Aboriginal peoples' health.* Prince George, BC: National Collaborating Centre for Aboriginal Health.

McKenzie, B. (1997). Connecting policy and practice in First Nations child and family services: A Manitoba case study. In J. Pulkingham & G. Ternowetsky (Eds.), *Child and family policies: Struggles, strategies and options* (pp 100–114). Halifax: Fernwood Publishing.

Muthén, L. K., & Muthén, B. O. (1998–2012). *Mplus user's guide* (7th ed.). Los Angeles: Muthén & Muthén.

National Council on Welfare. (2008). *First Nations, Métis and Inuit children and youth: Time to act.* Ottawa: National Council on Welfare.

Olesnavage, M., Preston, M. D., Sorrells, A. D., & Tadgerson, S. M. (2010). Disproportionate minority contact of American Indians/Alaska Natives in the child welfare system of Michigan. *Michigan Bar Journal, 89*(1), 31–35.

Public Health Agency of Canada (PHAC). (2010). *Canadian incidence study of reported child abuse and neglect 2008: Major findings.* Ottawa: PHAC.

Rossi, P. H., Schuerman, J., & Budde, S. (1999). Understanding decisions about child maltreatment. *Evaluation Review, 23*(6), 579–598.

Royal Commission on Aboriginal Peoples. (1996). *Report of the Royal Commission on Aboriginal Peoples.* Ottawa: Indian and Northern Affairs Canada.

Ryan, J. P., Garnier, P., Zyphur, M., & Zhai, F. (2006). Testing the effects of caseworker characteristics in child welfare. *Children and Youth Services Review, 29*(9), 993–1006.

Schuerman, J., Rossi, P. H., & Budde, S. (1999). Decisions on placement and family preservation. *Evaluation Review, 23*(6), 599–618.

Shdaimah, C. (2009). Rescuing children and punishing poor families: Housing related decisions. *Journal of Sociology & Social Welfare, 36*(3), 33–57.

Sinha, V. (2014). *National First Nations child welfare: FNCIS Advisory Committee.* Montreal: McGill University.

Sinha, V., Ellenbogen, S., & Trocmé, N. (2013). Substantiating neglect of first nations and non-Aboriginal children. *Children and Youth Services Review, 35,* 2080–2090.

Smith, B. D. (2006). *An examination of contextual factors that influence permanency decisions in the public child welfare system* (Unpublished doctoral diss., Howard University, School of Social Work.)

Standing Committee on Public Accounts. (2009). First Nations child and family services program—Indian and Northern Affairs Canada of the May 2008 report of the Auditor General: Report of the Standing Committee on Public Accounts. https://fncaringsociety.com/sites/default/files/docs/402_PACP_Rpt07-e.pdf

Sullivan, R., & Charles, G. (2010). Disproportionate representation and First nations child welfare in Canada. The Federation of Community Social Services of UBC. http://fpsss.com/wordpress/wp-content/uploads/2010/04/Disproportionate-Representation-and-First-Nations-Child-Welfare-Ap-10.pdf

Tilbury, C. (2009). The overrepresentation of indigenous children in the Australian child welfare system. *International Journal of Social Welfare, 18*(1), 57–64.

Tilbury, C., & Thoburn, J. (2009). Using racial disproportionality and disparity as an outcome measure for child welfare programs. *Children and Youth Services Review, 31*(10), 1101–1106.

Trocmé, N., Fallon, B., MacLaurin, B., Daciuk, J., Felstiner, C., Black, T., . . . Cloutier, R. (2005). *Canadian incidence study of reported child abuse and neglect, 2003: Major findings.* Ottawa: Minister of Public Works and Government Services Canada.

Trocmé, N., Fallon, B., MacLaurin, B., Sinha, V., Black, T., Fast, E., . . . Holroyd, J. (2010). Characteristics of children and families. In PHAC (Ed.), *Canadian incidence study of reported child abuse, 2008: Major findings* (pp. 36–43). Ottawa, ON: Public Health Agency of Canada.

Trocmé, N., Fallon, B., Sinha, V., Van Wert, M., Kozlowski, A., & MacLaurin, B. (2013). Differentiating between child protection and family support in the Canadian child welfare system's response to intimate partner violence, corporal punishment, and child neglect. *International Journal of Psychology, 48*(2), 128–140.

Trocmé, N., Knoke, D., & Blackstock, C. (2004). Pathways to the overrepresentation of Aboriginal children in Canada's child welfare system. *Social Service Review, 74*(4), 577–600.

Trocmé, N., MacLaurin, B., Fallon, B., Daciuk, J., Billingsley, D., Tourigny, M., . . . McKenzie, B. (2001). *The Canadian incidence study of reported child abuse and neglect: Final report.* Ottawa: Minister of Public Works and Government Services Canada.

Wilson, D., & Macdonald, D. (2010). *The income gap between Aboriginal peoples and the rest of Canada.* Ottawa: Canadian Centre for Policy Alternatives.

Wolock, I. (1982). Community characteristics in child abuse and neglect cases. *Social Work Research and Abstracts, 18*(2), 9–15.

Yoo, J. (2002). The relationship between organizational variables and client outcomes: A case study in child welfare. *Administration in Social Work, 26*(2), 39–61.

Zhou, A. Z., & Chilvers, M. (2010). Infants in Australian out-of-home care. *British Journal of Social Work, 40*(1), 26–43.

Decision-Making in Child Welfare and Protection in Practice

11

The Use and Usability of Decision-Making Theory in Child Welfare Policy and Practice

CORA BARTELINK, TOM A. VAN YPEREN, INGRID J. TEN BERGE, AND ERIK J. KNORTH ■

INTRODUCTION

Decision-making is an essential element of the work of professionals in child welfare and child protection. The concept represents a cognitive process of assessing a situation and identifying and choosing alternative possibilities, resulting in the selection of a course of action (Bartelink, 2018; Wang, Wang, Patel, & Patel, 2004). The assessment of the situation involves the problems, risks, strengths, and protective factors present—as well as their interactions— in children's lives. The whole process is aimed at reducing the problems and risks and reinforcing strengths and protective factors. Some of the situations to assess and the choices to make are uncomplicated and have limited impact, such as the decision to advice parents to offer the child a training in social skills because of a mild shyness. Other decisions are of vital importance, such as the recommendation to place a child in child protective custody and foster care because of severe child maltreatment.

Decision-making theories serve to describe and hypothesize on the mechanisms of deliberate, conscious and analytical strategies in decision-making, as

Cora Bartelink, Tom A. van Yperen, Ingrid J. Ten Berge, and Erik J. Knorth, *The Use and Usability of Decision-Making Theory in Child Welfare Policy and Practice* In: *Decision-Making and Judgment in Child Welfare and Protection.* Edited by: John D. Fluke, Mónica López López, Rami Benbenishty, Erik J. Knorth, and Donald J. Baumann, Oxford University Press (2021).
© Oxford University Press. DOI: 10.1093/oso/9780190059538.003.0011.

well as in unconscious and intuitive processes that may be involved (Evans, 2008; Hogarth, 2005; Kahneman, 2003, 2011; Sloman, 1996). Professional decision-making is often associated with a replicable, analytical process (Munro, 2008). In this respect, it can be distinguished from decision-making by laymen. Caseworkers base their decisions on sound observations and other data, and they build clear rationales that are explicit and can be critically evaluated for their validity. That is, in theory. In practice, however, decisions by caseworkers often tend to be made intuitively (Klein, 2000). Moreover, research has repeatedly indicated that decision-making processes in child welfare and child protection are flawed in several respects. First, it is found that caseworkers relatively often disagree about the assessment of the family situation (e.g., whether or not the child is exposed to or at risk of child maltreatment) and about the decisions to be made (what action should be taken; cf. Berben, 2000; Britner & Mossler, 2002; Gold, Benbenishty, & Osmo, 2001; Knorth, 1995; Rossi, Schuerman, & Budde, 1999; Ten Berge, 1998). Second, some studies have shown that caseworkers have difficulty making accurate assessments of the situation and predicting the future behavior of their clients (cf. Metselaar, Knorth, Noom, Van Yperen, & Konijn, 2004; Skeem, Mulvey, & Lidz, 2000).

There are several explanations for caseworkers disagreeing in their judgments and decisions and struggling with accurate assessment (for an overview, see Gambrill, 2005; Garb, 1998). First, caseworkers can rarely rely on clear empirical findings (i.e., evidence-based decision-making; Berben, 2000; Kaplan, Pelcovitz, & Labruna, 1999), unambiguous theories (Munro, 1998), or explicit professional knowledge or guidelines (Bartelink, Ten Berge, & Van Vianen, 2015; Drury-Hudson, 1999; Ten Berge, 1998). Rather, it has been found that personal beliefs and experience influence decision-making (Arad-Davidzon & Benbenishty, 2008; Benbenishty et al., 2015; Benbenishty, Segev, Surgis, & Elias, 2002; Brunnberg & Pećnik, 2007; Jent et al., 2011; Osmo & Benbenishty, 2004; Portwood, 1998; Rosen, 1994), as do contextual and individual circumstances, such as family poverty and the professional's mood (Baumann, Fluke, Dalgleish, & Kern, 2014; Dalgleish, 2003; De Vries, Holland, & Witteman, 2008; Gambrill & Shlonsky, 2000; Holland, 2000).

Second, caseworkers have difficulty processing complex and large amounts of information. Therefore, they may unconsciously use strategies to make the decision-making task easier. They may be prone to the use of heuristics as a way of dealing with the complexity of the decision-making task. *Heuristics* are simple, efficient rules that people often use to form judgments and make decisions (Gambrill, 2005). However, these strategies make them vulnerable to certain pitfalls. They are mental "shortcuts" that usually focus on one aspect of a complex problem while ignoring others. These heuristics are often based on non–case-related factors like the previous experience of the caseworker with other families. Because of the personal nature of these shortcuts, they may lead to differences in the decisions made by different caseworkers and to inaccuracy of the assessment.

In addition, caseworkers appear reluctant to revise their initial judgments (Munro, 1996, 1999). Munro (1996, 1999) found that caseworkers' first impression of a family strongly influenced their response to additional information. They were skeptical about information that did not correspond to this first impression and were less critical of information that corresponded to their first impression (Munro, 1996, 1999). Munro (1999) also found that caseworkers tended to make decisions based on evidence that was recent, vivid, or emotionally charged. As a consequence, they may suffer from phenomena such as tunnel vision and confirmation bias (Gambrill, 2005). *Tunnel vision* means that caseworkers become caught up in a narrow picture of the family's situation. *Confirmation bias* is the tendency to confirm professional assumptions rather than to falsify them. These phenomena might distort caseworkers' judgment of the situation and thereby lead to an incorrect judgment (i.e., a false-positive or false-negative decision).

This chapter discusses decision-making theories and how methods—based on these theories to support practitioners—could improve decision-making in child welfare and child protection, related to our studies into decision support systems in the Netherlands. In the next section, we discuss two theoretical frames that underpin the complexity of decision-making tasks in child welfare and child protection, followed by a reflection on methods that aim to support decision-making based on our findings. Then we move the focus to what seems to be a crucial factor: the decision-maker him- or herself. Later, we discuss some options that might be helpful to improve decision-making. Finally, we draw conclusions.

DECISION-MAKING THEORY AND METHODS IN CHILD WELFARE AND CHILD PROTECTION

Theory

DECISION-MAKING ECOLOGY

To obtain a better understanding of the complex nature of the process of decision-making, Baumann, Fluke, Dalgleish, and Kern (2014) proposed a framework for studying decision-making in child welfare and child protection which they called Decision-Making Ecology (DME) (see Figure 11.1). According to this framework, the decision-making process consists of both the assessment of the situation and the decision on the course of action. In particular, decision-making is described as a psychological process, one based on Dalgleish's *general assessment and decision-making model* (Dalgleish, 2003). As

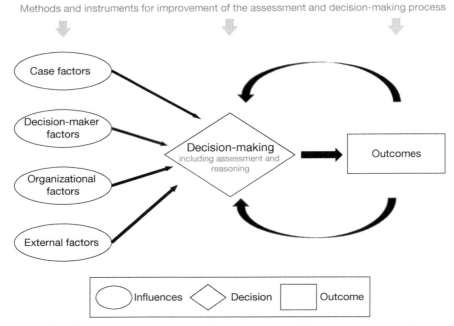

Figure 11.1 Decision-Making Ecology (Baumann et al., 2014). Gray items are added to the original model, as is explained in this section.

part of such a process, the reasoning of the decision-maker, be it implicit or explicit, connects the assessment of the situation to the decision to be made—it is more or less like a debate that caseworkers have with themselves (and possibly with coworkers) about the case and their professional knowledge, resulting in a choice about the course of action. Reasons, therefore, are the recognizable "products" of this reasoning process (see Gambrill, 2005). In addition, Baumann and colleagues (2014) assumed that the outcomes of previous decisions can influence caseworkers' future reasoning and decision-making. These outcomes may be actual as well as perceived costs and benefits to the decision-maker, the client, and/or the agency responsible for handling and supporting the case.

According to Baumann and colleagues (2014; see Figure 11.1), a range of factors relating to the case, the decision-maker, and the organizational and external contexts also influence the decision-making process and thereby the outcomes. These factors may combine in several ways. *Case factors* concern the child and family characteristics which influence assessment and decision-making, such parenting behaviors and children's health and psychosocial functioning. *Decision-maker factors* concern the characteristics of the decision-maker which influence assessment and decision-making, such as age, education, work experience, and attitude. *Organizational factors* concern the characteristics of an agency that influence assessment and decision-making, such as excessive caseloads, role ambiguity, and adequate or inadequate supervision. *External factors* mainly concern the broader environmental characteristics, such as the law and the availability of community resources.

The DME framework has been applied in a number of studies on the substantiation of maltreatment (Detlaff et al., 2011; Fluke et al., 2001), placement decisions (Fluke, Chabot, Fallon, MacLaurin, & Blackstock, 2010; Graham, Detlaff, Baumann, & Fluke, 2015), and reunification decisions (Wittenstrom, Baumann, Fluke, Graham, & James, 2015). These studies usually focused on the *context* in which professionals make their decisions (i.e., organizational factors and external factors; Baumann et al., 2010; Detlaff et al., 2011; Fluke et al., 2010). Less is known about the impact of decision-maker factors, although it has been argued that attitudes (e.g., Benbenishty et al., 2015; Jent et al., 2011) and work experience (Benbenishty et al., 2002; Brunnberg & Pećnik, 2007) may influence the decision-making process.

The DME is a relevant interpretive framework for research because it describes several sources that influence the decision-making process. However, it does not prescribe the characteristics of good-quality decision-making. In addition to the DME, we suggest that a good-quality professional decision-making process can be characterized as:

- *Structured*: Judgments and decisions are made systematically and are well-founded, verifiable, and transparent (Gambrill, 2005);
- *Evidence-based*: Judgments are based on relevant theories and empirical knowledge about the occurrence, causes, and factors that prolong child and family problems, and decisions about interventions rely on research-based evidence, professional practice-based knowledge, and relevant client experiences (Sacket, Straus, Richardson, Rosenberg, & Haynes, 2000), and the decision-making is based on case-specific knowledge (i.e., the assessment is used to inform the decisions);
- *Involving dialogue with parents and children (shared decision-making)*: Parents and children are active participants in the decision-making process (Faber, Harmsen, Van der Burg, & Van der Weijden, 2013; Joosten et al., 2008; Patel, Bakken, & Ruland, 2008; Poston & Hanson, 2010; Swift & Callahan, 2009; Westermann, Verheij, Winkens, Verhulst, & Van Oort, 2013).

These three quality criteria are based on common factors that are generally effective in child welfare and child protection (see Van Yperen, Van der Steege, Addink, & Boendermaker, 2010).

The DME does not provide leads for improvement of the decision-making process. Therefore, we added decision-making methods and instruments to the framework, though it is not yet clear how these methods may influence the assessment, the decision-making, and the outcomes (i.e., whether methods have an effect on the influencing factors or on the decision-making process). We assume that decision-making methods and risk assessment instruments have the potential to influence how caseworkers analyze and assess case factors and support the decision-making process. The use of these methods and instruments may lead to more agreement between professionals and fewer incorrect decisions (i.e., false-positive or false-negative decisions). Previous research has indicated that clinical judgments without the use of instruments are less reliable than judgments based on methods that support systematic information-gathering and analysis of the situation (see, e.g., Ægisdottir et al., 2006; Grove, Zald, Lebow, Snitz, & Nelson, 2000).

DECISIONAL CONFLICT MODEL

Another decision-making theory—probably one of the first that does not start with the postulate that a decision problem is "well-defined" (see Vlek & Wagenaar, 1979)—is the *conflict theory* of Irvin Janis (Janis, 1989; Janis & Mann, 1976, 1977; Wheeler & Janis, 1980). This theory is tailored to *consequential choices*: decision problems for which a choice has or can have far-reaching consequences and therefore have an emotional impact on the decision-maker.' Moreover, it deals with decisions that do not exclusively have positive consequences; no matter which choice is made, both benefits and disadvantages are to be expected. Having to choose between alternatives that have both pros and cons makes the decision situation conflicting.

There are more and less adequate ways of dealing with a decision conflict. The criterion that Janis and Mann (1977) use is the chance that a decision-maker will later regret the decision taken and, if possible, cancel the choice made. Janis and Mann have called the decision-making pattern that minimizes this chance of regret *vigilant*. (They distinguish, in addition to the vigilant decision pattern, four nonvigilant patterns: unconflicted inertia, unconflicted change, defensive avoidance, and hypervigilance.) A vigilant decision-making pattern is characterized by an attempt to answer a few key questions as well as possible *before* making a decision. The questions correspond to four phases in the decision-making process: (1) appraising the situation, (2) surveying alternatives, (3) weighing alternatives, (4) undertaking preparation/implementation. The phases and their specific questions are clarified in a table (see Appendix; adapted from Knorth, Van den Bergh, & Smit, 1997). In addition to general questions, the right-hand column specifies the questions for a specific decision; for example, for the decision to place a child in family foster care. A clear logic is evident in the sequence of the questions, but in vigilant decision-making it is more important *that* questions are dealt with than that this is done in a strictly logical sequence (Knorth, 1994).

A crucial moment in the decision-making process is weighing a decision alternative (phase 3 in table): What are the arguments in favor of and against the distinguished alternatives? In the model, it is, after all, the balance between pros and cons in the opinion of the decision-maker that determines whether a decision will be made to go ahead with an alternative. To promote vigilant decision-making, Janis and Mann developed a paper-and-pencil method for the weighing phase, the *Decisional Balance Sheet* (DBS), which supports the decision-maker in systematically considering the relevant factors in a situation in which a choice must be made. With respect to "drawing up the balance," the authors distinguish between anticipations regarding the decider (practitioner) him- or herself and the people concerned (child, parents, referring agency, etc.) as well as anticipations in the utilitarian and appreciative areas. *Utilitarian* anticipations relate to expected practical advantages and disadvantages of an alternative. *Appreciative* anticipations refer to the question of whether those involved in decision-making (parents, children, teacher, caseworker) approve or disapprove of the option at hand.

Methods for Decision-Making

There are several methods to support decision-making. We discuss three of them: structured decision-making methods ORBA and LIRIK, the clinical DBS methodology, and actuarial methods.

STRUCTURED DECISION-MAKING: ORBA AND LIRIK

As discussed earlier, caseworkers' assessment and decision-making may benefit from the use of protocols and diagnostic tools. In the Netherlands, two have been widely implemented: ORBA (Onderzoek, Risicotaxatie en Besluitvorming AMKs [Investigation, Risk Assessment and Decision-Making by Advice and Reporting Centres for Child Abuse and Neglect]) and LIRIK (Licht Instrument Risicotaxatie Kindveiligheid [Light Instrument for Risk Assessment of Child Safety]). ORBA (Ten Berge & Vinke, 2006a) is a structured decision-making method containing guidelines, criteria, and checklists that aim to support caseworkers in collecting relevant information, making judgments on a child's safety and risks, and deciding whether or not child protection is needed. The LIRIK (Ten Berge, Eijgenraam, & Bartelink, 2014) is a checklist that guides caseworkers in their assessment of signs, risk factors, and protective factors for the child's safety. It helps to systematically check relevant factors and to conclude whether or not the safety of children is at risk.

Effects of ORBA on decision-making in child protection. The effects of ORBA have been investigated in its use for the Advice and Reporting Centres on Child Abuse and Neglect (ARCCAN; Ten Berge & Vinke, 2006b). The objective of the first empirical study (De Kwaadsteniet et al., 2013) was to investigate the transparency and systematicity of the decision-making process in the case records of ARCCANs. We compared case records before ORBA had been implemented to case records after ORBA had been implemented. The analyses in this study concerned (1) content aspects, (2) process aspects, and (3) rationales for conclusions and decisions in records from 2010. We found that the case records showed clear improvements after ORBA implementation in terms of both content and process. ARCCAN professionals considered more risk assessment elements (i.e., risk and protective factors, estimation of chance of reoccurrence of child maltreatment), provided more explanations for the problems present in the family, had more elaborate investigation plans, and made more explicit decisions. However, they did not present their conclusions about whether or not the child was maltreated and whether or not help was needed any more frequently than before. Nor did they more frequently provide rationales for their conclusions and decisions in the case records. It was concluded that the case records demonstrated a more systematic and transparent decision-making process after ORBA implementation. However, further improvements are necessary as important elements are still often lacking.

The objective of a second empirical study (Bartelink et al., 2014) was to investigate whether ORBA led to more uniform judgments and decisions. We performed a vignette study and compared trained and untrained ARCCAN caseworkers. We found that agreement on judgments and decisions of both trained and untrained caseworkers was low. While we found some differences between trained and untrained caseworkers, the former did not always agree more on judgments and decisions than the latter. Therefore, we cannot conclude that ORBA leads to more uniform judgments and decisions.

Interrater reliability and predictive validity of LIRIK. In a third study (Bartelink, De Kwaadsteniet, Ten Berge, & Witteman, 2017), we investigated the interrater reliability and predictive validity of the LIRIK, a risk assessment instrument (Ten Berge et al., 2014). LIRIK is a checklist that supports professional judgments on current child safety and future risk of child abuse and neglect. LIRIK is based on the scientific knowledge about risk and protective factors and supports caseworkers to reach stepwise conclusions about actual safety and future risks by systematically addressing relevant cues in relation to parent–child interaction, child functioning, and risk and protective factors. In a vignette study, we examined whether caseworkers agreed about safety and risk judgments with and without the use of LIRIK. We found that agreement about safety and risk judgments was low, both with and without LIRIK. We concluded that reliability was insufficient. In a study in organizations for child welfare and child protection, we examined how well safety and risk judgments with and without LIRIK predicted future abuse and neglect. Caseworkers made safety and risk judgments in the cases assigned to them in the regular care process (i.e., not specifically selected for this study). After 6 months, we analyzed the case records to see if caseworkers reported unsafe outcomes (i.e., child maltreatment reports, child protective orders, out-of-home placement, safety, or crisis interventions). We found that caseworkers' safety and risk judgments moderately predicted an unsafe outcome 6 months later, both with and without LIRIK. As there were no clear differences between caseworkers who used LIRIK and those who did not, we concluded that LIRIK did not lead to better (i.e., more reliable and more valid) judgments than without the use of this instrument.

CLINICAL DBS METHODOLOGY FOR PLACEMENT DECISIONS

The DBS is the basic structure on which a clinical instrument was developed to support placement decisions in child and youth care (Knorth, 1991, 1994; Knorth, Van den Bergh, & Smit, 1997). Based on some small-scale studies, Knorth and Veerbeek (2007) concluded that the utility value of the DBS consists of three qualities: (1) the decision-maker is encouraged to explicate all considerations in proposing a particular alternative, including pros and cons for all those concerned and comprising utilitarian as well as apprecia-tive consequences; (2) the mapping of considerations, including the assess-ment of risks and potential setbacks, facilitates the identification of specific areas of concern for care and treatment thereby forming the foundation for a supervision or treatment plan; and (3) if applied in a team setting, the DBS helps to structure the group discussion and avoid "groupthink" (Janis, 1972). ("Groupthink is a psychological phenomenon that occurs within a group of people in which the desire for harmony or conformity in the group results in an irrational or dysfunctional decision-making outcome. Group members try to minimize conflict and reach a consensus decision without critical evalua-tion of alternative viewpoints by actively suppressing dissenting viewpoints, and by isolating themselves from outside influences" [https://en.wikipedia.org/wiki/Groupthink.])

In contrast with other applications (e.g., political decision-making, solving ethical dilemmas, choosing study programs, choosing cancer treatment, con-sidering abortion, personal counseling; see Knorth & Veerbeek, 2007) the re-search on implementation in the field of child protection and child welfare is very limited.

ACTUARIAL METHODS

Actuarial decision-making can be considered as a research-based method guided by an assessment instrument containing items that statistically predict clinical conditions and best decisions. Cutoff scores are based on research.

Evidence from several disciplines shows that actuarial prediction methods are more accurate than clinical judgment (Ægisdottir et al., 2006; Grove et al., 2000). Although the difference with clinical judgment is not very large (on the average, the actuarial method leads to 10% more accurate decisions), one could argue that any improvement is important. A serious drawback, however, is that these studies do not pertain to the field of child protection and child welfare. Although there is some research showing that the use of algorithms and databases may lead to improvements in clinical decision-making (Barth et al., 2012; Weisz et al., 2012), and a recent review shows that actuarial methods outperform clinical judgments (Van der Put, Assink, & Boekhout van Solinge, 2017), other studies on the use of actuarial instruments in complex cases of child maltreatment (see Bolton & Lennings, 2010; Herman, 2005; Keary & Fitzpatrick, 1994) do not show consistent results. Actuarial methods also have their flaws, especially when it comes to offering cues for the treatment plan. Because actuarial instruments focus on the statistical relevance of factors in making predictions, they may ignore factors that are relevant for change in the situation of the child. In all, decision-making in child welfare and child protection may benefit from actuarial decision support systems. However, we are just beginning to understand what those benefits and pitfalls are.

General Message

These studies show that decision-making methods and instruments—focused on case factors in cases of suspected child abuse or neglect—have only a limited effect on the decision-making process and the reliability and validity of judgments and decisions made. Actuarial methods may be more precise in making valid judgments but may ignore factors that are relevant for treatment and intervention decisions. Methods and instruments like DBS, ORBA, and LIRIK may have higher clinical relevance, but our studies on two of these approaches show that professionals still often disagree in their judgments and decisions, and the predictive validity of their judgments remains limited. Although case factors play a central part in the decision-making process, the DME framework shows that other factors also influence the decision-making process and outcomes. Structured decision-making, as well as actuarial methods and instruments, do not address these factors.

The finding that decision-making methods have a limited effect is not unique (e.g., Ægisdottir et al., 2006; D'Andrade, Benton, & Austin, 2005; Grove et al., 2000). Previous studies on structured decision-making methods in child welfare and child protection show that these methods support a comprehensive assessment of the situation within families (for an overview, see Léveille & Chamberland, 2010). Our findings indicate that caseworkers take a more holistic view and make more complete assessments when they use instruments like ORBA. However, in line with previous research, we also found that interrater agreement did not improve (Kang & Poertner, 2006; Regehr, Bogo, Shlonsky, & LeBlanc, 2010). With respect to risk assessment instruments, our results are not exceptional (e.g., Barlow, Fisher, & Jones, 2012). Instruments that support structured clinical judgments are often criticized for their lack of consistency and validity (D'Andrade et al., 2005; Van der Put et al., 2017). Recently, Schouten (2017), for example, found that a child abuse screening instrument used by medical doctors in out-of-hours primary care and emergency departments had low predictive validity.

In conclusion, using methods and instruments such as DBS, ORBA, and LIRIK is useful, but certainly not enough to substantially improve decision-making. In terms of the DME (Baumann et al., 2014), our findings indicate that methods focused on case factors have only a limited effect on the interrater agreement and predictive validity of the decisions.

INFLUENCES OF THE DECISION-MAKER

The limited effect of decision-making instruments like ORBA and LIRIK on the quality of caseworker decision-making led to a shift of our focus from these instruments to the reasoning and attitudes of the decision-makers. With this shift of focus, we intended to gain more insight into the reasoning processes and attitudes that may influence the decision-making process. The aim was to further explore why decision-making methods have such limited effects. We hypothesized that the rationales of decision-makers may be the link between personal characteristics on the one hand and their assessment and decisions on the other. Rationales provide insight into the reasoning process of decision-makers.

The main research question of this study (Bartelink et al., 2018) was to determine to what extent rationales play a part in intervention decisions in addition to risk assessment, attitudes, and the work experience of decision-makers. Professional caseworkers and students were asked to assess a vignette presenting a suspected case of child maltreatment and decide whether the child needed to be placed in out-of-home care (foster care).

Caseworkers and students mentioned a wide range of reasons indicating a great diversity in reasoning. The mean number of reasons mentioned per person was low (2.9). Moreover, as a group, students and professionals hardly differed from each other in the rationales provided. For both groups, the risk assessment and attitude toward placement predicted the placement decision: assessment of high risks and a positive attitude toward out-of-home placement was associated with a high chance that foster care was recommended. The attitudes of the participants toward out-of-home placement and their rationales (such as "information lacking," "the effectiveness of earlier interventions," "the degree of cooperativeness of the parents") were strong predictors for a placement decision. Work experience was not a significant predictor.

These results are in line with previous research (Arad-Davidzon & Benbenishty, 2008; Arruabarrena & De Paúl, 2012; Bartelink et al., 2015; Font & Maguire-Jack, 2015; Horwitz, Hurlburt, Cohen, Zhang, & Landsverk, 2011; Jent et al., 2011; Lambert & Ogles, 2004; Minkhorst et al., 2016). Our study shows that important reasons—such as the endangered development of the child and the inadequacy of the parenting—are often missing and rationales are unconvincing. Participants mostly focus on the advantages of their recommended intervention. Disadvantages and alternatives are seldom discussed. In this sense, the workers' reasoning seems biased; it may be cognitively too demanding to consider the many factors related to a case and deliberately argue on the pros and cons of different recommendations.

In accordance with other studies (Garb, 1989; Lambert & Ogles, 2004; Minkhorst et al., 2016), work experience did not influence the quality of the reasoning in our study, although other studies did find a relationship (Benbenishty et al., 2002; Brunnberg & Pećnik, 2007; Portwood, 1998). A few studies show that work experience may add little or nothing, especially in case of complex decisions (Devaney, Hayes, & Spratt, 2017; Spengler et al., 2009). The study of Devaney et al. (2017), however, showed that the picture is still quite puzzling. They found that experienced and less-experienced professionals did differ in their decisions, whereas experienced caseworkers and students did not. In all, the influence of work experience on the quality of decision-making seems too complex to draw any firm conclusions.

WHERE TO GO FROM HERE?

Decision-making methods and instruments that focus on case factors have only a limited effect on the decision-making process and the judgments and decisions made. Although the process becomes more transparent and systematic, caseworkers still often disagree in their judgments and decisions, and the predictive validity of their judgments remains limited. Attitudes and individual reasoning processes appear to substantially influence the decisions made. This means that decision-maker factors (i.e., attitudes and reasoning) play an important part in the decision-making process.

The research shows how difficult it is to improve individual decision-making, thereby raising the question of whether it is possible to further optimize decision-making in child welfare and child protection, and, if so, how and to what extent. Although systematic methods and instruments have a certain value, we see several additional options to improve decision-making.

Critical Thinking

One way to become less prone to decision pitfalls is *critical thinking* (Gambrill, 2005; Munro, 1996; Toulmin, Riecke, & Janik, 1984) or *vigilant decision-making* (Janis & Mann, 1977; Knorth, 1991). Munro (1996, 2008) states that the single most important factor in minimizing error in child protection practice is to admit that you may be wrong. Critical thinking is characterized by critical self-reflection and thinking about alternative explanations as well as the pros and cons of the proposed intervention and possible alternatives. Several strategies can be used to stimulate critical thinking, such as hypothesis testing, taking the opposing point of view (Munro, 1999), and scrutinizing evidence for strengths and weaknesses in a structured and systematic way (Duffy, 2011; Knorth et al., 1997). Through self-reflection, caseworkers critically investigate what underpins their decisions (e.g., the attitudes, feelings, and assumptions they have in relation to their cases). The DBS methodology is a tool for caseworkers that supports self-reflection and critical thinking. Critical thinking may ensure that people remain receptive to new information. Mistakes could be minimized if caseworkers are aware that they regularly need to revise their views when they receive new information and their knowledge base alters. Training and ongoing on-the-job supervision may support the development of critical thinking skills (see Duffy, 2011; Pelaccia, Tardif, Triby & Charlin, 2011).

Team Decision-Making

Another way to possibly improve decision-making is to use team decision-making. Although team decision-making can be prone to the same pitfalls as individual decision-making (e.g., Pijnenburg, 1996; Van den Bossche, Gijselaers, Segers, & Kirschner, 2006; Van Diest, 1994; West, 2004), it may strengthen decision-making when coworkers purposely interrogate each other critically about their reasons, motivations, and attitudes; possibly address alternative explanations; and explore the limitations of the preferred solution and the advantages of alternative interventions (Nouwen, Decuyper, & Put, 2012). We assume that critical thinking is very useful in and easy to adapt to team decision-making. The DBS may be a tool that supports critical thinking in team decision-making as well.

Systematic Feedback

Systematic feedback on the effects of judgments and decisions may improve the validity of the decision-making process (see Spengler et al., 2009). Outcome monitoring may be a useful tool to increase feedback on judgments and decisions made (Van Yperen, 2013). It supports reflection on the decisions made, raises caseworkers' awareness that their interventions do not always result in the desired outcomes, and provides them with the opportunity to adapt their intervention strategy (Delicat, 2011; Hutschemaekers, 2010; Lambert & Shimokawa, 2011). Outcome monitoring systematically increases professional practice knowledge and provides new information to caseworkers that may lead to adaptations in the decisions made.

Shared Decision-Making

Shared decision-making is of special interest because it deals with the personal influences of the decision-maker, and it is a motivational strategy to engage clients in sharing their values and definitions of the child's well-being. Shared decision-making is characterized by the reciprocal process of decision-making between professional and client in which both the client and the caseworker share relevant information and discuss together what may be the best way to progress. This process leads to shared assessments and decisions about treatment or other interventions. The caseworker shares information about the diagnosis, prognosis, and treatment options and their pros and cons. Clients contribute to the discussion by sharing their view on their situation, thoughts on their preferences, and previous experiences related to treatment options (Ouwens, Van der Burg, Faber, & Van der Weijden, 2012). Shared decision-making consists of three phases (Elwyn et al., 2012):

1. *Information exchange and exploration of the treatment or intervention options ("choice talk").* Both caseworker and client exchange their assessments of the situation and can come up with options that may be considered in the further discussion. The caseworker's proposals may arise from scientific evidence or practice knowledge; the client's input arises from personal values or experiences or from experts by experience.

2. *Description and consideration of all options with their advantages and disadvantages ("option talk").* Caseworkers can share information about the possible positive or negative effects of treatment and intervention options. Clients can contribute to the discussion through their personal preferences or experiences with previous treatments.
3. *Joint decision of caseworker and client about the treatment ("decision talk").* Based on an analysis of the advantages and disadvantages, the caseworker and the client make a joint decision about the most appropriate treatment.

Solid evidence of the positive effects of shared decision-making is found in the medical research literature. Shared decision-making with adult patients seems to result in more active participation in the treatment process, better fit between the treatment and the patient's needs and wishes, and higher client satisfaction with the treatment. Patients are more satisfied about the decision-making process, feel better informed, and have more knowledge about their diagnosis and treatment. They are more confident that the right decision is made. Shared decision-making may possibly decrease costs (Drake, Cimpean, & Torrey, 2009; Faber et al., 2013; Patel et al., 2008).

Research on shared decision-making in child welfare and protection is very scarce. A review of Barnhoorn et al. (2013) shows that an interactive approach, which is typical of shared decision-making, has a positive impact on the satisfaction of both clients and caseworkers in child welfare services and on the outcomes of treatments. Other studies confirm these results in child welfare (see Vis, Strandbu, Holtan, & Thomas, 2011; McLendon, McLendon, Dickerson, Lyons, & Tapp, 2012).

Methods such as Signs of Safety (Turnell & Edwards, 1999) and family group conferences (Merkel-Holguin, 2003), which are reasonably popular among caseworkers, demonstrate that shared decision-making in cases of suspected child maltreatment is possible. Although they may not result in more positive outcomes concerning child safety than other interventions, these methods increase parent and child participation (Dijkstra, Creemers, Asscher, Deković, & Stams, 2016; Vink, De Wolff, Van Dommelen, Bartelink, & Van der Veen, 2017). Further research is needed to investigate the effective elements of shared decision-making to improve child safety.

CONCLUSION

Decision-making in child welfare and child protection is not an easy task. Decision-makers are faced with often incomplete and biased information, time pressures, and choices that possibly have far-reaching consequences for children and families. Especially when dealing with issues regarding child safety and risks, caseworkers are under great pressure to decide on the course of action with the best possible outcome while at the same time being uncertain of which course of action will have the most benefits and least disadvantages.

Decision theory and past research has shown that not only case-related factors influence the decision-making process and outcomes, but also decision-maker, organizational, and external factors. Together with the pitfalls that come with intuitive decision-making, this results in a lack of interrater agreement on and a low predictive value of judgments and decisions.

The possible impact of false positives and false negatives on children and families when deciding on child safety and well-being justifies efforts to gain more insight into the complex nature of the decision-making process and into ways to improve decision-making in child welfare and child protection. In this chapter, we discussed some of these efforts. Based on our studies in the Netherlands, we concluded that structured decision-making methods and instruments result in a more systematic and transparent decision-making process but not in better (i.e., more consistent and valid) judgments and decisions. Actuarial methods result in somewhat better predictive value but have other limitations for child welfare practice.

Our study into the rationales for placement decisions confirms that decision-maker factors play an important role and that the reasoning process shows some serious flaws. We therefore argue that further improvement of decision-making could be found in a combination of three approaches. The first is to use methods of structured decision-making and instruments with the purpose of making the decision-making process more systematic and transparent.

The second is reinforcing critical thinking in both individuals and teams. Systematic feedback and outcome monitoring provide valuable input on the validity of judgments and decisions, and in this way can support a reflective attitude and critical thinking. Finally, instead of striving to reach a high level of objectivity and validity in the decision-making process, a more fruitful approach could be shared decision-making. Ultimately, the goal of the decision-making process is to choose the intervention or treatment that has the best results for the child's safety and well-being. Shared decision-making is promising in that it involves children and parents as important and equal participants in deciding on the best course of action, thus resulting in a broader perspective on their situation, as well as enhancing their motivation to change.

REFERENCES

Ægisdottir, S., White, M. J., Spengler, P. M., Maugherman, A. S., Anderson, L. A., Cook, R. S., . . . Rush, J. D. (2006). The meta-analysis of clinical judgment project: Fifty-six years of accumulated research on clinical versus statistical prediction. *Counseling Psychologist, 34*, 341–382. doi:10.1177/0011000005285875

Arad-Davidzon, B., & Benbenishty, R. (2008). The role of workers' attitudes and parent and child wishes in child protection workers' assessments and recommendation regarding removal and reunification. *Children and Youth Services Review, 30*, 107–121. doi:10.1016/j.childyouth.2007.07.003

Arruabarrena, I., & De Paúl, J. (2012). Improving accuracy and consistency in child maltreatment severity assessment in child protection services in Spain: New set of criteria to help caseworkers in substantiation decisions. *Children and Youth Services Review, 34*, 666–674. doi:10.1016/j.childyouth.2011.12.011

Barlow, J., Fisher, J. D., & Jones, D. (2012). *Systematic review of models of analysing significant harm.* Oxford, UK: Oxford University Press.

Barnhoorn, J., Broeren, S., Distelbrink, M., De Greef, M., Van Grieken, A., Jansen, W., . . . Raat, H. (2013). *Cliënt-, professional- en alliantiefactoren: hun relatie met het effect van zorg voor jeugd* [Client, professional and alliance factors: Their relationship with the effect of child and youth care]. Utrecht, the Netherlands: Verwey-Jonker Institute.

Bartelink, C. (2018). *Dilemmas in child protection: Methods and decision-maker factors influencing decision making in child maltreatment cases.* (PhD thesis). Groningen, the Netherlands: University of Groningen.

Bartelink, C., De Kwaadsteniet, L., Ten Berge, I. J., & Witteman, C. L. M. (2017). Is it safe? Reliability and validity of structured versus unstructured child safety judgments. *Child and Youth Care Forum, 46*(5), 745–768. doi:10.1007/s10566-017-9405-2

Bartelink, C., Knorth, E. J., López López, M., Koopmans, C., Ten Berge, I. J., Witteman, C. L. M., & Van Yperen, T. A. (2018). Reasons for placement decisions in a case of suspected child abuse: The role of reasoning, work experience and attitudes in decision-making. *Child Abuse and Neglect, 83*, 129–141. doi:10.1016/j.chiabu.2018.06.013

Bartelink, C., Ten Berge, I., & Van Vianen, R. (2015). *Richtlijn Uithuisplaatsing voor jeugdhulp en jeugdbescherming* [Guideline Out-of-home placement for child welfare and child protection]. Utrecht, the Netherlands: NIP/NVO/BPSW.

Bartelink, C., Van Yperen, T. A., Ten Berge, I. J., De Kwaadsteniet, L., & Witteman, C. L. M. (2014). Agreement on child maltreatment decisions: A nonrandomized study on the effects of structured decision-making. *Child and Youth Care Forum, 43*, 639–654. doi:10.1007/s10566-014-9259-9

Barth, R. P., Lee, B. R., Lindsey, M. A., Collins, K. S., Strieder, F., Chorpita, B. F., . . . Sparks, J. A. (2012). Evidence-based practice at a crossroads: The timely emergence of common elements and common factors. *Research on Social Work Practice, 22*, 108–119. doi:10.1177/1049731511408440

Baumann, D. J., Fluke, J. D., Dalgleish, L., & Kern, H. (2014). The decision-making ecology. In A. Shlonsky & R. Benbenishty (Eds.), *From evidence to outcomes in child welfare: An international reader* (pp. 24–38). Oxford, UK: Oxford University Press.

Baumann, D. J., Fluke, J. D., Graham, J. C., Wittenstrom, K., Hedderson, J., Riveau, S., . . . Brown, N. (2010). *Disproportionality in child protective services: The preliminary results of statewide reform efforts.* Austin, TX: Texas Department of Family and Protective Services.

Benbenishty, R., Davidson-Arad, B., López, M., Devaney, J., Spratt, T., Koopmans, C., . . . Hayes, D. (2015). Decision making in child protection: An international comparative study on maltreatment substantiation, risk assessment and interventions recommendations, and the role of professionals' child welfare attitudes. *Child Abuse and Neglect, 49*, 63–75. doi:10.1016/j.chiabu.2015.03.015

Benbenishty, R., Segev, D., Surkis, T., & Elias, T. (2002). Information-search and decision-making by professionals and nonprofessionals in cases of alleged child abuse and maltreatment. *Journal of Social Service Research, 28*, 1–18. doi:10.1300/J079v28n03_01

Berben, E. G. M. J. (2000). *Als iedereen hetzelfde was . . . Indicatiestelling in de jeugdzorg* [If everybody would be the same . . . Assessment in child and youth care] (PhD thesis). Maastricht, the Netherlands: Shaker Publishing B.V.

Bolton, A., & Lennings, C. (2010). Clinical opinions of structured risk assessments for forensic child protection: The development of a clinically relevant device. *Children and Youth Services Review, 32*, 1300–1310. doi:10.1016/j.childyouth.2010.04.022

Britner, P. A., & Mossler, D. G. (2002). Professionals' decision-making about out-of-home placements following instances of child abuse. *Child Abuse and Neglect, 26*, 317–332. doi:10.1016/S0145-2134(02)00311-3

Brunnberg, E., & Pećnik, N. (2007). Assessment processes in social work with children at risk in Sweden and Croatia. *International Journal of Social Welfare, 16*, 231–241. doi:10.1111/j.1468-2397.2006.00456.x

Dalgleish, L. I. (2003). Risk, needs and consequences. In M. C. Calder (Ed.), *Assessments in child care: A comprehensive guide to frameworks and their use* (pp. 86–99). Dorset, UK: Russell House Publishing.

D'Andrade, A., Benton, A., & Austin, M. J. (2005). *Risk and safety assessment in child welfare: Instrument comparisons.* Berkeley, CA: University of California at Berkeley, School of Social Welfare.

De Kwaadsteniet, L., Bartelink, C., Witteman, C. L. M., Ten Berge, I. J., & Van Yperen, T. A. (2013). Improved decision making about suspected child maltreatment: Results of structuring the decision process. *Children and Youth Services Review, 35*, 347–352. doi:10.1016/j.childyouth.2012.11.015

Delicat, J. W. (Ed.). (2011). *4+2=1! Opleidingsvereisten gedragswetenschapper in de zorg voor de jeugd* [4+2=1! Educational requirements for the behavioral scientist in child and youth care]. Utrecht, the Netherlands: NIP/NVO.

Detlaff, A. J., Rivaux, S. L., Baumann, D. J., Fluke, J. D., Rycraft, J. R., & James, J. (2011). Disentangling substantiation: The influence of race, income, and risk on the substantiation decision in child welfare. *Children and Youth Services Review, 33*, 1630–1637. doi:10.1016/j.childyouth.2011.04.

Devaney, J., Hayes, D., & Spratt, T. (2017). The influences of training and experience in removal and reunification decisions involving children at risk of maltreatment: Detecting a 'beginner dip'. *British Journal of Social Work, 47*, 1–20. doi:10.1093/bjsw/bcw175

De Vries, M., Holland, R. W., & Witteman, C. L. M. (2008). Fitting decisions: Mood and intuitive versus deliberative decision strategies. *Cognition and Emotion, 22*, 931–943. doi:10.1080/02699930701552580

Dijkstra, S., Creemers, H. E., Asscher, J. J., Deković, M., & Stams, G. J. J. M. (2016). The effectiveness of family group conferencing in youth care: A meta-analysis. *Child Abuse and Neglect, 62*, 100–110. doi:10.1016/j.chiabu.2016.10.017

Drake, R. E., Cimpean, D., & Torrey, W. C. (2009). Shared decision making in mental health: Prospects for personalized medicine. *Dialogues in Clinical Neuroscience, 11*(4), 455–463.

Knorth, E. J. (1991). Vigilant decision making in connection with residential admission of juveniles. In W. Hellinckx et al. (Eds.), *Innovations in residential care* (pp. 195–210). Leuven, Belgium: Acco Publishers.

Knorth, E. J. (1994). The conflict model of decision making. Process monitoring of practitioners' intervention decisions. In E. J. Knorth & M. Smit (Eds.), *Residential child and youth care: Opportunities for a systematic approach—Second edition* (pp. 41–54). Leuven, Belgium: Garant Publishers (in Dutch).

Knorth, E. J. (1995). Decision making on out-of-home placement in child and youth care: A review of the literature. *Kind en Adolescent, 16*(2), 64–87 (in Dutch). doi:10.1007/BF03060579

Knorth, E. J., Van den Bergh, P. M., & Smit, M. (1997). A method for supporting intake decisions in residential child and youth care. *Child and Youth Care Forum, 26*(5), 323–342. doi:10.1007/BF02589439

Knorth, E. J., & Veerbeek, H. J. (2007). Decision making under uncertainty: An application of the conflict theory in case of young people's placement in care. In E. J. Knorth & M. Smit (Eds.), *A systematic approach in child and youth care—Second edition.* (pp. 181–210). Antwerp, Belgium: Garant Publishers (in Dutch).

Lambert, M. J., & Ogles, B. M. (2004). The efficacy and effectiveness of psychotherapy. In M. J. Lambert (Ed.), *Bergin and Garfield's handbook of psychotherapy and behavior change* (Fifth edition). (pp. 139–193). New York, NY: John Wiley.

Lambert, M. J., & Shimokawa, K. (2011). Collecting client feedback. *Psychotherapy, 48*, 72–79. doi:10.1037/a0022238

Léveille, S., & Chamberland, C. (2010). Toward a general model for child welfare and protection services: A meta-evaluation of international experiences regarding the adoption of the Framework for the Assessment of Children in Need and Their Families (FACNF). *Children and Youth Services Review, 32*, 929–944. doi:10.1016/j.childyouth.2010.03.009

McLendon, T., McLendon, D., Dickerson, P. S., Lyons, J. K., & Tapp, K. (2012). Engaging families in the child welfare process utilizing the family-directed structural assessment tool. *Child Welfare, 91*, 43–58.

Merkel-Holguin, L. (2003). Promising results, potential new directions: International FGDM research and evaluation in child welfare. *Protecting Children, 18*(1), 1–2.

Metselaar, J., Knorth, E. J., Noom, M. J., Van Yperen, T. A., & Konijn, C. (2004). Treatment planning for residential and non-residential care: A study on indication-for-treatment statements as input to the care process. *Child and Youth Care Forum, 33*(3), 151–173. doi:10.1023/B:CCAR.0000029684.84484.4c

Minkhorst, F. A. M., Witteman, C. L. M., Koopmans, A. C., Lohman, N., & Knorth, E. J. (2016). Decision making in Dutch child welfare: Child's wishes about reunification after out-of-home placement. *British Journal of Social Work, 46*(1), 169–185. doi:10.1093/bjsw/bcu102

Munro, E. (1996). Avoidable and unavoidable mistakes in child protection work. *British Journal of Social Work, 26*, 793–808. doi:10.1093/oxfordjournals.bjsw.a011160

Munro, E. (1998). Improving social workers' knowledge base in child protection work. *British Journal of Social Work, 28*, 89–105. doi:10.1093/oxfordjournals.bjsw.a011320

Munro, E. (1999). Common errors of reasoning in child protection work. *Child Abuse and Neglect, 23*, 745–758. doi:10.1016/S0145-2134%2899%2900053-8

Munro, E. (2008). *Effective child protection.* London, UK: Sage.

Nouwen, E., Decuyper, S., & Put, J. (2012). Team decision making in child welfare. *Children and Youth Services Review, 34,* 2101–2116. doi:10.1016/j.childyouth.2012.07.006

Osmo, R., & Benbenishty, R. (2004). Children at risk: Rationales for risk assessments and interventions. *Children and Youth Services Review, 26,* 1155–1173. doi:10.1016/j.childyouth.2004.05.006

Ouwens, M., Van der Burg, S., Faber, M., & Van der Weijden, T. (2012). *Shared decision making & Zelfmanagement. Literatuuronderzoek naar begrippen* [Shared decision-making & self-management. Literature study of concepts]. Nijmegen, the Netherlands: UMC St. Radboud, IQ Healthcare.

Patel, S. R., Bakken, S., & Ruland, C. (2008). Recent advances in shared decision making for mental health. *Current Opinion in Psychiatry, 21,* 606–612. doi:10.1097/YCO.0b013e32830eb6b4

Pelaccia, T., Tardif, J., Triby, E., & Charlin, B. (2011). An analysis of clinical reasoning through a recent and comprehensive approach: The dual-process theory. *Medical Education Online, 16*(1), 5890–5899. doi:10.3402/meo.v16i0.5890

Pijnenburg, H. M. (1996). *Psychodiagnostic decision-making within clinical conferences: Exploring a domain* (PhD thesis). Nijmegen, the Netherlands: Catholic University Nijmegen, NICI.

Portwood, S. G. (1998). The impact of individuals' characteristics and experiences on their definitions of child maltreatment. *Child Abuse and Neglect, 22,* 437–452. doi:10.1016/S0145-2134(98)00008-8

Poston, J. M., & Hanson, W. E. (2010). Meta-analysis of psychological assessment as a therapeutic intervention. *Psychological Assessment, 22,* 203–212. doi:10.1037/a0018679

Regehr, C., LeBlanc, V., Shlonsky, A., & Bogo, M. (2010). The influence of clinicians' previous trauma exposure on their assessment of child abuse risk. *Journal of Nervous and Mental Disease, 198,* 614–618. doi:10.1097/NMD.0b013e3181ef349e

Rosen, A. (1994). Knowledge use in direct practice. *Social Service Review, 68,* 561–577. doi:10.1086/604084

Rossi, P. H., Schuerman, J., & Budde, S. (1999). Understanding decisions about child maltreatment. *Evaluation Review, 23,* 579–598. doi:10.1177/0193841X9902300601

Sackett, D. L., Straus, S. E., Richardson, W. S., Rosenberg, W., & Haynes, R. B. (2000). *Evidence-based medicine: How to practice and teach EBM* (Second edition). New York, NY: Churchill Livingstone.

Schouten, M. C. M. (2017). *Systematic screening for child abuse in out-of-hours primary care* (PhD thesis). Utrecht, the Netherlands: Utrecht University.

Skeem, J. L., Mulvey, E. P., & Lidz, C. W. (2000). Building mental health professionals' decisional models into tests of predictive validity: The accuracy of contextualized predictions of violence. *Law and Human Behaviour, 24,* 607–628. doi:10.1023/A:1005513818748

Sloman, S. A. (1996). The empirical case for two systems of reasoning. *Psychology Bulletin, 119,* 3–22. doi:10.1037/0033-2909.119

Spengler, P. M., White, M. J., Ægisdottir, S., Maugherman, A. S., Anderson, L. A., Cook, R. S., . . . Rush, J. D. (2009). The meta-analysis of clinical judgment project: Effects of experience on judgment accuracy. *Counseling Psychologist, 37,* 350–399. doi:10.1177/0011000006295149

Swift, J. K., & Callahan, J. L. (2009). The impact of client treatment preferences on outcome: A meta-analysis. *Journal of Clinical Psychology*, 65, 368–381. doi:10.1002/jclp.20553

Ten Berge, I. J. (1998). *Decision-making in child protective services. The development and evaluation of a checklist for decision-making at child protective services intake* (PhD thesis). Delft, the Netherlands: Eburon Publishers.

Ten Berge, I. J., Eijgenraam, K., & Bartelink, C. (2014). *Licht Instrument Risicotaxatie Kindveiligheid: Herziene Versie Juni 2014* [Light Instrument Risk Assessment Child Safety: Revised Version June 2014]. Utrecht, the Netherlands: Netherlands Youth Institute.

Ten Berge, I., & Vinke, A. (2006a). *Beslissen over vermoedens van kindermishandeling: Handreiking en hulpmiddelen voor het Advies- en Meldpunt Kindermishandeling* [Deciding about suspected child maltreatment: Guide and instruments for Advice and Reporting Centres on Child Abuse and Neglect]. Utrecht, the Netherlands: NIZW Jeugd/Adviesbureau Van Montfoort.

Ten Berge, I., & Vinke, A. (2006b). *Beslissen over vermoedens van kindermishandeling: Eindrapport project Onderzoek, Risicotaxatie en Besluitvorming Advies- en Meldpunten Kindermishandeling (ORBA)* [Deciding about suspected child maltreatment: Final report project Research, Risk Assessment and Decision Making Advice and Reporting Centres on Child Abuse and Neglect (ORBA)]. Utrecht, the Netherlands: NIZW Jeugd/Adviesbureau Van Montfoort.

Toulmin, S. E., Riecke, R., & Janik, A. (1984). *An introduction to reasoning*. New York, NY: Macmillan.

Turnell, A., & Edwards, S. (1999). *Signs of safety: A solution and safety-oriented approach to child protection casework*. New York, NY: Norton.

Van den Bossche, P., Gijselaers, W. H., Segers, M., & Kirschner, P. A. (2006). Social and cognitive factors driving teamwork in collaborative learning environments: Team learning beliefs and behaviors. *Small Group Research*, 37(5), 490–521. doi:10.1177/1046496406292938

Van der Put, C. E., Assink, M., Boekhout van Solinge, N. F. (2017). Predicting child maltreatment: A meta-analysis of the predictive validity of risk assessment instruments. *Child Abuse and Neglect*, 73, 71–88. doi:10.1016/j.chiabu.2017.09.016

Van Diest, C. (1994). Group decision making: The unfolding of "process loss." In E. J. Knorth & M. Smit (Eds.), *Residential child and youth care: Opportunities for a systematic approach–Second edition* (pp. 55–67). Leuven, Belgium: Garant Publishers (in Dutch).

Van Yperen, T. (2013). *Met kennis oogsten: Monitoring en doorontwikkeling van een integrale zorg voor jeugd* [Reap with knowledge: Monitoring and development of integral services for youth]. Utrecht/Groningen, the Netherlands: Netherlands Youth Institute (NJi)/University of Groningen.

Van Yperen, T., Van der Steege, M., Addink, A., & Boendermaker, L. (2010). *Algemeen en specifiek werkzame factoren in de jeugdzorg: Stand van de discussie* [Non-specific and specific working factors in child and youth care: State of the art]. Utrecht, the Netherlands: Netherlands Youth Institute.

Vink, R., De Wolff, M., Van Dommelen, P., Bartelink, C., & Van der Veen, S. (2017). *Empowered by Signs of Safety? Research on the effectiveness of Signs of Safety in child protection*. Leiden, the Netherlands: TNO/Netherlands Youth Institute (in Dutch).

Vis, S. A., Strandbu, A., Holtan, A., & Thomas, N. (2011). Participation and health: A research review of child participation in planning and decision-making. *Child and Family Social Work, 16*, 325–335. doi:10.1111/j.1365-2206.2010.00743.x

Vlek, C. A. J., & Wagenaar, W. A. (1979). Judgment and decision under uncertainty. In J. A. Michon, E. G. J. Eijkman, & L. F. W. De Klerk (Eds.), *Handbook of psychonomics II* (pp. 253–345). Amsterdam: North-Holland Publishing.

Wang, Y., Wang, Y., Patel, S., & Patel, D. (2004). A layered reference model of the brain (LRMB). *IEEE Transactions on Systems, Man, and Cybernetics (C), 36*, 124–133. doi:10.1109/TSMCC.2006.871126

Weisz, J. R., Chorpita, B. F., Palinkas, L. A., Schoenwald, S. K., Miranda, J., Bearman, S. K., . . . The Research Network on Youth Mental Health (2012). Testing standard and modular designs for psychotherapy treating depression, anxiety, and conduct problems in youth: A randomized effectiveness trial. *Archives of General Psychiatry, 69*, 274–282. doi:10.1001/archgenpsychiatry.2011.147

West, M. (2004). Do teams work? In M. A. West (Ed.), *Effective teamwork: Practical lessons from organizational research* (pp. 7–26). Oxford, UK: Blackwell.

Westermann, G. M. A., Verheij, F., Winkens, B., Verhulst, F. C., & Van Oort, F. V. A. (2013). Structured shared decision-making using dialogue and visualization: A randomized controlled trial. *Patient Education and Counseling, 90*, 74–81. doi:10.1016/j.pec.2012.09.014

Wheeler, D. D., & Janis, I. L. (1980). *A practical guide for making decisions.* New York, NY: Free Press.

Wittenstrom, K., Baumann, D. J., Fluke, J. D., Graham, J. C., & James, J. (2015). The impact of drugs, infants, single mothers, and relatives on reunification: A Decision-Making Ecology approach. *Child Abuse and Neglect, 49*, 86–96. doi:10.1016/j.chiabu.2015.06.010

APPENDIX

Table 11.1

Decision-making phases and questions based on a vigilant strategy

Decision-Making Phases	Questions	
	In General	Upon Placement of a Child in Family Foster Care
1. Appraising the Situation	What problems occur in the current situation? What risks does the decision-maker take by not changing the existing situation?	What problems occur with regard to the child and the family/environment? Would there be any serious risk for the child and the family/environment if placement in foster care did not occur?
2. Surveying Alternatives	What is the decision-maker trying to accomplish by changing the current situation (goals set)? What alternative or alternatives is/are acceptable in order to reach the goals set?	What is the purpose of possible placement of the child in foster care? Is foster care acceptable as an environment for help, knowing the goals set, the matching criteria used, and the possibilities for placement and support available? Are there other forms of support that deserve serious consideration as options for reaching the goals set?
3. Weighing Alternatives	What alternative can be considered the best (relatively), also bearing in mind requirements which are deemed essential?	What is the balance of pros and cons (positive and negative expectations) if the decision for placement is made? And what is the balance for alternative decisions? Is this balance so favorable that placement in foster care is the best possible help (relatively)?

4. Preparation/ Implementation	How is the best alternative put into practice, and how can possible negative consequences be anticipated?	What measures can contribute to the best possible realization of the placement in practice (if this is decided on) or can prevent anticipated negative consequences or risks?

12

The Voice of the Child in Child Protection Decision-Making

A Cross-Country Comparison of Policy and Practice in England, Germany, and the Netherlands

SUSANNE WITTE, MÓNICA LÓPEZ LÓPEZ,
AND HELEN BALDWIN ∎

INTRODUCTION

All children have the right to be protected from harm. Children can also play an important part in their own protection by participating in the decision-making processes that affect them. Ensuring the participation of children in the child protection system has become a priority worldwide (Cossar, Brandon, & Jordan, 2014), in accordance with the increased recognition of Article 12 of the United Nations Convention on the Rights of the Child (UNCRC; Committee on the Rights of the Child, 2009). Research evidence highlights the benefits for children who are afforded this right. Children's participation in decision-making processes in child protection has been shown to have positive effects on children's well-being and sense of safety (Vis, Strandbu, Holtan, & Thomas, 2011), their acceptance of out-of-home placement decisions, higher placement stability (Cashmore, 2002), reduced anxiety or anger toward care decisions (Ten Brummelaar, Harder, Kalverboer, Post, & Knorth, 2017), and more successful and stable reunifications with families of origin (Balsells, Fuentes-Pelaez, Pastor,

Susanne Witte, Mónica López López, and Helen Baldwin, *The Voice of the Child in Child Protection Decision-Making* In: *Decision-Making and Judgment in Child Welfare and Protection*. Edited by: John D. Fluke, Mónica López López, Rami Benbenishty, Erik J. Knorth, and Donald J. Baumann, Oxford University Press (2021). © Oxford University Press. DOI: 10.1093/oso/9780190059538.003.0012.

2017). Overall, the participation of children in their own protective processes seems to contribute to the success of interventions (Kriz & Roundtree-Swain, 2017) and therefore provides an opportunity for developing more effective child protection systems.

However, the actual participation of children in decision-making regarding their own child protection pathways seems to be very limited (Van Bijleveld, Dedding, & Bunders-Aelen, 2015). This has been explained by factors such as a country's policy concerning children's participation, professionals' knowledge and skills regarding how to involve children in decision-making (Horwath, Kalyva, & Spyru, 2012), or professionals' attitudes regarding the child as a relevant source of information (Alberth & Bühler-Niederberger, 2015). Moreover, some authors have pointed to organizational factors, such as time constraints, scarce resources, and professional turnover, as factors that could hinder children's participation in child protection (Kriz & Roundtree-Swain, 2017; Kriz & Skivenes, 2015). The quality of the relationship between the child and caseworker also has been identified as an important factor in child participation (Cossar et al., 2014).

Children's participation currently is conceptualized as a temporal process with a series of critical points at which children should be granted the opportunity for meaningful participation. Meaningful participation is defined as the experience of children being listened to and taken seriously (Bouma, López López, Knorth, & Grietens, 2018). This approach acknowledges that every child is an expert in their own experience, and that they can contribute in a valuable manner to every decision affecting their own lives. A recent model of the participation of children in the child protection system representing this approach is that proposed by Bouma et al. (2018), which includes three dimensions of meaningful participation (informing, hearing, and involving). The model summarizes the topics children should be informed about, the conditions that make children feel listened to, and the circumstances that enable them to influence decision-making in child protection.

This chapter focuses on the participation of children in child protection decisions and draws on two studies undertaken within the Hestia research project (funded by NORFACE) that compared policies and responses to child abuse and neglect in England, Germany, and the Netherlands. First, we analyze policy and public discourse regarding children's participation in the three countries using Bouma's meaningful participation model (2018). Second, we focus on the practice of including children in decisions following investigations into suspected child abuse and neglect based on an analysis of 1,207 child protection cases. Finally, the chapter concludes by contrasting policies and practices regarding participation in each country and deriving further implications.

POLICIES AND PUBLIC DISCOURSES ON CHILDREN'S PARTICIPATION

The promotion of children's rights to participate in decisions concerning their own lives has become more prominent in child protection policy in England, Germany, and the Netherlands in recent years. In this section, we examine how the three dimensions of children's meaningful participation operationalized in Bouma's model are embodied in relevant child protection legislation and policy documents in the three countries (Bouma et al., 2018).

England

The requirement to include children in child welfare decision-making was introduced by the Children Act 1989, specifically in relation to children subject to family court proceedings. This requirement was subsequently extended by the Children Act 2004 to all children defined as being in need of social care services. This change in legislation was made following the inquiry into the death of Victoria Climbié, which identified failures by professionals to prioritize the needs of children over those of adults and to take children's views of their situation into account in child protection decision-making (Laming, 2003). A subsequent independent review of child protection in England recommended that the child protection system become more child-centered and that the rights, wishes, feelings, and experiences of children should inform the provision of services (Munro, 2011). Current statutory guidance on safeguarding and promoting the welfare of children in England sets out ways by which local authorities are expected to include children in decisions about their welfare at various stages in the child protection process (HM Government, 2018).

According to this statutory guidance, local authorities are expected to *inform* a child about any actions to be taken following a child protection assessment, and, where a multiagency conference is to be convened, the child should receive information prepared for the conference in advance, where appropriate. Information is not to be shared with a child if doing so may jeopardize a police investigation or place a child at risk of significant harm.

The need to *listen* to children is emphasized within English child protection legislation and policy. The Children Act 2004 states that, before determining what services, if any, to provide for a child, a local authority must, "ascertain the child's wishes and feelings regarding the provision of those services" (Children Act 2004, Section 53). Statutory guidance states that children should be seen alone, wherever possible, as part of assessments and reviews. Social workers are encouraged to conduct interviews with children in ways that minimize distress to them while maximizing the accuracy and completeness of the information gathered.

The requirement to *involve* children in decisions is also clearly evident in English legislation and policy. After ascertaining children's wishes and feelings regarding the provision of services, local authorities are required to, "give due consideration (having regard to his age and understanding) to such wishes and feelings of the child" (Children Act 2004, Section 53). Statutory guidance states that a child's needs and wishes must be put first, irrespective of their age, and that professionals must take into account the level of need and risk present from the child's perspective. Furthermore, children are represented by independent persons at several stages in the child protection process. Local authorities are required to appoint an Independent Reviewing Officer to every child in out-of-home care or who is subject to a child protection plan, whose duty it is to ensure the child's views are heard, recorded, and responded to (National Association of Independent Reviewing Officers, n.d.). Meanwhile, children who are the subject of family court proceedings are appointed a Children's Guardian, an independent social worker who represents the best interests of the child in court (Children and Family Court Advisory and Support Service, 2017).

Germany

In general, the rights of children to participate in all matters that affect them are increasingly being recognized in Germany (Pluto, 2007). In relation to child protection, the participation of children is only discussed widely regarding the welfare of children and youth in educational institutions as a lack of participation is considered a risk factor for institutional abuse (BMFSFJ, 2015). The participation of children in decision-making in child protection is not central in child protection law. Yet the concepts of child protection have changed from a paternalistic toward a more participatory approach in recent decades (Liebel, 2009), and many regulations regarding participation are granted by law.

German law states that children need to be *informed* by the local child and youth welfare authorities about all matters that concern them. Furthermore, they should be informed about proceedings, possible decisions, and consequences during care planning conferences and family court proceedings.

The importance of children being *heard* during the child protection process is more strongly emphasized in relation to family court proceedings than in relation to child protection investigations. However, some rights mentioned in Bouma's model (2018) are granted by law: children have the right to receive counseling provided by local authorities, in some cases even without the knowledge of their parents, and the new child protection law stresses the need to gather information from the child directly during child protection investigations. In addition, children have the right to request an emergency placement without providing any reason and to inform one person of their choice during an emergency placement about the placement.

Child protection in Germany has been considered to be very family-oriented (Gilbert et al., 2009; Gilbert, Parton, & Skivenes, 2011) and *involvement* of the whole family in risk assessment and decision-making is seen as part of a nonjudgmental and holistic approach of social work (Wiesner, 2009). Thus, working together with the family is also mandated by law, which should include the child. Children have the right to be involved by the local child and youth welfare authorities in all matters that concern them. Children have the right to be involved in the assessment of child endangerment and care planning conferences along with their parents. In family court proceedings, children should be heard and are appointed guardians ad litem who determine the interests of the child and ensure that these are considered in family court decisions (Witte, Miehlbradt, van Santen & Kindler, 2019).

Within the law, some circumstances allow professionals to exclude children from decision-making, such as the age and the developmental stage of the child; as well, children are not informed, heard, or involved in decision-making when it might endanger their well-being. However, guidelines when one or the other reason applies are not given in German policy documents and thus are up to professional discretion (Wiesner, 2009).

The Netherlands

In 2015, new legislation regarding child protection (Jeugdwet, 2014) was introduced in the Netherlands with a focus on parents' and children's own strengths and responsibilities and the promotion of their participation in child protection interventions (for a detailed description, see López, Bouma, Knorth, & Grietens, 2019). Moreover, children's participation is gaining centrality in the policies of the two key child protection institutions in the Netherlands: the Advice and Reporting Centre for Domestic Violence and Child Maltreatment (in Dutch: *Advies- en Meldpunt Huiselijk Geweld en Kindermishandeling* [AMHK]) and the Child Care and Protection Board (in Dutch: *Raad voor de Kinderbescherming* RvdK]). Documents used by both agencies emphasize the need for professionals to guarantee children's participation and cooperation throughout the protection process.

Dutch child protection policy documents specify the need to maintain an open and transparent system, including for children. *Informing* children about their right to participate in their own protection process has become a central issue in the Dutch child protection system. However, the way in which the information should be delivered to children is yet to be operationalized. The RvdK has the duty to inform children and parents when there is an open investigation regarding them and to communicate the decision made to the children, who receive a section of the investigation report if they are 12 years old or older or the complete report if they are 16 years old or older. Age limits for participation are not consistent within Dutch policy (Bouma et al., 2018).

Dutch child protection policy emphasizes the need for children's views about their own protection process to be *heard*. For instance, the current legal framework refers to the importance of talking *with* parents and children instead of *about* them (Memorie van Toelichting Jeugdwet, 2013). The two main Dutch agencies consider listening to children a fundamental step for gathering information during a child protection investigation. Moreover, children should be given the chance to express their opinion about the situation under investigation and about possible solutions. The AMHK even refers to the children's right to have an individual meeting with a behavioral scientist.

Dutch child protection policy highlights the importance of *involving* children as active agents in deciding the most appropriate intervention for their situation. However, there are no guiding principles available on how to enable children's influence in the decision-making process.

Although recent child protection policy reforms in the Netherlands have led to greater consideration for clients' participation, there are no clear procedures on how children's views should be incorporated in decision-making processes. In practice, children are reportedly not informed or heard enough in decisions concerning their lives (Kinderombudsman, 2016), and the Dutch government has stated that the participation of children in child protection investigations needs to be improved (Tweede Kamer der Staten-Generaal, 2016).

THE PRACTICE OF CHILDREN'S PARTICIPATION IN CHILD PROTECTION

In this section, the practice of children's participation is further examined using data on investigations into suspected child abuse and neglect in England, Germany, and the Netherlands. After a short description of the study design, we (1) compare rates of participation in the three countries, (2) examine predictors of child participation in each country, and (3) examine associations between child participation and decision-making outcomes in each country.

Method

Study design. Child protection investigations are conducted by children's services departments in England and by the Jugendamt in Germany. In the Netherlands, there are two institutions in each region involved in child protection investigations, the AMHK for voluntary support and the RvdK for compulsory support measures. A case file study of these investigations into suspected child maltreatment and neglect was conducted in all three countries. Approximately 100 case files were selected from four local authorities in each country (i.e., approximately 400 in total per country). The cases sampled from the agencies in the Netherlands were proportionate to their caseloads (AMHK: 80%; RvdK: 20%). In total, 1,207 case files were analyzed (England: 400; Germany: 409; the Netherlands: 398) by trained case file abstractors using a standardized coding scheme developed within the project. Reliability testing yielded acceptable results (intraclass correlation coefficient [ICC]: .90 [.71; .99]; Fleiss' κ: .82). Throughout the coding process, difficulties were discussed between all case file abstractors. Furthermore, the data were cleaned carefully afterward, checking for bias in coding and plausibility.

Measures. Case files were analyzed in relation to the characteristics of the children referred and their families, the handling of investigations as documented by social workers, and the decisions made at the end of investigations in terms of risk of significant harm and need for support. Binary variables were created for whether or not a child had participated in the decision-making at the end of the investigation and whether or not the child's caregiver(s) participated in the decision-making. Participation was defined rather broadly; it included being present at the decision-making conference, being asked for an opinion on support measures, or being able to choose between support measures. We did not include informing the child or caregiver in the definition of participation as the information provided by the social worker to the child or caregiver is rarely documented in the case file. Moreover, we considered informing children and caregivers as a prerequisite of participation. If a child or caregiver is not informed about the process, involving and hearing are very unlikely to happen.

The Modified Maltreatment Classification System (English & the Longscan Investigators, 1997) was used to account for the nature of maltreatment investigated in cases when comparing levels of participation between countries. This measure allows the coding of physical abuse, sexual abuse, emotional maltreatment, failure to provide, lack of supervision, moral maltreatment, and educational maltreatment based on information in the case file. In this study, the information documented in the case file during the investigation was used to code maltreatment type.

Data analyses. Statistical procedures were carried out using IBM SPSS Statistics 22. Logistic regression analyses were used to predict the participation of children in the decision-making process. Two different models were used: model 1, which included child and case characteristics as predictors, and model 2, which included characteristics of the decision-making process as additional predictors. The variables included child age and whether or not the child had a chronic health condition as these are factors are frequently associated with thresholds for participation in the three countries. Child gender was dropped from the analysis as it was not a significant predictor in any of the countries. In addition, the number of types of maltreatment was used to adjust for case characteristics.

Logistic regression analyses were also used to examine associations between child participation and the outcomes of decisions. Three different decision outcomes were used, including whether the social worker decided (1) the child was at risk of significant harm, (2) the family was in need of support, and (3) the child required individual support to address his or her specific needs. In the regression model, we specifically controlled for child and case characteristics.

Predictors in all regression models included the country in which the data were collected, allowing for a comparison between countries. Furthermore, all predictors were modeled in combination with the country to identify predictors that were influential in some countries but not in others. Thus, specific predictors within each country could be assessed.

Results

Sample. The characteristics of the children in the sample are shown in Table 12.1. The average age of the children at the time of referral to the local authority was 7.2 years (standard deviation [SD] = 5.4). Children's ages did not differ substantially between countries ($F(2, 1,203) = 1.69$; $p = .186$; $n = 1,206$). However, there were significant differences between the children's age groups, with a greater proportion of children in England being unborn at the time of referral compared to the other countries. In the total sample, 48.8% of the children were female ($n = 589$), 50.5% were male ($n = 609$), and for 0.75% ($n = 9$) the gender was other, unknown, or not documented. No significant differences in the gender distribution emerged between countries ($\chi^2(2) = 1.84$; $p = .399$; $n = 1,198$). In addition, 20.7% of the children had a documented chronic health condition, which had either been confirmed or was under investigation ($n = 250$). There were no significant differences in the number of children with documented chronic health conditions between countries ($\chi^2(2) = 0.04$; $p = .981$; $n = 1,207$).

Table 12.1 CHARACTERISTICS OF THE CHILD AND INVOLVEMENT OF BIRTH PARENTS

	England		Germany		Netherlands	
Child age (years)	M = 6.9 (SD = 5.6)		M = 7.1 (SD = 5.2)		M = 7.6 (SD = 5.3)	
Child gender	n	%	n	%	N	%
Female	206	51.5	200	48.9	183	46.0
Male	194	48.5	206	50.4	209	52.5
Other/unknown/not documented	–	–	3	0.7	6	1.5
Child has a chronic health condition	82	20.5	86	21.0	82	20.6
Caregivers involved in the investigation						
Both birth parents	210	52.5	271	66.3	284	71.4
Birth mother only	170	42.5	120	29.3	103	25.9
Birth father only	10	2.5	10	2.4	11	2.8
Neither birth parent	10	2.5	8	2.0	0	0.0

In the majority of cases, the birth mother was considered to be important to the investigation (95.9%; $n = 1,158$). In 66.0% of cases ($n = 796$), the birth father was considered to be important to the investigation (Table 12.1). No significant differences occurred between countries regarding whether the birth mother was involved in the investigation ($\chi^2(2) = 2.75$; $p = .253$; $n = 1,207$), whereas there were significant differences regarding whether the birth father was involved ($\chi^2(2) = 34.57$; $p < .001$; $n = 1,207$). In England, birth fathers were less likely to be considered important to the investigation than in the Netherlands and Germany.

Participation. In 175 cases (14.5%), there was some documentation of the child having been involved in the decision-making process. The involvement of children in the decision-making process differed significantly between countries ($\chi^2(2) = 33.9$; $p < .001$; $n = 1,207$). Germany had the highest number of cases with child participation documented in the case files (22.3%; $n = 91$), followed by England (13.0%; $n = 52$); the Netherlands had the lowest number of cases in which child participation was documented (8.0%, $n = 32$). Participation rates for children of different age groups are presented in Table 12.2.

Predictors of child participation. Results of the logistic regression models to predict child participation are presented in Table 12.3. Cases from England and Germany had significantly higher participation rates than cases from the Netherlands.

Table 12.2 PARTICIPATION RATES FOR CHILDREN OF DIFFERENT AGE GROUPS

Age group	England			Germany			Netherlands		
	A	**P**	**%**	**A**	**P**	**%**	**A**	**P**	**%**
Under 1 year[a]	85	0	0.0	48	1	2.1	38	0	0.0
1–3 years	61	1	1.6	88	6	6.8	68	0	0.0
4–6 years	56	3	5.4	60	4	6.7	83	0	0.0
7–10 years	66	8	12.1	100	28	28.0	71	7	9.9
11–14 years	82	24	29.3	67	26	38.8	82	10	12.2
15–18 years	50	16	32.0	46	26	56.5	56	15	26.8
Total	400	52	13.0	409	91	22.2	398	32	8.0

[a] Includes unborn children. A, Absolute number of children within each age group for each country; P, number of children within each age group who participated in decision-making

No significant differences were found between English and German cases. In all three countries, participation in decision-making was associated with the age of the child. Older children were more likely to be included in decision-making. For England and Germany, no other significant predictors emerged at the level of the child or the case. For the Netherlands, the child having a chronic health condition increased the likelihood of participation in decision-making, as did suffering more types of abuse or neglect. In the second model, involvement of the caregiver in the decision-making process was included as predictor. This was a significant predictor in all countries. Bivariate analyses showed that, in most cases, children were only included in the decision-making process when their caregiver was also included. However, caregivers were included even when the child was not (cf. Table 12.4).

Participation and decision. In Table 12.5, the results of the logistic regression analyses to predict outcomes of the decision-making process are shown. According to the between-country comparison, in Germany a child was considered to be at lower risk of significant harm compared to the two other countries. Moreover, similarly, it was less likely that a family was seen as in need of support in Germany compared with the Netherlands. No differences in the decision for family support between England and the Netherlands emerged. No differences between countries were found regarding individual support need.

Younger child age was predictive of a child being considered to be at risk of significant harm in England and the Netherlands. In England, child age was also a significant predictor of the need for family support. However, older child age was predictive of the need for individual help for the child in England and

Table 12.3 PREDICTORS OF THE PARTICIPATION OF CHILDREN IN THE
DECISION-MAKING PROCESS

Predictors	Model 1			Model 2		
	Odds ratio	Lower level	Upper level	Odds ratio	Lower level	Upper level
Country[a]						
England	9.01*	[1.33;	61.00]	70.90*	[2.24;	2242.33]
Germany	20.16**	[3.46;	117.46]	44.82*	[1.46;	1379.75]
Child age with country						
England	1.30***	[1.20;	1.41]	1.37***	[1.25;	1.51]
Germany	1.25***	[1.18;	1.32]	1.32***	[1.23;	1.42]
Netherlands	1.30***	[1.16;	1.45]	1.43***	[1.23;	1.66]
Child has a chronic health condition with country						
England	0.46	[0.20;	1.06]	0.37*	[0.15;	0.93]
Germany	0.98	[0.53;	1.81]	0.85	[0.42;	1.72]
Netherlands	3.40**	[1.50;	7.69]	2.42	[0.81;	7.18]
Number of types of maltreatment with country						
England	0.88	[0.70;	1.10]	0.65**	[0.49;	0.85]
Germany	1.04	[0.85;	1.28]	1.30*	[1.00;	1.68]
Netherlands	1.45*	[1.05;	2.00]	1.36	[0.86;	2.16]
Involvement of caregiver with country						
England				24.40***	[8.36;	71.21]
Germany				37.44***	[13.95;	100.49]
Netherlands				181.89***	[22.46;	1473.18]
Nagelkerke's R^2	.32			.57		

[a] The Netherlands as reference category; *** p <.001, ** p < .010, * p < .050.

the Netherlands. Whether a child had a chronic health condition was predictive of the risk of significant harm in the Netherlands and the need for family support in Germany. In all three countries, a chronic health condition substantially increased the likelihood of the child needing individual support. The more types of maltreatment investigated predicted the decision regarding the risk of significant harm and the need for family support in all three countries.

Table 12.4 PARTICIPATION OF CAREGIVER AND CHILD

	No participation		Caregiver participation only		Child participation only		Caregiver and child participation	
	N	%	*n*	%	*n*	%	*n*	%
England	183	45.8	165	41.3	5	1.3	47	11.8
Germany	171	41.8	147	35.9	6	1.5	85	20.8
Netherlands	295	74.1	71	17.8	1	0.3	31	7.8
Total	649	53.8	383	31.7	12	1.0	163	13.5

Only in England were greater numbers of maltreatment also predictive of the need for individual support for the child.

In England, whether children participated in the decision-making process was not associated with any of the three decision outcomes. In the Netherlands, participation of the child increased the likelihood that the child was considered to be at risk of significant harm, as well as the likelihood that individual support for the child was necessary. In Germany, participation of the child was associated with a greater likelihood that family support would be considered necessary and that individual support for the child was considered important.

DIFFERENCES AND SIMILARITIES IN POLICY REGARDING CHILDREN'S PARTICIPATION

The findings of the policy analysis of children's meaningful participation in England, Germany, and the Netherlands demonstrate that the participation of children is receiving increased attention in child protection policy developments in these countries.

In the policy documents reviewed, the dimension of *informing* children seems to focus mainly on the content or specific aspects of child protection practice; the prerequisite of informing children about their right to participate and its potential impact is not specifically described in policy documents of the three countries.

Even though the importance of *hearing* the perspective of the child in child protection processes is stressed in policy in the three countries, this typically relates to family court proceedings and, more recently, to investigations but not to other parts of the process. However, in England and Germany the law requires children to be involved in help planning conferences while services are provided.

Table 12.5 PREDICTORS OF OUTCOMES OF THE DECISION-MAKING PROCESS

Predictors	Child at risk of significant harm			Family needs support			Child needs individual support		
	Odds ratio	Lower level	Upper level	Odds ratio	Lower level	Upper level	Odds ratio	Lower level	Upper level
Country[a]									
England	1.26	[0.67;	2.36]	1.37	[0.66;	2.88]	1.76	[0.73;	4.23]
Germany	0.12***	[0.05;	0.27]	0.41**	[0.21;	0.80]	1.30	[0.52;	3.26]
Child age with country									
England	0.89***	[0.84;	0.93]	0.93**	[0.88;	0.98]	1.08**	[1.03;	1.13]
Germany	1.04	[0.98;	1.11]	0.99	[0.94;	1.04]	1.06	[1.00;	1.12]
Netherlands	0.93**	[0.89;	0.97]	0.98	[0.93;	1.03]	1.16***	[1.09;	1.22]
Child has a chronic health condition with country									
England	1.63	[0.90;	2.96]	2.08	[0.91;	4.75]	3.97***	[2.24;	7.06]
Germany	1.40	[0.73;	2.65]	3.04**	[1.53;	6.03]	4.04***	[2.28;	7.14]
Netherlands	2.12*	[1.17;	3.85]	1.79	[0.82;	3.89]	2.30**	[1.27;	4.16]
Number of types of maltreatment with country									
England	2.18***	[1.79;	2.64]	2.33***	[1.73;	3.13]	1.78***	[1.50;	2.10]
Germany	1.81***	[1.46;	2.25]	2.03***	[1.59;	2.59]	1.10	[0.90;	1.35]
Netherlands	1.93***	[1.55;	2.40]	2.16***	[1.59;	2.95]	1.08	[0.86;	1.36]
Involvement of child with country									
England	0.69	[0.31;	1.53]	1.02	[0.45;	2.29]	0.89	[0.43;	1.87]
Germany	0.92	[0.46;	1.85]	2.37*	[1.21;	4.67]	2.84**	[1.54;	5.26]
Netherlands	9.76***	[3.30;	28.86]	7.04	[0.90;	55.39]	3.68**	[1.55;	8.73]
Nagelkerke's R^2	.35			.23			.30		

[a] The Netherlands as reference category; *** $p <.001$, ** $p < .010$, * $p < .050$.

Child protection policy does not always place emphasis on *involving* children. Policy documents in Germany and the Netherlands, two countries with a strong family orientation, mention children and parents together when specifying the need for participation. In England, however, where a more child-centered approach is adopted, policy states that the needs and wishes of each child should be put first and that children should be seen alone wherever possible.

Moreover, we have observed that child protection policy from Germany and the Netherlands provides age limits for participation. These limits differ per country and within country despite the fact that the UNCRC discourages the use of age restrictions for participation.

LINKING POLICY TO PRACTICE

Low rates of participation. Considering that the participation of children is considered important in law and policy in all three countries, it is surprising how low the rates of involvement of children in the decision-making process are. In the Netherlands especially, the gap between policy and practice seems to be very wide. This finding is even more surprising considering the rather wide definition of participation used in this study.

Predictors of participation. Child age was predictive of the involvement of children in the decision-making process in all three countries. This finding is in line with the findings of Kriz and Skiveness (2015). The authors found that caseworkers decided on participation based on the age and developmental stage of children. It is also possible that social workers were more likely to document the participation of older children as they were more likely to take part in decision-making conferences, while conversations with younger children in less formal contexts might have been less reliably documented. However, even in the older age groups, participation rates are not very high. In Germany, this may link back to guidelines and policy documents mandating involvement only for older children. In England, however, policy/law only states that children's age should be considered, but that all children should participate.

In the Netherlands, having a chronic health condition was predictive of participation. This finding is rather surprising as usually the threshold for participation is higher for children with chronic health conditions, and the participation of children with chronic health condition and possible difficulties for their participation is not considered explicitly in Dutch law. It might be possible that social workers consider these cases more severe or see a greater service need and thus put more effort into children's participation.

Children who suffered more types of maltreatment were more likely to be included in decision-making in the Netherlands.[1]

This finding might be due to caseworkers feeling a greater need to listen to the child in cases involving more types of maltreatment as more drastic measures might be taken in these cases.

One of the key predictors of child participation in all countries was the involvement of at least one caregiver in the decision-making process. Children

---

[1] Effects of the number of types of maltreatment investigated on child participation were also statistically significant in the English and German case files when the participation of at least one caregiver in the decision-making process was controlled for. However, these findings have to be interpreted carefully as the odds ratios in the model are biased due to unequal frequencies of the combinations between caregiver and child participation.

were only included in decision-making when at least one caregiver was included. However, the same does not apply vice versa. Thus, caregivers might serve a gatekeeping role for child participation. This might be due to the fact that it is hard for social workers to enable child participation without the cooperation of caregivers. Two other studies confirm our findings. Sanders and Mace (2006) found that parents being uncooperative or actively preventing their children's participation created barriers to participation. They also found that children's wishes and feelings were most often expressed at case conferences through their parents. Meanwhile, Cossar, Brandon, and Jordan (2014) found that children were getting information about child protection processes from their parents (and older siblings) and that sometimes this information was inaccurate and could undermine the relationship between the child and the social worker. Both of these studies also found that some children were unable to answer questions honestly in conferences due to their parents being present.

Effects of participation on decision outcomes. Child participation was associated with different decision outcomes in Germany and the Netherlands. In the Netherlands, child participation was associated with an increased likelihood that the child was seen as being at risk of significant harm. In Germany, child participation was associated with an increased likelihood that the family was considered to be in need of support. For both countries, child participation was associated with an increased likelihood that individual support for the child was considered necessary at the end of the investigation. This latter finding in particular highlights how caseworkers appear to focus more on children's needs when they involve them in the decision-making process. Yet the data do not allow us to draw causal conclusions.

Strengths and limitations. This study is the first to examine the participation of children using a standardized procedure for data collection in more than one country. Yet the conclusions drawn are limited to what was documented in the case files, and caseworkers might have included children in the decision-making process without noting it in the case files. However, as all countries have documentation guidelines and the participation of children is required by law, this is very unlikely. Furthermore, it was not possible to assess the participation of children in more detail with a quantitative case analysis design (e.g., using all dimensions of Bouma's model [2018]) or using a second data source, such as information provided by the children.

IMPLICATIONS FOR CHILD PROTECTION SYSTEMS

Further research on children's participation in child protection decision-making is necessary to expand the knowledge base on factors that can hinder or facilitate this participation. Particular attention should be paid to the barriers preventing younger children from being included in decision-making processes and how these can be overcome, with a view to increasing young children's participation in the child protection process while being sensitive to their age and developmental stage. Such research could include qualitative work with caseworkers to gather their insights into the reasons for the low rates of child participation observed here. These reasons might include some of those identified by previous authors, including negative attitudes toward child participation (Alberth & Bühler-Niederberger, 2015), incompetence in involving children in decision-making (Horwath et al., 2012), and perceived threat to professional discretion (Pluto, 2007). Research on the recording of child participation in case files is also warranted to explore the extent to which failure to document child participation accounts for the apparent low rates of child participation. Meanwhile, qualitative research with children exploring the extent to which they have been heard, informed, and involved in decision-making processes would increase our understanding of children's experiences of participation in such processes and inform strategies to increase their meaningful participation.

The rhetoric supporting child participation found in the laws and policies of the three countries included in this study must be followed-up by practice. Clear guidelines for children's participation must be developed to prevent any age discrimination against children in the participation efforts and with special attention paid to more disadvantaged groups in care, including refugee children and children with disabilities. Adult culture and its restrictive understanding of children's capacities form an important obstacle hindering participation in child protection (Collins, 2016; Alberth & Bühler-Niederberger, 2015). There is a need to identify and share best practices of meaningful and ethical participation of children in child protection internationally. Moreover, the meaningful participation framework (Bouma et al., 2018) guiding our analysis of policy and practice could be used for policy-makers as a tool to reflect on how children's rights to participate are embedded in their child protection policy and practice guidelines. With this framework, attention can be directed not simply to how children are informed and are heard, but also to how their voices are taken into account during the entire child protection process.

REFERENCES

Alberth, L., & Bühler-Niederberger, D. (2015). Invisible children? Professional bricolage in child protection. *Children and Youth Services Review, 57*, 149–158. doi:10.1016/j.childyouth.2015.08.008

Balsells, M. A., Fuentes-Peláez, N., & Pastor, C. (2017). Listening to the voices of children in decision-making: A challenge for the child protection system in Spain. *Children and Youth Services Review, 79*, 418–425. doi:10.1016/j.childyouth.2017.06.055

BMFSFJ. (2015). Qualitätsstandards für die Beteiligung von Kindern und Jugendlichen: Allgemeine Qualitätsstandards und Empfehlungen für die Praxisfelder

Kindertageseinrichtungen, Schule, Kommune, Kinder- und Jugendarbeit und Erzieherische Hilfen. https://www.bmfsfj.de/ . . . /kindergerechtes-deutschland-broschuere-qualitaetsstandards.

Bouma, H., López López, M., Knorth, E. J., & Grietens, H. (2018). Meaningful participation of children in the child protection system: An analysis of Dutch policy. *Child Abuse and Neglect, 52*, 279–292. doi:10.1016/j.chiabu.2018.02.016

Children and Family Court Advisory and Support Service. (2017). Public law cases. https://www.cafcass.gov.uk/grown-ups/professionals/public-law-cases/.

Cashmore, J. (2002). Promoting the participation of children and young people in care. *Child Abuse & Neglect, 26*, 837–347.

Children Act 1989. (1989). Chapter 41. https://www.legislation.gov.uk/ukpga/1989/41/contents.

Children Act 2004. (2004). Chapter 31. https://www.legislation.gov.uk/ukpga/2004/31/contents.

Collins, T. M. (2016). A child's right to participate: Implications for international child protection. *International Journal of Human Rights, 21*(1), 14–46. doi:10.1080/13642987.2016.1248122

Committee on the Rights of the Child (CRC). (2009). *General comment no. 12. The right of the child to be heard.* Geneva: United Nations.

Cossar, J., Brandon, M., & Jordan, P. (2014). "You've got to trust her and she's got to trust you": Children's views on participation in the child protection system. *Child & Family Social Work, 103–112.* doi:10.1111/cfs.12115

English, D. J., & the Longscan Investigators. (1997). Modified maltreatment classification system (MMCS). For more information visit the LONGSCAN website at http://www.iprc.unc.edu/longscan

Gilbert, N., Parton, N., & Skivenes, M. (Eds.). (2011). *Child protection systems: International trends and orientations.* New York: Oxford University Press.

Gilbert, R., Widom, C. S., Browne, K., Fergusson, D., Webb, E., & Janson, S. (2009). Burden and consequences of child maltreatment in high-income countries. *Lancet, 373*(9657), 68–81. doi:10.1016/S0140-6736(08)61706-7

HM Government. (2018). Working together to safeguard children: A guide to inter-agency working to safeguard and promote the welfare of children. https://assets.publishing.service.gov.uk/government/uploads/system/uploads/attachment_data/file/779401/Working_Together_to_Safeguard-Children.pdf.

Horwath, J., Kalyva, E., & Spyru, S. (2012). "I want my experiences to make a difference" promoting participation in policy-making and service development by young people who have experienced violence. *Children and Youth Services Review, 34*, 155–162. doi:10.1016/j.childyouth.2011.09.012

Jeugdwet. (2014, 1 March). http://wetten.overheid.nl/BWBR0034925.

Kinderombudsman. (2016). *Als je het ons vraagt. Kinderrechtentour 2016.* The Hague: Author.

Kriz, K., & Roundtree-Swain, D. (2017). "We are merchandise on a conveyer belt": How young adults in the public child protection system perceive their participation in decisions about their care. *Children and Youth Services Review, 78*, 32–40. doi:10.1016/j.childyouth.2017.05.001

Kriz, K., & Skivenes, M. (2015). Child welfare workers' perceptions of children's participation: A comparative study of England, Norway and the USA (California). *Child & Family Social Work*, 1–12. doi:10.1111/cfs.12224

Laming, H. (2003). *The Victoria Climbié inquiry*. Norwich: The Stationery Office.

Liebel, M. (2009). "Nicht über unsere Köpfe hinweg": Oder: Partizipation ist der beste Kinderschutz. *IzKK-Nachrichten*, 1, 52–56.

López, M., Bouma, H., Knorth, E., & Grietens, H. (2019). The Dutch child protection system: Historical overview and recent transformations. In R. D. Krugman, L. Merkel-Holguin, & J. D. Fluke (Eds.), *National systems of child protection. Understanding the international variability and context of developing policy and practice*. New York: Springer.

Memorie van Toelichting bij de Jeugdwet. (2013). http://www.rijksoverheid.nl/documenten-en-publicaties/kamerstukken/2013/07/01/memorie-van-toelichting-bij-de-jeugdwet.html.

Munro, E. (2011). *The Munro review of child protection: Final report: A child-centred system*. Norwich: The Stationery Office.

National Association of Independent Reviewing Officers. (n.d.) What Is an IRO? https://www.nairo.org.uk/what-is-an-iro/.

Pluto, L. (2007). *Partizipation in den Hilfen zur Erziehung*. München: DJI Verlag.

Sanders, R., & Mace, S. (2006). Agency policy and the participation of children and young people in the child protection process. *Child Abuse Review*, 15, 89–109. doi:10.1002/car.927

Ten Brummelaar, M. D. C., Harder, A. T., Kalverboer, M. E., Post, W. J., & Knorth, E. J. (2017). Participation of youth in decision-making procedures during residential care: A narrative review. *Child and Family Social Work*, 1–12. doi:10.1111/cfs.12381

Tweede Kamer der Staten Generaal. (2016). *Motie van de Leden Bergkamp & Kooiman*, 31 839, nr. 552.

Van Bijleveld, G. G., Dedding, C. W. M., & Bunders-Aelen, J. F. G. (2015). Children's and young people's participation within child welfare and child protection services: A state-of-the-art review. *Child and Family Social Work*, 20, 129–138. doi:10.1111/cfs.12082

Vis, S. A., Strandbu, A., Holtan, A., & Thomas, N. (2011). Participation and health – a research review of child participation in planning and decision-making. *Child and Family Social Work*, 16, 325–335. doi:10.1111/j.1365-2206.2010.00743.x

Wiesner, R. (2009). Partizipation als Modus des Kinderschutzes: Bedeutung der UN-Kinderrechtskonvention für die Verfahren der Kinder- und Jugendhilfe. *IzKK-Nachrichten*, 1, 21–24.

Witte, S., Miehlbradt, L., van Santen, E., & Kindler, H. (2019). Preventing child endangerment: Child protection in Germany. In L. Merkel-Holguin, J. D. Fluke, & R. D. Krugman (Eds.), *National systems of child protection. Understanding the international variability and context of developing policy and practice*. Switzerland: Springer.

13

Teaching and Learning Decision-Making in Child Welfare and Protection Social Work

BRIAN J. TAYLOR ■

> In nature we never see anything isolated, but everything in connection
> with something else which is before it, beside it, under it and over it.
> —JOHANN WOLFGANG VON GOETHE, *cited in Wood (1893)*

INTRODUCTION: MY DECISION-MAKING, ASSESSMENT, AND RISK JOURNEY

The time that I became aware that I was on a personal journey in relation to risk and decision-making in social work was in the early 1990s. I was a social work training officer in an organization responsible for public health and social care services. During the annual training needs analysis to inform our in-service training plan, social work managers began to ask for short courses on "risk." The training department would seek clarity from managers about the training requests: in this case about what managers meant by "risk" as well as for which staff groups training was sought. I was given the lead role for developing this

Brian J. Taylor, *Teaching and Learning Decision-Making in Child Welfare and Protection Social Work* In: *Decision-Making and Judgment in Child Welfare and Protection.* Edited by: John D. Fluke, Mónica López López, Rami Benbenishty, Erik J. Knorth, and Donald J. Baumann, Oxford University Press (2021). © Oxford University Press.
DOI: 10.1093/oso/9780190059538.003.0013.

aspect of the training program and thus began to investigate what was published and who was teaching in this area. Over the years of providing short courses on variations of this topic, it became clearer that "risk" (i.e., appraising the possibility of future harm as well as assessing presenting need, strengths, eligibility for services, statutory powers, etc.) was closely related to professional judgment, assessment, and decision processes.

During this personal journey, the wider world of decision-making study was evolving. Various disciplines sought to apply knowledge to uncertainty leading to understandings of risk (Althaus, 2005) in the context of the emerging "risk society" (Beck, 1992). The context of statutes, regulations, and guidance in child welfare led to increasingly prescriptive decision procedures (Leonard & O'Connor, 2018). Society became more risk-averse (the "blame culture"), influencing professional practice (Fleming, Biggart, & Beckett, 2014). The management of risk and decisions became more closely aligned with managing quality, sometimes conceptualized as *social care governance* (Taylor & Campbell, 2011). Quite separate from our social work professional and organizational focus on assessment and risk, the study of human judgment was proceeding in parallel in fields such as business, medicine, economics, psychology, and military studies.

Somewhere along this journey into risk and decision-making, I made the connection with the enthusiasm that I had when I was in practice for structuring my social work assessments (Fengler & Taylor, 2019; Taylor & Devine, 1993). There were few assessment tools required or provided for use in the 1980s, despite the time-honored recognition of assessment as a key social work process (Richmond, 1917). I hunted out assessment tools from wherever I could, including from other professions, one example being a tool designed for health visitors (community nurses with a focus on young children) to assess child development. I created my own templates for organizing the information that I gathered in order to form a judgment. Encouragingly, my efforts to structure information in my court reports were well received by the magistrates and judges charged with making decisions in contested child welfare cases. I began to conceptualize "assessment" as a process that supports professional judgment and decision-making and which is set in a context of risk or uncertainty (Taylor, 2017a, Glossary). This journey has continued (Killick & Taylor, 2020).

THEORETICAL UNDERPINNINGS FOR PROFESSIONAL JUDGMENT

In general, we do not have established models for "professional judgment" or "decision-making" (cf. Baumann, Fluke, Dalgleish, & Kern, 2014; Drury-Hudson, 1999; Hammond, 1996; Hill, McIlfatrick, Taylor, & Fitzsimons, 2017;

Taylor, 2012a; Taylor & Killick, 2013) as a basis for teaching this topic in the helping professions comparable to those which we have for interpersonal helping skills (e.g., Egan, 1997; Koprowska, 2010; Shulman, 2009). Initiatives such as structured assessment tools and organizational systems for assessment processes clarify decision-making and assist in ensuring the recording (and hopefully the appraisal) of relevant information. The rationales for professional judgments and decisions may be obscure (De Kwaadsteniet, Bartelink, Witteman, Ten Berge, & Van Yperen, 2013). However, the profession is now at a stage where attention is being paid to assessment not just as a process of engagement and the gathering and ordering of data, but also as a task requiring analysis of data (Barlow, Fisher, & Jones, 2012; Schwalbe, 2004) so as to inform professional judgment more explicitly (Macdonald, 2001; Taylor, 2006).

The cognitive task of analyzing data may be understood in terms of heuristic processes using a "psycho-social rationality" (Taylor, 2017b) as well as through application of Aristotelian logic or probability calculus. It is recognized, of course, that heuristic approaches to judgments might be regarded as biases (Benbenishty et al., 2015; Enosh & Bayer-Topilsky, 2015; Helm, 2011; Munro, 1999; Spratt, Devaney, & Hayes, 2015). Studies of biases highlight the way that practitioners use cognitive framing of decision situations that go beyond a mere aggregation of statistical data. However, this may be viewed positively as an integral aspect of the functioning of the human brain in making use of large amounts of information (Gigerenzer & Gaissmeyer, 2011; Simon, 1956). An essential component of learning is the creation of simple models, which may be described as *heuristics* and which give structure to what is sometimes referred to as intuition (Hogarth, 2008). Although there may be legal and ethical issues in formalizing heuristic models (Taylor, 2017b), sense-making strategies seem to play an integral part in professional judgment just as they do in everyday life (Brearley, 1982; Platt & Turney, 2014). The brain seems continually to remodel and reorganize its use of information, rather than adding to a store of memorized data that is accessed as needed, like books in a library.

There is a particular challenge in learning and using conceptual frameworks for decision-making. Learning any new conceptual framework for action requires the individual to incorporate the new concepts with those already used for similar situations (Meyer & Land, 2003). As an example, learning an interpersonal helping model requires adjustment to previous ideas about what will be helpful for people, including learning from what has been helpful for oneself and learning from experience in the helping role (Hertwig, 2012). Learning frameworks for appraising and analyzing our own cognitive judgment processes occurs at a deep conceptual level. Learning from experience involves cognitive processes that make sense of those experiences (Hackett & Taylor, 2014). This theoretical understanding is illustrated here from our experience of teaching about decision-making at two distinct social worker career stages. The structures for teaching will be outlined briefly so that the reader can make sense of the later description of teaching about decision-making.

REFLECTIONS ON DECISION-MAKING SKILLS WITHIN SOCIAL WORK EDUCATION

In the United Kingdom, professional social work qualifying courses are required to be generic (i.e., to train social workers in the generic knowledge and skills required to work with the main client groups, such as family and child care, mental health, disability, and elder care). In terms of child welfare, this includes preparing social workers for practice in teams such as child protection, family support, child and adolescent mental health, therapeutic and mandated family center work, residential care, fostering, adoption, and 16+ services for young people leaving state care. Post-qualifying courses may specialize in particular client groups or methods of practice.

All social work education programs in Northern Ireland, both qualifying and post-qualifying, are required by the professional regulatory body, the Northern Ireland Social Care Council (NISCC), to be managed by a partnership of at least one employer and at least one academic institution (Department of Health, Social Services and Public Safety, & the Northern Ireland Social Care Council, 2006; Taylor, 1998; Taylor, Mullineux, & Fleming, 2010). Social workers can achieve academic credits from a university in parallel with achieving a professional award. Since 2007, all those qualifying in social work receive a bachelor's degree from a university as well as certification by the professional regulatory body. (Those who already hold a sufficiently relevant degree—about half of those recruited— can complete their social work bachelor's in 2 years rather than 3.) Since that time, professional qualifications in social work in Northern Ireland meet the standards of the 1999 European Union framework (the Bologna agreement) for higher education qualifications (European Association for Quality Assurance in Higher Education, 2005; Froment, 2006), requiring (in essence): (1) a professional entry qualification of at least graduate level, embodying at least 3 years of relevant higher education study; (2) a protected title (such that those using the title "social worker" with intent to deceive or commit a criminal offence); and (3) a register of those entitled to practice with effective arrangements for disciplinary action, independent of the particular employer, to be taken as required.

As part of the registration required to practice, social workers in employment in Northern Ireland are automatically enrolled on a post-qualifying framework known as Professional-in-Practice, which is at the post-graduate level (Level 7) within the European Union framework. This is after their Assessed Year in

Employment (Department of Health, Social Services and Public Safety, 2015), which takes place when first appointed. The first stage of this post-qualifying framework is a professional Consolidation Award, which is primarily for social workers who have just completed the Assessed Year in Employment but is also designed for incoming workers trained in other jurisdictions, for those changing client group, and as refresher training for those who have been out of the workplace for a period.

Following the initiatives to develop "risk" as a topic within the in-service short courses mentioned earlier, the topic of risk and decision-making began to be called for within accredited (examined) post-qualifying training in the late 1990s and within qualifying training in the early 2000s. As one initiative, Ulster University partnered health and social care employers in providing a post-qualifying module: *Professional Decision-Making in Social Work*, as part of the NISCC Consolidation Award. This module is simultaneously a third of a University Postgraduate Certificate in Professional Development in Social Work. This module addresses the NISCC Consolidation Award Requirement: *Demonstrate consistent and sustained sound judgment and decision-making in the context of complexity, risk, uncertainty, conflict and contradiction* (Northern Ireland Social Care Council, 2012). Each year, approximately three-quarters of social workers in their second year of professional work in Northern Ireland attend this module. Approximately two-thirds of these are in child welfare work. From the perspective of a teacher, this has provided a valuable opportunity to develop our curriculum on professional decision-making in a context of risk. A textbook was written to support this module on professional decision-making for newly qualified social workers, now in its third edition (Taylor, 2017a). The chapter framework of that book will be used to consider key topics in the teaching of decision-making skills appropriate for stages of learning (see Table 13.1).

On the qualifying (undergraduate) social work program at Ulster University, explicit teaching on decision-making is included within a module on Assessment and Risk Assessment in Practice Settings. The learning outcomes include understanding the social work role in undertaking assessment and engaging in decision processes. Generic material on risk and decision-making is taught as a context for detailed learning about assessment tools and approaches used in the local service for particular client groups (family and child care, elder care, justice and youth justice, mental health, disability). Priority topics (see Table 13.1) take into account student feedback, employer perspectives from practice teachers, and continued attention to the literature by academic staff. The module takes place when students have completed about half of their training and have undertaken one of their two major practice placements. Elsewhere in the curriculum, students learn about

Table 13.1 COVERAGE OF DECISION-MAKING TOPICS ON QUALIFYING AND THE
NEWLY QUALIFIED SOCIAL WORKERS' COURSE OF ULSTER UNIVERSITY AND
EMPLOYER PARTNERS.

Chapter	Topic	Qualifying (undergraduate) social work course	Post-qualifying (postgraduate) course for newly qualified social workers
1	Terms, concepts and models of decision-making	✓	*
2	Client perspectives, emotions, and crises in relation to decision-making	~	✓
3	Legal aspects of decision-making	~	✓
4	Assessment processes and decision support systems	*	*
5	Bias and use of knowledge in professional judgement	~	✓
6	Safeguarding and service eligibility threshold judgments and use of risk factors to predict harm	✓	*
7	Risk-taking as intrinsic to care plan decisions; values, gains, hazards	~	*
8	Collaboration, communication, and contest in decision-making	~	*
9	Dynamics: incremental decisions and changing your mind	0	~
10	Managing decisions, assessment, and risk: organizational support, blame, learning, and supervision	0	0

* = substantial focus; ✓ = moderate attention; ~ = some coverage; 0 = no coverage

other skills relevant to decision-making such as engaging clients and families, working in an organizational context, and multiprofessional working in general. About two-thirds of graduates go into child welfare roles for their first professional job.

For the Initial Professional Development Program for newly qualified social workers, the teaching topics are illustrated in Table 13.1, which enables some approximate comparison between this career stage with those on their qualifying training. The post-qualifying teaching focuses on material that is directly relevant to practice, particularly as ascertained from detailed student feedback at the end of each teaching block and from line managers through employer training departments. The teaching is generic, with examples drawn from a wide range of practice contexts, although the principles have application across all client groups. Our focus is on the knowledge and skills for beginning practitioners and on strengthening the profession (which is under frequent assault from some media and politicians) so that it can better serve clients, families, and society.

EXPERIENCES IN LEARNING AND TEACHING DECISION-MAKING SKILLS IN SOCIAL WORK

During 2017–2018, as part of module evaluation, students on these programs were asked their opinions on what constituted challenging issues in relation to professional social work decision-making. The comments by students on the qualifying program (about two-thirds of whom are likely to undertake a job in family and child care services on graduating) and social workers on the post-qualifying program (about two-thirds of whom were working in family and child care services) are illustrated in Table 13.2.

It will be noted that social workers after a year of practice were identifying a more extensive and more finely nuanced list of issues than those on their qualifying training. Sustaining this increasing refinement of perception through post-qualifying study is a key way that expertise grows from the more rule-oriented (and textbook-oriented) approach of novices. It is important to develop the ability to take into account appropriately the decision context (Font & Maguire-Jack, 2015) and the decision task (Detlaff, Graham, Holzman, Baumann, & Fluke, 2015). Knowledge of risks and professional decisions is at an early stage during qualifying training and requires development during post-qualifying learning. This development of skills for decision-making is much broader than simply generating and testing hypothetical solutions, such as is sometimes conceived as constituting a clinical diagnostic judgment (Elstein & Bordage, 1979; Hassan, 2013). Supporting ongoing reflection on practice, utilizing theoretical concepts as a structure, is a key approach to developing such "process knowledge" (Sheppard, Newstead, Di Caccavo, & Ryan, 2000).

This chapter does not provide space to describe the examining processes or to analyze the assessed work produced by students. Two brief extracts, adapted

Table 13.2 ILLUSTRATIVE ISSUES IDENTIFIED BY SOCIAL WORK STUDENTS
ON QUALIFYING AND EARLY POST-QUALIFYING COURSES IN RELATION
TO PROFESSIONAL DECISION-MAKING.

Domain	Raised by students on qualifying course	Raised by social workers on post-qualifying course
Ethical	Ethical aspects	Balancing rights and risks; respecting self-determination; professional versus personal value conflicts
Accountability	Responsibility for clients and others	Managing the risk of an unmet need; concern at overreacting or underreacting; determining an acceptable risk; fear of making the wrong decision; being able to evidence good risk management
Managing the work	Time, resource, and organizational constraints	Time to consider properly the risks and other factors; managing self within an organizational context
Assessment and professional judgement	The challenges of multiprofessional working	Gaining information about parents in child protection cases; access to information via web systems; lack of information from police; diverse perspectives of family members; families not being open and honest; judging client decisional capacity
Appraising risks	Knowing what is a reasonable risk	Judging differential risk depending on the age of the child
Emotion	Fear of blame	Confidence, especially in risk-taking decisions with clients
Supervision and management	Having a good supervisor	Consistency of management decisions, in particular varying thresholds

for confidentiality and readability reasons, will illustrate the way that connections are made between the teaching of theoretical constructs and the realities of practice by a newly qualified social worker within an assessed assignment.

I was concerned about the emotional impact on the child Gary (aged 14 years) of being arrested despite the seriousness of the allegations about his sexual behaviour toward his step-sister. Placing him away from home, albeit with relatives, seemed harsh with hindsight as it now seems that he did not act in a predatory fashion. However it has to be recognised that at the crisis point, decisions have to be made based on the information available (Gigerenzer & Goldstein, 1996 in Taylor, 2012a). This type of professional judgments in social work are focused on making a safe decision with the least negative impact, within the constraints of limited information, time and resources (Taylor, 2012b). At the multi-professional Risk Management Meeting, the main aspects of the Family Safety Plan that I proposed were agreed.

Taylor (2017a) suggests that within decision-making, the outcomes are uncertain and the desired benefits may not be possible ... [and] describes the tension between risks and rights to ensure that they are located within the broad context of social opportunity and choice. Whilst, on one hand, I had a duty of care to other young people and staff to ensure that they are not placed at risk of harm as a consequence of my judgment and decision-making, on the other I wanted to focus on the resources and strengths John [young person aged 15 years] possessed [despite his aggressive outbursts. (Boyd, 2016, p. 10)

Although we have conducted no rigorous research, the main difference between students on qualifying training compared to the newly qualified stage could be conceptualized as relating to the application of knowledge to practice. Practice experience ensures that reflective comments—based on new "theoretical" insights—are meaningful and realistic, and they are intrinsically connected to improving the individual's cognitive processes and hence their skilled behaviors. Practitioners seem to learn best when building directly on their ongoing experience of closely related work.

FUTURE DEVELOPMENTS

The future for teaching and learning about decision-making in child welfare seems to embody four key dimensions: the art and science of decision-making, and how we improve and demonstrate the effectiveness of teaching on this topic. These will be considered in turn.

The Science of Professional Judgment: Learning to Use Knowledge About Risk Factors

Professionals of the future will be required increasingly to incorporate statistical knowledge within the art of their profession, requiring improved numeracy skills (Simms, 2016). This may require passing through the painful stage of "conscious incompetence" before reaching the more pleasant stage of "conscious competence" (Reynolds, 1942). Research (e.g., Dawes, Faust, & Meehl, 1989; Grove & Meehl, 1996) generally shows the superiority of mathematical models over human judgment for prediction tasks such as estimating the likelihood of child abuse given certain risk factors. The use of mathematical models within assessment tools to compute child abuse risk factors is developing gradually. There is potential for such approaches to provide a robust evidence base that can inform practice once we reach a stage of having factors that are agreed by the relevant professions as clearly defined, useful, and measurable with sufficient accuracy. Even then, creating a knowledge base that is acceptable for use in an argument for court is a further challenge (Duffy, McCall, & Taylor, 2006).

Mathematical models and computer algorithms will always be better—on average—than humans at computing accurately a large number of factors to calculate a numerical likelihood of a particular harm. The human brain is not designed to carry out multiple regression equations. However, the human brain can create and operate computer systems that can carry out such mathematical procedures. The challenge for professions in evidence-based decision-making lies in conceptualizing, specifying, and measuring useful risk factors; creating approaches to useful synthesis of these within usable assessment tools, models of professional judgment, and decision supports; and the development of learning processes for using these effectively and appropriately. Attention needs to be paid to ethical, legal, and technical issues so that professionals learn to use knowledge and exercise discretion effectively in this "new world" of knowledge-informed practice. Leaders in the profession need to understand the strengths and limitations of how factors are theorized and measured and to use appropriate implementation and evaluation methods (Taylor, Killick, & McGlade, 2015).

The Art of Professional Judgment: Conceptual Learning and Psycho-Social Rationality

Despite the incremental development of science (knowledge) to underpin decision-making in situations of risk (or uncertainty), we must not lose sight of the art of professional judgment and decision processes. The human dimension will still be an essential component of any human helping or safeguarding process, albeit increasingly integrated with and built upon a robust scientific evidence base (Potter, 2018; Van de Luitgaarden, 2009), perhaps mediated through a computer. Professional decision-making in relation to child welfare is much broader and more complex than the human ability to predict rare events and includes the following items:

Appraising the completeness, truthfulness, accuracy, and coherence of information;

Considering client and family information in the context (frame of reference) of law, standards of practice, regulations, guidance, policies, principles, ethics, and procedures;

Collaborating with other professionals, agencies, and the courts;

Making a reasoned and reasonable professional judgment and recommendations;

Seeing the connections between items of information and formulating a coherent mental picture of the family dynamics and risks; and

Appraising availability, acceptability, and effectiveness of possible interventions.

To support learning about decision-making, we need to conceptualize better the way that professionals use types of *psycho-social rationality* (Benner, 1984; Evans, 2011; Taylor, 2017b) and how they best use knowledge of risk factors within cognitive judgment processes (Hamilton, Taylor, Killick, & Bickerstaff, 2015). For example, the study by Pritchard and colleagues (2013) showed that, for child homicide, having a step-father figure in the family with a conviction for violence was a much larger risk factor than the mother's or the father's mental health problems (the second and third largest significant factors of those studied) or poverty (not found to correlate with child homicide). However, professionals need to understand that just 1 in 2,000 step-fathers with a previous conviction for violence went on to kill a child despite this being one of the largest (if not the largest) risk factors. Understanding the relative weighting of risk factors will help social workers to judge risk levels and make a proportionate response. However, this will require years of research (even assuming that research funding bodies are willing to invest substantially more than at present) to achieve a knowledge base that can inform practice effectively. The tradition of social work supervision (Field & Brown, 2016; Hawkins & Shohet, 2012; Howe, Gray, & Brown, 2013; Turney & Ruch, 2018) and reflective practice (Houston, 2015; Sicora, 2017) is very much a strength of the social work profession when viewed from the perspective of learning about decision-making.

Evidencing What Works in Teaching Decision-Making

There are few studies of the effectiveness of teaching interventions to improve decision-making in child welfare (Bartelink, Van Yperen, & Ten Berge, 2015), even by comparison with the number of rigorous studies of the effectiveness of child welfare interventions themselves (see Cochrane Developmental, Psychosocial and Learning Problems Group, 2018; Furlong et al., 2018).

There is some encouragement from research findings that some decision-making skills can be improved through training (Shamian, 1991) although evidence is sparse. Recently, Whittaker (2018a, 2018b) has created a randomized controlled trial (experimental study) where a student group on qualifying social work training in England is presented with realistic vignettes in a computer laboratory and must make judgments. Those in the intervention group will receive immediate video feedback after each judgment from a panel of experienced practitioners who explain the information to which they would have paid attention. Those in the control group do not receive this feedback. Such approaches to developing and testing an appreciation of multiple risk factors and their effective use within professional judgment need to be extended in order to improve our teaching of decision-making skills in the profession.

Developing the knowledge and skills for decision-making involves nurturing the professional artistry of useful "knowing," increasingly incorporating robust scientific evidence (Ghanem, Kollar, Fischer, Lawson, & Pankofer, 2018) of what is "known." The professional knowing required for decision-making incorporates cognitive, emotional, social, and reflective abilities. Enough external known knowledge—such as from research, theory, and the law—needs to be internalized to "know that you need to know it and where to find it." Enough retained internal knowing knowledge is required to create an effective cognitive *organizing framework* (or map) of concepts that can be operationalized through interpersonal skills. Practice is the focal integrating point for this growing external and internal knowledge base requiring reflective practice for continued learning and development.

Developing the Knowledge Base to Inform Teaching on Decision-Making

Educators need to make more connections between decision-making and other aspects of the curriculum, including assessment skills and processes; concepts of risk and use of risk factors; context of service provision, statutes, standards, and procedures; and knowledge drawn from psychology, health, law, sociology, etc. We need reflective models to support the integration of statistics with the uniqueness of individuals so that professional judgments are underpinned by the statistics *and* the story.

Wide-ranging research is required to provide an evidence base for the development of professional decision-making in a context of risk (Jansen, 2018; Killick & Taylor, 2012; Stevenson & Taylor, 2017; Taylor & Whittaker, 2019;

Whittaker & Taylor, 2018) where complexity, uncertainty, and emotional strains are likely to remain as substantial aspects of practice for the foreseeable future.

We need to build confidence in the profession, both in individual cognitive judgments and in engagement and leadership within decision processes while acknowledging the accountability appropriate in a democratic society. In this context it is pleasing that the profession is now being supported by, among other initiatives, the Biennial International Symposium on Decisions, Assessment, Risk and Evidence in Social Work (www.ulster.ac.uk/dare), which has taken place near Belfast every two years since 2010, and the Decisions, Assessment and Risk Special Interest Group of the European Social Work Research Association (http://www.eswra.org/decisions_sig.html; Taylor et al., 2017), both of which are creating a dynamic of international professional learning across cultures and jurisdictions.

CONCLUSION

The continuing development of good professional judgment and decision processes is a priority for public confidence in the professions that are committed to effective safeguarding for children and help for families on behalf of society. The development of social workers from novices to experts requires a broad approach embracing psycho-social rationality as well as statistics, interpersonal decision processes as well as individual judgment. As the potential of large-scale data gathering is developed, the art and science of decision-making in child welfare will require careful development and a new practice and educational paradigm for the ultimate benefit of the clients, families, and societies whom we serve.

REFERENCES

Althaus, C. E. (2005). A disciplinary perspective on the epistemological status of risk. *Risk Analysis, 25*(3), 567–588. doi:10.1111/j.1539-6924.2005.00625.x

Barlow, J., Fisher, J. D., & Jones, D. (2012). *Systematic review of models of analysing significant harm. Research Report DFE-RR199*. London/Oxford: Department for Education/Oxford University Press.

Bartelink, C., Van Yperen, T. A., & Ten Berge, I. J. (2015). Deciding on child maltreatment: A literature review on methods that improve decision-making. *Child Abuse and Neglect, 49*, 142–153. doi:10.1016/j.chiabu.2015.07.002

Baumann, D. J., Fluke, J. D., Dalgleish, L., & Kern, L. H. (2014). *The decision-making ecology*. In A. Shlonsky & R. Benbenishty (Eds.), *From evidence to outcomes in child welfare: An international reader* (pp. 24–37). Oxford: Oxford University Press.

Beck, U. (1992). *Risk society: Towards a new modernity*. New Delhi: Sage.

Benbenishty, R., Davidson-Arad, B., López, M., Devaney, J., Spratt, T., Koopmans, C., . . . Hayes, D. (2015). Decision making in child protection: An international comparative study on maltreatment substantiation, risk assessment and interventions recommendations, and the role of professionals' child welfare attitudes. *Child Abuse and Neglect, 49*, 63–75. doi:10.1016/j.chiabu.2015.03.015

Benner, P. (1984). *From novice to expert: Excellence and power in clinical nursing practice*. Menlo Park, CA: Addison-Wesley.

Boyd, M. (2016). *An analysis of risk and professional decision making in youth justice (custodial setting). Assignment submitted for post-qualifying Module SWK705: Professional Decision Making in Social Work*. Coleraine, Northern Ireland: Ulster University.

Brearley, P. (1982). *Risk in social work*. London: Routledge & Kegan Paul.

Cochrane Developmental, Psychosocial and Learning Problems Group. (https://dplp.cochrane.org

Dawes, R. M., Faust, D., & Meelh, P. E. (1989). Clinical versus actuarial judgment. *Science, 243*, 1668–1674. doi:10.1126/science.2648573

De Kwaadsteniet, L., Bartelink, C., Witteman, C., Ten Berge, I., & Van Yperen, T. (2013). Improved decision making about suspected child maltreatment: Results of structuring the decision process. *Children and Youth Services Review, 35*(2), 347–352. doi:10.1016/j.childyouth.2012.11.015

Department of Health, Social Services and Public Safety. (2015). *Assessed year in employment (AYE) of newly qualified social workers (NQSW): Implementation of the AYE Policy from 09 November 2015: Circular HSS (OSS) AYE: 2/2015*. Belfast: Author.

Department of Health, Social Services and Public Safety, & The Northern Ireland Social Care Council. (2006). *Northern Ireland post qualifying education and training framework in social work*. Belfast: Authors.

Detlaff, A. J., Graham, J. C., Holzman, J., Baumann, D. J., & Fluke, J. D. (2015). Development of an instrument to understand the child protective services decision-making process, with a focus on placement decisions. *Child Abuse and Neglect, 49*, 24–34. doi:10.1016/j.chiabu.2015.04.007

Drury-Hudson, J. (1999). Decision making in child protection: The use of theoretical, empirical and procedural knowledge by novices and experts and implications for fieldwork placements. *British Journal of Social Work, 29*(1), 147–169. doi:10.1093/oxfordjournals.bjsw.a011423

Duffy, J., Taylor, B. J., & McCall, S. (2006). Human rights and decision making in child protection through explicit argumentation. *Child Care in Practice, 12*(2), 81–95. doi:10.1080/13575270600618331

Egan, G. (1997). *The skilled helper: A systematic approach to effective helping* (6th ed.). Pacific Grove, CA: Brooks/Cole.

Elstein, A. S., & Bordage, G. (1979). Psychology of clinical reasoning. In J. Dowie & A. S. Elstein (Eds.), *Professional judgement: A reader in clinical decision making* (pp. 109–129). Cambridge: Cambridge University Press.

Enosh, G., & Bayer-Topilsky, T. (2015). Reasoning and bias: Heuristics in safety assessment and placement decisions for children at risk. *British Journal of Social Work, 45*(6), 1771–1787. doi:10.1093/bjsw/bct213

European Association for Quality Assurance in Higher Education. (2005). *Standards and guidelines for quality assurance in the European higher education area.* Helsinki: Author.

Evans, T. (2011). Professionals, managers and discretion: Critiquing street-level bureaucracy. *British Journal of Social Work, 41*(2), 368–386. doi:10.1093/bjsw/bcq074

Fengler, J., & Taylor, B. J. (2019). Effective assessment: A key knowledge and skill for a sustainable profession. *Social Work Education: The International Journal, 38*(3), 392–405. doi:10.1080/02615479.2018.1538333

Field, R., & Brown, K. (2016). *Effective leadership, management and supervision in health and social care.* London: Sage.

Fleming, P., Biggart, L., & Beckett, C. (2014). Effects of professional experience on child maltreatment risk assessments: A comparison of students and qualified social workers. *British Journal of Social Work, 45*(8), 2298–2316. doi:10.1093/bjsw/bcu090

Font, S. A., & Maguire-Jack, K. (2015). Reprint of "Decision-making in child protective services: Influences at multiple levels of the social ecology." *Child Abuse and Neglect, 49*, 50–62. doi:10.1016/j.chiabu.2015.02.005

Froment, E. (2006). The evolving vision and focus of the Bologna process. In European University Association (Ed.), *Bologna handbook: Making Bologna work* (section A 1.1-1). Berlin: Author. http://www.eua.be/publications/bologna-handbook/

Furlong, M., Stokes, A., McGilloway, S., Hickey, G., Leckey, Y., Bywater, T., . . . ENRICH Research Team (2018). A community-based parent-support programme to prevent child maltreatment: Protocol for a randomised controlled trial. *HRB Open Research, 1, 13.* doi:10.12688/hrbopenres.12812.2.

Ghanem, C., Kollar, I., Fischer, F., Lawson, T. R., & Pankofer, S. (2018). How do social work novices and experts solve professional problems? A micro-analysis of epistemic activities and the use of evidence. *European Journal of Social Work, 21*(1), 3–19. doi:10.1080/13691457.2016.1255931

Gigerenzer, G., & Gaissmaier, W. (2011). Heuristic decision making. *Annual Review of Psychology, 62*, 451–482. doi:10.1146/annurev-psych-120709-145346

Grove, W. M., & Meehl, P. E. (1996). Comparative efficiency of informal (subjective, impressionistic) and formal (mechanical, algorithmic) prediction procedures. *Psychology, Public Policy and Law, 2*(2), 293–323. doi:10.1037/1076-8971.2.2.293

Hackett, S., & Taylor, A. (2014). Decision making in social work with children and families: The use of experiential and analytical cognitive processes. *British Journal of Social Work, 44*(8), 2182–2199. doi:10.1093/bjsw/bct071

Hamilton, D., Taylor, B. J., Killick, C., & Bickerstaff, D. (2015). Suicidal ideation and behaviour among young people leaving care: Case file survey. *Child Care in Practice, 21*(2), 160–176. doi:10.1080/13575279.2014.994475

Hammond, H. R. (1996). *Human judgement and social policy: Irreducible uncertainty, inevitable error, unavoidable injustice.* New York: Oxford University Press.

Hassan, I. S. A. (2013). Cognitive schemes and strategies in diagnostic and therapeutic decision making: A primer for trainees. *Perspectives on Medical Education, 2*(5/6), 321–331. doi:10.1007/s40037-013-0070-3

Hawkins, P., & Shohet, R. (2012). *Supervision in the helping professions* (4th ed.). Maidenhead, UK: Open University.

Helm, D. (2011). Judgements or assumptions? The role of analysis in assessing children and young people's needs. *British Journal of Social Work, 41*(5), 894–911. doi:10.1093/bjsw/bcr096

Hertwig, R. (2012). The psychology and rationality of decisions from experience. *Synthese, 187*, 269–292. doi:10.1007/s11229-011-0024-4

Hill, L., McIlfatrick, S., Taylor, B. J., & Fitzsimons, D. (2017). Who decides what and when: A holistic understanding of decision making in implanatable cardioverter defibrillator deactivation. *European Heart Journal, 38*(suppl.1), 629–629. doi:10.1093/eurheartj/ehx504.P2983

Hogarth, R. (2008). On the learning of intuition. In H. Plessner, C. Betsch, C., & T. Betsch (Eds.), *Intuition in judgment and decision making* (pp. 91–106). New York: Lawrence Erlbaum.

Houston, S. (2015). *Reflective practice: A model for supervision and practice in social work.* Belfast: Northern Ireland Social Care Council.

Howe, K., Gray, I., & Brown, K. (2013). *Effective supervision in social work.* London: Sage.

Jansen, A. (2018). "It's so complex!": Understanding the challenges of child protection work as experienced by newly-graduated professionals. *British Journal of Social Work, 48*(6), 1524–1540. doi:10.1093/bjsw/bcx127

Killick, C., & Taylor, B. J. (2012). Judgments of social care professionals on elder abuse referrals: A factorial survey. *British Journal of Social Work, 42*(5), 814–832. doi:10.1093/bjsw/bcr109

Killick, C., & Taylor, B. J. (2020). *Assessment, Risk and Decision Making: An Introduction.* London: Sage.

Koprowska, J. (2010). *Communication and interpersonal skills in social work.* London: Sage.

Leonard, K., & O'Connor, L. (2018). Transitioning from "outside observer" to "inside player" in social work: Practitioner and student perspectives on developing expertise in decision-making. *Journal of Social Work Practice, 32*(2), 205–218. doi:10.1080/02650533.2018.1438998

Macdonald, G. (2001). *Effective interventions for child abuse and neglect: An evidence-based approach to planning and evaluating interventions.* Chichester, UK: Wiley.

Meyer, J. H. F., & Land, R. (2003). Threshold concepts and troublesome knowledge: Linkages to ways of thinking and practising in improving student learning; ten years on. In C. Rust (Ed.), *Improving student learning. Improving student learning theory and practice 10 years on* (pp. 412–424). Oxford: Oxford Centre for Staff and Learning Development.

Munro, E. (1999). Common errors of reasoning in child protection work. *Child Abuse and Neglect, 23*(8), 745–758. doi:10.1016/S0145-2134(99)00053-8

Northern Ireland Social Care Council. (2012). *Quality assurance framework for education and training regulated by the Northern Ireland Social Care Council.* Belfast: Author.

Platt, D., & Turney, D. (2014). Making threshold decisions in child protection: A conceptual analysis. *British Journal of Social Work, 44*(6), 1472–1490. doi:10.1093/bjsw/bct007

Potter, A. (2018, July). *Local authority social workers as professional witnesses in care proceedings (in England): Legal and social work evaluations of expertise.* Oral presentation at 5th Biennial International Symposium on Decisions, Assessment, Risk and Evidence in Social Work (DARE), July 2–3. Templepatrick, Northern Ireland.

Pritchard, C., Davey, J., & Williams, R. (2013). Who kills children? Re-examining the evidence. *British Journal of Social Work, 43*(7), 1403–1438. doi:10.1093/bjsw/bcs051

Reynolds, B. C. (1942). *Learning and teaching in the practice of social work.* New York: Farrar & Rinehart.

Richmond, M. E. (1917). *Social diagnosis.* New York: Russell Sage Foundation.

Schwalbe, J. (2004). Revisioning risk assessment for human service decision making. *Children and Youth Service Review, 26*(6), 561–576. doi:10.1016/j.childyouth.2004.02.011

Shamian, J. (1991). Effect of teaching decision analysis on student nurses' clinical intervention decision making. *Research in Nursing and Health, 14*(1), 59–66. doi:10.1002/nur.4770140109

Sheppard, M., Newstead, S., Di Caccavo, A., & Ryan, K. (2000). Reflexivity and the development of process knowledge in social work: A classification and empirical study. *British Journal of Social Work, 30*(4), 465–488. doi:10.1093/bjsw/30.4.465

Shulman, L. (2009). *The skills of helping individuals, families, groups and communities.* Belmont, CA: Brooks/Cole Cengage Learning.

Sicora, A. (2017). *Reflective practice and learning from mistakes in social work.* Bristol, UK: Policy Press.

Simms, V. (2016). Challenges in mathematical cognition: A collaboratively-derived research agenda. *Journal of Numerical Cognition, 2*(1), 20–41. doi:10.5964/jnc.v2i1.10

Simon, H. A. (1956). Rational choice and the structure of environments. *Psychological Review, 63*, 129–138. doi:10.1037/h0042769

Spratt, T., Devaney, J., & Hayes, D. (2015). In and out of home care decisions: The influence of confirmation bias in developing decision supportive reasoning. *Child Abuse and Neglect, 49*, 76–85. doi:10.1016/j.chiabu.2015.01.015

Stevenson, M., & Taylor, B. J. (2017). Risk communication in dementia care: Professional perspectives on consequences, likelihood, words and numbers. *British Journal of Social Work, 47*(7), 1940–1958. doi:10.1093/bjsw/bcw161

Taylor, B. J. (1998). Service needs and individual qualifications: Training social workers for the community care policy initiative and post-qualifying credits. *Social Work Education, 17*(1), 77–93. doi:10.1080/02615479811220071

Taylor, B. J. (2006). Factorial surveys: Using vignettes to study professional judgement. *British Journal of Social Work, 36*(7), 1187–1207. doi:10.1093/bjsw/bch345

Taylor, B. J. (2012a). Models for professional judgement in social work. *European Journal of Social Work, 15*(4), 546–562. doi:10.1080/13691457.2012.702310

Taylor, B. J. (2012b). Developing an integrated assessment tool for the health and social care of older people. *British Journal of Social Work, 42*(7), 1293–1314. doi:10.1093/bjsw/bcr133

Taylor, B. J. (2017a). *Decision making, assessment and risk in social work* (3rd ed.). London: Sage.

Taylor, B. J. (2017b). Heuristics in professional judgement: A psycho-social rationality model. *British Journal of Social Work, 47*(4), 1043–1060. doi:10.1093/bjsw/bcw084

Taylor, B. J., & Campbell, B. (2011). Quality, risk and governance: Social workers' perspectives. *International Journal of Leadership in Public Services, 7*(4), 256–272. doi:10.1108/17479881111194152

Taylor, B. J., & Devine, T. (1993). *Assessing needs and planning care in social work.* Aldershot, UK: Ashgate.

Taylor, B. J., & Killick, C. J. (2013). Threshold decisions in child protection: Systematic narrative review of theoretical models used in empirical studies (conference abstract). *Medical Decision Making, 33*(2), E145–E203. doi:10.1177/0272989X12455402.

Taylor, B. J., Killick, C., Bertotti, T., Enosh, G., Gautschi, J, Hietamäki, J., . . . Whittaker, A. (2017). European Social Work Research Association SIG to study decisions, assessment and risk. *Journal of Evidence-Informed Social Work, 15*(1), 82–94. doi:10.1080/23761407.2017.1394244

Taylor, B. J., Killick, C., & McGlade, A. (2015). *Understanding and using research in social work.* London: Sage.

Taylor, B. J., Mullineux, J. C., & Fleming, G. (2010). Partnership, service needs and assessing competence in post qualifying education and training. *Social Work Education, 29*(5), 475–489. doi:10.1080/02615470903159117

Taylor, B. J., & Whittaker, A. (Eds.). (2019). *Professional judgement and decision making in social work practice: Current issues.* London: Taylor and Francis.

Turney, D., & Ruch, G. (2018). What makes it so hard to look and to listen? Exploring the use of the Cognitive and Affective Supervisory Approach with children's social work managers. *Journal of Social Work Practice, 32*(2), 125–138. doi:10.1080/02650533.2018.1439460

Van de Luitgaarden, G. M. J. (2009). Evidence based practice in social work: Lessons from judgement and decision-making theory. *British Journal of Social Work, 39*(2), 243–260. doi:10.1093/bjsw/bcm117

Whittaker, A. J. (2018a). How do child protection practitioners make decisions in real life situations? Lessons from the psychology of decision making. *British Journal of Social Work, 48*(7), 1967–1984. doi:10.1093/bjsw/bcx145

Whittaker, A. J. (2018b, July). *Can real life decision-making skills be taught in the classroom? The Seeing Through the Eyes of the Experienced Practitioners (STEEP) study.* Presentation at 5th Biennial International Symposium on Decisions, Assessment, Risk and Evidence in Social Work (DARE), July 2–3. Templepatrick, Northern Ireland.

Whittaker, A., & Taylor, B. J. (Eds.). (2018). *Risk in social work practice: Current issues.* London: Taylor and Francis.

Wood, J. (1893). *Dictionary of quotations from ancient and modern, English and foreign sources.* London: Frederick Warne.

PART V

Future Directions

*Implications for Policy,
Practice, and Research*

14

Advancing the Field of Decision-Making and Judgment in Child Welfare and Protection

A Look Back and Forward

JOHN D. FLUKE, MÓNICA LÓPEZ LÓPEZ,
RAMI BENBENISHTY, ERIK J. KNORTH,
AND DONALD J. BAUMANN ■

In this final chapter, we present a summary of what appears to be established in the field of child welfare decision-making, and we raise some questions that still need to be answered. We also outline a series of research directions that could help in the further development of this field.

HOW HAS OUR KNOWLEDGE ABOUT DECISION-MAKING IN CHILD WELFARE EVOLVED?

An important feature of child welfare systems observed at the jurisdictional level (countries, states, provinces, counties, local authorities, etc.) is variability in the rates at which children and families experience no involvement to deeper involvement in the system. This funneling of families and children (Baumann, Dalgleish, Fluke, & Kern, 2011) characterizes the child welfare system, but, from a decision-making perspective, this variability can be viewed at least in part as a reflection of differences in case-level decision-making. For example, from the 2017 National Child Abuse and Neglect Data System (NCANDS) data

John D. Fluke, Mónica López López, Rami Benbenishty, Erik J. Knorth, and Donald J. Baumann, *Advancing the Field of Decision-Making and Judgment in Child Welfare and Protection* In: *Decision-Making and Judgment in Child Welfare and Protection*. Edited by: John D. Fluke, Mónica López López, Rami Benbenishty, Erik J. Knorth, and Donald J. Baumann, Oxford University Press (2021). © Oxford University Press. DOI: 10.1093/oso/9780190059538.003.0014 across US states, the average proportion of decisions to accept a child maltreatment referral is 0.42 (US Department of Health and Human Services [USHHS], 2019). However, the range of variability is from 0.16 to 0.98, encompassing nearly the entire set of possible values.

While not every decision point is as variable as intake, we are not aware of any studied child welfare decision point where variability has not been found across jurisdictions and sub-jurisdictions. These include key decisions to substantiate, to provide more services, to remove a child to out-of-home care, to reunify with the family of origin, to make a child available for adoption, and other similar decisions along the child welfare continuum.

What is more, variability in decision-making has been observed at not only the jurisdictional level, but also at the level of child welfare offices, supervisors, and individual workers. Of course it could be argued that this variability is to be expected given human involvement in the process and because of the differences in the ways that systems operate, but ideally one would like to be able to say that children and families who enter the child welfare system are being treated the same.

The variability in child welfare decisions rates across almost all conceivable units of analysis, whether jurisdictions or individual caseworkers, can be viewed as the manifestation of decision-making behavior in the child protection systems. Reasons for variability fit within the context of the theoretical frameworks we discuss in the chapter on theory (Chapter 1), particularly the Judgments and Decision Processes in Context (JUDPiC) and Decision-Making Ecology/General Assessment and Decision-Making (DME/GADM) models. As these theories assert, there are many underlying reasons for variability in decision-making. It is important and challenging to identify systematic causes for variability in decisions. Some of these causes for variability may be important and necessary because they reflect the particular context in which the decision is made. In fact, a lack of variability across different contexts may be a source of concern. For instance, if good foster families are scarce in one area and more available in another, we would expect that practitioners in these two regions would vary in their responses even when they face similar cases. Similarly, we expect practitioners to have a different risk assessment for children who would stay with their families if they operate in contexts that have very different access to family support services. The scientific exploration of sources of systematic variability may thus help inform when variability is the appropriate response to differences in context, when it may be due to lack of systematic use of information by practitioners, or to determine other unwanted sources of variability.

Assessments

Child protection systems have a history of relying on both formal and informal assessments of children and families. The underlying assumption, supported by research, is that case characteristics and circumstances should be the basis of child protection and child welfare decision-making. Some formal assessment processes are almost always required by policy and are sometimes supported by research. Less formal approaches emerge from "best practice" considerations.

Assessments and decisions in child welfare are recognized as highly complex tasks characterized by uncertainty, complexity, and high-stakes consequences. The information gathered to assist in those decisions is often scarce and ambiguous for a variety of reasons, and it is often used to make predictions for the future well-being of families and children. Errors and mistakes can happen in all stages of the assessment and decision processes. Some can be explained by the difficult circumstances in which professionals make assessments and decisions. Time limits, staff turnover, budgetary constraints, or limited availability of services present challenges at an organizational level. At a personal level, there are limitations in the psychological processes involved in decision-making that may create numerous errors (Kahneman, 2011). Compounding the assessment and decision-making process is a backdrop of public pressure to avoid any errors that may cause harm to children and families.

The chapters in this book have provided ample empirical evidence on the limitations of professional assessments and decisions in child welfare, as well as the challenges of improving professionals' decision-making skills through training (see, e.g., Chapter 13). The provision of assessments and decisions usually involves a group of professionals in consultation with a manager and external experts, who need to achieve consensus on what is best for the child and the family. There are sets of rules and procedures to be followed, which sometimes are difficult to accomplish (e.g., balancing the safety of children and preserving families). The severe shortcomings of assessment and decisions in child welfare supported by research have led to the development and implementation of assessment instruments such as those involved in risk of future maltreatment, placement, reunification, and the like (Bartelink, Van Yperen, & Ten Berge, 2015). Their implementation has been accompanied by an intense debate related to the restriction and limitation to professional practice that those instruments may promote and the low predictive accuracy and validity of many instruments. Moreover, there is a general lack of research evidence about the scientific and practical utility of these instruments (Baumann, Law, Sheets, Reid, & Graham, 2005).

Decisional Context

Our reading of the chapters and the current literature highlighted some new insights. While much of the psychological literature on decision-making focuses to a large extent on human abilities, limitations, and tendencies, the literature on child welfare decision-making emphasizes more the *context* in which decisions are being made. This is hardly a new phenomenon. The series of comparative studies of decision-making in multiple countries developed by Skivenes and colleagues (see, e.g., Berrick, Dickens, Pösö, & Skivenes, 2016; Burns, Pösö, & Skivenes, 2017) investigated how the characteristics of the child welfare system impact decisions made by practitioners in Europe and the United States. Benbenishty, Osmo, and Gold (2003) attempted to explain differences in the ways practitioners from Canada and Israel rationalized and argued about the different decisions they made about the same cases. Similarly, a large comparative study conducted in four countries showed cross-country variations among professionals who reviewed the same case (Benbenishty et al., 2015); and a comparative study by Witte, Baldwin, and López López (Chapter 12) focused, among other things, on the role of children in child protection decision-making in England, Germany, and the Netherlands.

What seems to be emerging more recently are attempts to both expand and nuance the conceptualization of context. Hence, the DME/GADM and JUDPiC models presented in this book demonstrate an interest in identifying and explicating multiple layers of context: organizational, regional (e.g., differences between counties), and nationally. These new efforts include more aspects of context than previous studies that employed context in more global terms. This work seems promising but quite preliminary. There is a need for more conceptualization of the different types of contexts and how they change over time. Developing these concepts will lead to the next stage in our research. Instead of post hoc interpretations of findings, we need to develop clear hypotheses about how certain characteristics of contexts would impact decisions. This is a necessary step if we want to provide useful suggestions about how we could change contexts so that decisions achieve better outcomes for children and families.

Decision-Makers

Individual Decision-Making

This book presents research addressing different types of decisions that are part of the decision-making continuum (Baumann, Fluke, Dalgleish, & Kern, 2014), including the initial decision of responding to a referral and additional decisions related to the type of services that children and families could be given, such as receiving an out-of-home placement.

The last type of decision, placing a child out-of-home, seems to be studied most frequently in connection to decision-maker characteristics, perhaps as a result of its being (potentially) the most intrusive type of decision in the continuum (Bartelink et al., 2018). In two US studies, female decision-makers seem to be more inclined to place the child out-of-home (Vanderloo, 2017) or to take custody (Rossi, Schuerman, & Budde, 1999) than male colleagues. Several studies presented in this book indicate that a "more pro-removal" attitude of the decision-maker improves the odds of an out-of-home placement decision—be it a placement in family foster care (Chapter 6, Chapter 11) or in residential care (Chapter 7). In the study by Bettencourt-Rodrigues and colleagues (Chapter 7), the removal favoring attitude was associated with a higher level of perceived risk, with positive "behavior beliefs" (the decision-maker expects a positive impact of the placement on the child and the family), with anticipating positive emotions (e.g., relaxation in the family), with perceived approval of the decision by significant others, and with a less positive value attributed to child protection and family preservation. Skills and work experience of decision-makers also seem to play a role. Vanderloo (2017) and Graham et al. (Chapter 5) found indications of a positive association between out-of-home placement decisions and a tenure or senior position of the caseworkers, respectively—with "seniority" as an indirect effect—and a study of Devaney, Hayes, and Spratt (2017) showed the less experienced practitioners to be more inclined to remove a child from the home. In line with this, Fluke et al. (2016) observed those practitioners who were longer employed by child welfare agencies to have a stronger orientation toward family preservation. A final factor that appears to be relevant is the perceived support in the professional environment by the decision-maker: less felt support seems to correlate with higher chances of children's out-of-home placement (Chapter 4, Chapter 5) or referral of the family to Family Group Conferences (Allan, Harlaar, Hollinshead, Drury, & Merkel-Holguin, 2017). On the other hand, approval by significant others enhances a placement intention, as specifically documented toward residential care (Chapter 7).

Another decision that has been connected to individual characteristics of the decision-maker is the one of substantiating child maltreatment. Research shows that the choice for a decision-maker to unsubstantiate seems associated with his or her being more experienced in the child welfare and protection field, showing a higher level of (self-assessed) skills, and having supporting relationships with colleagues and vice versa (Child Welfare Information Gateway [CWIG], 2003; English, Brummel, Graham, & Coghlan, 2002). Not feeling overworked and the perception of resources available to clients also correlate with unsubstantiation decisions (Fluke et al., 2001). Two other factors that seem to contribute to the decision to substantiate suspected child maltreatment are an advanced degree of the decision-maker in social/behavioral sciences (Chapter 8) and an attitude relatively favoring the option of removal of a child from the home in case of an unsafe family situation (Chapter 6). The last variable was found in three of the four European countries in the study concerned (Israel, Netherlands, Spain; not in Northern Ireland).

If we look at risk assessment, a more risky family situation for the child seems to be perceived by practitioners who feel more stressed by parents' confrontational behavior (LeBlanc, Regehr, Shlonsky, & Bogo, 2012); have lower levels of case skills; show more of an "external reference orientation," referring to the impact a decision might have on the child's and families' feelings (Chapter 5); and demonstrate a "more pro-removal" attitude (Chapter 6).

The decision to reunify the child and the family after a time in care has perhaps received less attention in research. However, this is precisely the focus of Chapter 9, where the authors suggest that there may be certain biases based in race and ethnicity that are operating in connection with other factors in reunification decision-making.

(Managing) Team Decision-Making

Team decision-making in child protection and child welfare remains an understudied topic. O'Sullivan (2011, pp. 65–68) elaborated on potential pros of team decision-making compared with individual decision-making, such as (1) sharing of information regarding clients, (2) the development of a fuller picture on the case, (3) sharing commitment to an action plan, and (4) the implementation of actions combining together to form a coherent and integrated intervention. The underlying assumption is that if a team meeting is well prepared, the communication between the team members is sufficiently open, the group climate is supportive, differences of opinion are managed constructively, and chairing the meeting is performed with great competence (O'Sullivan, 2011, pp. 77–78), then the process will improve upon the decisions made by individuals. That said, for the most part, this notion regarding team decision-making remains a compelling hypothesis in the child protection and child welfare arena as the evidence to support it is lacking and there are recognized threats to the validity of these claims.

One of the most frequently investigated phenomena in this context is group conformity: the pressure to conform to a particular view or choice. It can take the form of *apparent consensus*, which means that, on the surface, it appears that all team members do agree, "but in reality some or all are superficially conforming to a dominant view that they do not actually hold or that they find it convenient to acquiesce with" (O'Sullivan, 2011, p. 78). One way the phenomenon shows up is called the *Abilene paradox* (Harvey, 1974); it involves a common breakdown of group communication in which each member mistakenly believes that his or her own preferences are counter to the group's and, therefore, objections are not raised. (The name of the phenomenon comes from an anecdote that Harvey [1974] uses to elucidate the paradox: the trip of a family to Abilene, which no-one in the family actually wants to visit.)

Another manifestation of group conformity is known as *groupthink* (see also Chapter 13): group members try to minimize conflict and reach a consensus decision without critical evaluation of alternative viewpoints by actively suppressing dissenting viewpoints and by isolating themselves from outside influences (Janis, 1982). In contrast with the Abilene paradox, groupthink individuals are not acting contrary to their conscious wishes and generally feel good about the decisions a group has reached (Sims, 1994). The risk of the occurrence of biases like these seems to be associated with decisions that are important or novel and are promoted by time pressure and high levels of uncertainty (Jones & Roelofsma, 2010).

An important factor in avoiding variants of conscious or unconscious group conformity is the *leadership style* of the person who chairs the team meeting: "The chair of a meeting plays a crucial role in facilitating stakeholders to work together in a constructive and vigilant way" (O'Sullivan, 2011, p. 71). This was clearly demonstrated in one of the few recent empirical studies in the child welfare field on team decision-making that we could find. In a study by Nouwen, Decuyper, and Put (2012) in Flanders, the Dutch-speaking part of Belgium, two different child welfare and protection agencies were observed. The teams substantially differed in the amount of *structural discussion space* (SDS) for team members to talk about each case. The leadership style also differed. In team A (with the highest SDS), the chair practiced an *empowering* style, described as encouraging team members to speak up and to critique proposed decisions and plans. In team B (with the lowest SDS), the chair practiced a *directive leadership* style, corresponding with a higher level of autocratic leadership, which is about making decisions without consulting team members or without taking their opinions into account (cf. Burke et al., 2006). Some of the (other) characteristics on which team A in a positive sense differed from team B were functional leadership, trust, alignment, constructive conflict, team reflexivity, efficiency, and viability (Nouwen et al., 2012, p. 2107). Although not exactly the same, the two leadership styles come close to what was discovered by Falconer and Shardlow (2018) in their comparison of child protection decision-making system orientations in England and Finland. In England, the dominant approach was called *supervised judgment*, described as a hierarchical, top-down form of decision-making. In Finland, the most practiced approach was called *supported judgment*, described as a more horizontal and shared decision-making format (see also Taylor & Whittaker, 2018).

Generally, it can be argued that it is not self-evident that team decision-making generates "better" decisions compared with individually taken decisions, and the implementation and promotion of such processes do not appear to have been informed through the generation of empirical evidence. A pivotal concern seems to be team conditions, including the style of management or leadership. This area, team decision-making, remains among the most important gaps in child welfare decision-making research.

Connecting Decisions to Outcomes

Among the most challenging aspect of child protection and child welfare decision-making research is associating decisions with the actual outcomes of those decisions. To some extent this challenge ties back to the fundamental proposition that most child welfare decision-making occurs under uncertainty as opposed to risk. A key definition of this condition is that it is not possible to develop a verifiable probability of an outcome based on the decision-making circumstances. For example, the decision to remove a child could ensure that a child is safe, but, for some children, the consequence of the placement on eventual functioning, well-being, and even safety is unknown. The ultimate outcomes for a child depend on events and situations that may arise during the period of the placement that could not have been predicted at the time of the decision-making process given current knowledge.

Some decisions along the decision-making continuum may prove more appropriate to address from the perspective of evaluating outcomes; for instance, the decision to respond to a child maltreatment allegation referral (Mansell, Ota, Erasmus, & Marks, 2011). Other decisions may prove possible to explore from an outcomes perspective, but our ability to formulate valid studies may exceed our capacity to develop adequate research designs that are also ethical.

PROSPECTS FOR IMPROVING ACCURACY IN DECISION-MAKING: THE PROMISE OF CHANGING TECHNOLOGY

The advent of new technology in recent decades holds many promises directed to efforts to improve decision-making in child welfare and protection. Information systems and extensive databases are now an integral part of many child welfare agencies. These local databases can now begin to serve as a laboratory with which to model decision-making. With current technologies, what was once possible only on a state level is now feasible for counties and local agencies. This progress is especially important when we consider the growing understanding that local contexts do make a difference and that lessons learned in one context may not be necessarily applicable to others.

Related technological advances are the enhanced ability to connect and merge multiple databases. As evident in several recent projects, it is possible now to create large-scale databases that include information from multiple sources, such as physical and mental health, child welfare involvement, and police and judicial data. This is important to better understand the characteristics of children and their families and how they are associated with decisions. Furthermore, as this trend toward linkable data continues, it will be possible to connect databases that reflect long-term outcomes for children who were in care. By merging databases that contain information on issues such as adult employment, welfare dependence, criminal involvement, and education, it is possible to provide feedback on the outcomes of decisions and help inform future decision-makers. Such information includes better understanding of the complex relationships between children and family characteristics, decisions, interventions, life events (such a death of a parent), and long-term (adult) outcomes of decisions made on behalf of children.

Other technological developments are the various aspects of artificial intelligence, such as machine learning, and the enhanced capacities to explore large and complex datasets (Big Data). These new techniques can help produce algorithms for predicting outcomes that may be more effective when compared with traditional statistical approaches (Chapter 2).

This latest development, while promising to support decision-making, exemplifies some of the potential pitfalls of reliance on technology. As databases become larger and more complex and the new analytic technologies harder to follow intuitively, there is a concern that practitioners will be presented with recommendations for decisions with no rationale except that this is what came out of machine learning.

This challenge is yet another reflection of the tension between taking the fullest advantage of emerging technologies and their ethical implications. While the ability to collect vast amounts of data from numerous sources and create a very detailed and long-term picture on each child and family promises to enhance our ability to make decisions in the best interests of children, they should also raise concern and debate. Our ethical discussions need to be updated to include both the great new promises of the emerging technologies as well as their perils. Clearly, the child welfare field cannot overlook the great potential of technology to improve our decisions. It is also clear, however, that the safeguards against infringing on children's (and families') rights to privacy and confidentiality need to be updated given the extensive and long-term nature of the data collection, processing capacities, and, especially, application of the new technologies.

MOVING THE RESEARCH FORWARD

In the various chapters of this book, the authors have formulated numerous questions that will need to be answered by future research. Some of the most important research directions and problems to address in this field are summarized here.

The research body developed in the area of child welfare decision-making throughout the past few years compels the need to explore not only the impact of case factors in the decision-making processes, but also the personal factors of the decision-maker as well as the contextual factors, both organizational and external ones. While the study of the influence of professionals' personal attributes in decision-making processes and outcomes has received ample attention, research findings suggest a limited impact in decisions. Recently, some authors have pointed to limitations in the way we have traditionally studied these factors, proposing that a number of context factors (organizational and from the broader context) may work as mediators of professionals' personal attributes on decisions made (see Graham et al., in Chapter 5). Thus, the relationship between factors at different levels seems much more complex than considered in early research, and we can expect in the coming years a renewed interest in exploring the personal factors of the decision-maker through more sophisticated models that consider the context within which decisions are made. More specifically, an incipient research interest is noted for how the impact of decision-maker characteristics may differ depending on the context in which they are inserted (e.g., different child welfare regimes). Moreover, other decision-maker factors tied to workforce concerns such as secondary trauma, adverse work experiences, stress, and burnout and their impacts in the ways that professionals make decisions are receiving increasing attention.

One of the enduring research themes identified has to do with the decision-making processes that lead to disparities in child welfare and protection. A number of studies conducted during the past decade have been devoted to explore the overrepresentation of certain groups of children and families in the child welfare system and to understand the factors at the case and organizational levels that could produce disparities in decision-making processes (Fluke et al., 2011). For instance, in the study of King et al. (2017) in the Canadian context, black families were 33% more likely compared to white families to receive a child protection intervention following an investigation. In a study conducted in Texas by Dettlaff et al. (2011), suspected maltreatment at the beginning of an investigation was more often substantiated at case closure when child protection reports concerned black children compared to white children. In New Zealand, Keddell and Hyslop (2019) found that social workers judge the vignette about an indigenous Māori family as being at higher risk for future child maltreatment or harm compared to an identical description of a Pākehā (i.e., white) family.

Exploring the decision-making context has been one of the great advances in our field during the past decade. The context of the decisions has been defined by aligned theoretical models (see JUDPiC and DME models in Chapter 1) that have been applied not only to child welfare organizations, but also to broader contexts such as culture and country.

At the organizational level, a number of systematic methods and aids have rapidly expanded in child welfare agencies all around the world to improve decision-making. In their chapter, Bartelink and colleagues present and discuss what is known about four of them: critical thinking, team decision-making, systematic feedback, and shared decision-making. However, the evidence about these techniques is still very scarce, and, in coming years, we can expect rigorous assessments that will allow us to know the real value of this new wave of decision-making aids.

While the decisions to place children out-of-home have received most of the attention in research, more recently we have seen how the range of decisions along the decision-making continuum have been analyzed. That said, continuing to extend the research to other types of assessments, including maltreatment severity assessment and other decisions, will be an important advance for the field.

Finally, a rising research field receiving increasing attention has to do with the participation of children and parents in child protection decision-making. Policy developments in many countries have established the need of children to participate in accordance with Article 12 of the United Nations Convention on the Rights of the Child (UNCRC). Children's participation in decision-making processes offers an opportunity for improved child protection systems since it has been linked to a range of positive effects for children and the success of child protection interventions (see Witte et al., in Chapter 12). More research is needed to develop our knowledge base on the barriers and facilitators of children's participation in decision-making.

Quantitative Approaches

Given the importance of decision-making in child protection and child welfare, we are encouraged to see from the chapters in this book that more attention is being paid to the subject from a research standpoint. While it is still common to find a focus on case-level assessment rather than decisional context, that, too, has begun to shift. Despite improvements in our knowledge, we consider the state of research in this area underdeveloped. It is also important as an applied field to consider how this knowledge can and should be translated for implementation.

From a methodological perspective, Chapter 3 by Gautschi and Benbenishty provides a good grounding in the methods used to study decision-making. We tend to agree with the authors that one approach to advancing the methods overall is to develop designs to combine them. For example, given that vignette methods provide good experimental control, can they be combined with the actual decisions made by participants? In other words, are responses on vignettes actually reflected in behavior? If so, in what way?

Many of the chapters in this book base their knowledge claims on quantitative designs and methods. Predominately, these are based on correlational studies applying large-scale datasets (Fallon et al., Chapter 10; Font et al., Chapter 8; Graham et al., Chapter 5; Stepura et al., Chapter 2; and Wittenstrom et al., Chapter 9), while others rely on vignette methods (López López and Benbenishty, Chapter 6; Bettencourt-Rodrigues et al., Chapter 7). These studies offer refinements of models that include important cues about the leverage points for developing interventions. In some cases these may have implications for national or provincial policy (e.g., Fallon et al., Chapter 10), are related to workforce concerns (e.g., Graham et al., Chapter 5; Bettencourt-Rodrigues et al., Chapter 7), or are associated with racial bias (Wittenstrom et al., Chapter 9).

While practical suggestions are made in terms of the implications, what is lacking are experimental studies that could help to verify the efficacy of these claims. Is the field of decision-making research at a point where we could address certain key questions about these leverage points? For example, what is the anticipated size of the changes that could be attained by addressing a candidate leverage point, and could an implementation study be designed to determine if the implemented change achieves the anticipated result? Are certain training or staff development approaches that translate decision-maker factors identified in correlational studies actually effective at changing decision-making behavior? For example, would on-the-job training opportunities that systematically expose workers to a diverse group of families reduce disparities in decision-making and what dosage is needed? Would specific decision-making related improvements in the resource base or array of services result in changes in decision-making behavior?

Qualitative Approaches

Next to larger-scale quantitative survey studies a great deal can also be learned from more qualitative approaches in studying practitioners' decision-making in child protection and child welfare. In essence, this type of research can be briefly worded with the saying by Taylor and Bogdan (1998, p. 3): "go to the people," thereby presupposing that the researcher is getting as close as possible to the world and experiences of the people under study (i.e., their deciding on children at risk). This can be done by observing stakeholders (including practitioners, parents, other caretakers, children and young people), by interviewing them, by asking them to react to certain stimuli (case descriptions, pictures, assignments), by studying documents that represent personal experiences (diaries, reports), etc. Some of these methods and techniques were successfully applied in decision-making situations.

Several qualitative studies have been performed around the structuring and contents of arguments or rationales that (should) underpin or justify an intrusive decision like out-of-home placement of a child. In a recent study by Zeijlmans, López López, Grietens, and Knorth (2019), 20 Dutch matching practitioners in family foster care were interviewed using vignettes and a "think-aloud" methodology to generate an understanding of their reasoning. Two types of vignettes were created: hypothetical children and hypothetical foster families. The interviews were analyzed using a qualitative deductive content analysis focusing on key indicators of three classes of heuristics: recognition, one-reason, and tradeoff heuristics (cf. Gigerenzer & Gaissmaier, 2011). The results showed that the *recognition heuristic* did not play a decisive role in the matching process; practitioners considered more than one family before making a final decision. The findings for the *one-reason heuristic* revealed conjunctive decision-making rules: families were sometimes rejected based on one negative premise. This reminds us of the "trump card strategy" identified by Backe-Hansen (2003). The analysis of the *tradeoff heuristic* demonstrated that the number of positive premises and the ratio between positive and negative premises predicted the matching decision. However, the total number of premises also predicted the matching decision, which might indicate *confirmation bias* (Tversky & Kahneman, 1974). Indications for confirmation bias were also found in qualitative studies by Bartelink et al. (2018) and Spratt, Devaney, and Hayes (2015).

A growing body of research has been focused on the role that children and young people play in decisions that impact their lives: Do they *participate* in such decisions, to what degree, and what are the relevant factors that determine the level of participation? Recent qualitative studies were performed in cases of parental divorce (Hemrica & Heyting, 2004), in child protection and child welfare cases (Leeson, 2007; Van Bijleveld, Dedding, & Bunders-Aelen, 2014), and in out-of-home care (Bessell, 2011; Ten Brummelaar, Knorth, Post, Harder, & Kalverboer, 2018). One rather consistent finding is that children's participation in decision-making is far from a matter of course (see also Chapter 12). A second finding is that the role of the practitioners, especially their attitudes on child participation, is pivotal.

It seems that qualitative research should be considered a valuable approach in exploring and exposing professional strategies of decision-making in child protection and child welfare, including topics such as the ways of justifying and reasoning regarding these "hot" decisions, the use of mental "shortcuts" (heuristics and biases), or the role of stakeholders like children and young people themselves.

CONCLUSION

It is clear from the body and range of research found in this book that the interest in child protection and child welfare decision-making is growing. From a practice perspective, decision-making has moved from a focus on assessment to an increased interest in ways that policies, biases, attitudes, and beliefs operate to create the variability in decision-making found throughout the systems of service delivery. Despite this growth in our understanding, we lack a clear sense of the degree to which key factors, aside from case factors, influence decision-making practice. What we also lack are studies of interventions that might help to reduce not only variability but also studies that address the ability of the systems to improve decision-making in a way that will ultimately improve outcomes for children and families.

REFERENCES

Allan, H., Harlaar, N., Hollinshead, D., Drury, I., & Merkel-Holguin, L. (2017). The impact of worker and agency characteristics on FGC referrals in child welfare. *Children and Youth Services Review, 81*, 229–237. doi:10.1016/j.childyouth.2017.08.013

Backe-Hansen, E. (2003). Justifying out-of-home placement: A multiple case study of decision-making in child welfare and protection services. *International Journal of Child and Family Welfare, 6*(4), 151–166.

Bartelink, C., Knorth, E. J., López López, M., Koopmans, C., Ten Berge, I. J., Witteman, C. L. M., & Van Yperen, T. A. (2018). Reasons for placement decisions in a case of suspected child abuse: The role of reasoning, work experience, and attitudes in decision-making. *Child Abuse and Neglect, 83*, 129–141. doi:10.1016/j.chiabu.2018.06.013

Bartelink, C., Van Yperen, T. A., & Ten Berge, I. J. (2015). Deciding on child maltreatment: A literature review on methods that improve decision-making. *Child Abuse and Neglect, 49*,142–153. doi:10.1016/j.chiabu.2015.07.002

Baumann, D. J., Dalgleish, L., Fluke, J. D., & Kern, H. (2011). *The decision-making ecology.* Washington, DC: American Humane Association.

Baumann, D. J., Fluke, J. D., Dalgleish, L., & Kern, H. (2014). The decision-making ecology. In A. Shlonsky & R. Benbenishty (Eds.), *From evidence to outcomes in child welfare: An international reader* (pp. 24–38). New York: Oxford University Press.

Baumann, D. J., Law, J. R., Sheets, J., Reid, G., & Graham, J. C. (2005). Evaluating the effectiveness of actuarial risk assessment models. *Children and Youth Services Review, 27*, 465–490. doi:10.1016/j.childyouth.2004.09.004

Benbenishty, R., Davidson-Arad, B., López, M., Devaney, J., Spratt, T., Koopmans, C., . . . Hayes, D. (2015). Decision making in child protection: An international comparative study on maltreatment substantiation, risk assessment and interventions recommendations, and the role of professionals' child welfare attitudes. *Child Abuse and Neglect, 49*, 63–75. doi:10.1016/j.chiabu.2015.03.015

Benbenishty, R., Osmo, R., & Gold, N. (2003). Rationales provided for risk assessments and for recommended interventions: A comparison between Canadian and Israeli professionals. *British Journal of Social Work, 33*(2), 137–155. doi:10.1093/bjsw/33.2.137

Berrick, J. D., Dickens, J., Pösö, T., & Skivenes, M. (2016). Time, institutional support, and quality of decision making in child protection: A cross-country analysis. *Human Service Organizations: Management, Leadership and Governance, 40*(5), 451–468. doi:10.1080/23303131.2016.1159637

Bessell, S. (2011). Participation in decision-making in out-of-home care in Australia: What do young people say? *Children and Youth Services Review, 33*(4), 496–501. doi:10.1016/j.childyouth.2010.05.006

Burke, C. S., Stagl, K. C., Klein, C., Goodwin, G. F., Salas, E., & Halpin, S. M. (2006). What type of leadership behaviors are functional in teams? A meta-analysis. *Leadership Quarterly, 17*(3), 288–307. doi:10.1016/j.leaqua.2006.02.007

Burns, K., Pösö, T., & Skivenes, M. (Eds.). (2017). *Child welfare removals by the state: A cross-country analysis of decision-making systems.* New York: Oxford University Press.

Child Welfare Information Gateway (CWIG). (2003). *Decision-making in unsubstantiated child protective services cases: Synthesis of recent research.* Washington, DC: US Department of Health and Human Services. https://www.childwelfare.gov/pubPDFs/decisionmaking.pdf

Dettlaff, A. J., Rivaux, S. L., Baumann, D. J., Fluke, J. D., Rycraft, J. R., & James, J. (2011). Disentangling substantiation: The influence of race, income, and risk on the substantiation decision in child welfare. *Children and Youth Services Review, 33*, 1630–1637. https://doi.org/10.1016/j.childyouth.2011.04.005

Devaney, J., Hayes, D., & Spratt, T. (2017). The influences of training and experience in removal and reunification decisions involving children at risk of maltreatment: Detecting a "beginner dip." *British Journal of Social Work, 47*(8), 2364–2383. doi:10.1093/bjsw/bcw175

English, D. J., Brummel, S., Graham, J. C., & Coghlan, L. (2002). *Final report: Factors that influence the decision not to substantiate a CPS referral. Phase II.* Olympia, WA: DSHS, Children's Administration, OCAR.

Falconer, R., & Shardlow, S. M. (2018). Comparing child protection decision-making in England and Finland: Supervised or supported judgement? *Journal of Social Work Practice, 32*(2), 111–124. doi:10.1080/02650533.2018.1438996

Fluke, J. D., Corwin, T. W., Hollinshead, D., & Maher, E. J. (2016). Family preservation or child safety? How experience and position shape child welfare workers' perspectives. *Children and Youth Services Review, 69*, 210–218. doi:10.1016/j.childyouth.2016.08.012

Fluke, J. D., Jones Harden, B., Jenkins, M., & Ruehrdanz, A. (2011). A research synthesis on child welfare disproportionality and disparities. In Center for the Study of Social Policy (Ed.), *Disparities and disproportionality in child welfare: Analysis of the research* (pp. 1–93). Washington, DC: Center for the Study of Social Policy.

Fluke, J. D., Parry, C., Shapiro, P., Hollinshead, D., Bollenbacher, V., Baumann, D., & Davis Brown, K. (2001). *The dynamics of unsubstantiated reports: A multi-state study—final report.* Englewood, CO: American Humane Association.

Gigerenzer, G., & Gaissmaier, W. (2011). Heuristic decision making. *Annual Review of Psychology, 62,* 451–482. doi:10.1146/annurev-psych-120709-145346

Harvey, J. B. (1974). The Abilene paradox: The management of agreement. *Organizational Dynamics, 3,* 73–80.

Hemrica, J., & Heyting, F. (2004). Tacit notions of childhood: An analysis of discourse about child participation in decision-making regarding arrangements in case of parental divorce. *Childhood, 11*(4), 449–468. doi:10.1177/0907568204047106

Janis, I. L. (1982). *Groupthink: Psychological studies of policy decisions and fiascoes.* Boston, MA: Houghton Mifflin.

Jones, P. E., & Roelofsma, P. H. M. P. (2010). The potential for social contextual and group biases in team decision-making: Biases, conditions, and psychological mechanisms. *Ergonomics, 43*(8), 1129–1152. doi:10.1080/00140130050084914

Kahneman, D. (2011). *Thinking, fast and slow.* New York: Farrar, Straus and Giroux.

Keddell, E., & Hyslop, I. (2019). Ethnic inequalities in child welfare: The role of practitioner risk perceptions. *Child and Family Social Work, 24*(4), 409–420. https://doi.org/10.1111/cfs.12620

King, B., Fallon, B., Boyd, R., Black, T., Antwi-Boasiako, K., & O'Connor, C. (2017). Factors associated with racial differences in child welfare investigative decision-making in Ontario, Canada. *Child Abuse and Neglect, 73,* 89–105. https://doi.org/10.1016/j.chiabu.2017.09.027

LeBlanc, V., Regehr, C., Shlonsky, A., & Bogo, M. (2012). Stress responses and decision making in child protection workers faced with high conflict situations. *Child Abuse and Neglect, 36,* 404–412. doi:10.1016/j.chiabu.2012.01.003

Leeson, C. (2007). My life in care: Experiences of non-participation in decision-making processes. *Child and Family Social Work, 12*(3), 268–277. doi:10.1111/j.1365-2206.2007.00499.x

Mansell, J., Ota, R., Erasmus, R., & Marks, K. (2011). Reframing child protection: A response to a constant crisis of confidence in child protection. *Children and Youth Services Review, 33*(11), 2076–2086. doi:10.1016/j.childyouth.2011.04.019

Nouwen, E., Decuyper, S., & Put, J. (2012). Team decision making in child welfare. *Children and Youth Services Review, 34*(10), 2101–2116. doi:10.1016/j.childyouth.2012.07.006

O'Sullivan, T. (2011). *Decision making in social work* (2nd ed.). New York: Palgrave Macmillan.

Rossi, P. H., Schuerman, J., & Budde, S. (1999). Understanding decisions about child maltreatment. *Evaluation Review, 23*(6), 579–598. doi:10.1177/0193841X9902300601

Sims, R. R. (1994). *Ethics and organizational decision making: A call for renewal.* Westport, CT: Greenwood Publishing Group.

Spratt, T., Devaney, J., & Hayes, D. (2015). In and out of home care decisions: The influence of confirmation bias in developing decision supportive reasoning. *Child Abuse and Neglect, 83,* 76–85. doi:10.1016/j.chiabu.2015.01.015

Taylor, B., & Whittaker, A. (2018). Professional judgment and decision making in social work. *Journal of Social Work Practice, 32*(2), 105–109. doi:10.1080/02650533.2018.1462780

Taylor, S. J., & Bogdan, R. (1998). *Introduction to qualitative research methods* (3rd ed.). New York: John Wiley & Sons.

Ten Brummelaar, M. D. C., Knorth, E. J., Post, W. J., Harder, A. T., & Kalverboer, M. E. (2018). Space between the borders? Perceptions of professionals on the participation in decision-making of young people in coercive care. *Qualitative Social Work, 17*(5), 692–711. doi:10.1177/1473325016681661

Tversky, A., & Kahneman, D. (1974). Judgment under uncertainty: Heuristics and biases. *Science, 185*(4157), 1124–1131. doi:10.1126/science.185.4157.1124

US Department of Health & Human Services (USHHS), Administration for Children and Families, Administration on Children, Youth and Families, Children's Bureau. (2019). *Child Maltreatment 2017.* https://www.acf.hhs.gov/cb/research-data-technology/statistics-research/child-maltreatment.

Van Bijleveld, G. G., Dedding, C. W. M., & Bunders-Aelen, J. F. G. (2014). Seeing eye to eye or not? Young people's and child protection workers' perspectives on children's participation within the Dutch child protection and welfare services. *Children and Youth Services Review, 47*(3), 253–259. doi:10.1016/j.childyouth.2014.09.018

Vanderloo, M. (2017). *Caseworker factors that influence removal decisions in child welfare. Doctoral dissertation.* http://socialwork.utah.edu/wp-content/uploads/sites/4/2017/08/Vanderloo-Mindy.pdf

Zeijlmans, K., López López, M., Grietens, H., & Knorth, E. J. (2019). Heuristic decision-making in foster care matching: Evidence from a think-aloud study. *Child Abuse and Neglect, 88*, 400–411. doi:10.1016/j.chiabu.2018.12.007

Page numbers followed by *f* and *t* indicate figures and tables, respectively.